YUGOSLAVIA

FODOR'S TRAVEL GUIDES

are compiled, researched, and edited by an international team of travel writers, field correspondents, and editors. The series, which now almost covers the globe, was founded by Eugene Fodor in 1936.

OFFICES
New York & London

Fodor's Yugoslavia:

Area Editor: SYLVIE NICKELS
Editorial Contributors: ROBERT BROWN, E. GEORGE MADDOCKS, JOHN
    MAYOR, PETER SHELDON, DAVID TENNANT
Editor: RICHARD MOORE
Maps: ALEX MURPHY
Drawings: BERYL SANDERS
Photographs: PETER BAKER, SYLVIE NICKELS

FODOR'S®

Yugoslavia

1984

HODDER AND STOUGHTON
LONDON   SYDNEY   AUCKLAND

All the following Guides are current (most of them also in
the Hodder and Stoughton British edition.)

CURRENT FODOR'S COUNTRY AND AREA TITLES:

AUSTRALIA, NEW ZEALAND
  AND SOUTH PACIFIC
AUSTRIA
BELGIUM AND
  LUXEMBOURG
BERMUDA
BRAZIL
CANADA
CARIBBEAN AND BAHAMAS
CENTRAL AMERICA
EASTERN EUROPE
EGYPT
EUROPE
FRANCE
GERMANY
GREAT BRITAIN
GREECE
HOLLAND
INDIA
IRELAND

ISRAEL
ITALY
JAPAN
JORDAN AND HOLY LAND
KOREA
MEXICO
NORTH AFRICA
PEOPLE'S REPUBLIC
  OF CHINA
PORTUGAL
SCANDINAVIA
SCOTLAND
SOUTH AMERICA
SOUTHEAST ASIA
SOVIET UNION
SPAIN
SWITZERLAND
TURKEY
YUGOSLAVIA

CITY GUIDES:

BEIJING, GUANGZHOU, SHANGHAI
CHICAGO
DALLAS AND FORT WORTH
HOUSTON
LONDON
LOS ANGELES
MADRID
MEXICO CITY AND ACAPULCO
NEW ORLEANS
NEW YORK CITY

PARIS
ROME
SAN DIEGO
SAN FRANCISCO
STOCKHOLM, COPENHAGEN,
  OSLO, HELSINKI, AND
  REYKJAVIK
TOKYO
WASHINGTON, D.C.

FODOR'S BUDGET SERIES:

BUDGET BRITAIN
BUDGET CANADA
BUDGET CARIBBEAN
BUDGET EUROPE
BUDGET FRANCE
BUDGET GERMANY
BUDGET HAWAII

BUDGET ITALY
BUDGET JAPAN
BUDGET MEXICO
BUDGET SCANDINAVIA
BUDGET SPAIN
BUDGET TRAVEL IN AMERICA

USA GUIDES:

ALASKA
CALIFORNIA
CAPE COD
COLORADO
FAR WEST
FLORIDA

HAWAII
NEW ENGLAND
PENNSYLVANIA
SOUTH
TEXAS
USA (in one volume)

CONTENTS

FOREWORD

Facts at Your Fingertips

When to Go 1; Where to Go 2; What Will It Cost 5; Sources of Information—National Tourist Offices Abroad, Tour Operators 6; Package Tours 8; Travel for the Handicapped 9; Travel Documents 9; What to Take 11; Getting to Yugoslavia from North America by Air 11, by Sea 13; Getting to Yugoslavia from Great Britain by Air 13; by Train 13; by Car 14, by Bus 15; Getting to Yugoslavia from the Continent by Air 15, by Train 15, by Sea 16, by Bus 16, by Car 16; Customs 16; Yugoslavia National Tourist Offices 17; Guides 18; Money 18; Traveling in Yugoslavia by Sea 19, by Air 19, by Train 20, by Bus 20, by Car 21; Hotels 24; Roughing It—Camping and Youth Hostels 26; Restaurants 26; Tipping 27; Special Events 27; Summer Festival 28; For the Culture Minded 28; Fishing 29; Swimming 30; Boating 30; Hunting 30; Mountain Climbing 31; Winter Sports 31; Language 31; Holidays and Closing Times 32; Shopping 32; Mail and Telephones 33; Religious Services 33; Photography 33; Medical Services 34; Useful Addresses 35; Newspapers 35; Customs on Leaving 35; Duty Free 36

The Yugoslav Scene

Exploring Yugoslavia

Supplements

FOREWORD

One of the very first images that springs to mind at the mention of Yugoslavia, impelled no doubt by colorful illustrations in travel brochures, is that of the sunny Dalmatian coast with its innumerable islands. But there is much more to this fascinating country. It is a complex nation consisting of six autonomous republics and two territories of national minorities, and demonstrates the molding influences of different civilizations. Over the centuries, Yugoslavia absorbed the varying characteristics of successive waves of invaders.

But, though the country at large seems to be a homogenous unit to the casual visitor, the closer one looks, the greater the differences that can be seen between the provinces, with some areas vividly recalling bygone ways of life. Slovenia, for example, retains many facets of the Austro-Hungarian Empire. Istria and Dalmatia still recall the Venetian Maritime Republic. Bosnia and southern Serbia preserve the slower rhythm of life and Islamic color of the days of the Ottoman Sultanate. This fascinating, sometimes anachronistic mélange is heavily overlaid, of course, by a social system that adds interesting features of contemporary origin. The resulting mixture of old and new, together with the wonderful variety of landscape, make a trip to Yugoslavia uniquely rewarding. The Federal Socialist Republic of Yugoslavia, an association of Communist states, is *not* behind the Iron Curtain so far as tourist facilities go, and has placed no needless restrictions on foreign visitors for well over 30 years.

Over the last couple of decades, Yugoslavia has made huge efforts to provide facilities that will make the visitor's stay more pleasant. Standards of hotels and restaurants have been vastly improved, roads and transportation in general have developed by leaps and bounds with wide modern highways now sweeping through countryside that used to be served only by simple, gravel roads. Standards of service may not have kept pace with the building program and, it has to be admitted, Yugoslavia is no longer the budget destination on which it founded its current popularity. Yet generalizations are always dangerous, and you could easily find a genuinely warm welcome combined with a modest bill. In these matters, as in so many others, Yugoslavia is amazingly diverse.

The creation of the vast modern hotel complexes along the Dalmatian coast turned the country into one of the most popular goals for the package-tour operators of most of the European countries. Yearly, waves of tourists break on the coast, filling the huge interlinked hotels to capacity. If you are looking for a reasonably-priced holiday and do not mind being one of a multilingual crowd, then the benefits are considerable. If, however, you want atmosphere, like to find character and interest in your surroundings and enjoy uncluttered scenery, then keep away from the hurly-burly of the coast and head for the mountains of Slovenia, Bosnia-Herzegovina or Montenegro. There you will discover that the traditional fascinations of Yugoslavia are still very much alive.

All prices quoted in this Guide are based on those available to us at time of writing. Given the general volatility of European costs and the fact that Yugoslavia itself was heading into a period of general austerity—indeed, of rationing—it is inevitable that changes will have taken place by the time this book becomes available. We trust, therefore, that you will take prices quoted as indicators only, and will double-check to be sure of the latest figures.

We would like to thank Sylvie Nickels for her considerable assistance in preparing this edition. Our gratitude goes to Mr. Ivo Armenko, Director of the Yugoslavian National Tourist Office in London, his deputy, Mr. Boris Marelic, and to the staff, for their constant help, advice and kindness; also to the Yugoslavian National Tourist Office in Belgrade and the tourist associations of many individual Republics, regions and resorts for their assistance and cooperation.

Errors inevitably creep into any guide. Hotels and restaurants suddenly fail in their service, acts of governments and of God change the traveler's lot overnight, and suddenly our recommendations seem quite wrong. We greatly appreciate letters from our readers telling us of their experiences and chastizing us for our mistakes.

Our addresses are:

in the U.S.
Fodor's Travel Guides, 2 Park Avenue, New York, N.Y. 10016;
in the U.K.
Fodor's Travel Guides, 9–10 Market Place, London W1.

FACTS AT YOUR FINGERTIPS

 WHEN TO GO. July and August are the most popular months for holidays along the coast. They are also, of course, the most crowded and the hottest. In the majority of places the heat is tempered by the sea breezes, but one or two spots, notably the town of Split (not the surroundings), are sheltered by mountains and become rather airless. A fair amount of rain falls in the Kvarner Gulf region at the summer's height. It rarely lasts very long, however, and the climate at this period is too warm for it to be very noticeable. Bathing is possible on the coast from early May or June (depending on latitude of resort) to early October. Winters are pleasant, though it may rain a lot up to about May.

Summers can be very hot indeed inland, unless you contrive to spend at least part of your time in the mountains. Spring and fall are decidedly the best times for the interior. Winters there can be extremely cold. Winter sports in the inland mountain regions of all the Republics begin in December and last until April or May.

Average maximum daily temperatures in degrees Fahrenheit and centigrade:

Belgrade

	Jan.	Feb.	Mar.	Apr.	May	June	July	Aug.	Sept.	Oct.	Nov.	Dec.
F°	37	41	52	64	73	79	82	82	75	64	52	41
C°	3	5	11	18	23	26	28	28	24	18	11	5

Split

	Jan.	Feb.	Mar.	Apr.	May	June	July	Aug.	Sept.	Oct.	Nov.	Dec.
F°	50	52	57	64	73	81	86	86	79	68	59	54
C°	10	11	14	18	23	27	30	30	26	20	15	12

Here is a simple conversion chart to help you change Fahrenheit into centigrade and vice versa—

°Centigrade	°C or °F	°Fahrenheit
−18	0	32
−15	5	41
−12	10	50
−9.5	15	59
−7	20	68
−4	25	77
−1	30	86
2	35	95
4.5	40	104
7	45	113
10	50	122

Off-Season Travel. This can be rewarding in Yugoslavia, not only for bypassing the crowds and higher prices, but for the opportunity to meet and know the people of the country. Spring is particularly delightful for nature-lovers, and the most comfortable season for almost every kind of sightseeing. Fall and winter are best for hunting. Winters are cold inland, but very pleasant by the sea (though there are rainy periods). The average winter temperatures along the Dalmatian coast are higher than those on the French or Italian rivieras, but strong winds called the *bura* and *maestral* blow occasionally from inland.

The winter sports season is at its height, as elsewhere in Europe, from January until about the end of March.

WHERE TO GO. Regions and Cities. Yugoslavia, except for its coast, is a relatively unexplored area. Travelers today, however, encounter all of the comforts and facilities to which they are accustomed. Yet a journey to Yugoslavia remains an adventure; wherever you go, this is a land of bold bright contrasts. Scenically, the Alps of Slovenia and wild peaks of Montenegro contrast with the vast flat Danube plains of Serbia. Historically, the ancient Slav and Turkish cultures, everywhere in evidence, contrast with rapid economic and industrial growth. Holiday-wise, the sleepy sun-soaked siesta of a Dalmatian beach contrasts with a motor trip over the lovely mountain roads of Macedonia, or a journey by hydrofoil down the Danube from Belgrade to the Iron Gates. The extremes of physical tourist comfort range from the luxury of Dubrovnik to the rough-and-ready joys of a modest motel in Macedonia.

Yugoslavia is a sizeable country: its 98,000 square miles make it slightly larger than Great Britain, or Oregon; it has a population of over 22 million. Distances are made longer by the country's many mountain ranges. Fully three-fourths of its area consists of mountains and highlands. Most tourists prefer to concentrate on one region at a time. These (and main centers) are:

Istria and the Kvarner Gulf: Portorož, Pula, Opatija, Rijeka
Central Dalmatia: Zadar, Split
Southern Dalmatia and Montenegro: Dubrovnik, Herceg-novi, Budva
Inland Slovenia: Ljubljana, Maribor, Bled
Inland Croatia: Zagreb, Varaždin, Plitvice Lakes
Serbia: Belgrade, Niš, Priština, Novi Sad
Bosnia-Herzegovina: Sarajevo, Mostar, Jajce, Banja Luka
Macedonia: Skopje, Ohrid
Inland Montenegro: Titograd, Cetinje, Žabljak

All of these regions (except the coast, which is divided between Slovenia, Croatia and Montenegro) are autonomous Socialist Republics in the Federal Socialist Republic of Yugoslavia. Inside Serbia, Kosovo (largely Albanian) and the Vojvodina (partly Hungarian, but including many other nationalities) also enjoy autonomy. You will find that each region has its own character and traditions, and its own individual charm.

The Coast. If, like most tourists, you seek the sun, Yugoslavia offers one of the most deeply indented coastlines in Europe, 628 km. (400 miles) as the crow flies, but 6,116 km. (3,823 miles) of actual shoreline, including about 1,000 islands and 100s of attractive beaches set against a scenic background of blue skies, towering limestone mountains and a myriad of offshore islands, covered sometimes with pinewoods, sometimes with olive groves or vineyards, and sometimes with Mediterranean scrub and fragrant wild herbs. From north to south, some of the principal towns or tourist centers are: Opatija, a highly popular seaside resort with many fine hotels; Rijeka, Yugoslavia's main seaport; Zadar, noted for both Roman and medieval relics and ruins; Split, where the entire heart of the old city is formed by Diocletian's third-century Roman palace; peaceful Makarska; fabulous walled Dubrovnik with its ramparts, moat and drawbridges; Budva, a little walled Venetian town, recovering from the devastating earthquake of Easter 1979; Sveti Stefan, a one-time fishing village, now a luxury tourist complex; Bar, rapidly growing into a major seaport; and Ulcinj, a Moslem town with a splendid beach, close to the Albanian frontier.

You can cruise this marvelous coast on a comfortable Jadrolinija cruise steamer, starting from Venice or Rijeka. If you visit the islands you have to use hydrofoil, car-and-passenger ferries, or the passenger services run by Jadrolinija. You can also use the Jadranska Magistrala (Adriatic Highway) to travel up and down the coast by comfortable bus or private car, using the now numerous car ferries to reach the nearer islands. Either way you can visit such wonderful places as Rab in the north Brač, a short sea journey from Split; Hvar; magic Korčula, where some maintain Marco Polo was born; Mljet, which some claim to be the most beautiful of all Dalmatia's islands, and a host of other lovely places.

Inland Slovenia. If you prefer Alpine lakes and mountains, Slovenia is for you. Its capital, Ljubljana, is bright and mainly modern with a fascinating medieval citadel, built on the site of prehistoric and Roman settlements. Bled is beside a mountain lake reflecting the glaciers of the Julian Alps, featuring fine hotels, water sports and mountain trails. Higher up you come to Bohinj, by a larger lake nestled at the base of Triglav, Yugoslavia's highest mountain. Western Yugoslavia is noted for limestone caverns and underground rivers, characteristic of the karst that covers much of the country. One of the loveliest limestone grottos in the world is in Slovenia at Postojna, halfway between Trieste and Ljubljana. Here a tiny electric train carries sightseers for nearly five kilometers (three miles) through vast underground vaults richly adorned with crystal stalactites and stalagmites. The sumptuous illumination and awesome acoustics of these caverns remind one of some enormous cathedral.

Bosnia-Herzegovina. Perhaps your taste runs to the exotic? Then explore Bosnia-Herzegovina, a land of beautiful bare mountains, cut by fertile green valleys and spectacular river gorges. This remote mountainous province has retained a distinct Turkish character. You can reach Sarajevo, its capital, by air, train, or comfortable coach services and good roads. Here you will discover Turkish mosques, minarets, and bazaars, finely set off by well-designed modern structures, the latest of them created to cater for the 1984 Winter Olympics.

Here, too, stands another historic landmark: the bridge on which Archduke Franz Ferdinand of Austria was assassinated, an event whose repercussions finally exploded into World War I. The Bosnian hinterland is a wild region of mountains and valleys, waterfalls and Moslem communities. The last two are combined in the little town of Jajce, a medieval capital of Bosnia and a modern historic landmark as well, for it was here that Tito's partisans proclaimed the modern republic of Yugoslavia in 1943.

Inland Montenegro. Even more remote is the former kingdom of Montenegro, of which Titograd is the modern capital. Here, atop Mount Lovčen, is perhaps the most startling single panorama in Europe: a real Sputnik-eye view of the lovely Gulf of Kotor on the one hand, and the high-rearing Black Mountains of inland Montenegro on the other. At Cetinje, you'll visit the modest palace of Montenegro's former king. Beyond are the awe-inspiring gorges of the Tara and Piva rivers, and the exciting road over the Čakor Pass and through the Rugovo Gorge to Peć, gateway to Serbia and Macedonia.

Serbia. Serbia is of interest to students of history, art and folklore. In Belgrade (Beograd, meaning "White City") you are really in the heart of the Balkans. Few modern metropolises boast as romantic a city park as the Kalemegdan, where you can ramble freely through an ancient Turkish fortress built on a still more ancient Roman one, throw coins down a well from which people were drinking 2,000 years ago, or gaze out over the balconied cliffs to where the mighty Sava River pours its waters into the still mightier Danube. Beyond begin the endless plains of the Vojvodina. As Yugoslavia's capital, Belgrade is, of course, the point to which all roads lead. From it, you can head south for the monastery country of South Serbia and Macedonia, via Kraljevo, Niš (where the healing springs were used in Roman days), Skopje and Ohrid.

Macedonia. Macedonia—worth an expedition in itself—is a vast province where most roads follow deep mountain gorges. This backward province is being transformed into an exciting example of progress, industrial development, agricultural improvement, and education.

Skopje, its capital, has been tastefully reconstructed after the heavy damage inflicted by the earthquake of July 1963, and is once again the busy center.

In the southwest corner of Macedonia is amazing Lake Ohrid, where numerous church-frescos indicate a humanist revival of art in the early Middle Ages. Here too you can dine off a species of trout found nowhere else in the world, a "living fossil" which hasn't changed in 300 million years.

Inland Croatia. Between Belgrade and Ljubljana, on Yugoslavia's main inland highway, lies Zagreb, city of the Middle Ages and at the same time, as happens so often in Yugoslavia, a very up-to-date town. In many parts of Croatia, where ancient ruined castles and fortresses stand on steep hilltops, the Middle Ages and the 20th century seem very close together. This is an extremely prosperous industrial region.

South of Zagreb toward the coast lie the famous Plitvička Jezera (Plitvice Lakes), a chain of cascading mountain lakes, now a national park. Here, amid centuries-old forests, 16 jewel-like green-and-blue lakes spill mile after mile, one into the other, as down a flight of steps. The very last waterfall of all, 80 m. (264 ft.) lower than the highest, sprays up in a huge natural fountain. The area is lined with limestone caverns, and served by hotels and camp sites.

Spas, Hot Springs. These are found principally in Slovenia, Croatia, Serbia and Bosnia. Among the 100s of thermal stations are a number which are once more beginning to attract international clientele. Vrnjačka Banja is one of the largest and best-known. Rogaška Slatina, in Slovenia, is well-provided with hotels. Ilidža, close to Sarajevo, occupies a delightful situation. There are others scattered throughout the inland parts of Yugoslavia, especially in the north, in Croatia and Slovenia. Some have been or are being developed to international standards and are referred to in our regional chapters, though others do not have the range and quality of facilities of their Western European rivals. Information about specific disorders treated by Yugoslavia's curative springs can be obtained from any Yugoslav Information Office.

WHAT WILL IT COST. Because of a combination of improved, more sophisticated amenities and inflation, Yugoslavia is no longer the cheap country it once was, especially at the upper end of the accommodations scale. But a general raising of standards at all levels means that you can have an excellent, fascinating and moderately inexpensive vacation by choosing from the wide range of lower-priced accommodations now available.

You can make major economies by traveling out of season when hotel prices are lower. In a large tourist area such as Dubrovnik, for example, the cheaper rooms in a hotel may double in price for July, August and September, and the more expensive rooms will go up by 30–50%. Remember, too, that you have only to venture a little off the beaten track to find a sharp drop in prices.

Private house accommodations, available in four categories, cost substantially less than hotels. The general price range of a double room with bath or shower in a private home in the top category is from $12–20 depending on place and season; in lower categories, the price may be half these figures. In many cases, half- or full-board can also be provided.

The Yugoslavian National Tourist Board quotes *all* hotel prices in dollars or deutschmarks, though the hotels themselves must be paid in dinars. Consequently, as the exchange rate fluctuates, you may well find a difference between the advertised dollar price of a hotel and the actual dinar price. Watch out for these potential discrepancies.

At presstime, the exchange rate for the dinar was 65 to the U.S. dollar and 105 to the pound sterling. These rates will certainly change by publication time.

	Dinars
A typical day might cost one person:	
Good hotel, per person in a double room, breakfast, service and taxes included	750
Lunch in Moderate restaurant, with half-bottle local wine and coffee	400

Set dinner at hotel, with wine and coffee	500
Transport (4–5 tram/bus rides or 1 taxi)	60
Refreshments in a café	100
Evening entertainment	250
10% for contingencies	200
	2260

(Prices above for high season at main resort; at inland center in low season costs could be halved.)

Sample Costs. Tram or bus ticket about 12 dinars; taxi a basic 20 plus six per km. (but gas prices will force these figures up). Men's haircut 80 dinars, women's 200. Cinema 40 dinars, theater 100–200—but up to 300 dinars or more for special (e.g. festival) performances; opera tickets in Belgrade cost around 300 dinars. Beer 25–30 dinars, whiskey 80 and up, *šljivovica* 25–40; bottle of wine in Moderate restaurant from 120 dinars, in supermarket from 60. Coffee is currently rationed, but in a café should cost around 25–35 dinars.

SOURCES OF INFORMATION. You have now decided *when* you want to visit Yugoslavia, and probably have a fair idea of *where* you wish to travel in the country. Next thing to do is to seek the advice of a travel agent—that is, if you haven't done so already. Even experienced travelers will find it advantageous to do so. A good agent can save you endless time. For package tour bookings and transportation reservations his charge to you will be the same as you would pay direct, as he receives a commission from carriers and tour operators. If he works out for you an individual itinerary, he will make a service charge on the total cost of your trip—usually 10 to 15 percent, but it will more than likely *save* you money on balance. If you don't know of a reputable travel agent near your home, write:

In the United States: The American Society of Travel Agents, 711 Fifth Ave., New York, NY 10022.

In Britain: Association of British Travel Agents, 55–57 Newman St., London WIP 4AH.

If you want further details to plan your trip, here are the addresses of some of the Yugoslav government tourist offices abroad:

In the United States:

New York City: Yugoslav State Tourist Office, 767 Third Ave., NY 10020. Consulate General of the S.F.R. of Yugoslavia, 488 Madison Ave., NY 10022

Chicago: Yugoslav General Consulate, 307 N. Michigan Ave., Suite 1600, Illinois 60601.

Cleveland: Yugoslav Consulate General, 1700 East 13th St., Suite 4R, Ohio 44114.

Pittsburgh: Consulate General of the S.F.R. of Yugoslavia, 625 Stanwix

WE WANT AND APPRECIATE YOUR COMMENTS

Errors are bound to creep into any guidebook. Hotels and restaurants can suffer instant or gradual decline in the quality of their service, acts of governments or God can change the travel picture, and in many ways, items that we presented as gospel will now appear to be untrue.

For these reasons we greatly appreciate letters from you, the reader, telling us of your travel experiences, chastising us, if you will, for our errors, or advising us of our oversights. We want to know! (We also appreciate words of praise, and we receive a lot of those too.) Your letters help us improve our coverage, but they also give us that essential "consumer's eye view," which is so helpful. We want to produce the best-possible travel guide series—and you can help us do it.

Please send your comments to

Research Director
Fodor's Travel Guides
2 Park Avenue
New York, N.Y. 10016

St., Apt. 1605, Pa. 1522.

San Francisco: Yugoslav Consulate, 1375 Sutter St., Suite 406, Calif. 94109.

Washington: Yugoslav Embassy, 2410 California St., N.W., Washington D.C. 20008.

In Canada:

Toronto: Yugoslav General Consulate, 377 Spadina Rd., Ontario M5P 2V7.

Ottawa: Yugoslav Embassy, 17 Blackburn Ave., Ontario K1N 8A2.

In the U.K.:

London: Yugoslav National Tourist Office, 143 Regent St., London W1R 8AE. Yugoslav Embassy, Consular Section, 5–7 Lexham Gdns., London W8 5JU.

TOUR OPERATORS. Suggested **American** tour operators:
Atlas Ambassador, 509 Madison Ave., New York, NY 10022.
Kompas Yugoslavia, 630 Fifth Ave., New York, NY 10020.
Maupintour, 1555 St. Andrews Dr., Lawrence, Kansas 66044.
Olson Travelworld, P.O. Box 92734, Los Angeles, California.
Thomas Cook Ltd., 18 East 48th St., New York, NY 10017.
Trafalgar Tours, 30 Rockefeller Plaza, New York, NY.
Yugoslav Travel Agency Centrotourist International, 509 Madison Ave., New York, NY 10022.
Yugotours, 350 Fifth Ave., New York, NY 10001 (for charter flights, too).

Suggested **Canadian** tour operators:
Pierbusseti, 6 North Michigan Avenue, Chicago, Illinois 60602.
Sun Tours Ltd., 1470 Don Mills Rd., Don Mills, Ontario.
UTL Holiday Tours, 22 College St., Toronto, Ontario.
Yugotours of Canada Ltd., 100 Adelaide St. West, Suite 1350, Toronto, Ontario.

Suggested **British** tour operators:
Cosmos, Cosmos House, 1 Bromley Common, Bromley, Kent.
Global Holidays, Glen House, 200 Tottenham Court Rd., London W1P OJP.
Horizon, Broadway, Edgbaston Five Ways, Birmingham B15 1BB.
Phoenix Holidays, 29 Thurloe Place, London SW7 2HP.
Pilgrim Holidays, 3 Cork St., London W1X 1HA.
Saga Holidays (for senior citizens), 119 Sandgate Rd., Folkestone, Kent.
Seven Seas Sailing Club, Rodermsham Green, Sittingbourne, Kent ME13 ONG (Dalmatian Coast).
Thomson Holidays, Greater London House, Hampstead Rd., London NW1 7SD.
Yugotours, Chesham House, 150 Regent St., London W1R 5FA.

Naturist Holidays. These are operated on a package basis by Yugotours (address above) and other firms, for example Peng Travel, 86 Station Rd., Gidea Park, Essex RM2 6DB. Accommodations are in special camps and hotel villages, complete with beaches, restaurants, shops, sports facilities, parking lots, and sanitary facilities, such as at Punat (island of Krk), Poreč, Medulin, Rovinj, Koversada (near Vrsar in Istria), Rab, Srebreno (near Dubrovnik), Vrboska (on the island of Hvar), and Ada on an island on Montenegro's river border with Albania.

Congresses. Though special congress centers are only just beginning to appear in Yugoslavia, there are many towns and cities that are able to cater for most needs. Full information can be obtained through Yugoslav National Tourist Offices or Yugocongress, Kaptol 5, 41000 Zagreb.

Youth Travel. There is a special office which organizes holidays and travel for students and young people in Yugoslavia; it is the *Biro za medunarodnu razmenu omladine i studenta* (Bureau for the Exchange of Youth and Students), at Mose Pijade 12, Belgrade. It maintains a number of youth hostels as well as international youth centers in Dubrovnik, Rovinj, and Bečiči; and arranges holidays and educational trips throughout the country.

 PACKAGE TOURS. The most economical way to travel, at any cost level, is on the package tour. Thus, ex-London, a 14-day trip to Podgora is priced at £170–£298 (available from Yugotours); 14 days in Istria is £190–£300 (from Thomson); and 14 days in Dubrovnik is £198–£364 (from Phoenix). All these include air fare and half-board accommodations. Price variations are because of differing standards of hotel and seasonal rates.

From the U.S. a one-week all-expense tour can run from $539 up, including airfare, or from $290, land portion only; two weeks would be $693 to $749 for the land portion. Among typical packages offered recently were: *Globus Gateway's* 13 day Yugoslavia and Venice tour, with stays in Zagreb, Belgrade, Sarajevo, Dubrovnik and Split. Roundtrip from and to the U.S. is via Munich, Germany; land cost began at $600. *Percival* featured two tours—a 22-day "Balkan Holiday" that spent about a third of its time in Yugoslavia, land cost coming to about $1,740; and a 15-day budget "Adriatic Holiday" stopping in Yugoslavia before Austria and Greece. Land rate for the latter was $989. Although booked from the U.S., *Cosmos* has tours beginning and ending in London – one covering Yugoslavia, Greece, Turkey and Bulgaria in 15 days for $588. Prices and itineraries for 1984 were being set as we went to press, but the above are representative of the type of tours you are likely to come across. Prices are per person, double occupancy. All of the above tours are booked through a travel agent rather than directly through the packagers.

Centrotourist Yugoslav Travel Agency, 509 Madison Avenue, New York, NY 10022, has a Travel Chex voucher plan guaranteeing accommodations without advance reservations in any of 37 hotels in 18 cities. Hotels are Deluxe,

First and Tourist class. Centrotourist also has railpass and fly/drive packages. These plans all allow you some of the price advantages of package tours with the flexibility of independent travel.

The pay-as-you-go, go-where-you-please tourist is of course more difficult to budget for. His tastes may call for deluxe, comfortable, economy or rock-bottom roughing-it accommodations. "Deluxe" as here used, means staying in the best hotels; traveling by plane, car and first-class railroad sleepers; best seats at the opera, and paying reasonable attention to nightclubs. "Comfortable" travel involves staying at good hotels but not the palaces; eating in good restaurants, but not the most expensive ones, indulging in moderate amounts of nightlife and orchestra-seat entertainment; traveling by train or bus. "Economical" travel still lets you into clean comfortable hotels, but without style, and away from the larger resorts; you can eat good food, but in crowded restaurants, since places both cheap *and* good are bound to be crowded. You'll patronize more bars with jukeboxes rather than nightclubs. "Rock-bottom roughing-it" means picknicking, hitchhiking, cycling, or second-class on the train, cheap restaurants and staying in the least-expensive private houses.

On these four levels, daily expenses and hotel-plus-three-meals in high season, double occupancy per person, will come to approximately 4,500 dinars deluxe; 2,300 dinars first-class comfortable; 1,500 dinars economical; and 500 dinars roughing-it.

An important budgeting consideration is the *season.* In spring and fall there is a reduction on full-board prices, sometimes as much as 40%. Highest rates are in July and August, for which period it is also essential to make your reservations far ahead: many tours and hotels are completely booked up, with long waiting lists, months in advance.

 TRAVEL FOR THE HANDICAPPED. Flying Wheel Tours, P.O. Box 382, Owatonna, Minn. 55060, specializes in individual tours. Two definitive sources of information in this field are the books *Travelability* by Louis Reamy (Macmillan) and *Access to the World* by Louise Weiss (Facts on File, 460 Park Ave. S., New York, NY.); and the Travel Information Center, Moss Rehabilitation Center, 12th St. and Tabor Rd., Philadelphia, Pennsylvania 19141. For a complete list of tour operators who arrange such travel, write to the Society for the Advancement of Travel for the Handicapped, 26 Court St., Brooklyn, NY 11242.

In the U.K., useful sources of information on travel for the handicapped are the Royal Association for Disability and Rehabilitation, 25 Mortimer St., London W1N 8AB, and Mobility International, 62 Union St., London SE1 1TD.

 TRAVEL DOCUMENTS. To visit Yugoslavia, you should have a national passport, though tourist permits allowing you to enter the country and valid for 30 days can be issued on the strength of a national identity card.

National Travel Club

Over 75 Years of Service To Our members

Membership brings you 14 money-saving benefits and services INCLUDING a subscription to TRAVEL-HOLIDAY magazine AND $35,000 travel accident insurance coverage ($50,000 IMMEDIATELY with an initial 2-year membership) for ALL your travels ANY-WHERE in the world and for the ENTIRE TERM of your membership. You enroll JUST ONCE (at incredibly low annual dues) — No monthly payments to make or bother about.

NO OTHER TRAVEL CLUB GIVES YOU SO MUCH FOR SO LITTLE

Over a HALF MILLION members consider these benefits indispensable:

- $35,000 Travel Accident Insurance ($50,000 on renewal; Immediately with initial 2-year membership
- Subscription to TRAVEL-HOLIDAY magazine
- Travel Information Service
- Book Discounts (25% savings)
- Routing Service
- Travel Digest Evaluation Program
- Avis & National Car Rental Discounts
- Mediguide Service
- Discount travel film Library
- Mail Forwarding Service
- Discount Pharmaceutical Service
- Discount Film Processing
- Car/Puter-Discount Auto Pricing & Buying Service
- Membership Card & Club Emblems

Accident insurance provided by Nationwide Insurance Company, Columbus, Ohio.

PASSPORTS

U.S. residents must apply to the U.S. Passport Agency in Boston, Chicago, Detroit, Honolulu, Houston, Los Angeles, Miami, New Orleans, New York, Philadelphia, San Francisco, Seattle, Stamford (Conn.) or Washington DC, or to the local Federal or County courthouse. In some areas selected post offices are also able to handle passport applications. Take along proof of citizenship, proof of identity (Social Security and credit cards are *not* acceptable), birth certificate, two recent photographs two inches square, full-face, black and white or color, on non-glossy 24-page paper, and taken within the past six months, and $35 plus a $7 processing fee when applying in person (no extra fee when applying by mail); passports for those under 18 are $20. If you still have your previous passport, issued within the past eight years, you may use this to apply by mail, and the fee will again be $35. U.S. passports are valid for ten years and are not renewable. Apply several months in advance of your expected departure date. If you expect to travel extensively you may request a 48- or 96-page passport instead of the usual 24-page one at no extra charge. If your passport is lost or stolen, immediately notify either the nearest American Consul, or the Passport Office, Department of State, Washington, DC, 20524. Record your passport's number and date and place of issue in a separate, secure place.

If not a U.S. citizen, you will need a Treasury Sailing Permit (form 1040 D) certifying that all Federal taxes have been paid: apply to your District Director of Internal Revenue for this. You will have to present: 1) your blue or green alien registration card; 2) passport; 3) travel tickets; 4) most recently filed form 1040; 5) W-2 forms for the most recent full year; 6) most recent current payroll stubs or letter. Check to make sure that this is all. To return to the United States, you will need a reentry permit if you intend to stay abroad longer than one year. Apply for it at least six weeks before departure, in person at the nearest office of the Immigration Service, Washington DC.

British subjects must apply for passports on special forms obtainable from travel agency or any Head Post Office. The application should be sent to the Passport Office for your area (this is clearly indicated on the guidance form). Apply at least five weeks before the passport is required. The regional Passport Offices are located in London, Liverpool, Peterborough, Glasgow, and Newport (Mon.). Applications must be countersigned by your bank manager, or by a solicitor, barrister, doctor, clergyman, or Justice of the Peace who knows you personally. You will need two photos. The fee is £11 and the passport is valid for ten years.

The British Visitor's Passport, costing only £5.50, is valid for Yugoslavia (though many people will tell you that it is not), *provided* you obtain a Tourist Permit for a nominal fee at the frontier. The Tourist Permit is valid for 30 days. If you plan to stay longer and are using a British Visitor's Passport, you should obtain a visa before departure.

VISAS

Yugoslavia has abolished visas on a reciprocal basis. Nationals of most European countries, including Great Britain (who hold full passports), can enter Yugoslavia without formalities: American, Canadian and Australian citizens require a visa, but this is issued free without formality at any frontier post or airport.

HEALTH CERTIFICATES

Not required for entry into Yugoslavia. Canada, United States and U.K. do not require a certificate of vaccination prior to reentry. However, as the law changes from time to time and country to country, we suggest that you take advice about the current status of the need for vaccination before you travel.

 WHAT TO TAKE. More important is what *not* to take. Travel light: by packing only as much luggage as you can easily carry yourself, you simplify going through customs, avoid registering and checking baggage, and make it easier to arrive at hotels where there are no porters. There are currently two kinds of luggage restriction. For transatlantic air-travelers the limit is by size. In 1st class the two pieces allowed must not exceed 62″ in total height, width and length for each piece; in Economy the total for each of the two bags is 106″. For air travelers from other parts of the world the old 66 lb. (in 1st class) and 44 lb. (in Economy) still obtains.

Travel simply: Yugoslavia is an informal country, where a man not wearing a suit or tie will feel awkward in only the best restaurants. Lightweight clothes are, of course, essential in summer, with a light raincoat in case of sudden storms.

Other "musts" for your Yugoslav trip include: your own sports equipment; your favorite photographic film; some English-language books and magazines (though many can now be bought in large towns and resorts); and your own favorite make-up medicines. Pack a small first-aid kit and any medicines you may need and a reserve packet of toilet paper, of the flat type which is easy to pack or carry around. If you wear glasses, bring a spare pair.

 GETTING TO YUGOSLAVIA FROM NORTH AMERICA BY AIR. There are direct flights to Belgrade, Zagreb, Ljubljana and Dubrovnik from New York, or you can fly via several European cities to reach Yugoslavia's main airports: Belgrade, Zagreb, Ljubljana, Dubrovnik, Pula, Sarajevo and Split. Airports at Rijeka, Zadar and Tivat are also equipped to handle large commercial flights. Inside the country, an inexpensive domestic network links these airports with Maribor, Skopje, Ohrid, Osijek, Priština and Titograd. In North America, Yugoslav Airlines, JAT, has offices in New York, Chicago, Los

Angeles, Detroit, Cleveland, and Toronto, plus regular charter flights to Yugoslavia from Chicago, Cleveland and Toronto.

In effect, there are now three types of air fare: First Class, Economy and Charter (of one kind or another). Each has its advantages and disadvantages. Charter is the least flexible, but it is far cheaper than the others; and on regularly-scheduled airlines, charter-group passengers, while paying far less for it, receive the same Economy Class service as do their seat-neighbors who are flying as individuals. For most people who fly as individuals, the level of service and comfort in Economy Class will be quite adequate, and the luxuries of First Class will *not* be worth the considerable added expense. On purely charter-flight lines, the amenities may be more sparing, and the flying times may be longer. From Toronto, Yugoslavia Airlines and Yugotours operate charter flights to Ljubljana, Maribor, Dubrovnik, Belgrade and Skopje, late April to mid-October.

In the last several years the rules for charter groups have been relaxed, and the scheduled carriers have entered the charter/package field so much that the range of possibilities now available is too great to list here. Only you can decide what kind of schedule you have and what kind of trip you want to fit into it; after that, your travel agent can best advise you on the most economical rates and the best deals. Unless you want stopovers (see below), you will save greatly by picking one of the various kinds of excursion or package fares. It's a general guideline to remember that in mid-1981 the basic New York-Belgrade-New York airfare could begin as low as around $860 for 7- to 60-day Excursions. These special fares represent substantial savings when you consider the price of normal economy round trip, $890 (peak season) and $2568 first class.

An excellent survey of the charter flight business and directory of charter flights and their operators is *How to Fly for Less, a Consumer's Guide to Low Cost Air Charters and Other Travel Bargains,* by Jens Jurgen, published by Travel Information Bureau, 44 County Line Road, Farmingdale, NY 11735.

Bonus Stopovers. If you go by charter or package-tour you can save money. However, you are locked into the schedule and/or itinerary of that particular flight or group. If you travel as an individual, it will cost you more, but you can take advantage of various stopovers along the way, time permitting, then return by a circle route that lets you see even more. This is because when you buy a ticket from, say, New York to Belgrade, essentially you have bought the right to use up to 8,060 km. (5,406 miles) of transportation each way. Since the actual air distance is only 6,448 km. (4,505 miles), you have an extra 20% to use as you please, at no extra charge.

For example, here are some of the combinations possible on this particular ticket: New York-Lisbon-Madrid-Geneva-Zürich-Munich-Zagreb-Belgrade. These are by no means the only European cities that can be included, and we suggest that you investigate all the available possibilities, if you have the time to indulge in a really fascinating whistle-stop tour.

GETTING THERE FROM NORTH AMERICA BY SEA. You can take the *Queen Elizabeth 2* to Britain or France and carry on from there by any means you like— that being the only regular transatlantic liner left. Alas, there is no more freighter/passenger service to Yugoslavia.

 GETTING THERE FROM GREAT BRITAIN BY AIR. Belgrade, Zagreb, Ljubljana, Dubrovnik, Pula and Split airports are equipped for the largest international jets. Scheduled services are operated in summer by JAT Yugoslav Airlines to all these destinations. Charter flights go also to Rijeka (Krk).

Consult with your travel agent before booking, as there are always price-cutting battles being waged and fares change almost from month to month. JAT office in London: 201 Regent St., W1.

Stopovers. Travelers from Britain holding full-fare tickets (and *very* few budget-conscious people will travel full-fare) can use stopovers en route to Yugoslavia. Here are just a few examples. Leaving the British capital, you may fly first to Paris and then into Switzerland (Basel). Then you can continue to Zürich or Munich and Zagreb before arrival in Belgrade.

Another possibility is to fly to Brussels and then via Frankfurt and Vienna, or Frankfurt, Stuttgart and Munich, to Zagreb.

Brussels also may be visited in place of Paris and Basel. You can fly London-Brussels-Zürich and then continue via Munich and Zagreb to Belgrade.

 GETTING THERE FROM GREAT BRITAIN BY TRAIN. From London to Yugoslavia there is only one through service available. The main train is the *Tauern Express,* which runs from Ostend to Ljubljana, Zagreb and terminates at Split on the Adriatic coast. The connecting service from London departs from Victoria in the early afternoon. If you wish to pay the supplement and travel by Jetfoil from Dover to Ostend, then it is possible to depart from Victoria later, at 15.58. The *Tauern Express* leaves Ostend at 21.15 and travels across Germany overnight, arriving at Stuttgart at 06.18 the following morning. Thence it goes via Munich (09.00) and Klagenfurt (16.19), arriving at Ljubljana in mid-afternoon (15.47). The train then carries on to Zagreb (17.20) and finally reaches its journey's end, Split, at 05.44 the following morning. Sleeping accommodation is available in the form of 1st and 2nd class sleeping cars from Ostend to Salzburg and from Ljubljana to Split. There are also 2nd class couchettes from Ostend to Klagenfurt. A restaurant facility is provided from Munich to Villach; at other times a light refreshment service is available—no on train catering service is advertised for the Yugoslavian part of the trip.

For Belgrade probably the more convenient route is via Paris using the *Simplon Express,* although this does have the slight disadvantage of requiring a change of termini in the French capital. From London to Paris there is a choice

EUROPE AND
DON'T MISS

Now you can sail the legendary QE2 to or from Europe—
and fly the other way, free! That means you can begin or
end your European vacation with five glorious days and
nights on the last of the great superliners. And get a free
British Airways flight between London and most major
U.S. cities. (Specially reserved flights of the Concorde are
open to QE2 passengers at incredible savings.)

Only the QE2 offers four top restaurants and five
lively nightspots. A glittering disco, a glamorous casino,
and a 20,000-bottle wine cellar. The famed "Golden
Door" spa, with saunas and Jacuzzi® Whirlpool Baths.
And your choice of yoga, aerobic dance, jogging, swimming, hydrocalisthenics and massage.
• Regular crossings between England and New York,
some also calling at other U.S. ports. Sail roundtrip at big
savings.
• Cunard's choice European tours—varying in length,
attractively priced, either escorted or independent—all
include a QE2 crossing.
• Big discounts at all of Cunard's London hotels—
including the incomparable Ritz.
• Enchanting QE2 European cruises, which may be combined with a crossing.

For all the facts, including any requirements and
restrictions, contact your travel agent or Cunard, P.O. Box
999, Farmingdale, NY 11737; (212) 661-7777.

CUNARD

Certain restrictions apply to free airfare and Concorde programs. See
your travel agent.

The QE2:
The Magic.

British Registry

of routes and ways of travel. First of all the quickest—which is by rail/hovercraft, marketed under the name *City Link*. Departure is from Charing Cross at 11.00, arriving Paris (Nord) 17.41. Then there is the traditional route from Victoria—leaves 09.58 by rail, thence by ferry Dover/Calais, finally train arriving at Paris (Nord) at 18.25. Finally, for people on a tight budget, there is a coach service run by Hoverspeed, leaving London (Russell Square) 08.45, arriving Paris 17.40.

The *Simplon Express* pulls out of Paris' Gare de Lyon at 19.30 and reaches Venice around 8 the following morning. It then runs through Trieste, Ljubljana and Zagreb to reach Belgrade at 22.10. Full restaurant service Paris to Dôle and from Ljubljana to Belgrade. Overnight 1st and 2nd class sleeping cars available, as well as 2nd class couchettes.

If you don't want to change in Paris, there is a summer through-service from Calais (Gare Maritime) at 19.30 to Venice, arriving just before three the next afternoon. There is then a cross-platform interchange to the *Venezia Express* which arrives in Ljubljana by 23.00. The train travels on overnight to reach Belgrade at 07.44. The connecting service for this route leaves London (Victoria) at 13.58.

In all cases reservation of seats is recommended. The *Thomas Cook Continental Timetable* has an excellent coverage of mainline services throughout Europe and contains a section on Yugoslavia. It is published monthly—but be sure to buy the latest edition as train services change between summer and winter. Available in the U.S. from Forsyth Travel Library, 9154 West 57th St., PO Box 2975, Shawnee Mission, Kansas 66201. In Britain order from: Thomas Cook Ltd., Timetable Publishing Office, PO Box 36, Peterborough, PE3 6SB.

GETTING THERE FROM GREAT BRITAIN BY CAR. Your destination inside Yugoslavia may determine the highway-route that you choose from England at the outset. To reach the Dalmatian coast your best bet is to cross the frontier at Trieste in Italy. (The most enjoyable way to reach Trieste is to drive across France to Basel in Switzerland and then take the new St. Gotthard road tunnel into Italy. Count on two nights en route.) But if you are making for Yugoslavia's main *autoput* (which leads to Zagreb, Belgrade and the south) you would be better advised to take one of the mountain passes from Austria; there are nearly a dozen of these, but the principal ones are outlined on p. 16.

Car-Sleeper Expresses. Many hundreds of miles of tiring driving and hours of time can be saved by utilizing one of these summer express trains for transporting your car and your party. While the car-sleeper cost is apparently expensive, it is fairly reasonable when compared with the cost of hotels and meals en route by road. It is obviously more advantageous for a party of four than two.

Useful services for Yugoslavia-bound motorists terminate at such places as Villach, Salzburg, Belgrade, Rijeka, Ljubljana, or Zagreb. Internal Yugoslav services also carry cars and passengers on rail routes between main cities and the coast.

GETTING THERE FROM GREAT BRITAIN BY BUS.
The once-thriving trans-Continental bus scene is now a shadow of its former self. At least two major companies have collapsed and the others are finding the going difficult. For the latest information contact Europabus, 11 East 44th St., New York 10017; or Room 27, Eversholt House, Eversholt St., London NW1 1BG (tel. 01-388 6846).

GETTING THERE FROM THE CONTINENT BY AIR.
The Yugoslav national airline, known by its initials *JAT*, has a network of services radiating from Belgrade and, to a lesser extent, Zagreb. Many European capitals and other major cities are served. There are also direct flights from Dubrovnik to a number of European destinations. These are most frequent in the summer. In addition, the respective national airline of the country concerned also covers most of these routes.

GETTING THERE FROM THE CONTINENT BY TRAIN. From Western Europe there are two main arteries feeding into Yugoslavia. Firstly through Austria via Villach, entering Yugoslavia at Jesenice, and secondly the central route from northern Italy via Venice and Trieste which reaches Yugoslavia at Sezana. The more important of the two routes is that through Austria. It also has the advantage that the trains are composed of more modern and comfortable coaches. The services available from France (Paris) and Belgium (Ostend) have already been mentioned (pages 13–14).

A wide range of through train-services is available from Germany. The *Yugoslavia Express* from Frankfurt travels via Stuttgart and Munich to Ljubljana and Belgrade. The *Mostar Dalmacija* commences its journey at Stuttgart and runs to Split on the Dalmatian Coast. There is also the *Akropolis Express,* originating at Munich and running down the backbone of Yugoslavia, calling at Ljubljana, Zagreb, Belgrade, Skopje (among other stops) before continuing its journey to Thessaloniki and Athens. The *Hellas Express* covers much the same ground, but starts at Dortmund, through Cologne (where you can catch it via a London/Ostend connection), then on to Mannheim and Munich. A through service is also available from Hamburg; this one operates via Nurnberg (by-passing Munich) and Graz, running direct to Zagreb and Belgrade. The train takes slightly over 24 hours on the trip.

It is obligatory to reserve seats on all trains from stations in Germany to Yugoslavia. Trains are heavily loaded, especially at weekends and during holiday periods, with "guestworkers" going home to their families in Yugoslavia and Greece.

A through service operates from Zurich to Belgrade, running via Innsbruck to Ljubljana and Zagreb, taking a day and a bit to complete the journey. Sleeping accommodation is available. Zagreb and Belgrade can be reached also by through trains from Vienna (Sudbahnhof).

GETTING THERE FROM THE CONTINENT BY SEA. From Trieste and Venice, Yugoslav and Italian ferries cross the Adriatic to Dubrovnik and other Yugoslav ports. Three- and four-day cruises to Yugoslav ports operate from Ancona each week.

In the summer, passengers without cars can use the car-ferry services from Venice, Ancona, Pescara, and Bari to Pula, Zadar, Split, and Dubrovnik and Bar.

GETTING THERE FROM THE CONTINENT BY BUS. Numerous Yugoslav bus lines run from Austria, Italy, Romania, Bulgaria and also Istanbul. They are comfortable, fast and cheap. Details of schedules, however, are not always easy to come by. Enquire from any Yugoslav National Tourist Office.

Europabus has some services from capitals to Yugoslav cities: contact Europabus, rue de Miromesnil, 89 Paris 75008.

GETTING THERE FROM THE CONTINENT BY CAR. Tourists driving overland from Western European countries may cross the frontier into Yugoslavia on any road from Italy or Austria. The main routes lead from Udine through Gorizia to Nova Gorica; from Trieste to Kozina or Koper; from Villach either through Tarvisio in Italy to Rateče (a flattish road), or over the Würzen Pass (steep on Austrian side, less so in Yugoslavia) to Kranjska Gora; from Klagenfurt through the excellent Ljubelj (Loibl) tunnel to Trzič-Kranj; or from Graz by the somewhat flatter road to Maribor. There are also some fascinating steep mountain passes by which the frontier may be crossed between the Loibl Tunnel and the Maribor road.

Car-Sleeper Expresses. See above.

CUSTOMS. Frontier formalities for foreign tourists entering Yugoslavia are not at all irksome and take little time. Yugoslavian customs authorities observe the international customs convention and are generally lenient toward tourists. At the present time, you may bring into the country duty-free:

1. **Personal effects** (clothes, luggage, etc.) in reasonable quantities.

2. **Supplies** for personal consumption (tourists over 15 years of age): 200 cigarets or 50 cigars or 250 grams of tobacco; one liter of wine, ¼ liter of spirits; ¼ liter of eau de cologne and small amounts of other perfumes; and reasonable quantities of foodstuffs for the journey.

3. **Equipment** for personal use: two cameras with 12 plates or five rolls of film; a small cine camera with two rolls of film; and a pair of binoculars. Portable equipment: one each, tape recorder, record player (ten records), radio, TV set, musical instrument, typewriter, pocket calculator; camping equipment, bicycle and sports boat with or without motor; sports equipment—e.g. fishing tackle, pair of skis, two tennis racquets, scuba diving equipment, a hunting weapon with 50 rounds of ammunition (but you must have permission from either the Yugoslav consular or the diplomatic office in your country of residence).

If you bring in more items than the above (e.g. full range of professional camera gear), you must declare them on entry and present the Customs document on departure.

 YUGOSLAV NATIONAL TOURIST OFFICE. It is possible to plan various types of holidays with the help of the Yugoslav National Tourist Offices (addresses above), and they can advise on special-interest tours. In addition, each republic and every resort has its own tourist organization. The main problem is that it is often extremely difficult to get information in one area about another, and even local information is not always reliable. Be prepared to check and double check—and to exercise patience!

Note. If you or your local travel agent want to organize an itinerary through all or part of Yugoslavia, your best bet is to get in touch with the head office of one or other of the big Yugoslav travel firms. Though each specializes in the area where it has its headquarters, each has offices throughout the country, and can handle itineraries on a national scale.

On the whole you do best to book with the company whose head office is situated in the town or region where you *start* your journey, in order to deal with problems and changes in advance. Names and headquarter-towns of some of these are as follows:

Atlas, Pile 1, 50000 Dubrovnik.

Centroturist, Bulevar Revolucije 70, 11000 Belgrade.

Dalmacijaturist, Titova Obala 5, 58000 Split.

Generalturist, Praška 5, 41000 Zagreb.

Globtur, Šmartinska 130, 61000 Ljubljana.

Imterimpex, Ivo Ribar Lola 10, 91000 Skopje.

Inex, Trg Republike 5, 11000 Belgrade.

Intours, Mitra Brkića 1, 81000 Titograd.

Kompas, Pražakova 4, 61000 Ljubljana.

Kvarner Express, Maršala Tita 186, 51410 Opatija.

Montenegroturist, 86000 Budva.

Narom Travel, Youth and Student Travel, Moše Pijade 12, Belgrade.

Putnik, Dragoslava Jovanovića 1, 11000 Belgrade.

Srbija-Turist, Voždova 12, 18000 Niš.

Unis Turist, Morića han, Sarači 77, 71000 Sarajevo.

Vojvodina Turist, Bul. Maršala Tita 19, 21000 Novi Sad.

Yugotours, Djure Djakovića 31, 11000 Belgrade.

GUIDES. Once past the customs inspection, your first contact with Yugoslavia is likely to be the man or woman representing one of the numerous Yugoslav travel organizations such as Kompas, Generalturist, Kvarner Express, Putnik, Dalmacijaturist, Montenegroturist, etc. Their service covers not only the usual hotel and transport reservations, but the thousand other needs of a stranger in a strange land, especially when he cannot speak the local language. All have accredited agents in the U.S., Britain and other countries, whose addresses can be obtained from Yugoslav Tourist Information Offices.

In addition to the commercial travel agencies, many localities maintain a Turistički Ured (Tourist Promotion Office) or Turist Biro which specializes in helping travelers to find accommodations and to enjoy the attractions of the area. Note, however, that the accuracy of information provided is unpredictable! They can also, of course, put you in touch with commercial travel agencies which will either book excursions or arrange for specialized activities such as hunting.

MONEY. There is no limit to the foreign currency and travelers checks you may bring with you, but the import and export of more than 1,500 Yugoslav dinars is prohibited. Surplus Yugoslav money can be exchanged before leaving, provided that you produce official exchange receipts.

At presstime the rate of exchange was about 65 dinars to the U.S. dollar and 105 to the pound sterling. You can usually get a better rate by buying dinars in your own country, but you can only bring 1,500 into Yugoslavia (see above). These rates will certainly change before, and during, 1984.

Helpful Tips About Cash. Always carry a few single dollar bills; they will save you changing small travelers checks, as well as coming in handy for last minute airport shopping.

A very good idea indeed is to stock up with small denomination money for the countries you are going to visit. You can get this in packs of $10, $15 or more from some banks.

Once inside Yugoslavia, you may exchange your travelers checks or foreign currency at the tourist rate at official exchange offices located in travel bureaus, hotels, and railroad stations, as well as banks. Each time you change foreign currency you will receive a certificate, which should be kept to facilitate re-exchange on leaving the country. The dinar is divided into 100 *paras.* There are coins of 5, 10, 20 and 50 paras and 1, 2, 5 and 10 dinars. Banknote denominations are 10, 20, 50, 500 and 1,000 dinars.

Travelers checks are the best way to safeguard your travel funds. In the U.S. Bank of America, First National City, Republic Bank of Dallas, and Perera Co., issue checks only in U.S. dollars; Thomas Cook issues checks in U.S. dollars, British pounds and Australian dollars; Bank of Tokyo in U.S. dollars and Japanese yen; Barclay's Bank in dollars and pounds; and American Express in

U.S. and Canadian dollars, French and Swiss francs, British pounds, German marks and Japanese yen.

Note: You can also cash personal checks up to £50 a time with a British banker's card at most banks, hotels and shops participating in the Eurocheque scheme.

TRAVELING AROUND YUGOSLAVIA BY SEA. A number of comfortable Yugoslav shipping lines serve the main points on the country's Adriatic coast from Venice (in Italy) and Rijeka to as far south as Dubrovnik and Bar. Smaller vessels ply from main ports out to the islands and back. All of these lines are operated by the Yugoslav Adriatic shipping company Jadrolinija, with head offices, Obala Jugoslavenske Mornarice 16, in Rijeka. Cable address: Jadrolinija, Rijeka. General agent in U.S. and Canada: March Shipping Passenger Services, One World Trade Center, Suite 5257, New York 10048; 400 Craig St. West, Montreal, Quebec H2Y 1K1.

Summer season routes serve Rijeka, Zadar, Split, Dubrovnik, Bar and intervening ports. They make the run in 24 hours. Some continue to ports in Greece and Italy, and include car-ferries with drive-on facilities.

The fast coastal routes are operated as pleasure cruises as well as passenger routes. Buses offer an alternative along the Adriatic Highway. If you want to get quickly from A to B along the coast, take a bus; if you want to enjoy the journey specially, take a ship. Fares are moderate. Children under four travel free of charge, and those from four to ten at half fare.

There are many coastal and inter-island services, though on the remoter islands the boats set off very early in the morning, returning in mid-afternoon, so that if you start from the mainland you are obliged to spend at least one night away. You can also travel on the numerous car-ferries, whether you have a car or not.

Hydrofoils operate scheduled services and excursions from Poreč, Pula, Rijeka, Split and Dubrovnik, not only up and down the coast and to the islands, but also to Venice, Rimini and other points in Italy.

TRAVELING WITHIN YUGOSLAVIA BY AIR. Yugoslavia is a country chopped up by innumerable mountains. Air travel is a very practical means of transport, and among the most scenic as well. On the flight from Belgrade to Dubrovnik, for example, the plane spans in a little over an hour, the flat, level plain of the Danube, the rugged uplands of western Serbia and Bosnia, the lunar escarpment of the Dalmatian *karst,* and finally the island-studded Adriatic.

JAT, Yugoslavia's internationally-accredited airline, serves the country's principal cities several times daily. In the summer months, the main Adriatic resorts are well connected by air with Ljubljana, Belgrade, Zagreb and beyond, with the principal air traffic centers of Western Europe. Dubrovnik, Pula and Split have all-year-round daily service to Belgrade, Zagreb, etc., and seasonal services to many towns in Europe. There are airports at all the republics' capitals and Maribor, Tivat, Ohird, Rijeka (Krk Island), and Zadar, as well as Dubrovnik, Pula, and Split.

As part of the government's overall transport policy, the cost of flying internally in Yugoslavia is among the lowest in Europe and is well below that in western Europe. Children under four go free, and between four and 12 travel at half fare.

The free baggage allowance is 15 kilo. (33 lb.) per passenger on internal flights.

TRAVELING WITHIN YUGOSLAVIA BY TRAIN.

Yugoslavia's railway system has been extended and improved by electrification and the introduction of diesel express trains, many of which connect the chief cities almost non-stop. Such expresses, for instance, link Ljubljana–Zagreb–Belgrade; Belgrade–Split; Belgrade–Rijeka; Belgrade–Skopje–Bitola; Belgrade–Sarajevo–Ploče; Zagreb–Rijeka; Zagreb–Split; Zagreb–Zadar; Zagreb–Šibenik and Zagreb–Sarajevo. Most have restaurant or buffet cars, and there are sleeping cars or couchettes on the night trains. Overall speeds, however, are not high, because of the nature of the terrain, but the fastest expresses cover the flat 420 km. (260 miles) between Belgrade and Zagreb in well under five hours. The railway from Belgrade to Bar, which opened in 1976, is a major engineering feat. It crosses Yugoslavia's once remote mountainous center via Titovo Užice, Bijelo Polje and Titograd; its 480 km. (300 miles) include 253 tunnels and some spectacular scenery.

Branch lines run to other principal cities. Thus, Ljubljana is linked to Rijeka, Belgrade (via Vrpolje) to Sarajevo and Kardeljevo (this line following the gorge of the turbulent, though scenic, Neretva River via Mostar).

Four kinds of passenger trains ply the Yugoslav network: "ordinary" (i.e. slow, stopping at all stations), "fast," "express," and "rapide." On most of these though not all, there are both first and second class. A special supplement is charged on express and rapide trains.

It is possible to buy an internal timetable for Yugoslavia for just over 60 dinars. If you can't get it anywhere else, try the Belgrade railway station.

TRAVELING WITHIN YUGOSLAVIA BY BUS.

Coach travel is not only cheaper than travel by train, but faster and more comfortable as well. For example, the daily coach service between Belgrade and Ohrid costs about 500 dinars, considerably less than first-class rail accommodation. The trip takes 14 hours.

Principal Adriatic cities are connected with inland centers by overland bus routes. Wherever you may find yourself, you will probably be able to get by bus to any other point in Yugoslavia within 24 hours. In view of the mountainous nature of the country and the distances involved this represents a considerable achievement.

It is very advisable to have a seat reservation, though this may not be possible unless you are boarding the vehicle at the start of its itinerary. As there is often more than one company operating on the same route, be quite sure which bus you are traveling on and get to the terminus in good time.

Besides the principal long-distance luxury lines, there are of course any number of local services running out of the big cities to the small surrounding towns and villages.

 TRAVELING WITHIN YUGOSLAVIA BY CAR. Foreign tourists driving to Yugoslavia by motorcar or motorcycle may cross the frontier at numerous customs points. No special international documents are required for tourists entering Yugoslavia with a private car (up to nine seats) or motorcycle. Drivers from the U.S., Great Britain and most European countries need only their national driving licence and car registration document. These should be in English, French or German, or should be translated into one of these languages or into Serbo-Croat.

Drivers who are not owners of the vehicle they are using should carry the owner's permit; this document must be certified by a competent national automobile or touring club.

Trailer and motor caravans and small boats on trailers are admitted without special formalities.

Service stations and workshops for repairs exist in most towns and tourist centers. Spare parts for European-made cars can be obtained from appointed dealers, listed on the motoring maps obtainable free from any Yugoslav National Tourist Office. It may take some time to send your requirements from the nearest dealer to the place where you happen to be. Your best bet really is to hire a pack of spares from your car dealer or motoring association on the normal sale or return basis. Yugoslav mechanics, however, are very resourceful and repairs are dealt with quickly.

Automobile Associations. The National Yugoslav Automobile and Motorcycle Federation (headquarters at Belgrade, Ruzveltova 43, tel. 419-555) supplies information to motorists on road conditions, etc. So do regional Automobile Associations at:

Belgrade	Auto-moto savez Srbije	Ivana Milutinovica 58, tel. 456-456
Ljubljana	Auto-moto zveza Slovenije	Titova Cesta 138, tel. 342-378
Sarajevo	Auto-moto savez BiH	Boriše Kovačevića 18, tel. 517-713
Skopje	Auto-moto sojuz na Makedonije	Ivo Ribar Lola 55, tel. 226-825
Titograd	Auto-moto savez Crne Gore	Novaka Miloševa 12/11, tel. 43-555
Zagreb	Auto-moto savez Hrvatske	Draškovićeva 25/1, tel. 522-522

Yellow-painted patrol cars provide free help on all the main routes. You will be asked to pay only for spare parts supplied. If towing is needed, this is provided at fixed rates for members of foreign motoring organizations. In addition, help can be summoned by calling the number 987 in any one of 80 strategically-placed areas. Yugoslavia has roadside telephone kiosks on main roads; else-where you can ask a passing motorist to summon help for you.

Car Rental. International car rental firms have offices in most Yugoslav cities, and cars can also be hired through travel agents. Addresses are given under main centers, but are otherwise easily available from local tourist offices.

Insurance. Third-party insurance is compulsory, and the green card is recom-mended. The Yugoslav insurance companies offer short-term coverage at mod-erate premiums, with a seven-day minimum. They are members of the International Automobile Insurance group, and can act for your home insurers. Main address in Belgrade is 6 Kneza Mihaila; also offices in principal cities and at most frontier points. Apart from ordinary car insurance, it is advisable to have extra cover for the costs that may arise in the case of illness or accident. This can be arranged in Britain through Lloyd's, several of the large insurance companies, the motoring organizations, Thomas Cook Ltd., and also through Europ Assistance.

Rules of the Road. International signs are in use throughout Yugoslavia. You drive on the right, pass on the left, and yield right of way to all vehicles approaching from the right (except on posted main highways). Park on the right; overnight parking is prohibited on main thoroughfares. In and around built-up areas the speed limit is 60 k.p.h. (37 m.p.h.), elsewhere 80, 100 or 120 k.p.h. as indicated. On the Adriatic Highway, because of the sharp bends, it is advisable to keep below 80 k.p.h. (50 m.p.h.). On-the-spot fines are imposed for parking on the wrong side, entering any main road without stopping, crossing a solid white line when overtaking, etc. Penalties for driving under the influence of drink are very severe. Drivers should note two further points: in Yugoslavia a driver involved in an accident tends to be considered blameworthy until he is proved innocent, rather than vice versa; and, as in most countries, foreign drivers are thought not to know how to drive properly. The moral is: take a lot more care than usual and drive more slowly than you might do at home. Drivers and passengers in the front seat must wear seat belts; motorcyclists must wear crash helmets.

Fuel. Costs 37.50 dinars per liter for Super (98 octane). Petrol coupons sold in units of 400 dinars in exchange for *foreign currency only* entitle holders to a reduction of over 25%. The coupons can be obtained at foreign automobile clubs, some banks and at main frontier crossings. But *please note* that owing to the soaring cost of fuel all over the world these prices will certainly be higher by the time you read this. If you are contemplating a motoring holiday, be very sure to work out fuel costs at the time you want to travel. The National Tourist Office should be able to put you in the picture, or your motoring association. *Be certain to check in advance* as the current financial state of Yugoslavia makes the availability of gas episodic at best and rationing has caused enormous lines at gas stations. The resultant hours of waiting can turn a motoring holiday into a traumatic experience.

Road Conditions. Yugoslavia's road network is gradually improving and there are now substantial stretches of toll motorway, as indicated on the annually revised map of the Yugoslav National Tourist Office. Nevertheless, there remain long stretches which, though often well surfaced, are too narrow for the weight of traffic they must carry at the height of the season when hordes of visiting motorists join the heavy long-distance trucks and more-local traffic. The Adriatic Highway is a case in point, and so is the country's main artery, the *autoput* E94/E5 linking Zagreb–Belgrade–Niš—where it divides into the E5N east to Bulgaria, and the E5S south to Skopje and Greece. This road is gradually being widened and improved.

Some excellent lateral routes link this highway across the mountains to the coast, but they are still often relatively narrow. The network is best-maintained in the north and center of the country. Further advice on recommended routes is given in the regional chapters, but the best advice is to drive with special care and patience at all times—and enjoy the usually marvelous scenery. If you're of a nervous disposition avoid the roads indicated in green on the tourist map—but if you're not, they are often spectacular.

Between 8 A.M. and 8 P.M., the main roads throughout the country are now patrolled by an aid and information service (look for yellow cars bearing the word Pomoć-Informacije).

Signposting. In remoter parts of the country, signposting, even of important historical monuments and ancient sites, is rather poor. Unfortunately, the signposting of local sites is in the hands of local authorities, who are often reluctant to give clear indications to churches, monasteries or mosques.

The Coast by Car. If you do not want to drive either up or down the coast you can put your car aboard one of the comfortable fast vessels at very moderate prices. The ships have drive-on facilities.

From the Jadranska Magistrala it is easy to visit the islands by regular ferries. Krk and Pag are linked to the mainland by bridges, but the latter island is so long that driving all the way south to the bridge and then all the way north to the place where you may want to stay on Pag takes much longer than the short sea crossing.

Car Ferries. There are now many of these linking the mainland and islands, some of them seasonal. The Yugoslav National Tourist Office can give you the latest details.

Spare Parts. These are hard to come by in Yugoslavia. Before leaving home, ask your car dealer for a packaged kit of vital spares; if you find you don't have to open it on your trip, you can always return it. Repairs are undertaken in workshops at the gas stations along the highways, and the leading American and European automobile manufacturers have agents in the main cities of Yugoslavia.

Kilometers into Miles. This simple chart enables you to convert from either miles into kilometers (read from center column to the right) or kilometers into miles (from center column to the left). For example, five miles = eight kilometers, and five kilometers = 3.1 miles.

Miles		Kilometers	Miles		Kilometers
0.6	1	1.6	37.3	60	96.6
1.2	2	3.2	43.5	70	112.3
1.9	3	4.8	49.7	80	128.7
2.5	4	6.3	55.9	90	144.8
3.1	5	8.0	62.1	100	160.9
3.7	6	9.6	124.3	200	321.9
4.3	7	11.3	186.4	300	482.8
5.0	8	12.9	248.5	400	643.7
5.6	9	14.5	310.7	500	804.7
6.2	10	16.1	372.8	600	965.6
12.4	20	32.2	434.9	700	1,126.5
18.6	30	48.3	497.1	800	1,287.5
24.8	40	64.4	559.2	900	1,448.4
31.0	50	80.5	621.4	1,000	1,609.3

HOTELS. The Yugoslav tourist authorities officially grade the country's hotels into the following categories: L (for luxury), A (first class), B (second class), C (third class) and D (fourth class). Our own price gradings, shown in the table below, follow the Yugoslav example closely, Deluxe (L) equating with the Yugoslav luxury category, Expensive (E) with first class, Moderate (M) with second class, and Inexpensive (I) with the Yugoslav third- and fourth-class groupings. At the moment, very few hotels are included in our top (L) classification. On the whole, hotels in the (E) group deserve their rating, though service may sometimes lack polish away from main centers. (M) accommodations will suit the majority of ordinary travelers, and indeed some of the more recent ones qualify in all but some detail (e.g. lack of swimming pool) as (E)s. The (I) hotels cater adequately to those traveling on a budget or looking for an immediate overnight stop, although the bottom end of the category is strictly for those roughing it. Motels are now classified as I, II and III.

Hotel Room Costs
(double occupancy, with bath/shower; prices in dollars)

	Main resorts, regional capitals	Minor resorts, small towns
Deluxe (L)	$90–120	—
Expensive (E)	$50–80	$40–50
Moderate (M)	$35–50	$25–35
Inexpensive (I)	$15–35	$12–25

In the low season, prices can be up to 50% lower

A point that must be made clear is: Yugoslav hotels do not provide uniformly standardized service and accommodations such as are found in Holiday Inns, Hiltons, and other worldwide chains. Facilities and service in the best Yugoslav hotels are very good but they are not the same in all their details as those of any of the world's hotel chains.

A number of Moderate establishments have fewer rooms with private bath or shower than many modern Inexpensive hotels. In this respect, the point to note, at least in the cheaper establishments, is the hotel's age. Those that were built in the last two decades have been designed with full modern equipment. Also, large numbers of Yugoslavs who went to Western Europe a few years ago to work in hotels and restaurants have now returned to their own country and taken senior positions in hotels. International investment is being encouraged, and some of the international chains have invested in Yugoslavian hotels.

Service in better hotels in the main towns is usually good though receptionists are often badly overworked because separate hall porters are lacking—and there is a shortage of good reception staff anyway. In the coastal resorts service is rather more variable, especially in summer, when many part-time hotel staff are engaged. The main fault of most Yugoslav hotels is a slight shoddiness in the actual construction: paintwork, plumbing, and fittings may turn out faulty, and there is a shortage of skilled staff to undertake maintenance, though the situation has improved markedly over recent years.

If anything in your room, such as a light, or a tap, needs attention, tell the receptionist firmly and clearly what is wrong. Continue to badger him until it is put right. Delays are probably due to lack of workmen.

The only other main problem is one of noise. If you don't like dance bands, singing and loud talk, make certain to get a room which does not overlook the hotel's terrace. You can't close windows in summer, and there may be very little interval between the last drinking parties going home and early starters arriving for market. You may also have the noise of pop groups performing until the early hours running into the arrival-time of the first delivery lorries. Again, the powers-that-be are paying more attention to such details and late-night music is increasingly strategically placed at a greater distance from accommodations.

One thing almost completely lacking in all Yugoslav hotels is the personal touch given by family proprietors. The hotels, like all commercial enterprises in Yugoslavia, are managed by all those working in them. Managers and management committees are selected by the workers. If you want the personal, family touch you would do well to take rooms in a guest house or private house. These are also, of course, a great deal cheaper. Guest houses, which are usually privately run, are often charming and are particularly prevalent in Slovenia and Croatia, though increasingly in evidence elsewhere. Private house accommodations are well organized through local tourist offices (a list is also available from the Yugoslav National Tourist Office) and are divided into four categories, the top one providing private bath or shower (see p. 5).

Self-catering accommodations are growing and chalets are available for hire at many camp sites. A list of these sites from the Yugoslav National Tourist Office details all facilities and prices.

On-the-spot tourist offices will help you find accommodation on arrival. In large towns, however, and on the coast in high season, advance booking is essential—preferably through travel agencies. In resorts, tourists are charged a Visitor's Tax regardless of the type of accommodations they use, including camping sites. The tax is collected by hotels and tourist offices and averages from

4 to 15 dinars according to local regulations. In the off-season this tax is usually 50% lower.

 ROUGHING IT. There are over 200 camping-areas in Yugoslavia, more than half of them along the Adriatic coast and most of the others conveniently along main highways. Modern washing facilities, sanitation, electricity, shops and restaurants, organized entertainment, sports and recreational facilities, are standard for most of them, and medical and automotive services are usually available. In some areas there are bungalows and chalets for rent. In general, camping is allowed only on the official camp sites; anywhere else you must have permission from the local authorities or tourist bureau.

Camping equipment brought into Yugoslavia is free of customs duty provided that it is taken out again when you leave. Green card (third party) insurance is compulsory. Short-term policies for 7, 15, or 30 days may be obtained at the border when you enter the country. The premiums must be paid in foreign currency. You may, of course, already have such insurance as part of membership in a camping organization or motor club.

A directory of campsites, with detailed listing of facilities, services and prices along with a map and general information on regulations and requirements is available from Yugoslav tourist offices.

Youth hostels in Yugoslavia are now affiliated to the International Youth Hostel Movement. They are run by Naromtravel, the Travel Department of Yugoslav Youth and Students, 11000 Belgrade, Mose Pijade 12, which also operates various types of student hostels and restaurants in principal cities and summer holiday camps on the Dalmatian coast.

 RESTAURANTS. If you use restaurants frequented by tourists, whether in hotels or separate from them, you can reckon to pay the following for a three-course meal without drinks: Expensive (E) 500–800 dinars; Moderate (M) 200–350; Inexpensive (I) from 100; less for fixed-price meals.

All hotel restaurants, in theory, serve fixed menus. In practice, many—quite illegally—refuse to serve these cheaper meals to foreign visitors. Yugoslavia's National Tourist Association *(Turistički Savez Jugoslavije,* 11 001 Beograd, Moše Pijade 8) is keen to ensure that hotel restaurants fulfil their obligations to visitors. If you meet with difficulties of this sort, write immediately to the Association giving the name of the hotel, town, the date and time, as well as outlining your complaint.

Breakfast is served continental-style—coffee or tea (weaker than English tea) with bread and jam. You may order eggs for a few dinars more.

Food And Drink. Yugoslav cooking features huge portions of lamb, pork, veal and chicken, generously laid out with vegetables. Fruit and fresh salads are usually included. In most places you can of course get international dishes. Seafood is a Dalmatian specialty, and some local cheeses are worth trying.

WINTER GAMES
SUPPLEMENT

Sarajevo 84

The Winter Olympics

The history of the Winter Olympics has on the whole been rather unhappy and controversial. For one thing, their relations with the main Olympic movement have always been strained, mainly because separate Summer and Winter Games disrupt the unity of the movement. Similarly, the fact that competitors from only a few countries stand a realistic chance of success—for the simple reason that few countries have the snow and mountains necessary for training and practice—has also been a sticking point to the Olympic purist. Another commonly heard criticism is that the Games are unreasonably dependent on good weather (not a single Games has gone by without some panic about the weather, usually lack of snow). A major problem today is that the Games are big business and particularly vulnerable to commercial pressure, pressure that directly conflicts with the movement's amateur ideals.

Nordic vs. Alpine

In addition to these difficulties, the early days of the Winter Games were also dogged by a serious split between the major winter sports countries. Until the early 1920s, winter sports were confined largely to the Scandinavian countries and consisted only of the traditional Nordic events of cross-country skiing, ski jumping and ice hockey. As early as 1901, the Scandinavians had organized their own Nordic Games, which, like the Olympics, were held every four years, while the Norwegians held a national skiing week every year at Holmenkollen. Alpine, or downhill, skiing at this point was almost unknown and was practiced mainly by English tourists on trips to Switzerland. However, Alpine skiing was beginning to grow rapidly in popularity, and it was from the ranks of the Alpine enthusiasts that calls were made for winter sports to be included on the Olympic program. At first, these demands met with little success. In addition to the objections raised by the Olympic purists, the Scandinavians—the major exponents of the sports—were unhappy at the prospect of Winter Olympics, believing that their own championships would be superceded and their dominance ended.

In the event, of course, they bowed to the inevitable and the first official Winter Olympic Games were held at Chamonix, France, in 1924. However, it is a reflection of the acrimony that surrounded them that their status as official Winter Games was confirmed only retrospectively in 1926.

Professional Problems

Despite the controversy, the Chamonix Games were a success and from 1926 the Winter Games became an integral part of the Olympic movement. Unhappily, the launching of the Games did not signal an end to controversy. A small mishap was encountered in the planning stages of the 1928 Games when it became apparent that it would not be possible to hold both the Summer and Winter Games in the same country, as the International Olympic Committee (IOC) had originally intended. As Holland was the country in question, this is perhaps not surprising—that country's highest point is somewhere in the region of 300 meters (900 feet). In the event, the 1928 Games were held in St. Moritz, Switzerland.

A very much more serious problem arose in 1935, which in one form or another has plagued the Winter Games ever since. In that year, the IOC refused to allow ski instructors to compete in the 1936 Games on the grounds that they were professionals, despite an earlier understanding that they would be considered amateurs. Simultaneously, it was decided that the German team, which had been training together for months (at Hitler's expense) and was nothing if not professional, *was* eligible to compete. The self-evident contradiction of this ruling caused much muttering in the corridors of power.

After the war and the resumption of Olympic competition (the first post-war Winter Games were held at St. Moritz in 1948), the problem of professionalism grew more urgent. The Games provided manufacturers of skiing equipment with invaluable advertising, and they were not slow to take advantage. Competitors became walking advertisements, introducing a commercial element quite alien to the Olympic ethos. This was a development that deeply alarmed the new President of the IOC, American millionaire Avery Brundage. There was little love lost between Brundage and the International Ski Federation (FIS), and throughout the 1950s and 1960s relations between the two deteriorated. Many thought the crisis point had been reached in 1968 when, before the Grenoble Games in France, the FIS announced that, contrary to an earlier agreement, competitors would be allowed to carry advertisements. The Games went ahead, but in a strained atmosphere made worse by the disqualification of the popular Austrian Schranz in the giant slalom and the disqualification of three East German women in the bobsleigh for heating the runners on their sleds.

Brundage's crusade against professionalism reached a peak at the next Games, held in Sapporo, Japan in 1972. Schranz, by now the veteran of the Austrian team, gave an interview before the Games in which he admitted receiving several thousand dollars from ski manufacturers and attacked Brundage for his adherence to an outdated code of amateurism. The IOC promptly expelled Schranz from the Games, precipitating the resignation of the entire Austrian team (subsequently withdrawn). The massive cost of these Games—an unbelievable 555-million dollars—also caused concern, as it now appeared that only the richest countries could afford to host future Games.

Against all expectations, however, the next two Games, at Innsbruck in 1976 and Lake Placid in 1980, not only failed to raise the thorny issue of professionalism (the retirement of Brundage in 1972 may have contributed) but, as the Games were held in cities that had already hosted them, proved far less expensive than those at Sapporo, where practically all the facilities had been purpose-built.

The situation today regarding the amateur status of competitors is not quite the burningly sensitive issue it was in the days of Brundage. Nonetheless, commercial pressures on top competitors are greater than ever and it seems inevitable that they will follow the lead of track and field athletes who are now effectively professionals.

Greater realism seems also to have permeated the Winter Games with regard to their financing. It has long been an embarrassment to the IOC that they have been forced to preside over multi-million dollar events. The greater the prestige of the Games, the more diluted the original Olympic vision of simple, unaffected sportsmanship and international camaraderie becomes. The Sarajevo Games appear to be about to reverse this trend. Of course, the importance of the Games is such that it is impossible to recapture their original simplicity. But by trying to ensure that the Games are as nearly self-financing as possible and that their facilities will not become mere white elephants after the Games, it appears probable that the giantism of previous Games will be avoided.

Sarajevo and the Olympics

Sarajevo's preparations for the XIV Winter Games have been impressive. The city already had many winter sports facilities before being selected to host the Games (it is a regular venue for the annual skiing World Cup, for example, a series of winter sports competitions held over two months and some seven or eight different countries). But in addition to improving existing facilities, many new ones have been built.

The facilities the city had before the Games were the downhill ski-run at Jahorina, some 25 km. from the city center, an ice rink in the city center, and a cross-country ski track at Veliko Polje on Mount Igman, 26 km. from the city. All three have been modernized and improved. New press facilities and communications systems have been installed, and at Jahorina, new drag- and chair-lifts built. The Kosevo Stadium in the city center has also been largely rebuilt. This will be used for the opening and closing ceremonies.

The major new construction work in the city has taken place around the Kosevo Stadium. Here a new indoor ice rink has been built (the Zetra Hall), capable of seating 8,500 spectators. This will be the main Olympic Hall, and after the Games will be used for indoor athletics as well as for ice-skating. Next to the Zetra Hall, Yugoslavia's first-ever speed-skating rink has been built; this accommodates 10,000 spectators. A fourth ice rink has also been constructed next to the existing one in the city center by the main Skenderija press center.

Three other major new facilities have been provided at sites around the city. These are:

The 70- and 90-meter ski jumps at Malo Polje.

The men's downhill run at Bjelasnica, 22.5 km. from the city, with supplementary courses for the slalom and giant slalom. As at Jahorina, new drag- and chair-lifts have been installed.

ZETRA
»Koševo« Stadium
Olympic Hall
Speed Skating rink
Figure Skating
Ice Hockey

Speed Skating
SKENDERIJA
Main Hall
Auxiliary Hall
Figure Skating
Ice Hockey

Main press center
TREBEVIĆ
Bobsleigh and Luge track
JAHORINA
Women's Alpine events

BJELAŠNICA
Men's Alpine events
IGMAN-VELIKO POLJE
Cross country
and Biathlon

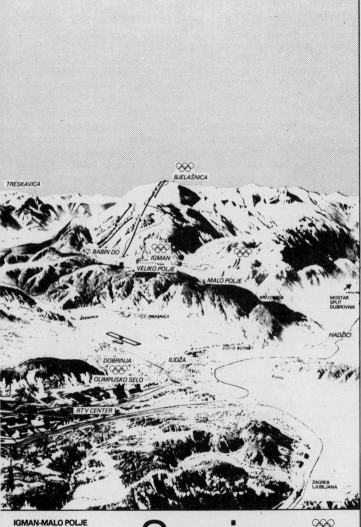

TRESKAVICA

BJELAŠNICA

BABIN DO

IGMAN

VELIKO POLJE

MALO POLJE

KRIŽOVICA

MOSTAR
SPLIT
DUBROVNIK

HRASNICA

VRELO BOSNE

HADŽIĆI

DOBRINJA

ILIDŽA

Busna

OLIMPIJSKO SELO

RTV CENTER

ZAGREB
LJUBLJANA

IGMAN-MALO POLJE
Ski jumping
OLIMPIJSKO SELO
Olympic village
RTV Center
Railway station

Sarajevo ❄

The bobsleigh and luge track at Trebevic, 10 km. from the city.

All the Olympic sites have been given lavish press and spectator facilities. Similarly, a complex timing system has been installed for the Alpine, bobsleigh and luge, and cross-country events.

The provision of accommodations has been equally impressive. In addition to the small Olympic village for competitors in the Nordic events at Veliko Polje, a main village has been constructed at Mojmilo on the western edge of the city. This will be able to house up to 2,300 competitors and their coaches in 639 apartments. The village has been funded partly by the organizing committee and partly by local labor associations. Workers from these associations will move into the village after the Games. The village will be able to supply 9,000 meals a day and has, among its many facilities, an outpatients surgery, a sports hall, plus a number of cinemas, discos, and press facilities. Similar accommodations have been provided for the journalists at Dobrinja, close by the Olympic village. The other major accommodations are those for officials in the brand new hotel Sarajevo, close by the Zetra Center.

A complex and ultra-modern communications system has been built to provide accurate and instantly available information for the press and to handle television transmissions to all corners of the globe. Each of the Olympic sites is linked to the press center in the Skenderija center, allowing results to be sent to and from the center the moment they become known.

Similarly, a network of buses and other transport facilities has been conceived to ferry competitors, officials, journalists and spectators to and around both the city and the Olympic sites. During the Games, some 500 buses will be brought to Sarajevo for this purpose.

Several U.S. tour operators are offering package plans to the Olympics that include airfare, accommodations, tickets, and transportation to the events. Among them are:

Jetset Tours, 778 Sixth Ave., Ridgewood, N.Y. 11385;

Megavent, 310 Madison Ave., New York, N.Y. 10017;

New York State Destinations, PO Box 432, Lake George, N.Y. 12845;

Yugotours, 350 Fifth Ave., New York, N.Y. 10118.

For prices and other details, talk to a travel agent.

XIV Olympic Winter Games
Sarajevo 1984

TIMETABLE OF EVENTS

Number	Sports	Code	Symbols	
1	Biathlon	BT		
2	Bobsleigh	BS		
3	Cross-country	CC		
4	Downhill	DH		
5	Figure skating	FS		
6	Giant slalom	GS		
7	Ice hockey	IH		
8	Luge	LG		
9	Nordic combined	NC		
10	Ski jumping	SJ		
11	Slalom	SL		
12	Speed skating	SS		
13	Opening ceremony	OC		
14	Closing ceremony	CL		

SPORTS			VENUE	TUESDAY 07	WEDNESDAY 08	THURSDAY 09
		OC	STADIUM KOŠEVO		14,30 — 16,00	
		SJ	MALO POLJE IGMAN			
		NC	MALO & VELIKO POLJE IGMAN			
		CC	VELIKO POLJE IGMAN			10 km W 9,00 — 10,00
		BT				
		DH	BJELAŠNICA			M 12,00 — 14,00
		GS				
		SL				
		DH	JAHORINA			
		GS				
		SL				
		LG	TREBEVIĆ			1 RUN M & W 9,00 — 11,00
		BS				
		BS				
		SS	ZETRA			1.500 m W 9,30 — 11,30
		FS	SKENDERIJA 2			
		FS	ZETRA			
		FS				
		IH	ZETRA	13,30/17,00/20,30		13,30/17,00/20,30
		IH	SKENDERIJA 1	13,00/16,30/20,00		13,00/16,30/20,00
		CL	ZETRA			
TOTAL EVENT PER DAY				1 (6)		5 (10)

M — MEN
W — WOMEN

D — ICE DANCING
P — PAIRS

SP — SHORT PROGRAM
CD — COMPULSORY DANCES

FRIDAY 10	SATURDAY 11	SUNDAY 12	MONDAY 13	TUESDAY 14
		70 m 13,00 — 15,00		
	70 m 12,30 — 14,30	15 km 12,00 — 14,00		
30 km M 9,00 — 11,30		5 km W 9,00 — 9,40	15 km M 9,00 — 10,40	
	20 km 9,00 — 12,00			10 km 9,00 — 12,00
	W 10,30 — 12,30			
				W 10,00 — 14,00
2 RUN M & W 9,00 — 11,00	3 RUN M & W 9,00 — 11,00	4 RUN M & W 9,00 — 11,00		
1 — 2 RUN 13,30 — 16,00	3 — 4 RUN 13,30 — 16,00			
W 500 m M 9,30-10,30/11,00-12,00		5.000 m M 9,30 — 12,30	1.000 m W 9,30 — 11,00	1.000 m M 9,30 — 11,30
			CF M 7,00 — 15,00	
CD 1 14,00 — 18,00		CD 2 14,00 — 18,00		SP M 15,30 — 18,30
SP P 20,00 — 23,00		FS P 19,00 — 23,00		FD 19,30 — 23,00
	13,30/17,00/20,30		13,30/17,00/20,30	
	13,00/16,30/20,00		13,00/16,30/20,00	
5 (7)	6 (11)	6 (7)	4 (9)	4 (5)

FS — FREE SKATING   FD – FREE DANCE
CF — COMPULSORY FIGURES

Chart continues on next page.

Code	WEDNESDAY 15	THURSDAY 16	FRIDAY 17	SATURDAY 18	SUNDAY 19
OC					
SJ				90 m 12,30 – 15,00	
NC					
CC	RELAY 4 × 5　W 9,00 – 10,30	RELAY 4 × 10　M 9,00 – 11,20		20 km　　W 9,00 – 12,00	50 km　　M 8,00 – 11,30
BT			RELAY 4 × 7,5 10,00 – 13,00		
DH					
GS	M 10,30 – 14,30				
SL					M 10,30/12,30
DH					
GS					
SL			W 11,30 – 13,30		
LG	DOUBLE 10,00 – 12,00				
BS					
BS			1 – 2 RUN 13,30 – 16,00	3 – 4 RUN 13,30 – 16,00	
SS	3.000 m　　W 9,30 – 11,30	1.500 m　　M 9,30 – 12,00		10.000 m　　M 9,00 – 13,00	
FS	CF　　　W 7,00 – 16,00				
FS		SP　　　W 14,00 – 18,30			EXHIBITION 18,00 – 20,00
FS		FS　　　M 19,30 – 23,00		FS　　　W 19,00 – 23,00	
IH	13,30/17,00/20,30		13,30/17,00/20,30		10,00/13,30
IH	13,00/16,30/20,00				
CL					20,00 – 21,00
	6 (11)	3 (4)	4 (6)	5 (5)	4 (5)

Events

The events at the Winter Olympics are divided into four basic categories: Alpine skiing; Nordic skiing; bobsleigh and luge; and skating.

Alpine events. Though Alpine, or downhill, skiing is synonymous in many people's minds with the winter Sports and is regarded as the most prestigious of all the events, it is in fact the baby of the Winter Olympics. Alpine skiing featured in the Olympics for the first time only in 1936, at Garmisch-Partenkirchen in Germany. Though both men's and women's competitions were held, only two medals were awarded. Combined points from the downhill and slalom races determined the winners. However, in 1948 at St. Moritz, the Alpine events were organized in their present form with three men's and three women's events: downhill, slalom and giant slalom.

At Sarajevo, the men's events take place at Bjelasnica and the women's at Jahorina.

Nordic events. Along with the skating, the Nordic events—cross-country, ski-jumping and biathlon—form the backbone of the Winter Games. With the exception of the biathlon, a gruelling off-shoot of cross-country skiing that combines shooting and cross-country racing, these events were featured in the Nordic Games that preceded the Winter Olympics and have formed part of the Olympic program since the first Winter Games in 1924.

There are two ski-jumping events (both for men only), the 70-meter and 90-meter jumps; four men's cross-country events (15 km., 30 km., 50 km. and the 4 x 10 km. relay); and four women's cross-country events (5 km., 10 km., 20 km. and the 4 x 5 km. relay). The women's races have been featured only since the war. In addition, there is a combined Nordic competition (for men only) which consists of a 70-meter ski-jump and a 15 km. cross-country race, the winner being chosen on combined placings. The biathlon (again for men only), introduced at the Squaw Valley, U.S.A., Games in 1960, has three events (10 km., 20 km. and the 4 x 7.5 km. relay).

All the cross-country events take place at Velko Pole on Mount Igman, and the ski-jumping at Malo Polje, also on Mount Igman.

Bobsleigh and luge. Bobsleighing, in varying shapes and sizes, has featured in the Winter Games since its inception in 1924. The luge, or toboggan, by contrast, has been an Olympic sport only since the Innsbruck Games of 1964. Both competitions are run over the same 1,200-meter track—before the 1976 Games, separate tracks, built at vast expense, were used for the two competitions—and four descents are required to determine the winner. There are two bobsleigh events (both for men only): the two-man and four-man; and three luge events: the men's and women's—both for one rider only—and the men's two-seater.

The bobsleigh and luge track at Sarajevo is at Trebevic.

Skating. There are three different types of skating competition in the Games, all of which have been included on the Olympic program since 1924 or earlier. Figure skating, both men's and women's and pairs, was featured at the London Summer Games in 1908 and again at the Amsterdam Summer Games in 1920. (Its absence from the 1912 Stockholm Summer Games was due only to there being no suitable artificial rink available.) Similarly, ice hockey was also featured in the 1920 Amsterdam Games. Having established their Olympic pedigrees, both were automatically selected for inclusion in the first Winter Games (1924). Men's speed skating, the third of the skating competitions, was also included in the 1924 Games. (Women's speed skating was adopted only in 1960 for the Squaw Valley Games.)

There are four events in the figure skating: men's and women's; pairs; and ice dancing (introduced at Innsbruck, 1976).

The speed skating has five men's events (500 meters, 1,000 meters, 1,500 meters, 5,000 meters and 10,000 meters). The women's speed skating has four events (500 meters, 1,000 meters, 1,500 meters and 5,000 meters).

The ice hockey competition is organized on a straight knock-out basis. All the skating events take place either at the Zetra or Skenderija complexes.

CHART OF MEN'S ALPINE RUNS

BJELAŠNICA

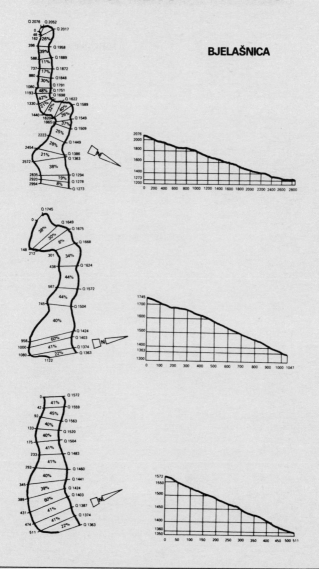

CHART OF WOMEN'S ALPINE RUNS

JAHORINA

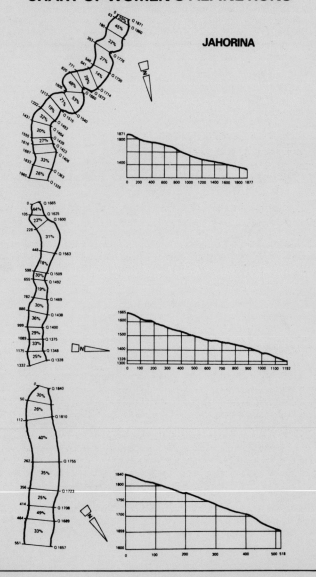

Wines are good and inexpensive; beers less good, but widely drunk. Bottled water, fruit juices and local soft beverages are excellent. The national beverage is *šljivovica,* a fiery transparent plum brandy. It is also known as *rakija.* Turkish coffee (*turska kafa*), strong, sweet, served in tiny cups, is a national beverage, though now rather expensive. You may order it in restaurants, after a meal, or drop into a *kafana* (coffeeshop).

Our chapter on *Food and Drink* gives more details on national and regional specialties.

TIPPING. In restaurants, add up to ten percent to your bill according to standard of service and the total involved. There is usually a specific charge quoted for the use of cloakrooms and the like. As is also the case with most people who do odd jobs for you, taxi drivers appreciate a little bit extra. But in no case is this obligatory.

SPECIAL EVENTS. Among events that attract foreign visitors to Yugoslavia is a full program of music, drama, film, and folklore festivals, as well as trade fairs and international sports events. Festivals of music and drama include the Split Summer (mid-Jun.–mid-Aug.) and the Ohrid Summer (12 Jul.–20 Aug.), both containing a little bit of everything, as do Opatija's Summer Festival (Jul.–Sept.) and Ljubljana's Cultural Summer (Jul.–Aug.). In similar vein are Zagreb Evenings (Jul.–mid-Sept.) and Belgrade's fairly extensive Bemus Musical Festival (mid-Oct.).

More specialized are: the International Jazz Festival at Ljubljana (mid-Jun.); the Yugoslav Children's Festival at Sibenik (19 Jun.–3 Jul.); Adriatic Melodies at Split (early Jul.); musical evenings in the 1,000-year-old church of St. Donat, Zadar (Jul.–Aug.); International Poetry Evenings at Struga (late Aug.); and varied cultural events and musical entertainments in Belgrade's Skadarlijske Večeri in the city's 19th-century quarter (May–Dec.). Pop and rock music can be heard at the Belgrade Spring in May and in many other places.

Folklore festivals include the Kmečka Ohcet (Peasant Wedding), in which large numbers of couples, including non-Yugoslavs, get married with the whole town *en fête;* you will find this at Plitvice (late May), Galičnik (about 10 Jul.), Bohinj (mid-Jul.) and Bled (early Aug.). Melodies from Istria take place in many Istrian and Kvarner resorts in June. Late July is the International Review of Original Folklore in the streets and squares of Zagreb. At Sokobanja there is the final round of the Yugoslav accordion competition (early Aug.). The Vojvodina Festival is held at Vrsac (late Sept.).

The Moreška sword-dance mime has been enacted in Korčula for centuries on 27 July. Performances now take place every Thursday throughout the summer. Outstandingly spectacular, it is still danced by the ordinary townspeople.

The highly recommended Yugoslav Feature Film Festival is held in the Roman amphitheater at Pula in late July, and there is also a film competition at Niš—this one in late August. The well-known Fest Film Festival of Belgrade occurs every February, while in March—again in Belgrade—there is a Documentary Festival. Theater-wise, September sees Belgrade's celebrated BITEF Festival, an annual event featuring avant-garde companies from many parts of the world.

Of the numerous trade fairs in Yugoslavia, Ljubljana Alp–Adria Fair is in late March; the same venue sees a Winter Sports Fair in November. The Zagreb Spring Fair is in April, the Autumn Fair in September, and there are specialized fairs at other times of the year. Belgrade has an International Car Fair in April and a Fashion Fair in October. Then there's the Agricultural Fair at Novi Sad in May. There are many other fairs held in various towns—the Yugoslav National Tourist Office or Embassy can supply full details.

The major sporting event in 1984 is, of course, the Winter Olympics, to be held at Sarajevo from 7–19 February. Otherwise, regular annual events include ski-jumping at Planica in March; international rowing on the lake at Bled (mid-Jun.); an international regatta on the Danube in early August, another at Split in the same month, and others elsewhere; a horse-riding tournament at Lipica in June, and the centuries-old riding competition at Sinj in early August. In addition, there are local events in all larger resorts during the tourist season, as we have indicated in the regional chapters.

DUBROVNIK SUMMER FESTIVAL. The ancient ceremonial marking the opening of Dubrovnik's annual Summer Festival takes place on 10 July in front of the Sponza Palace. The festival itself runs until around 25 August. A detailed description of planned events is published in the spring and can be obtained from Yugoslav Tourist Offices abroad, but each year the program includes about 100 performances of great plays and operas—by both Western European and Yugoslav dramatists and composers—as well as numerous presentations by Yugoslav folk-dance ensembles.

Most of the festival is staged out-of-doors, with the medieval palaces, fortresses and courtyards of Dubrovnik's Old City providing the perfect (and authentic) period setting.

FOR THE CULTURE-MINDED. For 5,000 years or more Yugoslavia has been at the crossroads of history: the evidence is clearly and beautifully visible today. Prehistoric cultures abound, especially in the Danube area. Greek and Roman ruins, strewn liberally throughout the country, are particularly striking at Celje, Zadar, Split (Diocletian's palace), Niš (thermal baths), Belgrade (Kalemegdan Park), Pula (second-century amphitheater, well preserved), Heraclea Lyncestis (ancient Macedonian-Greek city south of Bitola), etc. South Slav Christianity began building a mighty network of monasteries about 1,000 years ago. Years of study could easily be devoted to the frescos that have survived in the churches in southern Serbia and Macedonia, since many of these show all the characteristics of Renaissance paintings up to two centuries before the Italian Renaissance began. For five centuries, the Turks occupied much of Yugoslavia and more than three million Yugoslavs are still Moslems. They, too, have left their mark on Yugoslavia's architecture and town planning. In Sarajevo, Skopje, Tetovo, and many other towns, you can visit fine mosques, Turkish palaces, and *hammams* (baths).

Dalmatia's stone architecture is something apart, exemplified in magnificent walled towns and Catholic churches that date back in some cases to the ninth century. The celebrated modern sculptor, Meštrović, has a gallery devoted to him at Split, where he grew up, as well as in Zagreb.

All the principal cities have interesting museums; the Ethnographic Museum in Zagreb and National Museum of Belgrade are particularly well-known. Every major town too has a museum devoted to local antiquities.

Coach tours are organized by the largest Yugoslav travel agencies, covering the high spots of Yugoslavia's historical and art centers.

FISHING. A fairly wide range of sport fishing can be enjoyed in Yugoslavia's lakes, streams and rivers, as well as in the Adriatic Sea. While the variety of fish waiting to be caught is great, so are the detailed regulations for obtaining licenses. Information can be had by writing to *Sportski ribolovni savez Jugoslavije*, Alekse Nenadoviča 19–23, Belgrade. A leaflet obtainable from most Tourist Information Offices or from the Sport Fishing Association, above, outlines the principal sea fishing areas of the Adriatic, lists the main species of fish to be caught and summarizes the rather complex Yugoslav laws relating to sea fishing. Note especially that you are in all circumstances forbidden to sell the catch.

Sea fishing is possible and enjoyable from many points on the coast. Gamefishing, however, is not very highly developed, though fishing expeditions are organized by a number of Yugoslav travel firms. The area round Zadar and the Kornat Archipelago is especially popular, and Zadar is a good base.

Freshwater anglers have discovered that Yugoslavia's streams and lakes are well supplied with sizeable specimens of many kinds of fish. The choicest freshwater game belong to the salmon family: trout, huck and salmon parr. Huck often reach a weight of 20 kilo. (55 lb.). Salmon parr go up as high as four kilo. (about eight lb.). On Dojran Lake in southeast Macedonia, water birds are still used for fishing; this lake is especially rich in fish of the cyprinid family. Fishing permits are issued by district fishermen's unions, and can be obtained at some hotels and most tourist agencies.

You will find huck mostly in the Neretva, Soča, Zeta, Morača, and Beli Drim rivers, and in Lake Skadar. Salmon parr are numerous in the Drina River. The rivers of Bosnia-Herzegovina contain large numbers of salmonoids, while Croatian waters abound in trout. Visitors wishing to undertake any serious fishing should make early contact with one of the large Yugoslav travel agencies, most of whom are well equipped to organize trips of this kind.

SWIMMING. The sunny Adriatic coast provides superb bathing in crystal-clear water and picturesque surroundings. Most Yugoslav beaches are stony or pebbly, very hard on tender feet, but hotels and resorts make a regular practice of cementing over stretches of rock to make suitable sunbathing and diving platforms. The only really long stretch of sand is south of Ulcinj, close to the Albanian frontier. Some other resorts have small areas of sandy beach.

The Yugoslav coast is particularly well provided with beaches reserved for nudist bathing and there is a wide range of naturist holidays marketed by U.K. tour operators. Topless bathing is also becoming rather common in some places.

Bathing is best from June until mid-October, and is even possible from early May in the south. Lake swimming may be enjoyed in many inland waters, notably at Bled and Bohinj in Slovenia, Ohrid in Macedonia, and elsewhere. The clear warm depths of the Adriatic are ideal for skin diving, but be sure to bring your own equipment.

BOATING. For real excitement (and relaxation, too) take a canoe down the Drina, one of Europe's most beautiful rivers. Excursions (of interest to fishermen) may be arranged from Sarajevo and elsewhere. Raft trips on the river Tara in Montenegro are also available. Or you may prefer to take a kayak over the rapids of the Sava or Soča rivers in Slovenia. Aquatic sports of all kinds may be practiced on the lakes of Bled and Bohinj. Salt-water sailors, whether of yachts or motorboats, will find snug harbors at all the islands and coastal ports of the Adriatic. At the larger seaside resorts sailboats or motorboats may sometimes be hired. Wind surfing is becoming increasingly popular on the lakes and coastal bays.

HUNTING. If you like hunting, large and small game of all kinds await you in abundance in Yugoslavia, including such fine prizes as the hart, brown bear, wild boar, ibex, and chamois. The hart, specimens of which run as high as 300 kilo. (660 lb.), with horns weighing over ten kilo. (20–25 lb.), lives in the brushwood by the rivers Drava, Sava, and Danube. The chamois keeps to the high rocky mountains of Slovenia, Herzegovina, western Macedonia, Serbia, and Montenegro. In addition to the fairly high cost of a hunting tour, a tax of varying proportions has to be paid on all animals shot. Hare, fox, wolf, marten, and other animals also abound, as well as many species of wildfowl. In the numerous hunting preserves there are well-equipped lodges which afford comfortable accommodations and food. Further information is available through Yugoslav Tourist Information offices and from the main Yugoslav travel firms.

Make Your Trip More Enjoyable

"Try to speak the local language; it's really great fun. . . .

"The natives, who may not speak your language, will be proud and appreciative of your efforts to use *their* language.

"I can't think of a better way to break the ice---"

—*Eugene Fodor*

Fodor's / McKay has a wide list of Teach Yourself language and phrase books and foreign-language dictionaries. Most cost only a few dollars. If your local bookstore doesn't have the language book you need, write to us for a complete list of titles and prices.

Write to:
Sales Director
FODOR'S/McKAY
2 Park Avenue
New York, NY
10016

MOUNTAIN CLIMBING. Hikers and mountain climbers will find that in a normal year most of the snow has disappeared from the passes by the beginning of June, even in the Julian Alps and the other ranges along the northern frontier. The Dinaric Alps, lying parallel with the coast of Dalmatia, and inland ranges like the Lovčen of Montenegro and the Macedonian Šar Planina, are very hot in summer, even at high altitudes. The day's hike should start at dawn and finish by noon if you want it to be enjoyable and not an endurance test. Triglav, the highest peak in the Julian Alps at 3,000 m. (9,393 ft.), was first climbed in 1778. Other worthwhile peaks are in the Durmitor range, where altitudes reach up to 2,650 m. (8,301 ft.), in Montenegro, the Gorski Kotar region of Croatia, the Velebit mountains of Dalmatia, Treskavica near Sarajevo, and the Šar Planina of Macedonia. Splendid walking region around Maribor in the Pohorje Mountains, 1,150–1,400 m. (3,500–4,500 ft.). Even major cities such as Zagreb and Belgrade have good access to fine walking country.

 WINTER SPORTS. Some fine skiing awaits you in Yugoslavia, with the thrills enhanced by a rugged setting, less crowded than better-known tourist areas of Europe. The northern resorts of Slovenia are the more developed, Bohinj and Kranjska Gora especially. A 160-m. (525-ft.) ski jump draws the world's leading competitors to Planica. In Delnice (Croatia) a ski center has been developed in the mountains of Gorski Kotar. The vast bare plateau of Jahorina, near Sarajevo, offers perhaps the finest and most varied all-round ski terrain in Yugoslavia, and this area has undergone major development for the 1984 Winter Olympics, making it one of Europe's top winter sports centers. At the far end of Yugoslavia rises the majestic Šar Planina of Macedonia, 2,100 m. (6,560 ft.) high, with the resort of Popova Šapka. Snow is always plentiful in winter, and the ski lifts cost very little. Equipment can usually be rented in Slovenia.

 THE LANGUAGE. Luckily for the English-speaking tourists, English is now the most popular foreign-language study in Yugoslav schools. German is widely understood and used for basic needs. Older folk in Slovenia still speak good German, and on some parts of the coast, Italian.

Beside various dialects of Serbo-Croat, Slovenian is spoken in Slovenia, and Macedonian in Macedonia. All are Slav languages and bear a general family resemblance to each other, as well as to Russian, Polish, Czech, etc. (roughly as French resembles Italian or Spanish). Slovenian and Croatian are written in the Latin alphabet. Serbian, Montenegrin and Macedonian, however, are written in Cyrillic, both being official alphabets.

You will find the Latin and Cyrillic alphabets and a tourist vocabulary at the end of this guide. Main signs are always in the Latin alphabet, but a working knowledge of the Cyrillic alphabet is highly recommended if you're wandering off the beaten track in more southerly regions.

We can also recommend the *Language/30* cassette tapes: there is one for Serbo-Croat. As a handy, compact way of getting both expert tuition and a good command of a tourist vocabulary, the series is hard to beat.

 HOLIDAYS AND CLOSING TIMES. On the following national holidays, banks, shops, travel agencies and Government agencies are closed: 1–3 January; 1–2 May (Labor Day); 4 July (Partisan Day); 29–30 November (Republic Day). Additional regional holidays are: in Serbia 7 July; in Montenegro 13 July; in Slovenia 22–3 July; in Bosnia-Herzegovina and Croatia 27 July; in Macedonia 2 August and 11 October.

Business hours in Yugoslavia vary from season to season and from district to district; thus, Belgrade summer hours are as follows:

banks – 7 A.M. to 7 P.M., Sat. 7 to 1 P.M.

stores – 8 A.M. to 8 P.M., Sat. 8 to 3 P.M. (self-service stores open earlier and some operate on Sun., from 7 to 11 A.M.)

shops – either non-stop as above, or 8 A.M. to midday and 5 P.M. to 8, Sat. 8 A.M. to 3

food shops – 5.30 A.M. to 9.30 A.M. and 4 P.M. to 7; some open Sun. 7 A.M. to 11 A.M.

markets – 5.30 A.M. to 12.30 P.M., Sun. 6 A.M. to midday

offices – 8 A.M. to 3 P.M.

restaurants – 7 A.M. to midnight

cafés – 6 A.M. to 11 P.M. (later for those with music)

nightclubs – 10 P.M. to 3 A.M.

cinemas – 3 P.M. to 11 P.M. and from 10 A.M. on Sundays

travel agencies – 8 A.M. to 8 P.M.

Theater curtains rise at 7 or 8 P.M., depending on the show

 SHOPPING. Peasant and Oriental handicrafts still survive in present-day Yugoslavia, and you will find many beautiful and useful items available in the shops and markets, including costumed dolls, embroidered blouses, tablecloths, dinner mats, fine lace work, ceramics, woolen goods, carved wooden objects, filigree jewelry, leather items. Carpets, of fine brilliantly dyed wool, vary from small prayer rugs to huge floor coverings. Each region has its own carpet-weaving design. Gold, silver and copper metalwork, including items set with precious stones, are offered in the lively bazaars of Sarajevo (strike your own bargain), and good filigree work is found in many places.

In the large towns and resorts shops bearing the names Narodna Radinost, Jugoexport, Dom, Bosna Folklore and Minceta are reliable. A discount of 10% is granted in some stores on articles paid for by travelers checks or foreign currency. Prices are fixed in all shops and there is no haggling except in some open-air markets. Export of craft and souvenir items is not limited; you may take out any amount. Note that prices for similar items are often lower in the markets of big cities than in tourist resorts.

MAIL, TELEPHONES. (Main charges only.) Letters to Western Europe by airmail cost 8.80 dinars for 20 grams. Postcards for Europe by airmail cost 6.10 dinars.

To the U.S. and Canada (ten grams) an airmail letter costs 15 dinars, a postcard 12.50 dinars.

Allow as much time as possible for mail in each direction as the Yugoslav post, while usually reliable, is not noted for speed.

Local telephone calls usually cost 2 dinars for three minutes. Much of Yugoslavia is now on the automatic system and most calls within the country and to much of Europe can be dialled directly. Calls through the operator are best done from an hotel as delays can be considerable. Yugoslavia is one hour ahead of Greenwich Mean Time (GMT). In spring and summer it is five hours ahead of U.S. Eastern Daylight Time: in fall and winter it is six hours ahead of U.S. Eastern Standard Time.

RELIGIOUS SERVICES. The Serbian (Greek) Orthodox faith prevails in Serbia, Macedonia and Montenegro. The Roman Catholic religion is predominant in Slovenia and Croatia, including Dalmatia. Religion in Bosnia divides three ways: Orthodox, Catholic and Moslem. There are many Moslem communities in Macedonia and southwest Serbia. Protestant churches may be found only in major towns and cities.

PHOTOGRAPHY. Yugoslavia is very photogenic. Plan on bringing along your own film rather than buying the locally available products. Films imported to Yugoslavia are more expensive than in their countries of origin.

Black-and-white film can be developed and printed everywhere in Yugoslavia. However, if you are a camera enthusiast, you will probably prefer to keep your undeveloped films for processing at home. Color film and motion-picture footage are also better taken home for processing.

There are some restrictions on photography in Yugoslavia. Places where photographing is forbidden are indicated with signs showing a camera crossed out in red. As these signs are not always obviously placed, we seriously suggest that you always have a good look round before clicking the shutter.

Cameras and Film. Those once-in-a-lifetime holiday films are vulnerable to the X-ray security machines on airports. At some, such as London's Heathrow, extra-powerful equipment is used; at most, the machines are of the "low-dose" type. Both can cause films to be "fogged," and the more often the film passes through such machines, the more the fog can build up. Warning notices are displayed sometimes, and passengers are advised to remove film—or cameras with film in them—for a hand check. But many airport authorities will not allow hand inspection and insist that all luggage pass through the detection devices.

There are two steps you should follow. First, ask for a hand-inspection whenever you can. Second, buy one or more Filmashield lead-laminated bags, which are manufactured by the American SIMA Products Groups. These will protect films from low-dosage X-rays, but should not be relied on against the more powerful machines. The bags are also available in Britain.

 MEDICAL SERVICES IN YUGOSLAVIA. The I.A.M.A.T. (International Assoc. for Medical Assistance to Travelers) offers you a list of approved English-speaking doctors who have had postgraduate training in the U.S., Canada or Gt. Britain. Membership is free; the scheme is worldwide, with many European countries participating. An office call costs $20; hotel calls $30; night and holiday calls $35. For information and a directory of correspondent clinics and physicians apply in the U.S. to 736 Center St., Lewiston, N.Y. 14092; in Canada, 123 Edward St., Toronto; in Europe, Gotthardstrasse 17, Zug, Switzerland; in Australia, St. Vincent's hospital, Victoria Parade, Melbourne 3065. In Yugoslavia I.A.M.A.T. has member hospitals or clinics in Belgrade, Dubrovnik, Opatija, Split, Zadar and Zagreb.

Foreign tourists are entitled to exactly the same medical treatment as Yugoslav citizens, though small charges are made but only at the same rates as apply to locals. Your hotel or the local tourist office will tell you how to set about consulting a doctor, or will call one for you.

Despite these facilities, it is well worth taking out a medical insurance before you leave home. This will cover not only doctors' and hospitals' services on the spot, but also the cost of bringing you home, if necessary on a stretcher (paying for the extra aircraft seats occupied) and with someone to accompany you. You can buy insurance of this sort from Lloyd's, from major insurance companies, and if you've a car or caravan, from the AA or RAC, and the Caravan Club (who also cover your car and/or caravan very efficiently). But the cheapest service of all, and probably the most effective and comprehensive, is provided by Europ Assistance Ltd, 252 High St., Croydon, Surrey CRO 1NF. Outstanding advantages are the provision of a 24-hour telephone number in the U.K., from which advice and help can be obtained at any time, and of on-the-spot guarantees of payment to people who provide services for which you may not have ready cash. It has an air ambulance on 24-hour call, and uses it whenever advisable. Cover against all the expenses that may arise from a car accident or breakdown (flying out spare parts, hiring another car, bringing a damaged car back to the U.K., additional hotel bills, etc.) is also available. Charges vary considerably, but samples are £7.15 per person for up to 12 days, and £19.35 for a car. This scheme is only available to British residents.

USEFUL ADDRESSES. Belgrade: American Embassy, Kneza Miloša 50; British Embassy, Generala Ždanova 46; Canadian, Proleterskih Brigada 69. Zagreb: American Consulate, Braće Kavurića 2; British Consulate, Ilica 12. Split: British Consulate, Titova Obala 10.

NEWSPAPERS. In the large cities and most resorts, you'll find English-language newspapers. Supplies tend to depend on Yugoslavia's foreign currency situation.

CUSTOMS—RETURNING HOME. If you propose to take on your holiday any *foreign-made* articles, such as cameras, binoculars, expensive time-pieces and the like, it is wise to put with your travel documents the receipt from the retailer or some other evidence that the item was bought in your home country. If you bought the article on a previous holiday abroad and have already paid duty on it, carry with you the receipt for this. Otherwise, on returning home, you may be charged duty.

Americans who are out of the United States at least 48 hours and have claimed no exemption during the previous 30 days are entitled to bring $400 worth of purchases duty-free (up from $300). For the next $1000 worth of goods beyond the first $400, inspectors will assess a flat ten percent duty, rather than charging you different percentages for various types of goods. Above $1400 duties vary according to the merchandise. The value of each item is determined by the price actually paid (so keep your receipts). All items purchased must accompany the passenger on his return; it will therefore simplify matters at customs control if you can pack all purchases in one holdall. Every member of the family is entitled to this same exemption, regardless of age, and the allowance can be pooled.

Not more than 200 cigarets, or one carton, may be included in your duty-free exemption, nor more than a liter of wine or liquor (none at all if your passport indicates you are from a "dry" state or are under 21 years old). Only one bottle of perfume that is trademarked in the U.S. may be brought in, plus a reasonable quantity of other brands.

Antiques are defined, for customs purposes, as articles 100 years old and over, and are admitted duty free. If there's any question of age, you may be asked to supply proof.

Small gifts may be mailed to friends, but not more than one package to any one address, and none to your own home. The inscription on the package should read "Unsolicited gift, value under $25." Tobacco, liquor and perfume may not be mailed.

If your purchases exceed your exemption, list the most expensive items that are subject to duty under your exemption and pay duty on the cheaper items. Any article you fail to declare cannot later be claimed under your exemption.

Do not bring home foreign meats, fruits or plants, or soil or other agricultural items when you return to the United States. To do so will delay you at the port of entry. It is illegal to bring in foreign agricultural items without permission, because they can spread destructive plant or animal pests and diseases. For more information, read the pamphlet *Customs Hints,* or write to: "Quarantines," U.S. Department of Agriculture, Federal Building, Hyattsville, Md. 20782 for Program Aid No. 1083, *Travelers' Tips.*

Residents of Canada may, after seven days out of the country, and upon written declaration, claim an exemption of $150 a year plus an allowance of 40 ounces of liquor, 50 cigars, 200 cigarets and two lb. of tobacco. Personal gifts should be mailed as "Unsolicited Gift—Value Under $25." For details, ask for the Canada Customs brochure, *I Declare.*

Canadian Customs regulations are strictly enforced; you are recommended to check on the allowances and to keep receipts for whatever you may have bought abroad.

British subjects. There is a two-tier allowance for duty-free goods brought into the U.K., due to Britain's Common Market membership. *Note:* The Customs and Excise Board warn that it is not advisable to combine the two allowances.

If you return from an EEC country (Belgium, Denmark, Eire, France, W. Germany, Greece, Holland, Italy, Luxembourg) and goods were bought in one of those countries, duty-free allowances are:

300 cigarets (or 150 cigarillos, or 75 cigars, or 400 gr. tobacco); 1.5 liters of strong spirits (over 38.8 proof), or three liters of other spirits (under 38.8 proof) or fortified wines, plus four liters of still table wine; 75 gr. perfume and .375 liters toilet water; gifts to a value of £120.

If you return from a country outside the EEC *or if the goods were bought in a duty-free shop on ship, plane or airport* the allowances are less:

200 cigarets (or 100 cigarillos, or 50 cigars, or 250 gr. tobacco); one liter of strong spirits (or two liters of other spirits or fortified wines) plus two liters of still table wine; 50 gr. perfume and .25 liters toilet water; gifts to a value of £28.

 DUTY FREE is not what it once was. You may not be paying tax on your bottle of whiskey or perfume, but you are certainly contributing to somebody's profits. Duty-free shops are big business these days and mark ups are often around 100 to 200%. So don't be seduced by the idea that because it's duty free it's a bargain. Very often prices are not much different from your local discount store and in the case of perfume or jewelry they can be even higher.

THE
YUGOSLAV
SCENE

THE COUNTRY AND THE PEOPLE

A Panoply of Paradoxes

by
SYLVIE NICKELS

Yugoslavia is a superb, colorful mixture which makes fascinating fare for the visitor; but it is a good idea to know at least a little of what that mixture comprises. Underlying it is a unity that reveals itself whenever the Yugoslavs find themselves with their backs to the wall or in times of national sadness. It's something you don't learn from sitting on a beach or in the comfortable insulation of a modern tourist hotel. You learn it from staying with the Yugoslavs, from traveling in

39

the same buses and trains as they do, from eating in the same restaurants and taking part in the same activities—especially in that most favorite pastime, conversation.

All these things are open to anyone. Some of my most pleasant memories are of incidents that not even the best travel agent could ever have organized. One was of an early spring bus journey that should have taken seven hours and took 17. Crossing Cakor Pass between south Serbia and Montenegro, we got caught in an unseasonable blizzard which turned the landscape into one of Arctic grandeur. The entire busload, mainly Shiptars (Albanians), adopted me, as the only and very unsuitably-dressed foreigner, and entertained me and each other with traditional songs led by the conductor. On another occasion, I found myself spending Easter alone with a family in Belgrade as a paying guest. We had no common language, yet any possible loneliness was dispelled on Easter Sunday morning when a tray of special delicacies was brought in to me, despite the fact that the family was Orthodox and their Easter on a quite different date from mine that year. It was also in Belgrade that I was "picked up" in a most proper fashion by a young man who wanted to practise his English, and spent the next two days showing me round.

In a Roman Catholic monastery on an island off the Dalmatian coast, I became involved in an amicable argument between one of the priests and a local official, which ended, as a good argument should, with agreement to differ. The monastery had a fine collection of Roman and other treasures taken from the sea, a small (and I hasten to add imperfect) sample of which was slipped, quite unofficially, into my pocket, and which adorns a bookcase today. I left my scarf in the monastery on that occasion, and it was handed back to me by another young priest on the early morning boat to the mainland the following day. This monastic order had its headquarters on the mainland, and it subsequently became a regular bolthole whenever I was passing that way, for a cup of coffee and pleasant conversation in halting French.

It was in Ohrid, Macedonia, that I was sitting on a wall by a monastery one morning when a lady from a nearby first floor flat leant out to invite me up for coffee (the word *kava* is not too difficult to distinguish). She worked in the local post office and she, too, with her family and friends adopted me for the next two or three days, with only a few words of French and my two tiny Serbo-Croat dictionaries to help us along. We still correspond, each getting the other's letters translated in order to be able to answer them. In Montenegro, chance acquaintances have become old friends; and the same is true of a dozen or more Croats and Bosnians from all walks of life. Through them, I have had the privilege of joining in family events and outings in a way that has never quite happened to me anywhere else.

In a Nutshell

So how did the marvelous mix come about? It may be an old truism to say that Yugoslavia is one country with two alphabets, three religions, four (main) languages, five (principal) nationalities, six republics and a border with seven countries; but I know of no mnemonic that better summarizes a complex and fascinating situation. The fact that within about 60 years, interrupted by a world war and a total political upheaval, Yugoslavia has made for herself some kind of unity is one of the greater miracles in nation-making of the 20th century. The fact that she has grown into a respected small non-aligned power out of the utter disruption of that war is another miracle. The fact that she survived politically and—more or less—economically her unequivocal opting out of the Cominform in 1948 further compounds these miracles.

All of this does not mean of course that the Yugoslavs are saints. They have done terrible things to each other in the past, and intermittent dissent between Serbs and Croats, or the discontent of ex-patriots abroad, alas, still makes more impression on world headlines at times than the sheer effort of will that lies behind the country's growth into maturity. The Slovenes continue to object from time to time to helping to foot the bill for the less affluent Macedonians, and the Montenegrins still talk nostalgically of their tough and not always so romantic past. I doubt however whether many would choose to depart their homeland, except for a few years in order to make more money somewhere else; and that goes for most of the minorities, of whom there are many.

Let's begin with the seven national frontiers which, starting in the north and working round clockwise, are with Italy, Austria, Hungary, Romania, Bulgaria, Greece and Albania. You don't need to know much about European history to imagine what effect such an assortment of neighbors might have had on the Yugoslavs. Their history is described in another chapter of this volume, but certain facts are crucial to any attempt to begin to understand the kaleidoscopic nature of the Yugoslav way of life. The fundamental fact is that for centuries the country was split, in fluctuating proportions, between the Ottoman Turkish Empire and that of the Habsburgs, with the Venetians putting their spoke in along the coast from time to time.

Topography too has a considerable influence. In the north you have the towering splendors of the Julian and Karavanke Alps, in the south and southwest the Transylvanian Alps, and running parallel with the Adriatic coast, more or less linking these ranges, you have the Dinaric chain. Cutting through these mountains are rivers that often become glorious, raging torrents hemmed in between soaring rock faces. Because of the curious nature of some of the limestone formations, known as *karst,* some of these rivers disappear underground for considerable distances, carving out fantastic subterranean worlds like the Postojna caves, which are among the sightseeing wonders of the country.

Not many of these capricious and dramatic waterways flow into Yugoslavia's own sea, the Adriatic. Most of them head inland, eventually joining the mighty Sava, which in turn pours itself into the Danube below Belgrade. The mighty plains fed by these great rivers are simply an extension of the Hungarian *Puszta,* across which the Mongol hordes thundered toward Western Europe and the Turks advanced toward the very gates of Vienna.

A Look at the Yugoslavs

Take as an example an office or factory worker earning his daily bread in a city like Ljubljana, capital of Slovenia in the north of the country. Many of the more tangible aspects of his life have been influenced—architecturally, religiously, culturally—by centuries of association with neighboring Austria. Or take a shepherd grazing his flocks above some Bosnian or south-Serbian village in the mountainous center of the country. Here a dominant feature of the community is likely to be the slender minaret of a mosque, and the bazaar will resound to the hammering of copper or plaintive music that has more than a hint of the East in it. Or take Macedonia in the deep south, where the costumes change from one village to another. Here the architectural and spiritual essence is in the medieval Orthodox monastery echoing long-ago Byzantine strength and later Macedonian tenacity. Or consider a fisherman or a market gardener or a hotel waiter on the long, languid Adriatic coast. His ancestors were for centuries effectively barred from their fellow South Slavs by a mountain barrier and the politics that lay beyond. Multiply these examples some scores of times and you will see why it is impossible to generalize about the Yugoslavs.

But they have one important common heritage. Yugoslavia means "land of the South Slavs." The six republics into which it is divided are Slovenia, Croatia, Serbia, Bosnia-Hercegovina, Montenegro and Macedonia. Within the boundaries of Serbia, two autonomous provinces minister to the special needs imposed by history and the presence in them of large national minorities. Kosovo in the mountainous south has a majority population of Albanians. In Vojvodina in the Danube plains, Hungarians predominate, but there are other substantial minorities. For all these, Yugoslavia has done probably more than most other countries in a similar position in terms of safeguarding the language and culture of each group. It has not been without its less fortunate repercussions as in the case of the Albanians of Kosovo, some of whom resorted to violence in their efforts to effect closer union with Yugoslavia's austere little neighbor, Albania. Calm has been restored but to the outsider—and to most Yugoslavs—this outburst was astonishing as well as dismaying, especially given the vast investments pumped into this formerly backward region.

The South Slavs who first appeared in the area of present-day Yugoslavia in the sixth century brought with them certain social and cultural conventions and absorbed others from the indigenous Romanized Illyrians and Celts, which have survived many subsequent strains. The fundamental native feature was the *zadruga,* the tight-knit organization of a family unit, in which everyone had his place. This as much as anything perpetuated the strength of South Slav unity, and it survived as a legal entity right up to 1868. Remnants of its influence exist even today, though the demands of the later 20th century have probably put more pressure on it than all the horrific turmoils of the past ever did. Nevertheless, despite all the rapid changes that have swept the Yugoslavs from a primitive rural society to an industrial economy in a few decades, and in spite of the resulting strains that have been imposed on a slower, simpler way of life, there is still a feeling for family that has, alas, become much rarer farther west. People are concerned about each other, the old are not so readily left to the care of others, and you don't hear much about battered babies.

The five main nationalities are the Slovenes, Croats, Serbs, Macedonians and Montenegrins. The four principal languages (Slovene, Croat, Serb and Macedonian) are really three, since Croat and Serb—known to the rest of the world as Serbo-Croat—are very similar.

Three Religions, Two Alphabets

And so we come to the three religions. With the splitting of the Roman Empire into the Catholic West under the aegis of Rome and the Orthodox East under Byzantium, came the first major division of the future land of the South Slavs, before they even arrived on the scene. With the coming of the Turks, the division became dramatically incised across the map of Yugoslavia as the Orthodox regions were absorbed into the Ottoman Empire, some of them for over five centuries —indeed, right up to World War I. Contact between the South Slav inhabitants on either side of this political and cultural barrier was almost nonexistent. Orthodox churches and monasteries, with few exceptions, were turned into mosques or fell into disrepair. With a degree of coercion that varied in different parts of the region, the Moslem faith was adopted by many—but by no means by all. The fine novel *The Bridge on the Drina* by the Nobel prizewinner Ivo Andrić tells graphically of life over a 400-year span in a small Bosnian town under the Turks.

The use of the Roman and Cyrillic alphabets follows the divisions imposed by the splitting of the Roman Empire, the Roman or Latin alphabet being used as one would expect in the northern and western Catholic areas and the Cyrillic in the southern and eastern Orthodox regions. Cyrillic, which was developed by two brothers, the monks Cyril and Methodius, in the ninth century, was taught by their followers in a monastery in Ohrid, Macedonia, whence it spread across the rest of the Slav world, including, of course, Russia. In fact, today, the Roman alphabet has substantially infiltrated the Cyrillic areas of Yugoslavia.

Nowadays, the street names and other useful signs are usually printed in both alphabets, though it is well worth the effort of learning the Cyrillic letters, so that at least you can recognize a *PECTOPAH* for what it is: a restaurant. The knowledge of foreign languages has increased enormously of recent years, the older generation still tending to speak more German, but the younger ones English. Still, it has never done anyone any harm to learn a few words like "good morning" and "thank you" in the language of the country, nor the correct pronunciation of the names of people and places; the effort is often well rewarded.

So we have Yugoslavia, one country that combines most human and natural variety. And it should be clear by now why it is impossible to make any generalizations whatsoever, either about Yugoslavia or the Yugoslavs. It is one of the very good reasons why it would be a sad waste to confine your visit to one resort hotel (which tends anyway—in Yugoslavia as anywhere else—to be much like another). The small amount of energy needed to travel only a few kilometers can bring you into a totally different world. Combine this with a little planning, and you can participate in some of the rich folk traditions which here retain their authenticity, and have not yet grown tired and stale.

Events Great and Small

One custom which you can hardly avoid and which takes place every evening, when the weather is fair, is the *korzo.* You hear it before you see it: a faint hum in the distance, growing in intensity as you approach until it sounds like the buzzing of a million angry bees. In fact, it is nothing more than the local people taking their evening stroll, usually in the main square, sometimes up and down a main street, or along the waterfront of a fishing village or coastal center. In a square, the crowd mills about rather, but along a street or waterfront the townspeople stroll very slowly up one side and back along the other. The tradition goes back over many generations, and despite the lure of radio and television, it is kept up with as much enthusiasm today by the young as by the old. Usually it takes place at dusk, somewhere between 6 and 8 P.M., the scene rapidly filling and, later on, equally rapidly emptying, as if at an unseen signal. It is an opportunity to exchange the day's gossip, to meet friends, to see and be seen. Many a romance has its origins in the *korzo;* quite a few of my Yugoslav friends met their spouses in this way. But there are strict rules: young ladies do not stroll alone, always in couples or small groups. But eyes may meet across the crowd, a few words may be exchanged. Eventually the young man will suggest a coffee or a snack. So the timeless business of courtship begins.

At the other end of the scale, each republic has its special day, commemorating its integration into the Federal Republic; and the whole country celebrates 29th November as the day on which in the small town of Jajce in Bosnia, Yugoslavia was born as a Federal People's Republic in 1943 (today, Federal Socialist Republic). There are other national events, in particular the series of Youth Days that have their climax on President Tito's birthday on 25th May. This begins some time earlier, each year in a different place, when a specially carved *štafeta* (or baton) is carried on a journey of about 6,440 km. (4,000 miles) that will take it right through the country on its way to Belgrade for the birthday date. It is carried by a relay of young people, and as it passes there is a general holiday atmosphere, with the emphasis on youth, to the accompaniment of dancing and displays, and various cultural and sporting activities.

Many of the more local celebrations are associated with the rhythm of the seasons or with some dramatic, historical or legendary event. One of the best known in the latter category is the *Moreška* of Korčula island, a most vivid dance pageant depicting the struggle between the Black and the Red King for a beautiful princess. The kings may represent the Moors and Turks, and the princess the town of Korčula, but it is in any event a highly skilful (and exhausting) display, for which the local men and boys participating have to train rigorously. The traditional date for the event is 27th July but, because of its popularity, quite a few extra performances are arranged throughout the season. *Alka,* a spectacular tournament of costumed knights tilting at the ring, commemorates a victory over the Turks in 1715 at Sinj, on the Dalmatian coast near Split; this is on the first Sunday after 15th August.

In August or September, some of the mountain villages of Slovenia have special festivities—in the tradition of many other mountain areas —connected with the return of the cattle or sheep from the high summer pastures. In Macedonia, where weddings can still be very colorful, an enchanting multiple marriage ceremony takes place at Galičnik, a small place in the heart of the mountains not far from the Albanian border.

In most of these festivities traditional dancing plays a major part, and the Yugoslavs excel at it. Here folk dancing lives on not simply as a tourist attraction—though it is that, too—but because both young and old enjoy it. Thus many different kinds have survived, of which the *kolo,* a group dance reminiscent of a reel, is the most common, varying from region to region and even from village to village. Internationally, Yugoslav folk groups are quite outstanding, carrying off first prize in many a contest. Performances demonstrating dances from different parts of the country can be seen in numerous towns and resorts throughout summer, sometimes in beautiful natural or historic settings. But the small, spontaneous local celebration can be even more fun, and away from the beaten track you may find yourself the only foreigner there. Quite often there'll be a whole sheep roasting on a spit, and as the wine flows you might be surprised to find how much Serbo-Croat you can suddenly understand!

Of the more sophisticated summer cultural festivals, the most famous is Dubrovnik's, not only because of the quality of the performances (many international guest stars participate), but also because of some of the unsurpassed settings in this beautiful walled city. Medieval and Renaissance Dubrovnik produced its own fine artists and writers, among them Marin Držić whose play *Dundo Maroje* (Uncle Maroje) is often performed at the festival, and whose style has been likened to that of Molière. Other Yugoslav cities also make good use of their architectural heritage. The Ljubljana Festival, for example, centers upon Križanke, a fine complex combining a 16th-century monastery with remains dating from medieval and Roman times. In Split, various parts of the Emperor Diocletian's Palace provide wonderful settings for summer festival performances. In Pula, the great Roman arena is the annual scene of the Yugoslav Film Festival.

Communism and Private Enterprise

But now let's take a look at Yugoslavia's own brand of Communism, which they prefer to call Socialism. You have probably already heard that it is rather different from anyone else's. Indeed, the Yugoslavs might claim with quite a lot of justification that they are the only ones who are really putting Communism into practise. So what's so special about it?

You won't travel very far in Yugoslavia without hearing someone mention the term "workers' self-management," and therein lies the clue to the whole business. State ownership does not exist in Yugoslavia. All enterprises and services are owned and managed by the people who work for them, under the system of workers' self-management. "Workers" in this context means all who work, whether they are medical specialists, university professors, hotel managers or waiters, skilled artisans or the men who sweep factory floors.

Ownership in this sense does not mean that each worker contributes hard cash which he can remove if he gets fed up and leaves. It means that he gives his time and his labor in return for which he gets not only his wages, but the right to participate in decisions affecting every level of the organization of his enterprise: e.g. what is produced, methods of production, marketing, hours of work and wages, what to do with the profits, or how to overcome a loss. Basically, the organization works from the lower echelons upward like the building of a pyramid, rather than the other way round. Workers' councils are elected by secret ballot of all workers in each department and sub-department of an enterprise, each of these representing what is known as a basic organization of associated labor—more simply, a self-contained unit responsible for and to itself. Each council must report back to the workers' assembly it represents on major decisions before they are finally acted upon. In a large factory or group of factories these units can number as many as 50. Workers' councils take care of the general running of their unit, but major decisions are arrived at by a referendum of all the workers. In larger organizations, there are at progressive levels additional workers' councils representing groups of units, and so on, until one reaches the apex, the management workers' council for the whole enterprise.

Let's take the example of a factory producing its own yarn from which it then produces different types of carpet. The section producing a particular carpet design suddenly finds the bottom has dropped out of the market. It is the workers in that particular section who decide themselves what they are going to do about it: either to persevere with the same design and hope that demand can be re-stimulated, or to experiment with a completely different kind of product. In certain conditions, a unit can separate itself from its parent organization and set up on its own—though obviously, not if this will be to the detriment of the group as a whole.

These simple examples can be applied to virtually all forms of production, but the system works a little differently where there is no actual end product, such as in a school or hospital. Contributions to all these kinds of social services are made by every working member of the community from his or her gross salary, and in exchange he and his family benefit from the product—in this case the skills—of each service. The fundamental organization of a school, hospital, etc., however, is on the same lines as those of a commercial enterprise, each self-contained department or unit fulfilling its own specific function, and governed by the same system of workers' councils.

The philosophy of workers' self-management, in all its complex simplicity, has been the aim of Yugoslavia's form of socialism right from the beginning. It did not appear overnight, and its progress has been one of gradual expansion, consolidation and decentralization, culminating in 1974 in a new constitution, and in 1976 in the passing of the Associated Labour Act and subsequent amendments, the purpose of whose 670 articles is precisely to expand and define all that self-management means. Those who wish to know more on the subject should consult this formidable document, which is available in English.

As a working philosophy, I find it quite fascinating but you may wonder in what way it is likely to affect the visitor to Yugoslavia. The answer is that it depends on what your preconceived ideas of Communism, or your previous experience of a Communist country, might be. The degree of competition comes as a surprise to most people when they find, for example, two or three different bus companies operating similar services at different times and at slightly different prices. The same applies to all kinds of products and services.

From the tourist's point of view, the process of decentralization and the competitive nature of the system have their pros and cons. Healthy competition makes it well worth shopping around, whether it's for meals or mementos. On the other hand, things are sometimes so decentralized that it is not always easy to find out in one place what is going on in another!

One final example of the possible side effects of workers' self-management on the community at large might be of interest. This example occurred in a big industrial works near the town of Split, where a good deal of thought and discussion has been going on of recent years on the subject of pollution. The Yugoslav coast, so far, has been more fortunate than many, but the relatively heavy concentration of industry round Split makes it a higher-risk area. Programs of public education on the problem have been organized at different levels to increase awareness, and their effects had filtered through to the workers' councils of the enterprise concerned. Thus a decision was reached to invest a considerable sum into a plant for processing their industrial waste, certainly to the benefit of the city (and its visitors) as a whole.

And what of private enterprise? In a small way it flourishes and is encouraged, though one necessary move under consideration is the reassessment of the high taxes which have been the subject of long and loud complaint from the self-employed themselves. Anyone can run his own business, the maximum number of people employed, however, being limited by law to five. Thus far, among the most successful adherents of the private approach are restaurants, guest houses, and handicraft workshops, but there is also a move to encourage small light industries, involving private investment repaid with interest over a limited period. Such enterprises have already proved very successful in progressive Slovenia, and are now being taken up in less developed regions. Of agriculture there will be more to say later.

The Economic Recovery

As far as economic development is concerned, the change in Yugoslavia since World War II has been dramatic—notwithstanding the serious difficulties encountered since the death of Tito in 1980. As time goes on, that war for a rapidly increasing number of us is becoming an historical event rather than a remembered personal experience. But it is impossible really to grasp Yugoslavia's achievements without knowing something of the devastation she suffered. A few stark figures will serve to illustrate the point. By the end of World War II, Yugoslavia had lost ten percent of her population, *i.e.* 1,700,000 dead. Over 820,000 homes had been destroyed and 3½ million people were without a roof over their heads; two-thirds of the hospitals had been totally or almost totally razed; two-fifths of industrial installations were in ruins and the remainder seriously damaged; over half the railway lines were devastated and the rest unfit for use; thousands of road and railway bridges had been bombed out of existence and many thousands of kilometers of the roads themselves rendered useless. One can, indeed, use the word "holocaust" with justification.

These facts, of which little evidence remains in Yugoslavia today, help us to realize what amazing feats of recovery were achieved in a comparatively short time. For the phoenix did not merely rise out of the ashes, it emerged into a world that itself was undergoing great changes as it entered the era of technology. At the outbreak of war, three-quarters of the Yugoslav population were dependent on agriculture for their livelihood; today the proportion is less than a third.

It is important to remember too that especially during the earlier part of this period industry had to be totally reorganized, communications almost entirely rebuilt, the homeless rehoused and the production and distribution of practically every basic commodity arranged to fill empty shops and meet the needs of interminable queues. The foundations of the new Yugoslavia were laid by hundreds of thousands of her people rolling up their sleeves and working on short rations. This is worth remembering from time to time as we bowl along one of the new highways or gaze out of the window of our modern hotel at some idyllic holiday scene.

In Terms of Technology

Yugoslavia is fortunate in possessing rich resources of such useful raw materials as coal, iron ore, crude petroleum and chemicals, as well as great and fertile plains and river valleys for her now highly-developed agriculture. 84 percent of the latter is in private hands, but as landownership is limited by law to ten hectares/about 25 acres (and most peasant households own less), the result is rather unwieldy—many 1000s of small parcels of land. For this reason, there are continuing moves to revive the cooperative movement, by which private owners can benefit from modern technology, credit schemes and efficient marketing. In some of the more mountainous areas, the upper limit of private ownership has been increased to 20 hectares.

The skills and technology needed to turn raw materials and unworked products into semi-manufactured and finished goods had to be learned and developed, and it is in this field that the transformation has been most startling. Nowadays over 60 percent of Yugoslav exports are finished goods, compared with 5.4 percent pre-war, and these include an enormous range of items, from heavy machinery to furniture and footwear. The increase in exports of such capital goods as ships and complete power-generating and industrial plants, especially to developing countries, was another success of the 1970s. While the Soviet Union remains the country's most important single customer, the EEC is the biggest economic group trading with Yugoslavia, with Italy and West Germany at the head of the list. There is also quite substantial trade with the United States.

But alas economic miracles have their converse aspects. The recession which has affected the rest of the world has had a profound impact on the Yugoslavs too, who have had to face the fact that they have diversified too much and borrowed for too long. Rising inflation, a shortage of imported raw materials that need to be paid for in precious hard currency, and declining productivity have resulted in an economic uncertainty unknown in the recent past. There have been shortages of quite basic goods, including gasoline which has been subject to rationing at times (though visitors have been largely unaffected).

The Yugoslavs seem to be facing the facts with a sense of realism. A series of dinar devaluations to make Yugoslav exports more competitive have been combined with quite strict currency restrictions affecting Yugoslavs traveling abroad. Imports are being rationalized and a careful look is being taken at all investments. One wishes them well. But whatever the troubles of the present, it cannot be argued that technology has made its ineradicable marks on the Yugoslav landscapes, transforming whole regions or bringing ease of access to hitherto isolated areas. One example is the remarkable railway completed a few years ago to link Belgrade with the south Adriatic port of Bar. To achieve this, a way had to be cut through formidable mountain barriers, necessitating over 100 tunnels and 230 bridges. Thus, in addition to its economic value, it is today one of the most beautiful scenic railway routes of Europe. Another example is the Danube–Tisa–Danube hydroengineering scheme in the autonomous province of Vojvodina, resulting in a network of 930 km. (580 miles) of canals between these two great rivers. This network not only irrigates 50,000 hectares (over 120,000 acres) of productive land, but even more importantly, removes excess flood waters, from 700,000 hectares (over 1,700,000 acres). The increase in average yields of this "granary" of Yugoslavia has effectively made each field as productive as four were formerly. Yet another Danube project completed a few years ago, this time involving cooperation with Romania, was the remarkable Djerdap (Iron Gates) power plant and navigational system harnessing the river's turbulent waters to provide hydroelectric power for both countries. A second plant, Djerdap II, is currently under construction 80 km. (50 miles) downstream.

But in the end, especially in this materially-minded last quarter of the 20th century, a country's affluence (though sometimes more *apparent* than real) is perhaps most easily gauged by the proliferation of luxury goods. Thus the enormous increase in private traffic on the roads (with attendant parking problems in the cities!) becomes significant, as does the fact that almost every other family now possesses a television set. Go into things rather more deeply, and you find very much more fundamental changes: for example, that in 1952 there was only one physician on average for over 2,500 inhabitants and in 1976 this had become one for under 800; and that illiteracy has plummeted from almost 50 percent before the war to under 15 percent—mainly among older people and women in some underdeveloped parts of the country.

Accent on Youth

There has indeed been an educational explosion. Nearly 95 percent of all children of school age now have at least elementary schooling and, at the upper end of the educational scale, there are 25 times as many students (about 430,000) as there were before the war. Thus the sons and daughters of peasant farmers, fisherfolk and factory workers have become teachers and lawyers, doctors and scientists, politicians and journalists. It is significant that few of them forget their origins; going home to some small island community or remote mountain village is not simply the fulfillment of a duty: South Slav family ties are strong. It will be interesting to see what happens in the future.

One other very special feature of the Yugoslav educational system should be noted: the facilities available for ethnic minorities. There are schools teaching in the Albanian (by far the biggest group), Bulgarian, Italian, Hungarian, Romanian, Ruthenian, Slovak, Turkish and Czech languages. In regions with substantial minorities, additional means of education and amenities for national expression exist, such as the Albanian-language University in Kosovo, the cultural center ministering to Albanian and Turkish speakers in Skopje, Macedonia, and similar facilities for Hungarians in Novi Sad, Vojvodina. Similarly, newspapers and journals are available in most of the minority national languages, which also have their own television programs. The degree to which national forms of music, dancing, costume and customs have survived is quite remarkable and is one of the bonuses for the visitor to enjoy. And more recent forms of expression have been found. The splendid canvases of the naïve painters in the villages of the Danubian and Sava plains, whether they be Serb, Croat, Slovak or Hungarian, illustrate a whole folk-culture with a vividness that has won acclaim in international salons all over the world.

Sports fans will need no reminding of the Yugoslav enthusiasm for their two great loves: football and basketball. Recent failures in international football have indeed caused national dismay, but this has been more than compensated for by basketball successes. Athletics and boxing are other sports in which the Yugoslavs do well, and they have had a number of triumphs in a wide range of competitive activities ranging from bowling and table tennis to Graeco-Roman wrestling and judo. Chess has always been a popular pastime, and Yugoslavia holds the record for the number of international tournaments held in the country each year. When it comes to sporting activities for which visitors can expect ideal conditions, the most important include hunting, fishing, canoeing along the splendid rivers, sailing in the magnificent coastal waters, and winter sports.

You, the Tourist

But what of tourism in general? It is certainly no exception in illustrating the country's phenomenal growth. From 62,000 foreign visitors in 1948, the figure soared to well over 6½ million in 1980, and with rising affluence the increase in domestic tourism has been just as dramatic. Rapid growth can bring its dangers, and Yugoslavia, like many other countries suddenly projected into popular tourism, made its share of mistakes in indiscriminate building to standards that were not always as high as they should have been. The mass overdevelopment of stretches of coast suffered by some countries, however, has been avoided, and the sensible calling in of United Nations experts for advice on planning some years ago has been effective. Similarly, there is a lively and growing awareness of potential pollution dangers. Yugoslavia is a very active participant of the International Blue Plan for cleaning up the Mediterranean, and a number of conferences (in which all but one of the countries bordering the Mediterranean have participated) have already taken place on Yugoslav soil. For the moment, her Adriatic coast compares very favorably with many others; industry is limited to a few places like Rijeka and Split, and the currents weaving through the labyrinthine sea passages between 100s of islands act as a good cleanser. The treatment of industrial waste and of vastly greater amounts of sewage—one of the by-products of a healthy growth in tourism—is the subject of much discussion and more importantly of action, an example of which has already been mentioned.

For a short period in recent years, there was a tendency for the number of foreign tourists to remain static. Perhaps the success story had come too easily and too rapidly, and human nature being what it is, an infiltration of lower standards of service or higher prices for "extras" was becoming apparent. Whatever the cause, it gave the Yugoslavs pause for thought, resulting in the preparation of new laws on catering and tourism, both to ensure a higher standard of tourist services and to protect the consumer. Some resorts have even most laudably arranged meetings between visitors and local tourist agencies to exchange ideas and to resolve problems.

The Yugoslavs have realized that for many years tourist developments have concentrated almost entirely on hotel facilities with full pension, and plans are now in progress for providing half-pension or self-catering opportunities, and increasing recreational and special-interest amenities.

Spreading the Benefits

Much consideration has also been given to the fact that over 80 percent of visitors stay at resorts along the Adriatic coast. This is obviously serious neglect of the magnificent landscapes and cultural wealth of the rest of the country, especially when 75 percent of visitors come by their own transport, and therefore have the mobility to enjoy these attractions. To broaden the scope of tourism more amenities are needed, and the process is now under way. Some inland regions, such as the Slovenian Alps, the magnificent Plitvice Lakes of Croatia, the culturally mixed Sarajevo and other centers of Bosnia-Hercegovina, are already popular inland destinations, though often on a fairly short-term basis. Others, such as the mountain regions of Macedonia, South Serbia and Montenegro, have only recently begun to acquire such tourist accessories as first-class hotels, and some have yet to develop the standard of service normally expected.

The main point is that awareness of the needs exists, with regard not only to the standard but also to the variety of amenities required. Thus the outstanding cultural attractions of the medieval monasteries of Macedonia and South Serbia provide a theme for an increasing number of tours. So-called "village" tourism is being developed in a number of regions, featuring visits to shepherds' cottages, barbecue picnics, and participation in local folk events. In these various ways, a proportion at least of the devotees of sun-and-sea should be lured away from the beaches to see something of the rest of Yugoslavia. I'll wager they won't regret it.

THE PAST

The Ancient Story of a Young Nation

Yugoslavia officially became a single state only in 1918, after the 1917 Pact of Corfu. When Slav tribes entered the Balkans during the Dark Ages, at the time of the Wandering of the Peoples, they came in waves, with differing aims and under separate leaders. Having settled in the Balkans, they were at once subject to diverse influences, for they had settled across the dividing line of the Eastern and Western Roman Empires, Byzantium and Rome. Even more important for them was that the Balkan peninsula was a disputed territory between the Roman and Orthodox churches. The Serbs, Macedonians and Montenegrins adopted the Orthodox creed from Byzantium, the Croats and Slovenes the Catholic faith of Rome. The Bosnians had for a time a heretical religion of their own, Bogomilism, but after the Ottoman conquest in the 15th century they accepted Islam in large numbers.

Thus any attempt to summarize the history of the Yugoslavs is like the construction of a complex cable. Many strands of various colors are interwoven to form, in the end, a single unit.

Multicolored Mosaic

There are at least half-a-dozen such strands. Among the Yugoslav peoples themselves, there are the Serbians, the Croats, the Slovenes, the Bosnians, the Montenegrins and the Macedonians. Almost as varied at different periods are the peoples who have at one time or another been the overlords of the South Slav lands—the Byzantines, the Bulgarians, the Turks, the Venetians, the Hungarians and the Austrians. A most brilliantly colored thread, interwoven in the pattern for more than 1,000 years, traces the independent existence of the Republic of Ragusa, later Dubrovnik.

The large majority of these Slav peoples were hostile to one another for most of their history. They fought fiercely and frequently. They differed in social and cultural background, in historical traditions, in religion and in alphabet. They resembled one another in language, in racial memory and in the folk traditions of the common people. But the differences still exist. The ancient frontiers can still be roughly traced by those of the Socialist Republics. Nor have the years of unity always been years of internal peace. But deep-rooted racial tradition, tempered and annealed by years of war, has brought unity at last to the Yugoslavs. They are now a single people, albeit with marked provincial variations.

Until 1918, the Yugoslav lands were but once united under a single rule. The only time in history that this happened was before the coming of the Slav tribes, under the later Roman Empire. Then, for a time, the Balkan peninsula was a vital overland link with the rich eastern provinces, and supplied huge quantities of much-needed grain from the fertile Sava and Danube plains. Many of the great Emperors were of Balkan origin. The most impressive memorials of that time are the Palace of Diocletian at Split and the nearby ruined city of Salona. To British visitors the palace may seem strangely familiar. It was studied and sketched by the English architect, Robert Adam, in 1757. What he saw there became the model for London's original Adelphi buildings.

After the coming of the Slavs, these lands were once again almost united under the rule of the Ottoman Turks. But Turkish dominion, though at one time it stretched almost to the gates of Vienna, was not complete. Quite large areas of Croatia were unconquered military frontiers, and Slovenia was subject only to occasional forays. Also, two pockets of South Slav independence remained, in fact if not always in theory: the Republic of Ragusa-Dubrovnik and the State of Zeta (modern Montenegro or Crna Gora). Many of the Dalmatian cities remained subject to another foreign rule, that of Venice.

Until the end of the Middle Ages, nationality as we know it today did not exist, not even in some of the more centralized countries of Western Europe. Its place was taken by loyalty to a leader or to a creed.

The South Slavs were divided not only by tribal differences and history, but even more by the existence of three major religions, Catholic and Orthodox Christianity, rivals as much of one another as of Islam. These forces of division were stronger than any tending toward cohesion.

The idea of nationality began to emerge at about the beginning of the 19th century. At that time it had many names, for example, the Illyrian Movement, but for the sake of simplicity it may be called the "Yugoslav Idea." It was built at first upon shallow foundations.

Awakening of National Consciousness

In Slovenia the invasion of Napoleon's armies, the first major invasion of the Yugoslav lands from the west since that of Charlemagne's Franks, was hailed as a deliverance. The Slovenes, hitherto considered the boorish peasantry of an outlying Austrian province, had preserved their Slav language and little else. In fact, their continued existence as a racial group was largely due to their complex and archaic Slav tongue, and was little short of a miracle. Napoleon formed of Slovenia the short-lived Illyrian Province. The Slovene language was recognized as equal in administrative affairs with French and German, and Ljubljana became an administrative center.

National consciousness awoke, and there was a vigorous and patriotic outburst of Slovene literature. The great Slovene poet, Fran Prešern, hymned the Napoleonic armies (which had just crushed forever the political independence of Dubrovnik farther down the coast) as harbingers of a new kind of liberty. The Slovene Church (the Slovenes are devout Catholics) took up the cause of national liberty. When Slovenia reverted to being an Austrian province, the seed had already been sown. The Slovenes felt themselves to be a nation, and it was but one step further to feel themselves one with the other Yugoslav peoples. Attempts to "Germanize" the country failed. In 1870, the Croats and Slovenes made common cause of their Yugoslav aims, and after World War I, under their leader Father Antun Korošec, voted for union with the Serbs and Croats.

With the Croats the position was somewhat different. Memories of their early independence had died out among the peasantry and only a few scholars knew anything of the Croat kings of Dalmatia. Remembrance of the Military Frontiers had consolidated into a military tradition, but the Croat soldiers were almost always mercenaries. There was still, however, a strong tradition of separateness within the Habsburg Empire, as a sort of third force distinct from the dominant Austrians and Hungarians.

But in Bosnia and the Vojvodina, Orthodox Serb and Catholic Croat peasants lived and worked together, and despite religious rivalry still felt a community of race in their struggles with foreign overlords, which developed into active cooperation in the unrest of 1848 and at the time of the annexation of Bosnia by Austria-Hungary.

Bishop Štrosmajer of Djakovo, one of the great churchmen who preached the Yugoslav ideal, dreamed of a union of the South Slav peoples based on religious tolerance. But he was before his time. Another strong current of political consciousness demanded Croat independence within the framework of the Habsburg Empire. These nationalists hated the Serbs, whom they considered unlettered and schismatic barbarians.

These two main ideologies among the Croats bedeviled the whole of their later history, and led to the tragic fiasco of the Independent State of Croatia set up by the Axis during World War II.

The Montenegrins lived in their mountain stronghold in a state of almost continuous guerilla warfare against the Turks. Later a kingdom, they founded a theocratic state under prince-bishops, whose successors were chosen from collateral branches of the episcopal family of Petrović-Njegoš.

Of Traditions and Language

One of these prince-bishops, Petar Petrović-Njegoš, was the greatest poet of the Yugoslav peoples. His works were read far outside the boundaries of his petty state, and a quotation from one of them, "He is my brother, of whatever creed he be," became a rallying cry of Yugoslav patriots. The Montenegrins, incidentally, never considered themselves a separate people. The founder of the great Nemanja dynasty of medieval Serbian emperors was born in Montenegro, and the Montenegrins saw themselves as the élite, the free unconquered remnant of the Serbian people.

The Serb, Vuk Štefan Karadžić (1787–1864), worked unremittingly during the Serbian insurrections against the Turks, and his success was to make dreams of Yugoslav unity politically possible. Vuk wandered through the Yugoslav countryside collecting and publishing the rich store of peasant oral literature—ballads, songs, proverbs and folk-tales. He also compiled the first modern Serbian dictionary. The publication of these works had an immediate and startling effect, hard to understand in lands where there has been a long tradition of patriotic literacy. All the Yugoslav peoples remembered the past of which they had every reason to be proud. The beautiful and tragic cycle of the Kosovo ballads is filled with hope for the future, a future which many felt was about to dawn. The songs of the *haiduks* (patriotic outlaws who kept alive resistance to the Turks) reminded men that opposition to tyranny is glorious, while the cycle of Karageorge's revolt against the *dahis* (Turkish feudal warlords) showed them that it could also be successful.

A huge mass of national traditions, mainly but not exclusively Serbian in origin, was made the heritage of all Yugoslavs. Though not always true to history (the arch-figure of resistance, Marko Kraljević, a sort of Yugoslav Robin Hood, was less impressive in fact than in legend), these "traditions" were true to the spirit of the people, something more potent than literal accuracy.

An immediate and incalculably valuable effect of Karadžić's work was his simplification of the language, which for the first time in nearly 1,000 years made the spoken and written languages the same. As a result, all the Yugoslav peoples of that time (save the Slovenes) adopted a single literary dialect. The Croats, in particular, made a great and magnanimous gesture in abandoning their local idioms, though retaining their Latin alphabet. Thus, from the time of Karadžić onward, Serb and Croat have become almost the same language, though with minor dialect differences. The parallel of British and American English is evident and pertinent.

Serbia Independent

The writers and the dreamers created the pan-Yugoslav idea. The soldiers and the politicians were to make it viable. Their difficulties were even greater and their setbacks more serious. Yet they too succeeded. The first and greatest achievement was the liberation of Serbia. By the beginning of the 19th century, the highly-centralized structure of the Ottoman Empire had broken down.

Local warlords usurped power in the provinces and held it by force, cruelty and corruption. Four such men seized power in Serbia and began systematically to murder the Serbian leaders. The people, driven to desperation, rose in revolt under Karageorge, a peasant leader of military genius rather in the tradition of the medieval *haiduks.* He succeeded in liberating Serbia, but had to withdraw with most of his supporters when the Turks returned in force. One of his generals remained, Miloš Obrenović, who again raised the standard of revolt. Almost as great a soldier as Karageorge, Miloš was a better statesman. He knew the art of the possible. Under his rule, Serbia became a more or less independent principality, the Turks merely keeping garrisons in five fortresses. Karageorge tried to return, but was murdered by Miloš and his head sent to Istanbul, an act of political wisdom at the time, but which led to nearly a century of dynastic quarrels between the families of the two men. In 1867, the Turks were forced to leave their fortresses. Serbia became a free and independent kingdom.

As such she became the focus of Yugoslav hopes. Many of her greatest statesmen openly proclaimed federal ideals. Free Serbs cooperated with the Croats and with their countrymen under Hungarian rule in the troubles of 1848. Free Serbs, too, tried to help the patriots of Bosnia when that country was annexed by Austria-Hungary.

World War I

As a result, Serbia was regarded with ever-growing hostility by the Habsburg Empire, which ruled over many millions of discontented Slavs—Bosnians, Slovenes, Croats, Dalmatians, Serbs, Czechs and Poles. In Bosnia itself, hopes ran high. The "Young Bosnia" group was openly pan-Yugoslav in its ideas. The whole country was in a ferment of unrest which culminated in the assassination in 1914 of the Habsburg heir, Archduke Franz Ferdinand, at Sarajevo by a Bosnian student called Gavrilo Princip. That Princip had been supported and encouraged by the Serbian government is very doubtful and has never been proved; that his group had the sympathy, and perhaps the support, of patriotic Yugoslav groups on Serbian territory is most probable.

Austria-Hungary affected to believe in the involvement of the Serbian government, and sent an ultimatum so severe that its rejection was a foregone conclusion. Serbia, though recently victorious in the Balkan Wars, first against Turkey and then against Bulgaria, was so much weakened that she seemed an easy morsel to swallow. But the first Austro-Hungarian invasion was thrown back and the war spread. Austria-Hungary, instead of being faced with a localized conflict in which she expected rapid victory, was embroiled in a European war which brought about the downfall of her Empire.

In the last years of World War I, Serbia had indeed been defeated. Her country was occupied and her armies forced to retreat through Albania in conditions so hard that the Central Powers were ready to regard the Serbs as a force with which they need no longer reckon. But while the Serb armies, reformed and reequipped by Britain and France, were regrouping on the Salonica front, all was not well with the Habsburg Empire. Her Slav soldiers were unwilling to fight against their fellow-Slavs for the benefit of the Habsburgs, and deserted in considerable numbers when faced with Serbian or Russian troops. Her politicians continued to press for the eventual independence of the minority peoples. The South Slav deputies of the *Reichsrat* formed a Yugoslav Committee and demanded the unification of all the Serbs, Croats and Slavenes of the Empire in a single state. Later they signed a common declaration with the Serbian government, one of whose avowed war-aims was the liberation of all the Yugoslavs, and openly expressed their desire for a single, independent, democratic Yugoslav state under the Karageorgević dynasty. This was the declaration of Corfu, the basis of the creation of modern Yugoslavia.

Yugoslavia a Kingdom

The end of the war found the Yugoslav peoples in a state of hopeless confusion. The popular will had declared its desire for a unified state. The figure of President Wilson dominated the Peace Conference; his Fourteen Points had stressed the principle of self-determination. But there was much bitter argument about whether this principle should apply to the Yugoslav peoples individually or collectively; and if the latter, what form the new state should take—federal or centralized.

Events forced a degree of centralization. In 1915 the Italians had been promised large areas of ethnically Croat and Slovene lands in Istria and Dalmatia as a price for their entry into the war on the side of the allies. The promise was made before the collapse of the Habsburg Monarchy was foreseen and before America had entered the war. But President Wilson refused to recognize the treaty, as its terms were contrary to the principle of self-determination of peoples. The Italian armies entered the Yugoslav lands to take by force what they claimed was theirs by treaty. There were no Yugoslav forces to oppose them save the Serbian armies. Furthermore, there was no organized adminis-trative body to restore order in the post-war chaos except the Serbian civil secretariat. When the new Kingdom of the Serbs, Croats and Slovenes (S.H.S.) was created on 4th December 1918, its administrative and military forces were predominantly Serb. This was to be a cause of friction and discontent right up to very recent times, in fact up to the creation of Marshal Tito's Federal People's Republic of Yugoslavia on 29th November 1945.

The period between the wars may be summarized as a continual strain between the forces of centralism and those of separatism, cul-minating in the assassination of King Alexander at Marseilles in 1934, during a State Visit to France. The country was then in a most unstable political condition. Parliamentary democracy had failed, owing to ra-cial tension, inexperience and intolerance. King Alexander suspended parliament and ruled mainly by decree. The centralist faction had success after success, even in its breaking down of the old tribal and traditional frontiers by the creation of new administrative units—the *banovinas.* The Croats had almost withdrawn from the central administration and created a sort of state within a state under the powerful Croat Peasant Party. The governments in Belgrade were becoming less and less representative of the people—finally, they did not represent even the majority of Serbs.

In this atmosphere of smothered political discontent, two extremist groups became very powerful. One was the Macedonian Revolutionary Organization and the other the Croat Ustaše. Both were originally extremist patriotic organizations, but both sought external aid, each finally becoming mere executive organs of its own foreign sponsor.

Finally, as was inevitable, the two groups came to an understanding. King Alexander was killed by a professional M.R.O. gunman supported by Ustaše accomplices. Foreseeing the possibility of his assassination, King Alexander had appointed a Regency Council to rule the country in the name of his young son Peter. The only important member of this council was the young king's uncle, Prince Paul.

A former Oxford student and a distinguished esthete, Prince Paul was neither eager nor able to rule a divided and turbulent people at a time when the fate of Yugoslavia, and indeed of all Europe, was in the hands of two dictators, Hitler and Mussolini. Successive Yugoslav governments tried a policy of appeasement toward Germany and Italy, to which Yugoslav economic, and finally foreign, policy was closely linked. Under the Premier Milan Stojadinović, the government became openly fascist, with the artificial and somewhat comic Yugoslav Radical Union (J.R.Z.) assuming the rôle of the "single party." But a majority of the Serbs was hostile, the Croats were in open opposition and the other peoples largely non-cooperative. The experiment failed and Stojadinović was dismissed in 1938.

His successor, Dragiša Cvetković, tried to stop the rot by concluding an agreement, the *sporazum,* with the Croat leader, Vlatko Maček, but, though any slackening of tension within the country was welcome, it was soon clear that this was too little and came too late.

World War II

Thus Yugoslavia faced the outbreak of World War II in almost as disunited a state as it was at the close of the first, but with greater disillusion and less hope. Prince Paul, hoping to spare his country the fate of Poland, declared Yugoslavia neutral, but was forced to make greater and greater concessions to the Axis Powers. In March 1941 he paid a secret visit to Hitler at Berchtesgaden, and on the 25th of that month the Yugoslav Premier and Foreign Minister signed a treaty with Germany placing Yugoslavia in the Axis camp.

Events then moved with extraordinary rapidity. Cvetković had scarcely returned from Germany when the Serbs, ashamed and disgusted, rose against the government in the 27th March *coup d'état*, largely engineered by airforce officers and supported by the Serbian Orthodox Church. Prince Paul abdicated and fled, and the young Peter was proclaimed king. Yugoslavia reaffirmed her neutrality and repudiated her signature of the Axis Treaty. Though attempts were at once made by the new Prime Minister, Dušan Šimovič, to maintain Yugoslav neutrality, it was clear that Germany would attack very soon. Mobilization was ordered. In the early morning of 6th April 1941, German airplanes bombed Belgrade, and German mechanized forces crossed the frontier. The Italians also attacked from the west.

The king, the government and most of the service chiefs left Belgrade the same day. Plans were drawn up for a defense of the central mountain bastion of Serbia and Bosnia, and there was sharp fighting in Macedonia against German forces which had entered the country from Bulgaria in the east. But the Yugoslav mobilization had been too slow and too late. There had not been time to reorganize the cadres and remove the pro-Germans and separatists. There was much confusion and not a little treachery. Within ten days the Yugoslav armies had capitulated. The country was occupied and the "new European order" of Hitler and Mussolini established. The king and many political and military leaders escaped by plane. A government in exile was set up in London.

All Yugoslavia's external and internal enemies took advantage of the collapse. Slovenia and parts of Dalmatia were divided between Italy and Germany. Bulgaria annexed a large part of Macedonia. The rich farm lands of the north had a special German-Hungarian administration. Albania annexed certain frontier provinces with Albanian minorities. Montenegro, after an abortive attempt to restore the Petrović-Njegoš dynasty, found itself under Italian military government. In Serbia, a quisling government was formed under General Milan Nedić. In Croatia the extremists seized power and Ante Pavelić, the Ustaše leader who had been involved in the murder of King Alexander, returned from exile. An independent Croatian state was proclaimed and the worst features of Axis rule introduced.

The Resistance

Almost at once, however, resistance movements sprang up. Two of these became nationwide and of great importance. One, the Četniks, was commanded by Draža Mihailović; this was mainly Serb nationalist in spirit, and was regarded with suspicion and distrust by the other Yugoslav peoples. The other, the Partisans, was led by Josip Broz

(Tito), and was under the control of the Communist Party. Attempts to found a common front soon foundered on mutual distrust, and Yugoslavia experienced the unhappy fate of having two mutually hostile resistance movements facing four enemy armies—the Germans, the Italians, the Bulgarians, and the Ustaše-Croatians.

The Četniks had the backing of the Yugoslav government in exile, which appointed Mihailović their minister of war and a general. He had also the support of the Western allies at first, which was often considerable. The activities of the Partisans, however, were little known in Western Europe, and their dependence on Communist leadership was regarded with some suspicion. But as conditions in the resistance movements became clearer, it was evident that the Četnik movement was inconsistent, without inner cohesion and above all ineffective. Some of the Četnik groups collaborated with the enemy, and despite the undoubted courage and patriotism of many individual Četniks, it was obvious that the movement was a spent force of little military value. The Partisans, on the other hand, were rapidly developing their military forces, already had effective control of large areas of the country and above all were actively and continuously fighting the enemy. Allied assistance was transferred from the Četniks to the Partisans, and a military mission sent to Tito's headquarters.

The efficient organization and continued military success of Tito's Partisans drew to his support a large number of patriotic Yugoslavs whose opinions were not necessarily Communist, among them a number of former Četniks. Furthermore, his movement was successful in overriding regional jealousies (President Tito himself was, incidentally, a Croat), whereas the Četnik movement had been too predominantly Serbian nationalist. The formation of the new Yugoslavia was presaged at the meetings at Jajce in 1943 of the A.V.N.O.J. (Antifascist Council of the National Liberation of Yugoslavia).

The New Yugoslavia

There is no space here to enter in the complicated details of the Partisan campaigns. Suffice it to say that they held down large numbers of Axis troops in the Balkans, and thus contributed greatly both to Western and to Soviet victories on other fronts. The Partisans liquidated Axis puppet-states in the Balkans, including Ustaše-Croatia, and finally, after linking up with Soviet armies advancing from the east, liberated the whole country. After prolonged and rather acrimonious discussions with the exile government in London, the Communist Party won the day, the king not being permitted to return to the country. The new Yugoslavia was proclaimed the Federal Democratic

People's Republic of Yugoslavia (renamed in 1963 Socialist Federal Republic of Yugoslavia).

From the mid-60s on, Yugoslavia made rapid progress toward becoming a modern industrial state. The standard of living soared, but so have unemployment and prices. Roads have spun a network of communication across the face of the land, opening up the more remote regions. Under the leadership of President Tito, who remained amazingly alert and active almost up to his death in May 1980, the country maintained its precarious position between the Eastern and Western blocs.

Since his death, the system of revolving collective and rather anonymous leadership devised by Tito himself has had to face a resurgence of nationalism and severe economic problems, the result of overspending abroad and reduced productivity at home. Now strong measures to reduce inflation, rationalize imports and control investments have been introduced to reverse the situation. The nation is being asked to tighten its belt and roll up its sleeves, a need recognized by most thinking Yugoslavs. With these measures has emerged a new figure in the shape of the tough but respected Milka Planinc, who is also the first woman prime minister of any Communist country.

CREATIVE YUGOSLAVIA

From Phidias to Meštrović

Before the United Nations Plaza in New York stands Antun Augustinčić's magnificent statue, *Messenger of Peace*. A gift from the Yugoslav government, it represents a figure reminiscent of the Italian *condottieri* of the Renaissance; it is a work of tremendous power and virility.

Another contemporary Yugoslav sculptor, whose vigorous, lyrical works you will come across all over the country is Meštrović, and it comes as something of a surprise to visitors from Western Europe to discover these budding Michelangelos in what they believed to be a backward Balkan country. But Augustinčić and Meštrović are only two of the best among the many who are carrying on an ancient artistic tradition, European in its origin, which is the common heritage of countless artists and artisans in every corner of the land.

That heritage is manifested in a thousand different ways: ninth-century Croat ecclesiastical architecture; the Orthodox churches of Serbia and Macedonia; the metalwork of Kadar, belonging to the same period; the Bogomil tombs of Bosnia; the Renaissance buildings of the Dalmatian coast. Surely these alone are enough to prove the artistic genius of the southern Slavs. Upon these foundations their art evolved according to its own laws, and its refusal entirely to succumb to the influences of the country's Turkish and other rulers was a sure proof of its dynamism.

The earliest examples of the art of the inhabitants of what today is Yugoslavia belong to the Stone Age, sandstone vessels and crudely carved idols. The *situle* urn of Vače is one of the numerous relics of the Iron Age, and may be seen in Ljubljana Museum. The intensively vivid figures depicted upon it epitomize the civilization of Illyria, as rich in diverse ways as was the Etruscan in Italy.

The Greek occupation of Macedonia and the many Greek colonies founded along the shores of the Adriatic cut short the evolution of Illyrian art, and by the sixth century B.C. had transformed it into the Archaic Greek style, some of the best surviving examples of which may be seen in Belgrade, having been sent there from Macedonia. Classical Greek sculpture is represented by a copy of the statue of Athene, worked by the great Athenian sculptor Phidias in the fifth century B.C., which was found at the ruins of Heraclea, near Bitola. Two superb bronze statuettes of dancing satyrs came from the same site. Finally, there are various fine examples of ancient Greek workmanship from Ohrid, Trebenište, and other places. Of the Greek colonies on the Adriatic, little survives beyond the necropolis at Budva.

Roman art and architecture completely dominated not only the coastal regions but the interior also. Roman penetration began as early as the third century B.C., although it was not until the beginning of the Christian era that Yugoslavia was incorporated into the Empire. Soon good roads and beautiful cities made their appearance, and the campaigns of Tiberius and Trajan in the first and second centuries were celebrated in impressive public works that may still be seen today, notably along the Danube.

Other Roman buildings include the theater at Stobi in Macedonia; the temple and amphitheater at Pula; the majestic Palace of Diocletian at Split and the Roman town of Salona nearby. Roman sculpture is at its best in the statues at Stobi and Zadar, the reliefs of Šempeter, and the altars to Mithras at Ptuj. In a way Yugoslavia was a meeting-place of Hellenic and Roman art, and exemplifies a partial blending of the best in both.

The migratory waves of savage tribes from the northeast which followed the collapse of Rome brought the Huns, the Avars, and in the sixth and seventh centuries, the Slavs, from whom the present population of Yugoslavia is descended. Byzantium clung on for a while to the remnants of Imperial power, and the Emperor Justinian (A.D. 527–568) built the fortified town of Caričingrad in Serbia. This imposing site, which lies not far off the main Niš–Skopje road, reveals features of public building of the period, notably cisterns and water-conduits. It was while this descendant of Illyrian peasants was emperor that the Basilica of Poreč was built and decorated with precious mosaics.

The newly arrived Slavs were influenced by these Roman and Byzantine buildings in the design of their own simple churches, and produced a sometimes crude but nonetheless sincere imitation of their predecessors. These first examples of a native architecture are all to be found on the Dalmatian coast—St. Donat at Zadar, St. Barbara at Trogir, St. Michael at Ston, and the Holy Cross at Nin. Though all are small they perfectly exemplify pre-medieval monumental architecture, as is proved by the way the walls rise above the tetrastyle foundations.

The only church in Serbia possessing the same characteristics is that of St. Peter at Novi Pazar, which dates from the eighth century and was designed in the form of a Greek cross, topped by circular walls. In Macedonia there is the interesting church of St. Sofia at Ohrid, where beautiful frescos have recently been uncovered. It is a perfect example of Byzantine architecture, a forerunner of the blending of the Roman and Byzantine, which later became the native style of the country.

Serbo-Byzantine School

The most impressive examples of the architecture of the medieval Serb state are the monasteries of Serbia and Macedonia, built by their kings or high dignitaries as evidence of their piety.

During the second half of the 12th century, under the Nemanja dynasty, there was an exceptional upsurge of artistic activity among the Serbs, which found expression in the works of the Raška school in the neighborhood of the River Ibar, and spread to the Dalmatian coast and the nearer Byzantine provinces. Their typical combination of the Roman and Byzantine styles is obvious in the monasteries of Studenica, Žiča, Sopočani, Mileševo and others.

As their rule expanded southward the Serb kings introduced modifications in the monastic architecture of Macedonia, as a result of which the interior space is broken up by a complex system of supports for the slender cupolas. The Macedonian school is also distinguished by its preference for Byzantine-style decoration, the polychrome facade of various different materials being the principal form of external ornamentation. With the sole exception of the church at Dečani—the work of Vid of Kotor, a native of the coast—the Roman influence now disappears. Other examples of the Macedonian school are to be seen at Gračanica; in the little church of Panteleimon near Skopje; and at Staro Nagoričano, Lesnovo and Prizren, all of which possess the typical multiplicity of cupolas.

A further Serbian school grew up during the 16th century in the Morava valley, far removed from the Turkish threat. Its originators built the base in a clover-leaf configuration, and relied upon the skilful use of stone and brick for external decoration. The delightfully vigorous results have led most experts to agree that they represent the most original achievement of early Serb architecture.

The paintings in the earliest religious foundations of the Nemanja are in the aulic Byzantine style introduced into Serbia during the 11th century. However, the frescos at Studenica include (in addition to inscriptions in Cyrillic characters) other indications of a new national style, which developed rapidly during the course of the 13th century.

Serb mural painting reached its apogee during the 14th century, declining at the time of the Italian Renaissance, which also coincided with the disappearance of the last remaining traces of Serbian independence. At its height, however, Serbian mural painting was further advanced than any other of the same date.

In 1881, A. Ewans, the well-known art historian, published a series of articles in various British magazines and reviews on the subject of Serbian religious painting—a subject which seemed to fascinate him. In one of these he wrote, "It is almost incredible that the Byzantine form of art should have been able to find a place for its final flowering upon Slav soil, yet it is precisely there, and in Italy, that the cold forms of Byzantium acquired a special warmth. I will go even further, and state that if we had never known the buildings hidden away in the Balkan peninsula we should never have fully understood the significance of the great Italian Renaissance. To me nothing painted by Michelangelo surpasses the beauty of the image of the Angel of the Resurrection on the walls of Mileševo, founded by the Serbian kings."

Mural painting continued to develop at the same rate as architecture, the first native period of which began in the 12th century in the Ibar and Lim valley areas, and reached its greatest moment with the creation of the huge frescos in the Monastery of Sopoćani. Neo-Hellenistic work somehow seems even more striking when discovered among simple mountaineers, and becomes at the same time less formal and more human in such a setting. Mileševo, Ziča, Peć, Morača and the church at Gradac mark stages of a vigorous architectural development, into which a number of lay elements have now been introduced.

At the southern limits of the medieval Serb state a new style of mural painting appeared. Its subjects are of an epic character, richly-colored.

A notable example is the narrative calendar in the Monastery of Deča-ni, which contains a separate illustration for every day of the year. Other examples of this school of art may be seen in the Church of the Holy Virgin of Leviška at Prizren; at St. Nicetas near Skopje; at Gračanica and elsewhere.

Later, in the 15th century, new developments of the fresco were being used in the region of the River Morava. Brighter colored, and in a more original style than its predecessors, wholly independent of all foreign influences, this technique is exemplified in the monasteries of Manasija, Ravanica, and Ljubostinja. With the total eclipse of medieval Serbia, distinctive architecture also ceased to develop. Under the Turks, almost the only artistic achievement was in the painting of icons on wood, and in the illustration of manuscripts. If you are interested in icons, you should make a point of seeing those at Ohrid, Skopje and Sarajevo, or if in graphic art, the manuscripts at Peć.

Romanesque and Gothic Art

Under Turkish rule, Romanesque art in all its forms took refuge on the shores of the Adriatic, and survives in the churches of St. Krševan at Zadar; St. Tryphon at Kotor; the cathedrals of Trogir and Rab and the many lovely 13th-century spires of the Dalmatian coast. The plastic arts found two masters in Radovan and Buvina, whose finest works are respectively the carved portal of Trogir Cathedral, and the great wooden door of Split Cathedral.

The *ciborium,* the carved stone baldachin or canopy supported by columns, which disappeared from the rest of Europe with the appearance of Romanesque, survived on the Adriatic coast of Italy, and appeared soon after in such Dalmatian churches as those of Zadar, Rab, Kotor and Korčula.

Zadar became the center for gold- and silverware, the collections of church treasure that exist there being among the finest in the world, the silver sarcophagus of St. Simeon (Sveti Šimun) especially being an absolute masterpiece.

The members of an heretical religious sect in Bosnia, the Bogomils, produced a unique kind of sculptured tomb for their dead and many of these strange memorials are to be seen, the stones ornamented with geometric designs, or figures of huntsmen, mounted soldiers or groups of dancers. The artists are unknown, and the reason for these elaborate gravestones is a mystery, but those at Radimlje, near Stolac, at Borot-nice and Ubosko, are of great artistic merit. A few of the best examples are on view in the State Museum at Sarajevo.

This brief outline would be incomplete without mention of Turkish architecture, introduced into Macedonia, Serbia and Bosnia-Herzegovina during the 15th century. The most notable mosques are those of Sarajevo, Banja Luka and Tetovo. The graceful bridges at Mostar and Višegrad are also of Turkish workmanship.

Gothic architecture as we know it developed only in Slovenia and Croatia. There, every town built its Gothic church, sometimes in open country or upon some steep hill, and they were more sanctuaries and places of pilgrimage than for daily use—a proof, perhaps, of the greater spirituality of those times. Good examples are Sveti Primož in the Kamnik Alps and Ptujska Gora in Slovenia, both being decorated with touchingly naïve frescos. In Beram, Istria, the murals by Vincent of Kastav, painted in 1474, presage Renaissance art.

Šibenik Cathedral is a delightful blend of Gothic and Renaissance styles, while the Rector's Palace and the old Customs House in Dubrovnik are typical of the Dalmatian, inspired by Venice, of which there are countless lesser examples everywhere along the coast. The great architects of this period were the native George of Dalmatia; the Andrijić brothers; and the Italians Michelozzi, Sammicheli, and Nicholas of Florence. The city of Dubrovnik is an architectural entity almost unequaled throughout Europe.

Two great painters from Dalmatia contributed to the Italian Renaissance, Juraj Ćulinović (Giorgio Schiavoni) and Andrija Medulić (Andrea Medolla). The late architectural flowering which is to be seen in Kotor is entirely indigenous, and reached its zenith at the beginning of the 18th century. The dead city of Perast and the noble buildings of Prčanj and Dobrota recall the period of fame and prosperity ushered in by the renowned navigators making their homes here.

Advent of the Baroque

Italy was responsible for the advent of the baroque in Croatia and Slovenia, and of the Venetian style in Dalmatia. The so-called Vojvodina baroque found north of Belgrade is little more than a variation of the form found in Austria.

The principal monuments of the period are the *iconostases,* huge screens covered with the images of saints, worked in the traditional way, with precious wood carving framing richly-colored paintings on panel. Baroque painting is at its best in Slovenia in the works of Cebej, Jelovšek, Bergant and Layer.

During the 19th century all European artistic movements had their followers in Yugoslavia, the greatest figures of the period being Konstantin Danil, Ðuro Jakšić, Vlaho Bukovac and Anton Azbe. Sculpture flourished later, and it was not until the start of the present century that Ivan Meštrović, the "Yugoslav Rodin," became known. He was born in 1883 and has achieved world renown, his brilliant virtuosity inspiring a school of gifted disciples, such as Antun Augustinčić, Frano Kršinić, Toma Rosandić and Petar Palavičini. Insofar as painting is concerned, the influence of Parisian schools is apparent in the works of, for instance, Petar Dobrović, Milo Milunović, Petar Lubarda and Milan Konjević.

We should also make mention of the naïve, or "primitive" painters of Yugoslavia. The Hlebine Group has become particularly well known beyond the confines of the country (Hlebine is a village in Northern Croatia). Krsto Hegedušić influenced these primitive painters most, among whom Ivan Generalić, Mirko Virius and Franjo Mraz are the most celebrated. Naïve painting first attracted critical attention in the 1930s.

Literature

The earliest Yugoslav literature dates from the times of Cyril and Methodius, two Greek monks familiar with the Slav dialect of Macedonia. They were sent to Bohemia and Moravia by the Emperor Michael of Byzantium, at the request of Prince Rastislav, to preach Christianity to the inhabitants in the vernacular tongue. The two missionaries set to work to translate the Scriptures and prayer books, but to do so they had first to invent the Glagolitic alphabet so as to be able to reproduce the sounds of the Slav language. They were accused of heresy on this account by the German clergy, so carried their case to Rome, where the Pope ruled in their favor and approved their employment of the old Slav language for their missionary work.

When Cyril retired to a monastery in Rome to die in 869, his disciples Kliment and Naum, both from Ohrid in Macedonia, replaced the Glagolitic with the far more commonly used Cyrillic, named in honor of their master. The Cyrillic alphabet was rapidly adopted wherever the Christian Slav-Orthodox rites were followed and, today, is almost universally used in the Soviet Union, the Baltic languages, Lithuanian and Lettish, being the only exceptions.

The Catholics forbade the use of the national language in their Slav churches, but the Croats, who by this time had created their own independent kingdom, continued to use Glagolitic characters in various parishes, and even in modern times the Slav Liturgy was used on the island of Krk, and in churches along the Adriatic coast.

A relic of that period is the "Text of Freising" discovered in the Bavarian town of that name, which is a Confession written in Latin and Slovene. "The Annals of Father Dukljan" belong to the 12th century, and are of greater literary than historic worth. The "Vinodol Code" of 1288 is the earliest collection of Croatian laws in existence.

First Expressions of National Consciousness

Literature was encouraged at the court of the medieval Nemanja kings of Serbia. Popular literature then included many cycles of epic chants, recited by wandering minstrels, the communications medium of their day. The best known are *The Marriage of Tsar Dušan* and the *Maiden of Kosovo,* both of which movingly relate the brave struggle of a small people against the mighty Turks. Those that tell of the heroic exploits of the *haiduks* (outlaws) are vivid with the yearning of a whole nation to be free of foreign domination.

At the same time the literature of philosophy developed in the city-state of Ragusa (Dubrovnik), at first only reflecting the Humanist ideas of the Renaissance, but later achieving a native individuality.

Drama reached its golden age in the comedies of Marin Držić. The epic poetry of Ivan Gundulić, *Osman,* covers the period of the first Christian victories over the Turks at the beginning of the 17th century. Two patrician contemporaries were the moralist Marko Marulić of Split and Hanibal Lucić, the poet of the island of Hvar.

For Primož Trubar, son of a Slovenian serf, the Reformation was not so much a question of differing dogmas as a chance to bring spiritual help to an oppressed people. He was forced to escape to Germany where, in 1551, he published the first two books written in his mother tongue, a catechism and an elementary reading manual. The first liturgies in old Slav were printed in Montenegro in 1493.

The Romantic period saw a radical reformation of the Serb language brought about by Vuk Karadžić, and the appearance of such writers as Petar Petrović-Njegoš in Montenegro. The epic *Gorski Vijenac* ("The Laurels of the Mountain") of Petrović-Njegoš appeared in 1847, a kind of hymn to liberty of a lyric beauty unequaled in Yugoslav letters. The Illyrian Movement was not only militantly political in its efforts to form a Southern Slav Union, but was also literary in character, bringing into prominence such writers as Ljudevit Gaj in Croatia and Fran Prešern in Slovenia, second only to the movement's great leader Karadžić.

Most of the writers of the 19th century found their inspiration in Russian and French literature, notably the dramatists Nušić and Vojnović, and the novelists Lazarević, Cankar and Čipiko.

Among modern writers we should mention the poets Oton Župančić and Vladimir Nazor, the essayist Miroslav Krleža and the novelist Ivo Andrić, who most brilliantly uses the tragic history of his native Bosnia as the background of his work. Ivo Andrić received the Nobel Prize for Literature in 1961.

The Theater

Before World War II there were probably not more than a dozen theaters in the whole of Yugoslavia while, today, this country of only 22 million possesses over 70, including several opera houses. The many new companies of actors necessary to supply so greatly increased a public began as amateurs after the war, but even so the theater would have continued to languish had it not been for the fact that the state covers up to 75 percent of the deficit of each theatrical run. The result, as far as theatergoers are concerned, is that you can buy tickets for a price that is only a fraction of what you would be charged if each company had to pay its way without state assistance. Similarly, the charge for a seat at a performance of grand opera is less than the price of a cinema ticket in London or New York.

Yugoslavia has reason to be proud of her theatrical past. The little theater on the island of Hvar was opened in 1612, and is still in business (though mainly as a concert room). Dubrovnik today runs an annual Summer Festival from about the beginning of July until the end of August every year. Ballet and music of every sort are included along with drama, and foreign artists from all over the world are invited to take part. Belgrade's September Theater Festival, BITEF, is already world-famous. Smaller but similar openair festivals take place each summer at Split, Ljubljana and in the Roman amphitheater of Pula.

Sophisticated theatergoers from the great Western capitals of Europe and America will find the staging and acting of modern plays very exciting, and the quality of performances in classical works particularly, notably good. Similarly, a single visit to the opera in Zagreb, Belgrade or Ljubljana will convince you that the Yugoslavs are born singers, and you will hear performances that will bear comparison anywhere. Where the Yugoslavs excel is in the singing of their own magnificent folk songs. In Dalmatia especially, everyone sings: a man or woman without a good voice seems unthinkable here.

Music and Science

It is a curious fact that, unlike the northern Slav peoples, such as the Russians, the Czechs and the Poles, the Yugoslavs have never produced any world-famous composers. However, they are highly gifted performers, and their massed choirs are outstandingly good.

The four centuries of Turkish occupation seriously hindered the development of formal music in Yugoslavia. However, in Dalmatia, under the more benign Italian influence, a truly inspired musician appeared in the person of Ivan Lukačić (1574–1648), composer of motets that were sung in the cathedrals of Split and Šibenik. The Slovene Jakub Petelin (1550–1592) was a great master of the polyphonic, and in the 19th century Stevan Mokranjac became a recognized composer for massed choirs. The neo-Romantic style of music found expression in the now classic ballet of Stevan Hristić, entitled *The Legend of Ohrid,* and in the works of Krešimir Baranović and Josip Slavenski.

The incessant struggle of the Yugoslav people to achieve their independence left them with little time or opportunity for scientific work, although the eminent philosopher, mathematician and astronomer Roger Bošković (1711–1789) was Yugoslav born. He lived for many years in London, and was elected a member of the Royal Society. His greatest work, *Theory of Natural Philosophy,* was published in Venice. In this he based his beliefs on the universal understanding of natural science. The book appeared in seven editions in Vienna, Paris and London during the course of the next seven years, and was instrumental in Diderot's formulation of the Materialist philosophy of the period.

Nicola Tesla (1858–1943) is acknowledged as one of the leading figures in the development of wireless communications. Pavle Savić was one of the principal assistants of Mme. Joliot-Curie in the years between the two world wars. Today Yugoslavia's universities provide an eager new army of young investigators, and three institutes train specialists in nuclear engineering. The country is determined to make up for all the years lost in war and enforced idleness.

YUGOSLAV FOLKLORE

Somber Beauty—Bright Patterns

Yugoslav folk culture is a complex and fascinating tapestry in which it is often easy to recognize the threads of many influences from different directions imposed on or absorbed by the native artistic skills of the south Slavs themselves in the course of their checkered history. Much of it survives to a remarkable degree, either as an integral part of everyday life in the remoter areas of the country, or enthusiastically kept alive by groups or societies or cooperatives in the towns and resorts of what has developed in a few decades into a thoroughly modern state.

For the visitor this means that performances of folkloric music and dance are very much part of the Yugoslav holiday scene, and often of an unusually high standard; also that the availability of attractive handicrafts abounds in markets, bazaars and specialist shops. Among them are examples of popular art that are relevant to the day to day life of at least some of the people, such as the shepherd's goblets and the engagement distaff, which a woman will often carry with her to her grave; also beautiful handwoven carpets, blankets and bags, and superb embroidery that lasts for generations. Such artifacts are made without haste and with living care, for permanent use by the persons to whom they are given, and it is perhaps just this intimate quality that goes into the making which accounts for the inimitable warmth and charm they seem to possess, and which is so signally missing in commercial goods.

There are many traces of the Illyrian tradition within the Byzantine, just as Slav characteristics appear in the Turkish-Oriental work, as though the people had always sought to retain something essentially their own through the long centuries of foreign occupation.

Handicrafts and Costumes

Craftsmanship of high quality is common in Yugoslavia, and in the mountain districts, many ancient trades still thrive—weaving, for instance—the women being the only producers of textiles in their villages, as was universally so in medieval times. The beautiful embroidery decorating the cloth woven by the peasants is wholly typical of their life, revealing all the natural, vigorous joys and sorrows of a simple people.

Though you will have to go well off the beaten track in most areas to see peasant costume in everyday use, it is clearly in evidence at folkloric performances. The costume is essential to good folk dancing, for the music as well as the spirited movements is incomplete without its display, the costume of each district being entirely different from that of its neighbors.

In the Alpine province of Slovenia, the native costumes are similar to those in neighboring Austria, and are worn only occasionally, at folk festivals, pageants and parades. The men usually wear short trousers and large-brimmed hats, the women, a dirndl-type dress, richer in color and embroidery than their other Alpine counterparts, and special styles of headdress. Descending into the rich plain of central Croatia and the Serbian Vojvodina you will immediately notice many women wearing multiple skirts that flare out from the hips, and richly embroidered blouses with wide sleeves, while the men's hats are small, round and brimless. The men also wear linen trousers over Russian-style boots.

In the mountains inland from the Dalmatian coast, where the winters are hard, costumes are of embroidered wool. Both men and women wear round forage caps, and aprons, those essential additions to feminine attire being delicately embroidered. The embossed leather belts give the men a virile air, and the older men still wear *opanci* (pumps), or slipper-like shoes worn with brightly-colored knitted stockings.

The baggy trousers clasped at the ankles, the small shawls and embroidered blouses of Bosnia-Herzegovina clearly reveal Turkish influence. South of Belgrade the men wear dark brown suits ornamented with black lace, and military-style forage caps. Here the leather *opanci* with turned-up toes, found throughout the Balkans, are held in place by highly ornamented leather thongs.

Farther south the costumes become increasingly Turkish in appearance, filigree jewelry and hand-embroidered shirts being generally worn. In Macedonia Greek influence appears, the men wearing short kilts, and in the mountains to the west the clothes are of heavy wool, admirably made. Sometimes leather is used instead of cloth, and is decorated with rich and many-colored appliqué-work.

In Zagorje, Dalmatia, and also in Montenegro, you can still see old, finely-chiseled guns, swords and knives, which are purely decorative, adding interest and distinction to the regional costumes. Bronze and silver are much employed in the chasing, gold rarely. The metal itself is inset with many fragments of colored glass or precious stones or, occasionally, pearls or coral.

In Bosnia and Macedonia the women continue to wear necklace-crowns composed of coins to "draw men's eyes away from their faces," and there is a further reminder of the Orient in the remarkable gold and silver filigree work.

Lacemaking is Italian in its form in the coastal regions and oriental in Macedonia. It is easy to distinguish between lace made by the Moslem Yugoslavs and that produced by their Christian compatriots. In either case, you can still acquire the most exquisite handmade lace at moderate prices.

In old times the principal wood carvers were the shepherds, but today it has become a domestic handicraft. The remarkable gourds and drinking cups decorated with both Turkish and Slav motifs make excellent, though not inexpensive souvenirs, as does the pottery work, which is at its best in northwest Croatia. If you can find paintings on glass with a religious motif you may have discovered collectors' pieces of some value, as many of these go into folk-museums.

A specialty of Slovenia are the famous beehives, whose entrances are decorated with historic scenes painted on wood.

Handmade pottery is giving way to factory-made products. The best surviving hand-thrown examples come from Croatia and Macedonia.

Wall Carpets

The often beautiful wall carpets, still found in old farm houses, are made with ewes' wool. In the Lika, carpets are long-haired and shaggy, and dyed all one color. In the east, on the other hand, they are close-cropped, and ornamented with geometric patterns or stylized forms of animals and vegetables, the colors being very varied. The Lika also produces carpets made of feathers sewn together with hemp. The best centers for carpets are Pirot in Serbia, Lazaropolje and Kruševo, both in Macedonia. Kelim carpets are made in Sarajevo.

Folk Dances

The popular dances of Yugoslavia can be divided into groups according to the role of the women-dancers. In Serbia and Croatia the women play a part equal to the men's in the dancing of the *kolo*. In Bosnia, Macedonia and Montenegro, on the other hand, the influence of Oriental tradition requires them to keep in the background.

Serb dances are vigorous and exuberant, reflecting the intense vitality of the people. Generally the dance is led by the acknowledged best male dancer in the village accompanied by his fiancée. The round dance is a kind of *farandole* accompanied by flute and violin, and more recently, by accordion.

The *kolo slavon* is danced in the parts of Croatia between the Sava and the Drava. This is the most prosperous and fertile region in the country, which probably accounts for the dance's robust optimism. With backing provided by violin or accordion, a young girl sings certain couplets, which are then picked up by both men and women and sung by them together in a kind of chorus.

The Dalmatian *kolo* is a round dance to the music of a single-stringed violin at a rapid rhythm, comprising a number of original and often difficult figures set by the lead dancer. There may be an accompaniment of recited verses.

The Bosnian *kolo* is danced in silence, perhaps because under the Turkish occupation these men of the hills had no wish to attract attention to themselves, and so danced in the forests without music.

The people of Macedonia are particularly devoted to music, and in addition possess an innate sense of timing and rhythm, which probably explains why Macedonia is choreographically the most interesting part of the whole country. In the mountainous region of Galičnik and Lazaropolje you will find not only the *kolo*, but also the *lesnoto* and the *teskoto*, danced at marriage feasts, which incidentally often continue for three whole days and nights. These dances begin at a slow and solemn pace, and gradually accelerate to a wild finish.

Montenegrin dances are performed by couples, and include a number of enormous leaps by the man toward his partner. In moments of amorous enthusiasm the male partner may pull a pistol from his belt or sash and fire into the air. It is perhaps as well, therefore, that such performances usually take place out of doors.

At the end of September, when the cattle return from summer pasture on the high Alpine meadows, there are always great celebrations by the mountaineers of Slovenia, and there are a number of dances special to the occasion. Slovenian dances usually have a 3/4 beat, similar to the Austrian-Bavarian *Ländler* (country dances) and are accompanied by a peasant band comprising accordion, trumpet and bass. In the Bela Krajina or "White Borderland" region (so called because the people there wear white costumes similar to those of the Croats) of the southeastern part of Slovenia, the only existing Slovenian type of *kolo* is danced during the festival of Zeleni Jurij ("Green George"), which celebrates the coming of spring, and dates back to pre-Christian times.

The war dances of Macedonia which feature large groups of "contestants" armed with long swords, are tremendously impressive and are known as *Rusali.* In spite of their geographic proximity these bear no resemblance to the Albanian dances from the Rugovo district, not far from Peć, which are violently aggressive.

One of the most important features of Serbian folklore is becoming increasingly rare. The *guslari,* or wandering minstrel, is now found only very occasionally. He is a direct heritage of the Middle Ages, and chants the heroic exploits in the struggle against the Turks. The long, romantic tales are accompanied by a single-stringed violin, known as a *gusle.* These epic ballads often have tens of thousands of verses, pathetic in telling of defeat, exultant in victory and tender in love, and are beyond all price as revealing life as it was lived in those harsh and distant days of oppression. During the 19th century a collection of these ancient oral epics was made, so that the message of the fast-disappearing itinerant minstrel has not wholly been lost.

Folklore Shows and Discs

Yugoslavia is in many ways in a happy position. The old order has changed very suddenly. A generation ago there were millions of Yugoslavs who had never been outside their own villages and were still so poor that even a radio set was an unattainable luxury. Today they have television—and take it for granted. At the same time they remember very clearly all the old songs and the old dances and the old ways.

Neither they nor their children, the new generation, have had to be taught their own folklore by ardent revivalists. No one has had to roam their country collecting the old songs as Cecil Sharp did in England, so that younger folk could learn to sing them. They've been in the family (the same family) for generations, and with a little care, won't be lost.

The old ways emerge at the oddest moments. A Yugoslav pop group from Dubrovnik, for instance, represented their country at a Eurovision Song Contest in London. At a party on the following night an English friend struck up a traditional Dalmatian song. The boys from Dubrovnik took it up, and for the next two hours these apostles of pop regaled those present with a magnificently-sung impromptu concert of Dalmatian folk songs. The same thing happens frequently with folk dances. Strike up the music, and any and every Yugoslav present will be up and ready to take part. No one has taught them these traditional ways. It's in their blood.

So, if you find that a display of folk dancing is billed for the following evening, you can be quite sure it will be authentic. The performers may all be young people who are now attending technical colleges and universities and as up-to-date and technologically contemporary as the most ardent modernists could wish. Nevertheless, the old dances are still as real and as meaningful for them as anything else in their world.

The same applies in most respects to folk music, except that there are far fewer musical performers than there are dancers. You can hear some staggeringly lovely performances. But, alas, these occur far more rarely than good dancing. Some quite wonderful recordings have been made by various Yugoslav record companies. They are worth hunting out, if you have the time. Many of the songs, in particular, have inexpressibly moving melodies that affect you deeply, even though you don't understand a single word of the text.

The "Slava"

The populations of Serbia, Macedonia (mostly) and Montenegro belong to the Orthodox Church, and attach great importance to the family celebration known as the *slava*. This is half-pagan, dating from the time of the conversion to Christianity of the Slavs. Each family has its own patron saint, and celebrates the saint's day with great pomp and hospitality, sometimes in a style that they can only achieve as the result of many personal sacrifices.

On the morning of the great day the whole family goes to church to attend a special ceremony. Then accompanied by all their friends, who wish them good luck and good health—for their cattle—they return home and the celebrations begin.

FOOD AND DRINK

Both Full of Zest

Cooking in Yugoslavia admirably illustrates the effects of history and geography. The already varied local dishes of Bosnia and Macedonia show additional influences from Turkish cuisine, while food from northern Croatia and the Serbian Vojvodina has an unmistakable Hungarian flavor, and that of Slovenia an undeniable touch of old Vienna. Italian pasta and risotto (*rizoto* in Serbo-Croat) have both crossed the Adriatic.

In Bosnia-Herzegovina and Macedonia there are a considerable number of Moslem restaurants, as in both provinces there is still a strong Mohammedan minority. Some may look shabby by any standard, but nevertheless serve the most succulent food. The preparation of each dish is carried out before the eyes of the client in enormous cooking kettles. If you do decide to try one of these establishments (and you should do so at least once) then ask for an *aščinica.*

Serbian cooking is unquestionably the richest in regional dishes, with highly seasoned meats prepared in lard—not, as in so many countries, in butter or oil. Lunches tend to be more interesting than dinners, as Yugoslavs generally take their main meal at midday, before their siesta. However, main towns and resorts have plenty of attractive restaurants, many privately run, where you can eat well at any time. There has also been a marked improvement in the variety of dishes, including special-ties, available in quite a few tourist hotels.

Soups and Entrées

Let us observe the accepted order of dishes and begin with soups. The clear soups are prepared with chicken *(pileća supa),* beef *(govedja supa),* or a kind of bouillabaisse or fish soup *(brodet* or, in Serbia *alaska čorba).* The paste-like *Kacamak, palenta* or *mamaljuga* is ground maize cooked in salt water and eaten either with milk and sugar or with cream and cheese and usually accompanied by maize bread cooked without yeast. It is first-cousin to the Italian *polenta* and the Romanian national dish of *mamaliga.*

Hors d'oeuvres *(meze)* are served both hot and cold. The most familiar item is *gibanica,* which is simply a hot pâté of vermicelli cooked with the cream taken from boiled milk and eggs and cream.

We recommend the *piktije,* jellied pork or duck, and the *pogačice sa čvarcima,* which is a kind of oven-browned cake containing a great deal of pepper, that is supposed to arouse the appetite, and quite certainly makes it essential to drink. Do not miss the *dalmatinski pršut,* which is lightly smoked ham, or *užička pršuta,* beef smoked until it is hard, but be sure to leave room for the *salama Gavrilović,* certainly the equal of the very best Hungarian or Italian salami.

Now come a variety of dishes that are really neither hors d'oeuvres nor the main course, though they may be made to serve as either. Most popular of these is *ražnjici,* small squares of pork grilled on a skewer and eaten on a slice of bread. *Ćevapčići* is similar, except that the meat (pork, beef or lamb) is minced before grilling, and shaped into sausages. If you are not afraid of the consequences of an enormous thirst (or of social downfall if anyone should come within range), follow the unin-hibited Yugoslav custom and eat this dish with finely chopped raw onion. The *ćevap* is not unlike *ćevapčići* but is of thick slices of heavily spiced pork.

Conservative eaters may decide to play safe and ask for a steak, in which case they should keep their fingers crossed and ask for a *čulbas-tija*—though they may not recognize it as steak when they see it.

Try *pljeskavica,* which consists of a dozen small morsels of *ćevapčići,* already described, mixed with a similar amount of lamb and strips of sweet pepper, all grilled together.

A variation of this, known as *pljeskavica sa kajmakom,* differs only in that it is cooked in *kajmak*—a kind of cheesy butter made of the salted cream from boiled milk, which replaces ordinary butter in summer in country districts.

All the dishes described above are accompanied by salads, of which the best available is the *srpska salata,* which consists of slices of red and green peppers, cucumber and lettuce leaves. Note, however, that if you want this you must ask for it specially, as it always appears on menus as a separate dish. *Ajvar* is a spicy mixture of sweet peppers and egg plant, chopped up together with garlic.

Main Dishes

One of the most delightful things to be found on a Yugoslav menu is *punjene tikvice,* zucchini (or vegetable marrow) stuffed with minced beef and pork mixed together with rice. In Bosnia the same dish is served with a fresh cream sauce called *sogan dolma*—this you should be sure not to miss. A variation is *punjena paprika,* in which a sweet pepper replaces the zucchini, tomato mixed with the rice stuffing, and a thick, fresh tomato sauce added.

An excellent Serb dish is *djuveč,* a mixture of egg plant, carrot, potato, rice and meat, roasted with grated cheese. *Musaka* is entirely Turkish, and is made of alternate slices of meat and potato, though often egg plant and zucchini replace the potato. At the moment of putting the dish into the oven the cook pours over it a mixture of beaten eggs and sour cream. Yugoslav experts insist that the musaka made with egg plant is the finest, not only to eat, but also because the blend of colors pleases the eye as well as the palate.

You may have heard the Arabic word *pilav.* It is the almost universal name throughout the Near East for any meat dish prepared with rice. In Yugoslavia the meat is either minced or cut into small squares, and mixed with variously seasoned rice before being grilled. In the days of the Turkish occupation the outlaws produced *hajdučki ćevap* (the haiduk was the maquis of the period), which was as easy to make and tasty. It consists of pieces of meat, potatoes and smoked lard stuck on a skewer and roasted over a roaring fire. If you like oriental delicacies, then try *kapama,* squares of lamb, the stalks of green onions and spinach stewed together.

The savory stews of Yugoslavia nearly always contain a touch of cream and the yolk of an egg. The veal *râgout* is called *teleća čorba,* the chicken *pileća čorba.* In all cases the meat is stewed very slowly with sausage, red and green peppers and tomatoes, the yolk of an egg being added at the last moment. The result is a *lešo*.

In the same family as the *râgouts*, though with the emphasis on vegetables, are the *podvarak*, which is a kind of sauerkraut, combined with various different meats, and also the *kalja*, a subtle combination of cabbage with saddle of mutton. There is also *lonac*, which has a whiff of garlic—a dish that is found outside the frontiers of Yugoslavia under the name of *papazjanija*, a *râgout* of vegetables in season.

An attractive and nourishing Slovene dish is the *ričet*, made up of white beans slowly stewed with a morsel of smoked meat. Somewhat similar to an item of our perhaps less imaginative cuisine is breaded fried chicken under the name of *pohovano pile* in Croatia and *pohana piška* in Slovenia.

Fish and Shellfish

Although in both Istria and Dalmatia fish and crustacea are excellent and plentiful, their preparation seems to be a weak spot in the Yugoslav cuisine—all the more remarkable when you consider the exceptional skill revealed in the preparation of meat. If you can persuade the cook to serve them, we can recommend such grilled fish as red mullet *(barbuni)* and mackerel *(skuše)*. Ink-fish and squids *(lignje)* are delicious fried, though here they are served more often as small snacks to accompany such strong liquor as *šljivovica*.

Lobster *à la dalmatienne (jastog)* is simply cold boiled, and most people prefer the crayfish *(sufle od rakova)*. In Serbia, however, there is considerably more interest in freshwater fish, and there is a delicious dish consisting of a mixture of two Danube fish, sturgeon *(jesetra)* and the boneless sterlet *(kečiga)*. There is a great deal of trout *(pastrmka)* to be had from Yugoslavia's turbulent mountain rivers, the most delicious probably being those caught in Lake Ohrid in Macedonia, a special variety of salmon-trout found nowhere else in Europe, and of an unforgettably fine flavor.

Incidentally, lumpfish from Lake Ohrid also provide a red caviar, as do the Danube fish.

Desserts—Heavy and Sweet

Various rich fillings are included with desserts in Yugoslavia. A blend of pastry and fruit produces the superlative *štrudla*, with apples *(sa jabukama)* or cherries *(sa trešnjama)*. Served warm these are delightful, but hardly to be recommended for those with delicate digestions.

A popular Slovene dessert is ribbon noodles *(rezanci)* with fresh cheese and grated nuts or poppy seeds, heavily sugared. *Struklji* is a preparation of nuts and plums stuffed into balls of cheese before being boiled together.

Fortunately there are a number of cakes and tarts which make less serious demands upon your digestive powers, and we strongly recommend to you the local light cakes sprinkled with nuts or poppy seeds. The style of cakes in Croatia is more familiar to Western eyes and palates, while those of Slovenia reveal the beneficent influence of Vienna. A Slovenian specialty is *potica,* a kind of coffee cake made with several layers of nut filling. Many visitors fall to the temptations of *doboš,* which is of Hungarian origin, and is garnished with coffee and caramel. In the areas of the country longest under Turkish rule you will find plenty of *lokum* or Turkish delight, *kadaif, baklava* and *gurabije*— none of them recommended to anyone not possessed of a very sweet tooth. Macedonia produces *alva* which is made of egg whites, sugar and nuts, and *ćeten-alva,* which consists of sesame crushed in honey.

Wines

Yugoslavia is a great wine-growing country, and there are several areas almost wholly dedicated to the cultivation of the vine. You will come across local wines that change name according to their color, namely *crno,* which is dark red; *belo,* white; and *ružica,* which is rosé. These wines are obtainable everywhere, are drunk by the local people in great quantities, and are extremely cheap. In Dalmatia particularly, most families own their own vineyards, and until the recent emergence of large wine-shipping firms there was nothing they could do with their own wine except drink it.

The ordinary table wines are both cheap and agreeable, and can be ordered in jugs of various sizes, according to requirements.

Probably Yugoslavia's best-known wines are those grown in Slovenia, the *Ljutomer, Traminer* and *Riesling* being comparable to Alsatian wines.

Jerusalem is the name of a well-known wine-growing village in Slovenia. There is a legend that it was so called by fainthearted Crusaders, who hoped that they would thereby have completed their oath "to reach Jerusalem"!

From the vineyards of the Slovenian coast come the red *Teran* and *Pinot,* each having an excellent bouquet. In Istria there is an admirable strong red wine known as *refošk. Malvazija,* a malmsey, is also made in Istria, and elsewhere on the Croatian coast you will come across a sparkling, fruity wine, "the little water of Bakar" *(Bakarska Vodica).* In Split you will find the light red *opal* and the sweet muscatel called

Omiš. The best Slovene wines are exported, and it is often easier to get them abroad than in Slovenia.

Nearly all the Dalmatian islands grow wine. The red varieties are often called *Dingač,* though strictly speaking this is produced only on the peninsula of Pelješac. Of the white wines, the best in our opinion are the *Vugava* grown in Vis, and *Grk,* which means "Greek." This is produced on the island of Korčula and is of a particularly clear amber color. The island of Vis produces a number of wines.

From the vineyards of Herzegovina, near Mostar, comes the international-award-winning dry, white *Žilavka.*

Everywhere in Serbia you will meet the faintly effervescent *fruškogorski biser,* which is good when drunk iced. *Smederevka* is made from grapes grown on the banks of the Danube. *Prokupac* and *Negotin* are equally Serb, and resemble light Burgundies. Macedonia produces *kavadarka,* a heavy, rather coarse, red wine. The list could be extended indefinitely, as there are literally 100s of local vintages.

As sometimes happens in wine-growing countries, beer is relatively expensive, not very good and apt to be tepid. A possible substitute is *špricer,* one-third white wine and two-thirds soda water.

Numerous non-alcoholic fruit syrups are available, which can be mixed either with tap water or with one or other of the bottled mineral waters, of which there is a profusion in Yugoslavia. Even better are the small bottles of pure fruit juices—cherry, strawberry, raspberry, blackberry and many others. These are astonishingly refreshing in hot weather.

Tap water in all main towns and resort areas is perfectly safe—better, in fact, than in many more affluent countries. But beware of well water in remote districts.

Coffee and Rakija

This is the land of *turska kava,* the authentic Turkish coffee, which improves in quality the nearer you get to the center of the country, though in many places it is rapidly being challenged by the ubiquitous *espreso.* Turkish coffee is made of finely ground beans, rapidly boiled and very sweet—in fact it accords with the classic definition of perfect coffee. "Hot as hell, sweet as sin, and black as a woman's heart." If you don't like sugar you must ask for it *bez šećera.* In hot weather it is thirst-quenching, and a good pick-me-up. Except when you are in Slovenia or Croatia, avoid the local *café au lait* with your breakfast *(doručak);* it is nearly always poor, and you will do better to stick to Turkish coffee at all times. Tea is regarded as some kind of witches' brew for anyone suffering from stomach disorders, so if your cup of tea means something in your life, then take along a tea-making outfit with you.

All Yugoslav spirits are extremely strong, but a glass is often taken together with the first Turkish coffee of the day, whatever the hour. The generic name for most of these distilled drinks is *rakija*, though what you will most usually be given will be *šljivovica*. Nearly all *rakija* drinks are taken before eating, the cocktail habit being more or less unknown outside luxury hotels.

The best distilleries in Yugoslavia are at Zadar, where every kind of liqueur is manufactured in more or less successful imitation of all the well-known French brands. However, in our opinion, originals are always better than imitations, so you should try the liqueur of the country, which is called *maraskino*. Its special bouquet comes from the stones of the morello cherries from which it is made. "Maraškino" is better known in Western Europe under its Italian name of *maraschino*. It was invented in the still flourishing Maraska distillery in Zadar. Other well-known liqueurs are *vinjak*, a sort of cognac, and *pelinkovac* and *mastika*, which are spiced. Take a bottle home with you: it will make an inexpensive, unusual and much appreciated gift.

The old harbor of Rovinj on the Istrian coast, dominated by the Cathedral and its Venetian campanile

A peaceful old street in the island town of Korčula

The coastal town of Trogir, near Split, and below, the Serbian fortress
of Kalemegdan on the junction of the Sava and Danube rivers.

Kotor Cathedral backed by part of the Lovćen massif

EXPLORING YUGOSLAVIA

ISTRIA AND THE KVARNER GULF

Where Austria, Venice and Yugoslavia meet

We start our detailed description of Yugoslavia with the coast. It is justly regarded as being one of Europe's most beautiful holiday areas. However, there's a great deal of it. If you drive your car from the Italian frontier just south of Trieste to the Albanian border south of Ulcinj you will have covered all of 1,125 km. (700 miles), and this despite the road's not taking you out to the tip of every headland nor closely round the shore of every bay. Still less does this overall distance include side trips to any of the 1,000 or so islands off the coast, over a dozen of which are highly developed holiday areas in their own right, and not all of them specially close to the mainland.

Finding a satisfactory way of covering this long and lovely vacation strip is almost impossible. When we come to deal with inland Yugoslavia things are simple enough. We follow the boundaries of the Republics that make up the Yugoslav federation, because they are based on understandable geographical limits. The River Sava, for instance, is the dividing line for many kilometers between Croatia and Bosnia-Herzegovina. Slovenia ends and Croatia begins where the northern Alpine ranges give way to less rugged country. Many of these boundaries are not, however, immediately obvious. For instance, you will certainly have little impression of passing from one Republic to another as you drive the plain of Slavonia in Croatia onto the Vojvodina plain that forms part of Serbia. Nevertheless, these demarcations are practical and easy to understand. Along the coast the situation is different.

The first 30 km. (20 miles or so) of coast that you see after leaving Trieste form part of Slovenia. The next 965 km. (600 miles) are part of Croatia, with the exception of a 16 km. (ten miles) stretch just east of the port of Kardeljevo; this corridor was ceded to Bosnia-Herzegovina in the 18th century to allow it an outlet to the sea. Subsequent overlords Austria-Hungary, and, since 1918, Yugoslavia, have confirmed the arrangement. The port of Kardeljevo is, therefore, Bosnia-Herzegovina's road and rail outlet to the Adriatic, and is being rapidly developed. The final 110 km. (70 miles) or so of coast, to the Albanian frontier, are Montenegro's. If you look at an ordinary map, you will think this arrangement very strange. Surely, you will ask, Montenegro and Bosnia-Herzegovina, and possibly Slovenia as well, deserve a larger share?

The answer to the conundrum lies partly in geography and partly in geopolitics. Take a map on which the contours are clearly marked, and you will see that high mountain ranges run all along the coast from the Gulf of Kvarner's eastern coast to a little north of Albania. The islands are simply the peaks of largely submerged parallel ranges. Until the 1960s only a few difficult tracks crossed those mountains, and only a military cart-track built by Napoleon's troops ran along the coast. Almost till 1965 the coast was a place apart, completely different from the inland areas and where the best form of travel was by boat. In this same period it was not unusual for country folk to travel 30 km. (about 20 miles) or more down the coast in the little passenger steamer to see the doctor and to be quite content to stay overnight in his waiting room till morning surgery began. It is hardly surprising that the history of the coastlands and islands is markedly different from the interior's.

The earliest coastdwellers of whom we know anything were Illyrian, Liburnian and Dalmatian tribes whose civilization is only now being revealed by excavation. From the sixth century B.C. onward, trader-colonists from Greek city-states settled at points on the coast and islands such as Cavtat, Korčula, and Trogir. In the second century B.C. Rome expanded across the Adriatic and in time colonized the interior as well as the coast. When Roman power waned some 600 years later Slav invaders moved in overland from the north. Gradually their tribal organization developed into feudal kingdoms, the Croat kings ruling most of the coast. In time their territory was merged with Hungary's, and it was a Hungarian king who sold the whole of Dalmatia to Venice in 1410. By this time the Turks were establishing their rule through modern Yugoslavia's interior except for Croatia and Slovenia. A treaty between Turkey and Venice defined their common frontier as the line of mountain crests nearest the coast, except at the southern end, where the Turks held Bar and Ulcinj. Dubrovnik, then called Ragusa, contrived to remain independent. Venice controlled the rest of the coast, including all the major seaboard towns in Istria.

In the early 19th century Napoleon overthrew Dubrovnik as well as Venice. When Napoleon in his turn was defeated Austria-Hungary claimed its former territories of Slovenia and Croatia—including all the coast. Just as the preceding 400 years of Venetian occupation left its mark on what were then the region's main ports and towns (each with its main square like a miniature Piazza San Marco, a tiny clock tower modeled on the Campanile, an open-air loggia which acted as law courts—several have survived—and plentiful reliefs of the Lion of St. Mark, Venice's patron saint) so the Austrian occupation left its own traces. In the latter part of the 19th century the Austrians began to develop "watering-places" along the coast (better health was the objective in those days, rather than rest and recuperation, as now). They built hotels at selected points as far south as Hercegnovi. Some are still in use—in Pula, Opatija, Crikvenica, Split, Hvar and Dubrovnik, for instance, as well as Hercegnovi.

When Austria-Hungary went the way of Napoleon and Venice in 1918, the entire Istrian peninsula was ceded to Italy as part-payment for joining the Allies. She later seized Zadar and some of the islands. The rest were returned to the now independent former provinces, with Montenegro extending its control northward to embrace the whole of the Gulf of Kotor. In 1944, the whole of the coast and all the islands became Yugoslav.

So—to return to the original question—how can we divide our description of the coast into manageable parts? The answer is that we have disregarded all the administrative and political divisions, and taken as separate entities those areas which tourists and Yugoslavs connected with tourism feel belong together. We consider first the coast of the whole Istrian peninsula and the Kvarner Gulf, together with the islands in the gulf and off the Istrian coast. We call our second "Central Dalmatia": it runs from just north of Zadar to the River Neretva and a line produced due west from the river's mouth, to include a large number of offshore islands. Our third section is called "Southern Dalmatia." It includes the coast and the islands that belonged to independent Dubrovnik at the height of its power, together with the stretch that is now Montenegrin.

Thus we have Central and Southern Dalmatia, "Northern" has apparently got lost. This isn't the case. Strictly, our first chapter does not include any of Dalmatia, though the term Dalmatian is as often applied to this part of the Yugoslav coast as to all the rest. Northern Dalmatia begins (or used to begin) at the Velebit mountain's southern end: Zadar was its capital, with Split and the region round it comprising Central Dalmatia. Southern Dalmatia was in reality the area once governed from Dubrovnik—and the Montenegrin coast was not in Dalmatia at all. However, words change, like everything else. It seemed sensible to accept the new meaning assigned to Dalmatia. At least it spares us the presence of long and cumbrous chapter-titles.

Istria and the Kvarner Gulf

We have already given a brief historical summary of this area—Venetian till the early 19th century, Austro-Hungarian till 1918, partly Italian and partly Yugoslav between the wars, and wholly Yugoslav since 1944. Now we must describe it. Briefly, the coast has limestone hills, sometimes covered with woods, sloping down to a very blue sea. The islands are simply the tops of part-submerged mountains like those on the mainland. The coast has been worn into attractive coves and bays, with picturesque old fishing towns and ports in some of them and very modern holiday resorts in others: sometimes ancient town and modern resort are pleasantly combined. Olives and vines and other Mediterranean crops grow inland and on the slopes above the sea.

In appearance, the coastal and island towns range from almost pure medieval-Venetian (Rab, for example, with its fine stone buildings, church belfries and solid fortifications) to Austrian-Venetian (for example Piran), 19th-century Austrian (the older parts of Opatija) and pure 20th-century modern holiday Mediterranean (Medulin, Veruda, etc.). Each has its appeal, the new as well as the old, and each includes the timeless joy of flowers and fine trees. There are not many sandy beaches, but the bathing is excellent, as hundreds of thousands of visitors from Europe and beyond discover each year.

Poreč, with its huge tourist complexes providing some 13,000 beds, with another 2,500 in private houses plus camping sites, has replaced Opatija as tourist capital, at least in summer, followed by Portorož and Rovinj. Pula is the cultural center, and Rijeka is both an industrial and a communications center, as well as being Yugoslavia's main port.

Istria's Western Coast

Koper has a fine 15th-century Town Hall, a Gothic-Venetian style loggia and a cathedral, all of them to be found in the main square. The narrow and tortuous streets of the old town are in striking contrast to the wholly modern port and beach resort area, but in both you will find the symbolic lion of St. Mark that signifies former Venetian rule.

Koper was the Roman Capis, and in Italian, Capodistria. Like Trieste, Koper was once a warm sea port at the service of landlocked central Europe, but with the passing of sail, she was soon eclipsed by her larger rival. Today the town is a pleasant and quiet little backwater, and in some respects a suburb of Trieste, just across the Italian border.

A quarter of an hour from Koper by motorboat is one of the most perfect bathing beaches on the north shore of the bay. It is called Ankaran, and is now not only a well-equipped resort but also a lovely spot for a camping or self-catering holiday.

The coast road (much lovelier than the inland E27) runs between Roman saltpans to Izola, a former fishing village now completely changed by modern building developments. Once it was an island, but it has lost the benefits of its isolation now that it has been connected to the mainland. It is a mixture of small industrial center and holiday resort. Between Izola and Piran there are two small bays, Strunjan and Fijeso, the latter remarkable for the fact that only 20 m. (65 ft.) from the sea there is a lake of perfectly fresh water.

Piran is really charming: it is centered on a tiny medieval city perched on a rocky headland, birthplace of the Italian violinist and composer Tartini in 1692. The Municipal Theater is named after him. The two basins of the harbor are filled with many brightly painted sailboats, and the pure Venetian-Gothic buildings seem almost untouched by the hand of time. An odd reminder of long dead lovers is in the form of an inscription over one of these old houses which reads *Lasa pur dir*—"Let them talk." The story behind this is that a passionate love was poisoned by the scandalmongering neighbors.

Piran Cathedral has a Venetian campanile from which there is a wonderful view of the whole of the Gulf of Trieste, and an octagonal baptistry. If you walk for a few minutes through this strange little town you will come across remains of its medieval walls and numerous noble mansions in Venetian-Gothic or Austrian baroque. Here, too, you can see works by such masters as Carpaccio and Tintoretto, though to most visitors it is primarily a specially attractive resort for swimming and sunbathing, and enjoying the Mediterranean summer.

The shoulder of a hill hides Portorož until the moment of arrival in what is one of the most popular watering places in Yugoslavia. Because the town is completely sheltered by hills from the north winds the many parks of Portorož are filled with subtropical plants and flowers. There is a good beach, and the atmosphere is generally lively and more sophisticated than in other resorts. Portorož dominates this part of Istria with its casino, its entertainments, and its sociability. It is not a town that has notable historical associations, but the openair exhibition of modern stone sculpture—a collection of the works of sculptors who have participated in the annual International "Forma Viva" Symposium—is well worth a visit.

There are excellent motorboat excursions to be made from either Portorož or Piran, to places like Savudrija, once a tiny fishing village and today a pleasant modern holiday resort, set among pine woods and having a perfect beach. Behind it rises the 36 m. (117 ft.) high lighthouse, round which gulls and petrels scream and wheel against the clear blue of the Adriatic summer sky.

South of Savudrija is Umag, until as recently as the 1960s an undistinguished and decaying little fishing village but now a flourishing sea resort that plays host to more than 16,000 visitors at a time. Not the least of its attractions is a gently-shelving beach which is excellent for children. The tourist settlement is surrounded by olive groves and vineyards. The next town to the south is Novigrad. The name means "Newtown"—the Newtowns are as common in Yugoslavia as in English-speaking countries. This one is known as Novigrad (Istra) to distinguish it from other places of the same name. Like Umag, Novigrad was an almost totally decayed fishing village, with very few remaining inhabitants, till new hotels were built there. It had some importance, under Venetian rule, however, as well as in Roman times —as a museum of Roman carvings and inscriptions, some fine old houses and a Venetian loggia testify.

The road to Poreč turns inland skirting the River Mirna's estuary. Founded in the first century A.D. and called Parentium, Poreč still has the ruins of Roman temples of Mars and Neptune, as well as traces of its pentagonal-plan city walls. Its most imposing monument, however, is the magnificent basilica built in about A.D. 550 by Bishop Euphrasius. The basilica, which is now a museum, contains some superb gold mosaics. Today the whole of the area round this once-tiny town is studded with large modern hotels and what the Yugoslavs call "tourist complexes"—concentrations of hotel blocks, restaurants, bars, swimming pools, chalets, nightclubs, etc., all under the same management. At the season's height the vacation population of Poreč is far higher than the number of people the town contained when Euphrasius designed his beautiful church.

Beyond Poreč the road turns inland again to go round the long, V-shaped Limski fjord with the village of Vrsar (which has one of the country's largest naturist colonies) on its northern bank. Back again on the coast there is another lovely old town, Rovinj. Its center is a maze of shadowed, crooked streets beneath the baroque cathedral and the delicate silhouette of a Venetian campanile. The bright colors of houses and boats are reflected in the little harbor that was once the center of its life and livelihood. Today the two islands close to the coast here, Sveta Katarina and Crveni Otok, have been developed for modern holidaymakers. You reach them by motor launch.

Yet once more, on the way to Pula, the rocky coast forces us inland through the village of Bale and the ancient town of Vodnjan. Away out to sea we can pick out the idyllic-looking island of Brijuni, where President Tito had a secluded summer home. This is the only point on the coast totally untouched by tourist development as access was forbidden to the public. In medieval times quarries on Brijuni (Brioni in Italian) provided the stone for some of the finest buildings in Venice.

For our tour of the Istrian peninsula's eastern coast we will do as many other visitors do—make our base at Opatija. The 80-km. (50-mile) long southeastern coast of the Istrian peninsula bordering the Gulf of Kvarner is punctuated by numerous attractive, flower-decked little seaside resorts that have grown up there because of the excellence of the climate and the bathing. Among these Lovran is the oldest, and has a 12th-century church and tower, but its greatest attraction lies in the large and luxuriant gardens that surround the hotels and villas, and the many laurel and chestnut groves in the outskirts. Two perfectly-kept bathing beaches lead away north to Opatija, while southward lies Medveja, with another beach situated at the mouth of a ravine that pierces the flanks of Mount Učka. Next come Mošćenička Draga and Mošćenice, both pleasant small resorts, and after them Plomin and the modern resort of Rabac. Today, it is one of the largest of the new resorts on the Istrian coast—and one of the most popular.

North of Rabac, roughly halfway between Opatija and Pula, is the old mining village of Labin, mentioned in a number of Latin chronicles. Its picturesque houses are built on the slope of a hill that is crowned by a remarkable 15th-century church and a well-preserved fortress keep, or tower. If you climb to the top of the tower, you will have a lovely view across most of the Bay of Kvarner. Beyond is the strange fjord of Raša, which is well worth a visit.

Leaving the sea away to the right, the road now runs direct for the last 27 km. (17 miles) to Pula, a port and industrial center with a long history, called Pietas Julia in the third century B.C. and, later, Respublica Polensis. There is plenty of evidence of Roman occupation, of which the most remarkable is undoubtedly the relatively-intact oval amphitheater, designed to seat at least 23,000 people anxious to watch such spectacles as gladiatorial combat. You will have no difficulty in finding it, as its great walls rise imposingly above the port.

Some time ago the acoustics of the amphitheater were discovered to be excellent, and it has for many years been employed as the setting for an annual International Song Competition and an annual Film Festival as well as performances of opera.

Though the amphitheater must take pride-of-place, the Temple of Augustus, built a few years before the Crucifixion, is also of great interest. It stands next to the medieval Town Hall. If you are an enthusiast, you will find the splendid Roman and Byzantine mosaics in the little Archeological Museum of exceptional quality.

But this is not all, for behind the 15th-century basilica and beneath the walls of the Venetian citadel, you may still see the exquisite Porta Aurea, built in 30 B.C., and also the remains of two Roman theaters and the "Herculean" and "Twin" Gates. Incidentally, several Roman columns were used in the construction of the basilica.

But despite her great heritage from the past, Pula is also a flourishing industrial and shipbuilding city, as well as a port and the center of a modern tourist area, with excellent hotels and several charming beaches. A number of pleasant excursions can be made from the town to places as far afield as Venice, and other Italian localities, the Postojna Caves and the Plitvice Lakes, as well as to other modern resorts.

Medulin, 11 km. (seven miles) south, is a holiday village on a long sandy beach. Premantura is a tourist settlement on Istria's southwestern tip.

Opatija, Leading Resort

Opatija the Opulent, Istria's oldest resort, has all that is most loved by the poster artist. Across the long, deep bay the islands of Cres and Krk emerge from the intensely blue sea. Behind the town the leafy heights of Mount Učka rise to a majestic 1,370 m. (4,500 ft.). Moreover, Opatija has preserved some old-world comfort and even a trace of elegance amid the brash modernity of the coast.

Just over a century ago there was little here but a modest fishing village—still intact as the northern suburb of Volosko. Then, about 1880, doctors began recommending its healthy climate. Luxury hotels were built, and within a few years Opatija was a fashionable holiday resort of the Austrian and Hungarian nobility.

This region has the supreme advantage of an extraordinarily equable climate, with a mean annual average temperature of 57°F. The lowest and highest mean monthly temperatures ever recorded here are 48°F. and 79°F. respectively. This is partly explained by the fact that the mountains to the north protect it in winter from cold winds, and regular sea breezes keep it from really oppressive heat. The sun shines for four months of the year and fog, frost and snow are unknown. In winter rainy days are rare. There are actually quite heavy falls of rain in summer, but on relatively few days.

Naturally this privileged climate means that Opatija is a paradise of flowers, fruit and sweet-scented shrubs and plants—palms, lemon and orange groves, bamboo and yucca. A great variety of cacti lends a subtropical air to the many delightful little parks and gardens.

The town's rapid growth toward the end of last century explains the rather Edwardian air of some of the hotels. This was when real comfort (as opposed to labor-saving gadgets) was perhaps better understood than it is today. Most are built close to the beach, and nearly all have their own beautifully kept gardens, with views of sea or mountain framed by trees.

Tito Avenue, Opatija's main street, has fine shops and several luxury hotels, and not far away is Volosko, the picturesque small village of 18th-century houses, which is somewhat reminiscent of the French Riviera. Here begins the unique coastal path that stretches for around nine km. (six miles) along the Kvarner Riviera. A favorite walk is to Lovran through the fishing villages of Ika and Ičići, and there are plenty of benches if you feel like resting and admiring the view.

Opatija has several separate beaches, of which the most popular is the Kvarner Lido: the bathing is ideal. In the evenings there are concerts or folk-dancing displays in the large openair theater. In short Opatija affords every opportunity for the enjoyment of sun, peace, comfort and perfect sea bathing amid beautiful surroundings.

Opatija is also a good center for excursions that combine a short journey by bus or private car with some walking. The most popular of these are along the coast southward to Lovran, or to climb Mount Učka. This may sound strenuous, and on foot will take over four hours each way, but it is possible to cover a good part of the distance by road. As might be expected, the view from the top, of the 65-km. (40-mile) width of the Istrian peninsula to the west, and to the north almost to the Italian frontier at Trieste, is splendid.

All manner of excursions by coach and boat can be made from Opatija, to Venice, Postojna Caves, Plitvice Lakes, the islands of Krk, Cres, Lošinj and Rab, and to other resorts nearby.

Rijeka and the Croatian Littoral

The Yugoslavs consider the "Croatian Littoral" to be limited to the 160 km. (100 miles) or so of Adriatic stretching from Rijeka (known before the end of World War II as Fiume, when it was part of either

Italy or Austria-Hungary; both words mean "River") to just north of Zadar, where Dalmatia proper begins.

The coast is deeply indented, with delightful bays facing the intense blue of the open sea backed by steeply-rising mountains. Towns and villages are perched far above the water, but the dramatic element in the scene is softened by the warm beauty of the island-flecked sea. Since 1965, many modern tourist resorts have been built along this part of Yugoslavia's Adriatic coast, to join the much older (but now also modernized) watering place of Crikvenica.

The city of Rijeka was occupied in a daring raid by the poet D'Annunzio in 1919 and remained Italian until 1945, even though its Sušak district on the opposite side of the river was Yugoslav. Today the frontier no longer divides the city, and it has become Yugoslavia's most prosperous port.

Rijeka's tourist importance is in its being the port from which to take ship, either to explore the Dalmatian coast, or because it is a main point of departure for the Adriatic islands and Venice. Additionally, many roads lead from Rijeka to the charming seaside villages and numerous beaches of the Croatian coast.

Rijeka will seem to most visitors to be just an industrial town and major seaport. But the city can boast a pleasant medieval center, and there are other attractions too. From Titov Trg (Tito Square), for instance, 412 steps lead up to Trsat with its medieval castle and church now a museum and restaurant.

The fortress was built by the once powerful Counts of Frankopan, and the church was also erected at their orders to commemorate the Miracle of Trsat. The church was built in 1291 on the spot where the angels from Nazareth were supposed to have deposited the humble building in which the Virgin Mary gave birth to Jesus Christ. Traditionally, after an interval of three years, the angels continued their journey to Loreto in Italy, but Trsat has always remained a place of pilgrimage.

The *Jadranska Magistrala,* the well-surfaced but narrow Adriatic Highway, runs, often high above the sea but never very far from it, to Senj and Zadar. Between Rijeka and Senj, the road skirts a wide bay. The cliffs behind the bay are criss-crossed with ladders used as lookout posts. These are for the tuna fishermen who, as soon as a school of the great fish is sighted, first block their escape out to deeper water with huge nets, and then drive them slowly toward the shore.

Bakarac and tiny Bakar are sited at opposite ends of a long bay. Both have become holiday spots in recent years. Bakar is perched on a rock and largely medieval in character, despite its modern buildings. Here there is a remarkable 12th-century church and also one of the many castles of the Counts of Frankopan. Fortified castles of this kind are often to be seen here, reminders that until recent time fighting was a perennial hazard along much of this coast. The local wine, *Bakarska Vodica*, is very drinkable.

Next comes the little seaside resort of Kraljevica at the mouth of a narrow bay, sheltered by the mountains that almost encircle it. Tourist settlements and camp sites are set among vineyards. There is a new bridge to Rijeka's airport on Krk Island.

Crikvenica and Senj

Crikvenica's pebble beach, bounded at one end by the last outlying foothills of the Kapela range, can be unpleasantly crowded in summer. But at other times, the bathing is very pleasant here, and the sun decidedly warm. But don't be misled by older publications that describe the beach as "sandy." Serbo-Croat has only one word to mean both sandy and "gravelly." There are many pleasant walks and well-kept little parks, which combine to make Crikvenica a good holiday resort. It has all the usual seaside amusements. The once-unnoticed little fishing port of Selce nearby is now a busy resort with a number of hotels.

Novi Vinodolski, 11 km. (seven miles) south, is also pleasant and popular. It has a medieval castle of the ubiquitous Counts of Franko-pan. It was here that the earliest Croat Constitution, known as the Vinodol Code, was drawn up in 1266. Novi also has a remarkable 14th-century church, which was designed to recall the earliest kind of Christian basilica found occasionally in Asia Minor. It is only half-an-hour's drive from Novi to the little town of Senj, whose church, with its Romanesque dome, and Gothic and Renaissance buildings, is guarded by the Nehaj fortress. Senj has been important since ancient times because it stands at the foot of one of the few routes by which the gaunt Velebit ridge, 1,525 m. (5,000 ft.) above the town, can be crossed.

The people of Senj proudly recall the heroic rôle that their town played during the Turkish occupation of the surrounding country. Late in the 15th century a band of Serbs, who rose to notoriety as the Uskoks, successfully defied the Ottoman armies. With the old fortress as their base, protected on one flank by the mountains and on the seaward side by the windswept narrows of Senjska Vrata, these bellicose patriot-pirates and their descendants not only held off the attacks of a powerful enemy, but were themselves for 200 years a scourge to all the shipping of the Adriatic. The Venetians used to say of them *"Che Dio vi guardi delle mani dei Segnani"*—"God preserve you from falling into the hands of the men of Senj"—and this almost superstitious dread of the Uskoks was more than justified.

Two of their outstanding leaders were Petar Kružić and Ivo of Senj, whose deeds lived on in the ballads of the wandering minstrels, who until recently celebrated their exploits. However, despite their valor and cunning, they survived as long as they did only by playing off the rivalries of Venice and Constantinople against each other, and by the skill with which they handled their small, swift and maneuverable galleys. The Uskoks could always outwit their enemies, the vessels of whose fleets were heavy and unwieldy.

From Senj you will probably be able to identify the 70 m. (2,275 ft.) high Vratnik Pass, which pierces the wall of mountains that shut the town in toward the sea. That road leads away inland to the Plitvice Lakes and the heart of Croatia.

The restful little seaside town of Jablanac, dominated by a medieval castle of (as you will have guessed) the Counts of Frankopan, lies in the lovely fjord of Zavratnica, at the foot of the mighty Velebit Mountains. A few kilometers farther south is Karlobag, with its Capuchin Convent and its ferry services to the islands of Rab and Pag. Below the Velebit Ravine in the Paklenica National Park is Starigrad-Paklenica—with another Frankopan castle, and always given its full title to distinguish it from a Starigrad pod Valebit some kilometers north, and from the better-known Starigrad na Hvaru on the island of Hvar.

Farther on, the main Adriatic Highway turns west and crosses a superb bridge over the Maslenica Channel to reach Zadar 32 km. (20 miles) away over flat coastal land. Obrovac, off the main road, and now a bauxite-mining center, though formerly no more than a tiny market-town, can be made the base for many delightful climbs in the Velebit.

Visitors who like the sea or have time to spare may well prefer the sea journey from Rijeka to Zadar. The ship is never out of sight of the coast, and there is a fascinating succession of coastal views. The only trouble about sea travel is that all the time you are on board looking at the coast you are also wishing you were on the land seeing it at close quarters.

The Islands of Krk and Rab

Several large islands are to be found in the Kvarner Gulf. The northernmost is Krk, wide and ringed with broad, sandy bays. The scenery is majestic, the eastern part being arid and wild, the soil stony and poor. However, the southern and western areas are quite different, the land being richly fertile and for that reason more thickly populated. Krk was colonized by the Romans, fought over by Caesar and Pompey in 49 B.C. and subsequently changed its masters with each fluctuation of the balance of power in the Adriatic. The charming seaside village of Baška has right-of-place in Yugoslav history as the site where the famous 11th-century Baška Tablet engraved with Croat inscriptions in Glagolitic characters was found.

The little capital town of Krk clusters round the head of a bay: Roman baths supplied the building-materials for its sixth-century cathedral. Nearby is the delightful Dražica beach. Excursions can be made to the interesting old villages of Malinska (which is rapidly being spoilt by concrete overbuilding), Punat, Vrbnik and Omišalj—this last particularly rich in folk traditions. Vrbnik is becoming something of an artists' colony because of its picturesque situation on the summit of a rocky promontory, and because of the extraordinary beauty of the eastern coastline. Košljun Islet, facing the sandy beach of Punat, has a particularly fine Benedictine Monastery. All these villages have now been developed as resorts, and the island—linked to the mainland by fast motorboats, hydrofoils and the bridge in the north—is the site of Rijeka airport, which serves the whole of the region. For the holiday-maker, Krk combines the advantages of easy accessibility with the peace that comes from remoteness.

The island of Rab is among the best-known of the Croatian islands and is famous, among other things, for its delicious lobster. The Phoenicians were the first to install themselves here and then, as in so many places throughout the Mediterranean, the Greeks, Romans and Byzantines followed. Later it became part of Croatia and so lived under Venetian and, finally, Austro-Hungarian rule until Yugoslavia was born, in 1918. Most older buildings on the island in one way or another reflect these different influences.

Rab is in the same latitude as the French Riviera, and enjoys a similar climate. It is a perfect setting for the rich profusion of flowers and subtropical vegetation that grows everywhere.

The capital town was founded in Roman times on a narrow tongue of land, so that, approaching by sea, the traveler sees it set at the head of the bay, its ancient ramparts above, and the sails of many ships at its feet. It is a town of rare charm with its fine old private houses built by noble Venetian families centuries ago, and its 13th-century cathedral—one of the most remarkable on the Adriatic. Its bell-tower soars above every other building. From the top there is a view not only of the old town, but over kilometers of the neighboring coastline.

From here the 14th-century Palace of the Princess, the Benedictine Convent, founded in the sixth century, the magnificent library and the 15th-century Madonna of Vivarini are all to be seen.

The former Nimira Palace, built in the 14th century, is a restaurant now—and a very good one. Further reminders of Rab's proud past are to be seen in the Town Hall, a loggia, and in one of the old city gates.

But Rab is not wholly given over to things of the past, for there are plenty of modern villas and even naturist camps set among umbrella pines; and there are also several well-appointed beaches. If bathing is one of the main objects of a visit to Rab, then a day spent in the idyllic bay in the north of the island is to be recommended. Here nestles the small, quiet summer resort of Lopar, according to legend the birthplace of the Dalmatian stonemason Marino, who founded the Italian Republic of San Marino. Rab is reached by ship from Rijeka in 3¼ hours. There are also ferry services from the neighboring island of Krk and from Senj and Jablanac on the mainland.

Also in the Gulf of Kvarner facing the east coast of Istria are the two islands of Cres and Lošinj, both of them Italian until 1945. The eastern side of Cres is bare, but its western slopes are covered with excellent vines and dark pine woods. Cres is also the name of a charming little fishing village with an excellent beach, a 15th-century loggia and a fortified tower. Almost in the center of the widest part of this long, thin island there is a mysterious freshwater lake called Vrana, as much as 83 m. (273 ft.) in depth at one point—far deeper than the sea anywhere within kilometers of the island's coasts. Geologists have discussed the possibility of the source of the lake being an underground river connected with the Istrian peninsula by a channel under the sea.

A road runs the length of the island from Porozina in the north, connected by ferries to Brestova and Rijeka, to Osor in the south. In Roman times Osor was an important port-of-call for ships on the route from Aquileia, in the Bay of Trieste, to Split, Salona and Greece. It was attacked by the Genoese in the Middle Ages, and later became the base of a band of bloodthirsty pirates. For 1,000 years from the sixth century it was the seat of a bishop and from the end of that period date the Renaissance cathedral, the townhall, which also houses a museum, and several palaces.

A bridge spans the shallow channel only some 12 m. (40 ft.) wide between Cres and the island of Lošinj, where orange and lemon groves descend to the edges of the many excellent bathing beaches. This is an ideal place for deep-sea fishing, and there are adequate accommodations here.

The little town of Mali Lošinj is most attractive. It is built round the curve in a narrow bay, its gardens bright against the ancient buildings, and there are also 16th-century fortifications to hint at former greatness in what is today a quiet fishing village-cum-holiday resort. Alternatively, cross the three km. (two miles) to the opposite side of the island—Lošinj though some 30 km. (20 miles) long is rarely more than a tenth of that distance in width—until you come to Veli Lošinj, an ancient village with each of its houses in its own flower garden, leading down to a beach.

Everywhere in Lošinj are clumps of the neatly-shaped umbrella, or Mediterranean, pine. These trees also line the five km. (three miles) of beach stretching from Mali Lošinj to Čikat, yet another peaceful spot more or less off the average tourist's map.

There is an interesting excursion to be made from Lošinj to the neighboring, much smaller island of Susak, where some excellent wines are produced.

Susak is said to be the only sandy island in the Adriatic. There are perhaps no more than seven family names on the whole island, and the villagers still wear traditional peasant dress. There are no hotels, though accommodations can be arranged in private houses, and only one restaurant—a good one if the order for the midday meal is given immediately on arrival at the island. Most famous of the excellent local wines is the sweet pink *prošek*.

Among the island groups to the south, only Ilovik is inhabited and merits a visit.

Practical Information for Istria

WHEN TO GO. The tourist season in this region is from May until October. Because of the protection provided by Mount Učka against cold north winds the whole of Kvarner Bay, and in particular Opatija, also has a wonderfully mild winter climate. As a result, visitors come here in winter to avoid the cold, and in summer to escape the inland heat with the help of cool sea breezes. The mean summer temperature on the Istrian coast is 77°F. In spring it is made even more attractive by the mass of hazel, almond, and cherry trees in blossom.

There are small casinos at Opatija, Portorož, Rovinj and Umag. Opatija has almost every night during the high season, opera, concerts or folklore dancing and singing in an openair theater. At Pula a Yugoslav Cinema Festival is held in late July, and performances by the Ljubljana and Zagreb Opera Companies alternate with concerts and folk music, songs and dancing throughout the summer. The Istrian Song Festival in June and the Yugoslav Folklore Festival in mid-July have offshoots in all the bigger resorts. The artistic and sports events at Portorož last from May through September.

HOTELS AND RESTAURANTS. First a word of warning: virtually all the larger hotels on this coast cater primarily for package-tour visitors. Thus a possible drawback of such hotels is that the big battalions claim —and get—all the staff's attention. The guest who is paying just for himself, or himself and his family, can find it difficult to compete with people who represent, say, 200 visitors a week for three months every year.

If you want individual attention you may do better in smaller establishments, or in private homes, which are also much cheaper. What they lack in comfort and facilities they often make up for in friendliness and personal contact. Tourist Information Offices *(Turistički Ured* or *Turistički Biro),* often indicated by the letter "i," are found in nearly all resorts, and will take care of bookings and sometimes also of payments—though families prefer cash in hand.

Food and Drink. The region's cooking blends Italian and Austrian cuisine—not too heavy, and particularly good in its preparation of fish. The oysters of Vrsar are delicious, as also in their season are the locally caught crab—these are excellent and surprisingly inexpensive. Adriatic prawns *(škampa)* are also recommended, either boiled or fried and breadcrumbed. Most fish is grilled. However, mussels cooked in wine *(ostrige)* are a specialty. Fish soup *(brodet)* is somewhat similar to bouillabaisse, and is usually very good.

Cheese is not a particularly strong suit in Yugoslavia, but Istria produces one of the best in the country, a kind of gruyère. Another specialty is smoked ham *(pršut),* which goes very well with dark wines such as *Teran, Refošk, Vipava, Rebula,* and the delicious *Malvazija* from the island of Susak.

ISTRIA

ANKARAN. A good beach in the Bay of Kopor; season Apr.–Sept. *Adria* (M), 304 rooms in annexes round a converted Benedictine monastery. Pool, minigolf, bowling. *Convent* (M), about 150 rooms in various annexes.

BAKARAC. *Motel Bakarac* (I), 9 rooms. *Neptun* (I), 18 rooms. Both with a few showers.

IZOLA. Small beach resort fairly close to industrial area. *Belvedere* (M), 73 rooms. Tourist settlement. *Haliaetum* (M), 180 rooms. Annexes, two pools. *Marina* (M), 50 rooms. *Riviera* (I), 30 rooms.

KOPER. Picturesque seaside resort and port with yachting etc. *Žusterna* (M), 154 rooms. Pool. *Triglav* (I), 88 rooms. With terrace overlooking the sea.

LOVRAN. Beach resort just south of Opatija. *Beograd* (M), 102 rooms. Set in a fine park on the seafront. *Jadran* (M), 83 rooms. With annexes. *Miramare* (M), 32 rooms. *Park* (M), 55 rooms. *Primorka* (M), 24 rooms. *Splendid* (M), 83 rooms. With several (I) annexes. *Villa Elektra* (I), 61 rooms. *Villa Zagreb* (I), no showers.

MEDULIN. 11 km. (seven miles) from Pula. *Belvedere* (M), 460 rooms, pool. *Medulin* (M), 190 rooms. Annexes and chalets with kitchens. *Mutila* (M), 172 rooms. *Kažela* (I), 157 rooms. Naturist tourist settlement.

MOŠĆENICKA DRAGA. Particularly suitable for children; season Apr.–
Oct. *Marina* (M), 200 rooms. *Biser-Rubin* (I), 44 rooms. *Draga* (I), 43 rooms,
19 with bath.

NOVIGRAD (Istria). Excellent center for fishing enthusiasts; season Apr.–
Oct. *Emonia* (M), and annex *Stella Maris* (I), 175 rooms. *Laguna* (M), 228
rooms.

OPATIJA. All the hotels and particularly the tenth-floor restaurant of the
Ambassador are in national style, serving local specialties. *Ambassador* (L), 204
rooms. Some apartments, convention facilities, openair and covered pools, spacious. *Kvarner* (E), 56 rooms. Very comfortable, but older than the Ambassador.
With private beach, pool, tea and dinner dances. Charming *Amalia* (E) annex,
30 rooms.

Adriatic (M), 333 rooms. *Astoria* (M), 70 rooms. *Atlantic* (M), 23 rooms.
Avala (M), 60 rooms. *Bellevue* (M), 108 rooms. *Belvedere* (M), 67 rooms. Large
garden. *Brioni* (M), 62 rooms. *Continental* (M), 64 rooms. *Dubrovnik* (M), 43
rooms. *Imperial* (M), 121 rooms. *Istra-Marina* (M), 76 rooms. *Jadran* (M), 90
rooms. *Kristal* (M), 136 rooms. *Opatija* (M), 160 rooms. *Palme* (M), 100 rooms.
Panorama (M), 60 rooms. *Paris* (M), 90 rooms. *Resident* (M), 45 rooms. *Slavija*
(M), 116 rooms. *Zagreb-Esplanade* (M), 100 rooms.

Restaurants. Apart from those in the hotels, there are the following. *Lido,*
on Kvarner beach, has a terrace with a dance floor. *Mali Raj* (meaning "little
paradise") is on the outskirts; there is a natural beach beside the restaurant.
Ribliji Restoran specializes in seafood. In the port, try the *Café Jedro,* which
has a huge terrace.

PAZIN. A small, historic town in the center of the peninsula; season Apr.–
Oct. *Motel Lovac* (I), 25 rooms, 15 with bath.

PIRAN. Delightful small port, half Venetian, half Austrian in atmosphere;
season Apr.–Oct. *Piran* (M), 56 rooms, all with bath. *Punta* (M), 65 rooms, all
with bath.

POREČ. Lovely old town, center of the largest beach resort; season Apr.–
Oct. *Diamant* (M), *Neptun* (M), *Poreč* (M) and *Riviera* (I) are all in or near
town. Farther out are the vast, though well-organized, tourist complexes of
Bellevue; Brulo with the large, excellent *Kristal* and *Rubin* hotels; *Lanterna,*
including the rather expensive naturist *Solaris Pavilions; Masterada; Pical; Plava
Laguna; Spadići;* and biggest of all, *Zelena Laguna.* All various ranges of (M).

On the island of **Sveti Nikola** (St. Nicholas), opposite the quay: *Miramare*
(M), 60 rooms; and the *Splendid* chalets, with hotel annexes, including the
18th-century castle, *Istra,* with 24 rooms. Also motels *Lim* (I) and *Tarska Vala*
(I).

Restaurants. *Riblji Restoran,* overlooking the quay, offers seafood specialties. About 1½ km. (a mile) north of the town there is *Villa Materada,* which has snacks with wine.

PORTOROŽ. *Grand Hotel Emona* (E), 254 rooms. Slightly cheaper than the Grand Hotel Palace below. *Grand Hotel Metropol* (E), 103 rooms. *Grand Hotel Palace* (E), 207 rooms. All three with private beaches and pools.

All (M) are: *Apollo,* 96 rooms; *Bernardin,* 273 rooms, pool; *Lucija,* 112 rooms; *Marita-Suisse,* 82 rooms; *Mirna,* 96 rooms, pool; *Neptun,* 89 rooms, pool; *Palace,* 180 rooms, pool; *Park Villas,* 240 rooms; and *Riviera,* 454 rooms, annexes, pool. Other (M)s without their own pools but all with private beaches are *Barbara,* 75 rooms; *Roža,* 115 rooms; and *Vesna,* 52 rooms, no restaurant, and over-expensive.

Restaurants. *Jadran* and *Ljubljana,* both on the seafront, specialize in fish dishes.

PULA. *Brioni* (E), 223 rooms. Pool. *Park* (M), 141 rooms. *Riviera* (M), old but renovated; centrally located. Five km. (2½ miles) from Pula is the tourist complex of *Zlatne Stijene,* with 400 rooms. 1½ km. (a mile) farther out, at **Veruda,** are the *Park* (M), 144 rooms, and the *Verudela* (M) hotel complex, 336 rooms, 16 villas, 20 apartments. Also *Splendid* (M), 355 rooms in hotel complex. All of these are (M). (I) is *Ribarska Koliba,* with 110 rooms. There are campsites and chalets farther south at **Banjole** and **Premantura.**

Restaurants. *Ribarska Koliba* (the "Fishermen's Hut"—see above) is recommended. Also outside town is the attractive *Stoja,* with beach, music and dancing; and *Sakordjana,* beside a beach five km. (2½ miles) from Pula. The *Excelsior* is in Matko Laginja St.; dancing on the terrace. *Gorica* is in its own garden. *Zagreb,* serving local brown "stone" mussels, and *Jadran* are both good.

RABAC. Fishing port and major resort; season Apr.–Oct. *Apollo* (M), 54 rooms. *Fortuna* (M), 70 rooms. *Hedera* and *Narcis,* each with 133 rooms, form with the superior *Mimosa,* which has 147 rooms, a self-contained complex with indoor pool and nightclub; all (M). *Istra* (M), 40 rooms. *Lanterna* (M), 151 rooms. Also (M) are the vast *Girandela* and *St. Andrea* tourist settlements. *Marina, Mediteran* and *Primorje,* all (I), some private showers.

ROVINJ. Attractive old town and lively resort. *Eden* (E), 332 rooms. Indoor pool. *Istra* (E), 177 rooms. *Lone* (M), 170 rooms. *Monte Mulin* (M), 120 rooms. *Park* (M), 183 rooms. Also (M) are the *Rubin Villa Complex* at **Polari,** with 950 rooms, and the tourist settlements *Monsena,* with 620 rooms, and *Valalta,* 650 rooms.

On the neighboring islands of **Sveta Katarina** and **Crveni Otok** there are (M) hotels bearing the islands' names.

SAVUDRIJA. A simple seaside resort just under eight km. (five miles) from Umag; season May–Oct. Hotels and campsites are located in a delightful large pinewood running down to the shore. *Savudrija Bungalows* (M), 103 rooms. *Savudrija Hotel* (I), 64 rooms, some with showers.

STRUNJAN (near Koper). *Salinera* (M), 48 rooms. Has an (M) annex.

UMAG. A formerly tiny fishing village that has expanded into a vast popular modern beach resort. *Adriatic* (E), 142 rooms. Pool and casino. *Aurora* (M), 206 rooms. *Istra* (M) and annex, 550 rooms. *Koral* (M), 206 rooms. *Kristal* (M), 95 bungalows. *Umag* (M), 129 rooms. Also (M) are *Polynesia Villa,* at **Katoro,** with 686 apartments offering all facilities; the *Stella Maris* tourist settlement, with 533 bungalows; and the *Zagreb Hotel Complex,* with 450 rooms and 40 bungalows at **Punta.**

VERUDA. See Pula above.

VRSAR. Old fishing village and popular modern resort at the mouth of the River Lim, famous for its oysters; season Apr.–Oct. *Funtana* (M), 238 rooms. *Panorama* (M), 188 rooms. *Pineta* (M), 100 rooms. Pool. The *Anita Tourist Settlement* (M–I) is an extensive naturist/tourist settlement, with chalets, restaurants etc.

EAST KVARNER COAST AND ISLANDS

BANJOL (Rab Island). *Kontinental* (I) and annexes, 70 rooms.

BARBAT (Rab Island). *Barbat* (I), 16 rooms, none with shower. Simple.

BAŠKA. On picturesque Krk Island, good beach. *Corinthia* (M) and annexes, 290 rooms. *Velebit* (I), 30 rooms, none with shower.

CRES. Island in Gulf of Kvarner. *Kimen* (M), 226 rooms.

CRIKVENICA. Crowded beach with numerous hotels. Best is the *Omorika* (M), 117 rooms, plus 129 in pavilions. Also recommended is the modern *International* (M), 53 rooms. *Esplanade* (M), 88 rooms. *Mediteran* (M), 72 rooms, most with shower. *Miramare* (M), 92 rooms, some with shower. *Therapia* (E), 129 rooms. Pre-war hotel in gardens on hill; with pool. *Zagreb* (M), 72 rooms. Best buy is the *Ad Turres* (M), 283 rooms, tourist settlement, in pine forest with own beach.

At **Dramalj,** *Riviera Pavilions* (M) and annex, 100 rooms, most with shower. On the Kačjak promontory, *Tourist Settlement,* 226 rooms. *Crikvenica* (I), 36 rooms, none with shower. In port.

Restaurant. *Jadran* is a noted for its seafood.

JABLANAC. Ferry to Rab Island. *Jablanac* (I), 50 rooms, none with shower. *Zavratnica* (I), 10 rooms, none with shower.

KARLOBAG. Fishing village. Ferry to Pag Island. *Velinac* (I), 20 rooms.

KRALJEVICA. Bridge to Krk Island. *Oštro-Villas* (M), 40 rooms. Chalet-style. *Uvala Scott* (M), 338 rooms. *Praha* (I), 44 rooms, none with shower.

KRK. Capital of island of the same name. *Dražica* (M) and annex, 183 rooms. *Koralj* (M), 183 rooms. *Lovorka* (M), 94 rooms. *Bor* (I), 23 rooms, none with shower.

LOPAR (Rab Island). *San Marino* (M), 557 rooms, all with bath. Situated outside the village.

MALI LOŠINJ (Lošinj Island). *Alhambra* (M) and annexes, 84 rooms. *Aurora* (M), 404 rooms, *Bellevue* (M), 226 rooms; both with pool. *Helios* (M), 138 rooms. *Helios Bungalows* (M), 258 rooms. *Punta* (M), 167 rooms. *Vespera* (M), 404 rooms. *Čikat* (I), 60 rooms, *Istra* (I), 23 rooms; neither with showers.
Restaurants. *Gurman, Hajduk* and *Tri Palme,* all adequate.

MALINSKA (Krk Island). *Slavija* (M), 70 rooms. *Triglav* (M), 53 rooms. *Malin* (M–I) and annexes, 200 rooms.
At **Haludovo,** *Palace* (E), 220 rooms, pool. *Tamaris* (M), 289 rooms. Also apartments and villas.

NJIVICE (Krk Island). *Beli Kamik* (M), 375 rooms. *Flora* (M), 272 rooms. Tourist settlement. *Jadran* (M), 92 rooms.

NOVI VINODOLOSKI. Opposite Krk Island; season Apr.–Oct. *Horizont* (I), 70 rooms. *Lišanj* (I), 50 rooms. On private beach. *Povile* (M) and *Zagori* (M) tourist settlements, south and north of the town respectively, are better.

OMIŠALJ (Krk Island). *Adriatic* (M), 350 rooms, all with shower; annexes. *Jadran* (M) and annexes, 51 rooms.

PUNAT (Krk Island). *Park* (M) and annexes, 268 rooms. Naturist beach is just a short boat trip away.

RAB. Capital of lovely, densely wooded island of the same name. *Imperial* (M), 156 rooms, 83 with bath. *International* (M), 125 rooms and 4 apartments. Newer than the Imperial. *Istra* (M), 105 rooms.
Five km. (three miles) from the town in the woods, *Suha Punta* (M), tourist settlement with 430 rooms in bungalows. *Carolina* (M), 150 rooms, pool. *Eva* (M), 196 rooms.

RIJEKA. The country's main port and a partly industrial area. *Bonavia* (E), 154 rooms. In town center about 200 m. (220 yards) from quayside. With garden restaurant, café, and dancing on roof terrace. Old-established and the best in town. *Jadran* (M), 81 rooms, most with bath. By the sea in the Susak district, with private beach. *Motel Lucija* (I), 81 rooms, 40 with bath. *Neboder* (I), 52 rooms, 17 with bath. Well-situated in the town but noisy. *Panorama* (I), 60 rooms. *Park* (I), 47 rooms, 16 with bath. Outside town.

Restaurants. You will eat well at the *Gradina* in Trsat Castle, which also offers fine views. Also recommended is the *Gradski Restoran* on the wharf near the Narodni Trg. In the same neighborhood the *Zlatna Školjka* specializes in seafood.

SELCE. *Varaždin* (E), 186 rooms. Pool. *Jadranka* (M), 188 rooms. Pool. *Marin* (M), 100 rooms, pool. *Slaven* (M) and annexes, 250 rooms. *Selce* (I), 15 rooms, none with shower.

SENJ. Stopover opposite Krk Island. *Nehaj* (M), 43 rooms, 21 with bath. *Velebit* (I), 15 rooms, none with shower.

VELI LOŠINJ (Lošinj Island). Season Apr.–Oct. *Punta* (M), 167 rooms.

HOW TO GET AROUND. Krk's international airport is linked by bridge to the mainland, and there are rail terminals at Koper, Pula and Rijeka. Frequent bus services run between the coastal towns. All major agencies in Opatija organize trips in comfortable motorcoaches to the Postojna Caves, the Plitvice Lakes, and to Venice by launch, passenger steamer, or hydrofoil. Motorboat excursions are run from the coast towns, numerous car and passenger ferries operate between the mainland and the islands, complemented by hydrofoil services in summer.

WHAT TO SEE. Inland the main attractions are the fantastic Postojna Caves and Plitvice Lakes. There are also a number of attractive old fortified towns and many beautiful churches. Visitors with artistic leanings will particularly admire the little church of Beram, near Pazin, especially its extraordinary frescos. Then there are the art towns of Rovinj and Poreč, now also bustling seaside resorts. The islands of Rab, Krk, Cres and Lošinj are well worth visiting.

Pula, at the southern tip of the Istrian peninsula, is renowned for its magnificent Roman remains, not only the amphitheater seating 23,000 people, which is partly ruined, but also the Temple of Augustus, which has remained virtually intact.

SPORTS. First and foremost—swimming. The Istrian beaches are nearly all gently sloping and shallow, and thus—though more often pebble than sand—absolutely safe for children. Among the best are those of Medulin 11 km. (seven miles) from Pula, also Savudrija, Lovran, Lošinj and Opatija. There are heated fresh or salt water pools in some of the better hotels in winter.

The clear warm waters of the Adriatic in summer are ideal for underwater fishing, and there are plenty of fish to choose from. The best centers for this sport are on the islands of Cres and Lošinj. At Mali Lošinj there is an annual International Underwater Fishing Contest at the end of December. Fishing excursions are organized by travel agents, though if you prefer you can go on your own for a night's fishing with any of the fishing boats for hire at almost any resort.

Water skiing, wind surfing, and yachting can be arranged in many resorts, most of which possess fully-equipped marinas. Tennis, minigolf and bowling are available nearly everywhere.

 CAMPING. The Istrian Coast is ideal for camping. Official sites are to be found at virtually all resorts, though the quality does vary. Facilities of each are detailed in the Yugoslav National Tourist Office's camping leaflet. It is illegal to camp away from organized sites unless you have permission from the local Town Hall.

 SHOPPING. Examples of every kind of peasant handicraft are on sale in the shops of Opatija, Pula and many of the other larger resorts. The best buy is leather, suitcases, handbags, portfolios, etc. Most of these are handmade and even the factory-made articles are beautifully finished. Handmade lace is a specialty of Istria, and not expensive. Wood carvings and embroideries are also good bargains.

 USEFUL ADDRESSES. Every town and resort has a tourist information office. Istria's largest travel agency is Kvarner Express, which also owns several of the better hotels. Head office is at Maršala Tita 186, 51410 Opatija, with branches in most resorts. These offices organize hunting, fishing and sailing excursions.

CENTRAL DALMATIA

The Heart of the Coast

The section of the coast which we cover in this chapter is not long, barely 320 km. (200 miles), but it includes everything ever brought to mind by the name Dalmatia. Here you can see gaunt limestone mountains sloping sharply to the shore—sometimes direct into the sea. Here you have 100s of small, scrub-covered islands sharply etched against the intense blue of sea and sky, and colorful little villages tucked into bays and inlets, their red pantiled roofs glowing warmly. A number of lovely small stone-built towns, little larger than the villages but embodying high standards of civilized living and whose Roman remains blend harmoniously with predominantly Venetian architecture, are scattered along the coast, often perched picturesquely on small peninsulas. And almost every few kilometers there are modern hotels or "tourist complexes," with chalets and restaurants to welcome the visi-

113

tor and give him the opportunity of sampling the region's delights in modern comfort.

Preeminent among the towns is Split, centered upon a vast fortified palace built by the Roman Emperor Diocletian for his retirement. In the north the main town is Zadar, in plan still much the same as when it was designed by Roman civil engineers 20 centuries ago. Šibenik, south of Zadar, has much of beauty still too little appreciated, including a magnificent cathedral. Medieval Trogir, though overshadowed by Split and its modern airport, remains beautiful. South of Split, Makarska and the lovely coast on either side of it have now deservedly recovered their former popularity as centers of tourism. On the islands, Hvar and Korčula are outstanding among the region's "Venetian" towns. The appeal of these ancient places is quite different from that of the more modern holiday resorts that have grown up beside or between them. In bygone centuries the tiny towns were the only places that offered comfort and civilization. Today you can find all the comfort you could wish for in the resorts and holiday-complexes which were once primitive fishing villages whose inhabitants were still often barefoot, sometimes illiterate as well, uptil the 1950s.

Approaching Zadar

As we travel south toward Zadar, the character of the coast changes. The mountains gradually recede, and the coastlands for once become a flat and fertile plain, though the actual shore is still for the most part rocky and stony. Separated from it only by a narrow channel, the myriad islands of the Kornat (or Kornati) Archipelago spread out from the coast for several kilometers, providing a sheltered stretch of sea where fish thrive and boating enthusiasts can enjoy themselves. Most of the coast can be seen easily enough from the Adriatic Coastal Road. But to enjoy the islands to the full you need to spend long days exploring them by boat. If you have the good fortune to approach them across the sea from the west on a course of your own choosing, sail up under the fantastic cliffs of Dugi Otok's western side. This is a sight that not many people ever see, but once you have seen it you will never forget its majesty.

Exploring Zadar

Zadar, the ancient capital of Dalmatia, is built on a small peninsula. Its origins date from a long way back, and it still has many monuments of its glorious past to show. As early as Roman times it was already important, called at that time Jadera; it later became for a while a Byzantine stronghold. Following eight years of Napoleonic occupation it became part of the Austrian Empire in 1814, until under the 1920 Treaty of Rapallo it was handed over to Italy. Only in 1944 did it finally become part of Yugoslavia.

Zadar was much damaged by air-raids during World War II, but has been pleasingly rebuilt. The circular ninth-century Church of St. Donat luckily escaped serious damage: it is one of the earliest surviving buildings in Dalmatia. Its foundations were laid upon a Roman forum, and the outward effect is massively imposing, though its interior is austere. As might have been expected, the Croatian architects made good use of the already dressed Roman masonry they found on the spot, and on many of the columns you can still make out the original Latin inscriptions. If you climb the 55-m. (182-ft.) tower, you will be rewarded with a fine view of the Velebit Mountains and the nearer islands. The Archeological Museum, containing mostly Roman objects, stands opposite.

The Church of St. Anastasia is a Romanesque basilica with a small treasury. Other medieval churches include that of St. Simon, the town's patron-saint whose bones are kept in a sarcophagus richly decorated with silver and copper bas-reliefs, presented by Elizabeth of Hungary in 1380. There are many other churches of interest, among them Sveti Krševan, built in 13th-century Romanesque style, with a richly-decorated 16th-century altar, also some interesting frescos belonging to the original building, only recently rediscovered.

Among the medieval remains are the ruined but still impressive fortifications such as the Bovo de Antona tower and the Terraferma gate, both to be found close to the Church of St. Simon. The familiar 16th-century Venetian influence is present in the Loggia, the Guard House (now an ethnographical museum) and the "Five Wells."

An important modern industry is represented by the tall square building on the other side of the old harbor from the ancient walled town. This is the famous Maraska distillery, where maraschino was invented, and where a great variety of excellent modern liqueurs is still made.

Around Zadar

The ancient village of Nin, 16 km. (ten miles) north of Zadar, was known to the Romans as Aenona. There are traces of a forum and other Roman remains but they are rather unimpressive. There is also a very early Illyrian tomb though it is hard to find. St. Nicholas and the tiny ninth-century Church of the Holy Cross are curious examples of pre-medieval Croat architecture.

During the ninth and tenth centuries, Nin was the capital of the Kingdom of Croatia, and it was from here that Bishop Gregory of Nin (commemorated in the impressive bronze statue by Yugoslavia's foremost sculptor, Mĕstrović) conducted his campaign against the abolition of the Slavic liturgy. Having decided that the use in celebrating mass of a "barbaric" language written in the difficult Glagolitic characters was tantamount to heresy, the Holy See suppressed the practise. Gregory however triumphed, and the Glagolitic mass remained in use for two centuries.

The walls of Nin may still be seen as they were left after having been deliberately broken down by the Venetians in the 16th century so as not to fall intact into Turkish hands. A bridge leads to the barren island of Vir.

Another excursion from Zadar takes us 30 km. (19 miles) east to Novigradsko More, the so-called Sea of Novigrad. This is a wide, almost enclosed bay, linked with the Adriatic by a narrow, deep channel. On the shore of the bay is the charming little town of Novigrad. From here you can hire a boat to take you through the wild gorge of the River Zrmanja as far as Obrovac, where there is a splendid view from the old walls of a Turkish fort down the famous Zrmanja canyon.

From Obrovac you can continue inland, over the magnificent Alan Pass across the Velebit into the Lika, or return to the coast and turn north to the Starigrad-Paklenica National Park on the Velebit slopes. The little village of Posedarje lies just off the main road on the shore of the Novigrad Sea. Also to the north, a bridge connects the main road with the long, low island of Pag, which lies parallel with the Velebit range on the mainland. The island's capital is also called Pag, and is a fascinating old town. Both the capital itself and Novalja to the north have been developed as modern resorts. This is a quiet and peaceful part of the coast, with good opportunities for sailing and boating as well as swimming.

South from Zadar

25 km. (16 miles) south of Zadar the coastal road passes the beach of Filip Jakov, near Biograd na Moru (the "White Town on the Sea"), a walled town where once the Croatian kings were crowned, now an up-and-coming beach resort. Just beyond it are the tourist center of Crvena Luka and the village of Pakoštane. The coast in this area is unusually flat, and has quite extensive pinewoods, and other trees.

Continuing south the road follows a ridge between the sea and the wide lake Vransko. A branch left leads to the little town of Vrana, dominated by the impressive ruins of another Turkish fortress where there is one of the best preserved medieval "caravan-serais" to be found in the Balkans. The little church of the neighboring village of Miranje is concealed within the walls of another Turkish tower.

Crossing the narrow strip of land that separates Lake Vransko from the sea you glimpse rocky islands sunk in the rich blue of the Adriatic. Between the coast resorts of Pirovac and Vodice, a branch road crosses the promontory left (west) to Tijesno, a picturesque fishing port sited on both sides of the narrow channel separating the island of Murter from the coast.

You reach Šibenik by a bridge over the Krka, from which there are splendid views. The old town is built of a particularly attractive golden stone, and from the port it seems like a vast amphitheater crowned with formidable 17th- to 19th-century fortifications. Its narrow streets climb past the many ancient churches and medieval palaces.

Šibenik was founded in the 11th century and reached the height of its prosperity and power during the Middle Ages though, like nearly all the coastal towns of Dalmatia, it suffered during the protracted wars between the Turks and Venetians. The town was sold to the Venetians by Ladislas, King of Naples and Hungary, in 1410 but its citizens denounced the sale and resisted the Venetian troops sent to take possession.

Šibenik Cathedral was the work of four architects, and took a century to complete. The work was begun under the direction of the Italian di Giacomo, but he soon gave way to Orsini of Zadar, who completed the walls in Venetian Gothic. His successor, Nicholas of Florence, continued in Tuscan Renaissance style, and George of Dalmatia completed the task in the Gothic.

The vault and great cupola are formed of stone tiles of a kind found nowhere else in Europe, and the body of the cathedral is built entirely of the beautiful local stone. The frieze outside the apse is particularly interesting because of the carved heads of contemporary workmen, masons, fishermen, and so on.

You may wish to make an excursion, either by road or by sea, 18 km. (ten miles) north to the Krka waterfalls near Skradin, surrounded by vineyards. The water plunges sheer from a height of over 50 m. (160 ft.), and it is an unforgettable experience to look down through the iridescent spray to the basin of the falls far below. Modern hydroelectric works have somewhat reduced the force of the waterfalls.

The Franciscan Monastery of Visovac, on an islet in the Prukljan Lake, is famous for its manuscripts, incunabula and old paintings. Primošten, originally an island village, is now connected to the mainland on whose shore are a number of modern hotels. The 15th-century church was restored in the 18th century. A heated sea-water pool under a glass dome makes the town suitable for a winter holiday. Rogoznica is flanked by excellent beaches on several inlets opposite a tiny wooded island.

The Island Route from Zadar to Split

Before we come to Split we must mention the islands that lie along the Adriatic coast between the city of the Emperor Diocletian and Zadar, to the north. Opposite Zadar is the long narrow island of Ugljan which can be reached in half an hour. You land at the little port of Preko, over which an ancient fortress broods. From its walls there is a fine view across the straits to Zadar. The entrance to the port is almost blocked by the small island of Galovac, the thick woods that cover it encircling the ancient monastery. Near the southern tip of the island, there is the picturesque fishing hamlet of Kukljica. There are tourist chalets in the pinewoods here, and a central restaurant terrace and entertainments complex. The village has restaurants where, on Sundays, whole sheep are roasted on the spit.

Between Ugljan and Dugi Otok are several inhabited islets. Iž, the largest, is rich in olives, figs and vines. If you are a fisherman it is worth knowing that good simple accommodations can be obtained in the center at Iž Veli—and the fish are plentiful and varied.

Dugi Otok, literally "Long Island" (New Yorkers please note), supports seven small communities: Veli Rat, Soline, Božava (hotel), Luka (hotel), Žman, Zaglav and Sali (named after medieval saltpans). From these you can explore the Kornati archipelago, made up of 125 islets, most of them uninhabited. At one time some of the islands were pirates' lairs, and during World War II sheltered wounded partisans from Italian or German patrols. There are hidden creeks, deep caverns, grottos and wild rocks abounding, remotely beautiful and providing superb fishing. The great cliffs at the southwestern end of Dugi Otok form one of the coast's most magnificent sights and are well worth the effort of making a special excursion by boat or even on foot to see them.

The island of Pašman is connected to Ugljan by a bridge at the northern end. Tkon faces the mainland town of Biograd. There are the ruins of a ninth-century monastery in which you may see many inscriptions in contemporary Glagolitic.

Murter Island, joined to the mainland by a mobile bridge at Tijesno, is another good base from which to explore the Kornati archipelago. The capital village, which, as is customary, has the same name as the island, is within easy reach of several quite good bathing beaches, the best at Slanica cove backed by pines and olive groves.

Another pleasant little bathing resort is Zlarin, situated on a small island in the group of 30 extending to Šibenik. This is one of the few places in Europe where you can still buy coral from fishermen who have won it from the sea.

Approaching Split

As we approach Trogir and Split, we find ourselves entering a bay bounded by a stretch of flat land on the north (Split's international airport is situated here) and, on the south, by the peninsula beyond which lies the center of Split itself. The city is in the lee of the island of Čiovo lying right across the bay's mouth, and sheltered by the mountains which increasingly encroach upon the coast. A defile up which an ancient road, now asphalted, runs inland to Sinj and beyond is guarded by the formerly Turkish hilltop fortress of Klis, only a few kilometers from the heart of the city. South of Split, the mountains Mosor and Biokovo come closer and closer to the sea, in places appearing to drop sheer into the water from their 1,500-m. (5,000-ft.) ridges. Offshore, the islands of Šolta, Brač and Hvar provide excellent shelter for the inshore channel. This is a strikingly picturesque and varied section of the coast.

The Historic Town of Trogir

Trogir is a uniquely beautiful little medieval town set on an island about 400 m. (440 yards) long by 140 m. (150 yards) wide. A stone bridge makes it accessible from the mainland, a mobile bridge connects it with the Island of Čiovo, and numerous boats ply from Split.

Because of its relative isolation Trogir is largely unchanged, though modern hotels rise in the vicinity. Its tiny main square, in particular, still looks much as it must have done 300 years ago.

In the third century B.C. the Greeks founded a city here which they called Tragurion, perhaps because of the great herds of goats or *tragoi*, which are still a feature of the district, and both Strabo and Ptolemy refer to the importance it soon acquired. In the seventh century it somehow escaped the barbarian raids that sacked neighboring Salona. Before long, the newly arrived Croats colonized it, and with the erosion of the power of Constantinople between the ninth and 11th centuries, the Croatian kings granted Trogir municipal autonomy. After the death of King Zvonimir in 1089 the city developed rapidly under the Hungarian-Croat dynasties. In 1242 King Béla IV of Hungary, in flight from the Tartars, took refuge within its stout walls, and in gratitude for his escape confirmed it in all its rights and privileges. But Venice had long coveted Trogir and, in 1420, captured it after a desperate resistance. The Venetians remained until 1797, to be succeeded by the French under Napoleon's Marshal Marmont. This régime lasted until 1814, when the Congress of Vienna awarded Illyria to the Austrian Empire. Under Austrian rule it again rapidly declined and, when the

Austrian régime ended in 1918, Trogir had lived through 1,000 years of foreign occupation.

This almost forgotten city possesses however one claim to fame long recognized by classical scholars. In the 17th century the fragment of the Latin poet Petronius' *Satyricon* known as "Trimalchio's Feast" was discovered. The *Satyricon,* written in Nero's time, is an earthy, riotously funny satire dealing with Rome of the first century, and is now in the Paris Bibliothèque Nationale. Again, in 1928, a magnificent bas-relief of Kairos, the God of Opportunity (or Luck) was found, face down, on the kitchen floor of an old house. This dates from the first century B.C. and is on view in the Benedictine Convent of Trogir.

Exploring Trogir

Fortunately, cars are banned from the walled Dalmatian towns, so Trogir is entered on foot through the narrow Renaissance gate of St. Ivan. More picturesque still is the Porta Civitatis beside the little loggia (today the fish market) where, in former times, strangers had to wait until the City Magistrates had examined their papers. The gate itself is the same heavily nail-studded wooden one placed there 400 years ago. A few steps lead us to the main square, where the walls of the surrounding buildings have been weathered by the centuries; and there the Town Hall and its tower speak with the unmistakable accents of Venice and Florence. When long ago the open loggia was the center of the city's public life, it served alike as a Law Court, a provisional prison and as the site for public festivities. The Clock Tower was built by Donatello's brilliant pupil, Nicholas of Florence, in 1477. Trogir's oldest church is that of St. Barbara, dating from the ninth century and decorated in the now rarely found early Croat style.

Opposite the cathedral (of which more later) you will note the richly decorated Venetian Gothic façade of the 15th-century Cipiko Palace. On a little covered platform there is the painted wooden head of a cockerel, taken from a Turkish ship at the battle of Lepanto by Alviz Cipiko, commander of the Trogir squadron. Beside it is the wooden figurehead of the Goddess of Fortune, which ornamented Admiral Alviz's ship at the same battle.

Unquestionably the most remarkable building in Trogir is the 13th-century Cathedral of St. Lawrence. A Romanesque basilica with three naves, it is one of the most perfect examples of medieval architecture in the country. Enter by the Radovan portal, which is flanked by two lions surmounted by statues of Adam and Eve carved in 1240. The columns above bear representations of the apostles and various saints, and then there are carvings of animals and grotesques. The tympanum of the portal is decorated with the miracle of the Nativity, and while the outer side of the arch illustrates scenes from the New Testament, the inner illustrates the story of the Annunciation.

Probably the most remarkable part of the cathedral is the Chapel of St. John of Trogir, the masterpiece of Nicholas of Florence, built in 1480. The Sacristy contains a number of treasures, not the least among them being some of the works of the Venetian painter Bellini. Climb the clock tower for the view across the ancient roofs of the city, golden brown, but with the special patina of mellow old age.

Apart from St. Barbara and the cathedral, Trogir contains the 13th-century Romanesque Benedictine Abbey of St. John the Baptist, and a 14th-century Gothic Dominican church and convent, both housing notable art treasures. Domestic architecture is represented by the various palaces built by noble families in the Middle Ages, chief among them the Renaissance Lučić and Fanfogna palaces, both of which contain richly illustrated manuscripts. Lastly, the Kaštel-Kamerlengo fortress is a fine and well-preserved example of 15th-century military architecture from whence, in times of war, strong chains crossed to Čiovo and blocked the entrance to the harbor. A maritime power like Venice naturally preferred the familiar style of yet another island to the hazards of the mainland, thus Trogir extended across the wider channel to Čiovo. Čiovo features the fine 15th-century cloisters of Holy Cross Monastery.

Before abandoning Trogir, where the list of ancient buildings is necessarily rather formidable, we must just mention the temple-like gloriette built by Marmont during the Napoleonic occupation, which stands near the Venetian fort of Kamerlengo at the far end of the island.

The Kaštela Riviera

The *Jadranska Magistrala* follows a wide curve through the plain round the Bay of Split, but a narrower road hugs the coast for 16 km. (ten miles) through the Kaštela Riviera ("Castle Riviera"), so called after the seven castles built by the nobility of Trogir to guard their islands against the Turks.

The charm of the fine churches, with their campaniles set among vineyards and orchards, is threatened by Split's rapid industrial expansion and by the proximity of the airport. There are factories and ship-building yards on the side of the bay facing the Castle Riviera, but they do not seriously interfere with the region's peace.

On our way to Split we pass Solin, once the first-century Roman town of Salona. The original city was built by the Illyrians in the second century B.C., reaching its greatest importance after the Roman conquest in about 30 B.C., when it rapidly became a city of 60,000 inhabitants. Diocletian, the first of the great Illyrian commanders who tried to halt the barbarian incursions, was born nearby in about A.D. 245, son of a freedman. In 615 Salona was sacked by the Avars. Nevertheless, you may still see the ruins of its arena, public baths and immense Roman theater, also the foundations of many important early Christian churches.

Exploring Split

Split lies almost exactly halfway between Rijeka and Dubrovnik and is the official administrative capital of Dalmatia. It is rapidly becoming one of Yugoslavia's major industrial centers, with shipbuilding and cement works among its main industries. All this is spread around the remains of Diocletian's tremendous palace.

Diocletian became Emperor at the age of about 40, after a brilliant career as a soldier of Rome. His first task was to reorganize completely both the army and the civil administration, as a preliminary to undertaking the series of victorious campaigns which firmly reestablished even the remotest frontiers of the Empire. Though married to a Christian wife, he found it politically expedient to persecute the Christians.

Work on the palace was begun in A.D. 295 and it took ten years to complete. As soon as it was ready Diocletian abdicated, though still only 61, and spent the last eight years of his life in the peace of his native Dalmatia. His attempts to secure a stable succession failed, however.

After his death it was difficult to know how to make use of the great palace and it became successively a military camp, a market, and the shopping center of the city. The last reference to it in old chronicles relates how the Emperor Julius Nepos drove out these commercial tenants just before he himself was assassinated there in A.D. 480.

When Solin was sacked by the Avars in A.D. 615, such of the inhabitants as managed to escape fled first to the neighboring islands, and then when the raiders had gone, sought more permanent shelter within the walls of Diocletian's Palace, eventually building houses in the spacious courtyards, with any kind of material that came to hand. The Roman Palatium became medieval Spalato, and in 1918, the modern town of Split.

The enormous palace rectangle covers approximately 30,000 square yards. It is in a surprisingly good state of repair. In the 18th century it was visited by, and proved a potent influence upon, many artists and antiquarians, including the Scottish neo-Classicists John and Robert Adam.

The south front of the palace faces the sea, and it was here that the imperial apartments were placed so that for visitors arriving by sea, the first sight is of the outside of the main hall. The thickness of the walls

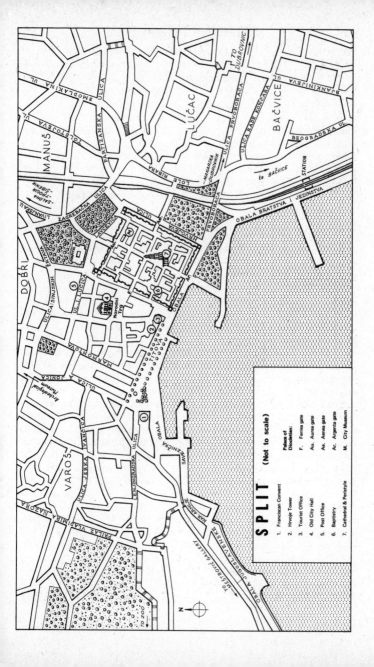

SPLIT (Not to scale)

1. Franciscan Convent
2. Hrvoje Tower
3. Tourist Office
4. Old City Hall
5. Post Office
6. Baptistry
7. Cathedral & Peristyle

Palace of Diocletian:
F.   Ferrea gate
Au. Aurea gate
Ae. Aenea gate
Ar. Argenta gate
M.   City Museum

makes it clear that the palace was originally designed to serve at all times as a fortified castle. Once inside the building you realize that you are looking at a military encampment. The east and west walls are each some 188 m. (618 ft.) long, the north wall measuring 150 m. (491 ft.), and the south some 155 m. (510 ft.). The four corners were capped with high square towers, of which three are still standing, and each of the four walls is pierced with a central gate. The largest of these is the Golden Gate (Porta Aurea), which faces Meštrović's statue of Bishop Gregory of Nin, defender against Rome of the Slavic Liturgy during the tenth century. The entrance through the western wall is the Iron Gate (Porta Ferrea), that through the south wall the Silver Gate (Porta Argenta), while the Bronze Gate (Porta Aenea) is in the east wall. The area is laid out somewhat after the model of a Roman military encampment.

The underground halls in the southern part of the palace, built as vast storerooms on ground sloping to the sea, now house exhibitions and souvenir shops. They correspond in plan to the upper halls, later destroyed.

The northern wing was the quarters of the Palace Guard, and also housed the permanent staff of 100s of slaves and servants needed to run the vast establishment. Medieval buildings flank one side of the central courtyard, or peristyle, but the original columns have been reerected on the other side. A stone stairway leads from here past a 3,500-year-old Egyptian sphinx of black granite to what was designed as the Emperor's grandiose mausoleum, but which was in the seventh century converted into the Cathedral of Our Lady, when it was encircled by a colonnade.

The interior of this building is circular, with square or semicircular niches designed to hold the illustrious dead. Massive granite pillars with Corinthian capitals carry the dome, with the added support of slender columns of red porphyry. Beyond these is the original antique frieze of an exceptional beauty.

The choir is a masterpiece of eighth-century Romanesque workmanship, and you should be sure not to miss the magnificent carved wooden reliefs in the main door. These were the work of the 13th-century Dalmatian sculptor Buvina, and depict scenes from the life of Christ. One of the best ways of appreciating the original plan and design of the palace is to climb to the belfry where, from a height of close on 182 m. (200 ft.), the great enterprise lies plainly revealed below.

In the seventh century the first Bishop of Spalato, John of Ravenna, converted the Jupiter Temple into the bapistry on the other side of the peristyle. Here you will find the mausoleum in the form of a square upon a raised foundation, with richly-decorated columns and door lintel. The vault crowning the hall of the vestibule of the palace displays an unusual 11th-century Croat relief.

Under the Venetians the humble refugee dwellings gave way to stately mansions, among which the Gothic-Renaissance Papalić Palace, which houses the Split Museum, is outstanding. This unique blend of antique and medieval splendor contains at present at least as many inhabitants as in the days of the palace's imperial glory; far from being artificially preserved, it pulsates with the intense life of the 20th century.

There are numerous humble little medieval churches dotted around the city, and the Franciscan Convent contains a superb Stations of the Cross. In the area surrounding the palace you will find much that is picturesque and surprisingly beautiful. The main square of Narodni Trg, with its Venetian Gothic Town Hall, now the Ethnographic Museum, stands immediately outside the palace limits, and a few yards beyond it is the octagonal Hrvoje Tower, once part of the 15th-century defenses. In the little square in front of it is a statue of the poet Marko Marulić by Meštrović.

So much sightseeing will probably make you thirsty and, after a full morning, you can do no better than visit the cafés temptingly placed on the promenade flanking the palace's southern wall.

There is a fine archeological museum on Tito Quay, near the palace, containing priceless records of Dalmatia's earliest days. There are Greek, Roman and early-Christian tiles, mosaics, ceramics and a numismatic collection.

Only a few kilometers inland is the supposedly indomitable fortress of Klis, for centuries a Turkish stronghold. From its towers you can look across open country all the way from Trogir in the north to beyond Split and the islands of Šolta and Brač.

30 km. (20 miles) inland, at Sinj, a great folklore festival known as *Akla* is held every year in early August in commemoration of the great victory in 1715 of a peasant army over a Turkish force of 60,000. The big moment is provided by a kind of equestrian tourney, the contest consisting of aiming a lance full tilt through a small ring. The men are dressed and the horses caparisoned in early 18th-century fashion, and the performance is exciting and colorful.

The Makarska Riviera

The *Magistrala* south from Split leads through the port of Omiš, at the mouth of the River Cetina, after which there is a road that follows the river upstream for six km. (four miles) through a tremendous gorge. Once a pirate lair, the bay is hidden between cliffs rising steeply to a height of nearly 300 m. (1,000 ft.), presided over by an old fortress. On the right bank, at Priko, stands the Old-Croat Church of St. Peter, and in the town itself are the Renaissance Church of the Holy Spirit and the Baroque parish church.

This region is popularly known as the Makarska Riviera, a coast of modest little fishing villages—some of which have burgeoned into holiday resorts—backed by thick pinewoods, olive groves and vineyards. The small coastal plain ends abruptly at the foot of the impressive Biokovo Mountains.

A pleasant detour may be made along a small road running inland from the village of Dubci, through Zadvarje, to the Cetina waterfall.

Back on the Makarska Riviera you will come first to Brela, and then to Baška Voda, bowered in pines, vines and figs; both are equipped with sizable hotels.

Makarska, since it gives its name to the district, is its "capital," and was once the favorite summer playground of the Croatian aristocracy, but today it is a very popular and bustling coastal base, owing to its gentle climate, 1½-km.-long (one-mile) pebble beach and its girdle of sweet-scented pines. Mountain climbers find the 1,745-m. (5,726-ft.) Sveti Jure a challenge—one of the many in the Biokovo range behind the town—but they are advised to start at dawn so as to reach the peak in time to spend the hottest hours of the day enjoying the view across the islands and coast. It is far too hot for climbing in summer after about 11 A.M.

However, Makarska does not appeal only to those anxious to escape from their offices or to the would-be alpinist. Many more come here to fish in the warmth of the Adriatic. Thus aquatically-favored, it comes as no surprise that the former Franciscan monastery has been converted into a Shell Museum. The fish available are unusually varied and plentiful.

The port, sheltered between two headlands, can be unpleasantly hot in high summer, but often a *maestral* rises to cool the midday hours. Four km. (2½ miles) farther south the Romanesque-Gothic Church of Tučepi is surrounded by olives and vineyards. There are large hotels along the pebble beach.

Podgora is picturesque but its beach is not big. A large monument here commemorates the founding of the Partisan Navy.

From here the appearance of the surrounding country changes abruptly to become no less beautiful, but far wilder and rougher. Fishing villages, clinging to the steep foothills of the Biokovo, like Igrane, Zaostrog and Živogošće, are exploiting their holiday potential. With magnificently sheltered water off their shores, these are delightful places in which to spend a quiet holiday. Excursions can be made to Mostar, Sarajevo and Split, and many other places of interest. After bypassing the large port of Kardeljevo (which is administered by the inland Republic of Bosnia-Herzegovina) the *Magistrala* crosses the River Neretva by way of a fine new bridge, skirts the town of Metković, and crosses the vast marshy estuary that is a fisherman's and wild-fowler's paradise. Various small villages border on the delta, and the people often use boats to travel around on the channels in the marsh. A railway runs inland from Kardeljevo to Sarajevo, Zagreb and Belgrade.

The Islands

The Central Dalmatian islands form a little world apart from the rest of the coast. Till the 1960s they were remote. It was not the remoteness alone, however, that made this quite palpable difference. Korčula and Hvar always were, and still are, ports-of-call for long-distance ships sailing the coast. Some aspects of attachment to the sea rather than to the land have given the islands a distinctive atmosphere, which they still keep intact—although now linked by many regular services to the mainland, or the subject of numerous day trips. To spend a few days in Korčula or Hvar or the even more distant town of Vis is to experience to the full the extraordinary tranquility of this coast. Even Orebić, the charming small resort on the peninsula of Pelješac opposite Korčula town, exudes the same feeling of peace. Though Pelješac is actually part of the mainland, it is so long and narrow that you feel detached, as if on an island.

Orebić is something of a rarity on the coast: it is one of the very few places where you can see a sizable number of middle-class houses from past centuries. It was, in fact, the chosen home of large numbers of sea captains till steam put sail out of business, and we will return to it after we have described the islands.

Šolta, Brač, Vis and Biševo

Opposite the Bay of Split lies the island of Šolta, famous for its wines, and to the south its far larger and much more visited neighbor of Brač. The quarries on Brač were once renowned throughout Europe. Marble from here has been provided for buildings as varied and famous as Diocletian's Palace at Split, the White House in Washington and the United Nations Building in New York, as well as for the construction of many local towns. Brač is touristically developed, but Šolta, despite the Illyrian, Roman and Venetian miscellanea in vineyards and olive groves, is still relatively unvisited.

Remote though it is, Vis has witnessed events which have profoundly affected the destiny of the whole of the Dalmatian coast, notably a naval battle between British and French squadrons in 1811, and another between Austrian and Italian fleets in 1866. During World War II the island of Vis was for a time partisan headquarters, and a staging-post through which British and American ships supplied Marshal Tito's forces with the material to carry on their struggle in the interior of the country.

The "capital" town of Vis is dominated by its 19th-century Austrian fortifications above the Convent of the Little Brothers and the dignified Delupis Palace. At the opposite end of the island is the charming little fishing village of Komiza.

Today Vis is a military area and you need a written permit to visit it. Such a visit should be combined with the rocky, cave-filled islet of Biševo, less than eight km. (five miles) south—a miniature Capri, with its own, still more colorful Blue Grotto. An overnight stop on this faraway island involves staying in a private house as there are no hotels.

Hvar

Hvar—the ancient Greek *pharos,* or lighthouse, of which there is today no trace—is also the name of the "capital" near the island's western tip. Hvar conforms to the general shape of these islands, long and narrow; it has been inhabited since the dawn of time, even before its primitive Neolithic settlement. It was a Greek merchant colony that founded Pharos in the fourth century B.C., while Romans, Illyrians, Croats and Austrians were successively its masters.

The little town lies at the heart of a bay backed by a ring of green hills and protected from the open sea by a scatter of small islets known as Pakleni Otoci—meaning the Tar Isles or the Accursed Isles. Far above its red tiles tower the 16th-century Španjola and 18th-century Sveti Nikola fortresses. There is also a third belonging to the period of the Napoleonic occupation.

Both islands and mainland of this region are as picturesque as anything to be seen on the Dalmatian coast, but Hvar itself is perhaps the most perfect of all. Rosemary, lavender and laurel surround the pale stone houses, which rising from the margin of the intensely blue water, combine to produce one of those rare moments of visual delight that stay in the mind for ever.

The architecture of Hvar is unmistakably Venetian in inspiration, the effect wholly Mediterranean. The city was largely destroyed by the Turks in 1571, so that most of its principal buildings are of late 16th- or early 17th-century construction, notably the Renaissance cathedral with its attractive campanile. The Arsenal built in 1612 encloses one of the oldest theaters in Europe, still in use, although mainly for concerts.

There is a Loggia designed by the Veronese Sammicheli, and not far away a Franciscan Convent which faces on to the bay and contains many art treasures, including works by Titian, Tiepolo and Bassano.

Hvar still has its 13th-century walls, and there is, besides, an impressive Spanish fort. There is a seeming multitude of magnificent old palaces to explore, still displaying the armorial bearings of their former chatelains. The town that has grown up outside the walls does not lack for either charm or color. There is a leafy avenue which leads past an old monastery garden to the large bathing beach.

Because of its beneficent climate Hvar has earned the nickname "Madeira of the Adriatic." There are many delightful places within easy bus-excursion distance of the old town, such as Stari Grad (famous for its medieval castle and 14th-century Church of St. Stephen), Jelsa, another charming coastal village, and Vrboska, which has a fine fortified church, and a baroque church also, which has remarkable paintings, including some by Veronese and Bassano. We would recommend any visitor to Hvar to take a boat across to the tiny island of Sv. Kliment (St. Clement), specifically to the bay of Palmizana where there is an extraordinary collection of tropical plants gathered from the Far East and South America. There is a splendid beach here, and a naturist bathing-establishment on an island opposite the town of Hvar. But don't forget that Hvar is yet another center of modern mass tourism with the drawbacks that such developments bring.

Korčula

Korčula is the last island port called at by most coastal steamers before Dubrovnik, and is situated due south of Hvar. The island has been continuously occupied since prehistoric times, largely because the thick woods that covered it provided the raw material for shipbuilding. Greeks from Cnidos settled here, as is proved by an inscription dating from the fourth century B.C., calling it Korkyra Melaina (Corcyra the Black) in allusion to its dark forests, and to distinguish it from the better-known island they called Korkyra, now Corfu.

The "capital" is situated on a headland which commands the strait that separates Korčula from Pelješac and is set within still-formidable defensive walls. It is one of the most picturesque towns of any on the entire Dalmatian coast. Crooked and narrow medieval streets open out suddenly into little squares where nobles' palaces glow golden-brown in the sun. The layout of these streets is specially fascinating. They form a sort of herring-bone pattern on either side of the main street-central axis, but the streets are offset from each other to prevent the north and south winds that blow up and down the strait from whistling unimpeded through the town. When the plan was devised we have no idea, except that the very fully-preserved medieval town records make no mention of any rebuilding. A Greek inscription of the fourth century B.C. makes reference to Korčula as a "stone town." It is at least possible that Korčula's layout is another example of the Ancient Greeks' town-planning skill.

One of the palaces may have been the birthplace of Marco Polo, who commanded a Venetian fleet of ten galleys which fought a battle against the Genoese within sight of Korčula in 1298. He was beaten and taken prisoner, together with the Doge of Venice, Andrea Dandolo. Once he had regained his liberty, Marco set out on his travels across a still-unknown world. Polos still live on the island, and one of the old palaces is debatably known as Marco Polo's house.

Korčula's 14th- to 16th-century Cathedral of St. Mark is an interesting example of the transition from the Romanesque to the Gothic style of architecture. Its greatest treasures are one possible and one definite Tintoretto and a Bassano. In addition, there is a beautifully-carved stone door, the work of a wandering French artist, Antoine de Vienne (about 1500). Near the cathedral, the 11th–12th-century Church of St. Peter (Sv. Petar) has a collection of baroque wooden statues of the Apostles.

Among other notable churches in Korčula, All Saints is remarkable for its collection of 14th–17th-century Greek icons brought back after the Candia war in the 17th century.

There are also the 17th-century Triumphal Arch by the 16th-century Town Hall (still in use), a quayside loggia, the old fortifications, any number of narrow streets between lovely stone-built houses. There are fine views across the strait of Pelješac. Of two small museums in the little square where the cathedral stands, one has a collection of church treasures, housed in the Bishops' Palace, and the other, the Town Museum, contains local relics.

It is hardly surprising to find that the island, with so long and remarkable a history, has kept alive many ancestral customs and costumes. One of the most colorful of these is the procession by three religious brotherhoods which takes place every Good Friday.

But the Good Friday procession is by no means the only traditional manifestation that you will find in Korčula. There is the symbolic sword dance of the *Moreška,* originally held on 27th July, and now every Thursday in summer—the Korčulani in dance and mime recall the incidents of a great battle between the kings of the Moors and the Sultan of Turkey for possession of a beautiful princess. The dancers wear magnificently colorful costumes and are armed, each with two swords. One represents attack, and the other defense. Though nothing certain is known of its origins, it is supposed that the Moreška was introduced into their folklore early in the Middle Ages by sailors returning from Spain. Another similar, though less colorful, event is the *Kumpanija,* the commemoration of the island's successful defeat of a pirate raid, which takes place in Blato every 23rd of April.

A popular excursion from Korčula is to cross to the islet of Vrnik, less than 3½ km. (two miles) away, where the Romans built an important stone quarry still in use today, from the highest point of which you can see no less than 12 neighboring islands, on one of which there are ruins of an ancient monastery.

Korčula island possesses several first-rate bathing beaches, one of them near the village of Vela Luka at the western tip of the island, where the deep bay provides excellent fishing and curative baths as well. Another attractive little fishing-village on the island is Lumbarda, where there is one of the finest sand beaches to be found in the entire length and breadth of the Yugoslav Adriatic. It also produces the potent amber-colored *Grk* wine. The fishermen of Korčula occasionally take out tourists who wish to join an expedition into deep waters.

From Korčula you can also visit the glorious island of Mljet, described in the next chapter.

Pelješac

Separated from Korčula by a narrow channel, Pelješac possesses all the climatic and geographic characteristics of a Dalmatian island. A branch of the *Magistrala* runs the entire length of the peninsula through most of the 40 villages. Increasingly popular are the bathing resorts of Orebić and, 15 minutes away, facing Kardeljevo on the mainland, Trpanj. Both have pleasant beaches in attractive settings. In addition, Orebić has an entertaining small Marine Museum. Some of the houses in the village date back to the 15th century, and the little streets are worth exploring. If you want to see what a middle-class sea captain thought was a fine house in the 19th century, the one belonging to the Maritime Museum's Director, Matko Zupa, is well worth visiting. It has been in his family for generations. The backbone of the peninsula is formed by a rocky mountain range which rises to well over 915 m. (3,000 ft.). Enthusiasts tackle the steep climb very early in the morning to watch dawn rise over Dalmatia and to refresh themselves afterwards with the famous *Dingač* wine, produced at Potomje some 20 km. (about 12 miles) away. Other expeditions can be made by motorboat. Many people like the way in which Orebić combines all the charms of Dalmatia (including a magnificent view across the sea to the lovely medieval town of Korčula, and entertaining excursions) with almost perfect peace. The hotels have been beautifully placed on the beach so as not to interfere with or even to be visible from the old village.

Lastovo Island, just south of Korčula, is a sleepy little place, center of a small independent archipelago visited chiefly for its fishing. There are no hotels in the two small villages of Ubli and the "capital," Lastovo.

Practical Information for Central Dalmatia

WHEN TO GO. The Dalmatian season now lasts throughout the year. Winters are mild, though rainy, summers rarely unpleasantly hot. The heat is kept within limits by a light sea breeze known as the *maestral*.

In high season, from May until October, regattas are held at many places on the coast. Performances of folk music and dances are also organized.

From mid-July to mid-August the Split Summer Festival of drama, concerts, opera and ballet takes place; it is preceded by a Festival of Light Music called "Melodies from the Adriatic Shores" early in July. From late June to early July, Šibenik hosts the Yugoslav Festival for Children, while in July and August concerts are held in Zadar's St. Donat church.

On 27 July and each Thursday from April through September, the *Moreška* is danced in Korčula town. It is an extremely spectacular mimed sword dance. On the first Sunday in August, the "Sinjska Alka," an equestrian festival commemorating a battle against the Turks in 1715, is held in Sinj.

HOTELS AND RESTAURANTS. This is one of the major tourist regions of Yugoslavia, with a great concentration of hotels and some of the country's better restaurants. Demand in season is, of course, great, and you will find that booking in advance is wise.

Food and Drink. Fish and all shellfish are plentiful in Dalmatia, and there is a fish soup called *brodet.* As an hors d'oeuvre try *dalmatinski pršut,* which is a delicious smoked ham, or the unbeautiful, but delicious fried ink-fish *(lignji).* Local restaurants are at their best preparing a mixed grill of fish known as *ribe pržene na ulju.* We recommend red mullet *(barbuni),* mackerel *(skuše),* Dalmatian lobster *(jastog)* is simply plain cold-boiled, as is the crayfish *(rak).* Try cheese after dinner: Primorški sir, Krčki sir or Paški sir.

Do not overlook the wines of the district, most of which are bottled commercially. The largest vintners are Dalmacijavino, with headquarters in Split. There are no vintage years, but expert supervision ensures that wines from the big firms maintain the same character and quality each year. Dalmacijavino's best red wines include *Postup, Plavac* (which has a unique bluish tinge) and cheapest of all, *Crno Vino* (Black Wine). *Dingač* is a heavy red wine from the Pelješac Peninsula, though the name is applied fairly indiscriminately to any heavy red wine. The most popular white wine is *Grk,* from Korčula. Lighter white wines include *Pošip* and *Vugava*. A rosé *(ružica)* is also available. A popular dessert wine is *Prošek*, though knowledgeable visitors prefer *Maraština*, an excellent local dessert wine, which many Yugoslavs seem not to know.

ZADAR AND NEARBY ISLANDS

BIOGRAD NA MORU. Season Apr.–Oct. *Adriatic* (M), 110 rooms, and *Ilirija* (M), 180 rooms, stand side-by-side in a seaside park in the town. *Crvena Luka* (M), 240 rooms. Tourist settlement three km. (two miles) to the south. *Kornati* (M), 88 rooms. *Motel Biograd* (M), 52 rooms. On the highway, 800 m. (half mile) from the sea. Open all year.

BOŽAVA (Dugi Otok Island). Season May–Oct. *Božava* (M), 122 rooms. *Palma* (M), with annexes. *Agava* (I). *Mirta* (I), 100 rooms, some with shower.

FILIP JAKOV (south of Zadar). Season May–Oct. *Mayica* (I), 76 rooms, 60 with bath.

IŽ VELI. Fishing village on Island of Iž; season Jun.–Sept. *Korinjak* (I), 78 rooms, none with shower. Simple.

LUKA (Dugi Otok Island). Season Jun.–Sept. *Luka* (I), 62 rooms, none with shower. Basic facilities.

NOVALJA (Pag Island). *Liburnija* (M), 136 rooms. *Loža* (M), 41 rooms. Also private house accommodations.

NOVIGRAD (near Zadar). Tiny town on Novigrad "inland" sea. *Mediteran* (I), 50 rooms. Simple.

PAG (Pag Island). Apr.–Oct. *Bellevue* (M), 166 rooms.

PETRČANE (13 km./eight miles northwest of Zadar). *Pinija* (M), 302 rooms, 5 apartments. Private beach on wooded promontory. Bowling. *Punta Skala Tourist Settlement* (M), 665 rooms.

PRIMOŠTEN. *Adriatic-Slav* (E), 161 rooms. Pool. *Adriatic-Zora* (E), 145 rooms. Also with pool. *Adriatic-Raduča* (M), 90 rooms. On wooded peninsula near picturesque fishing village.
Restaurant. *Villa Fenč,* in Old Primošten, is recommended for fish.

SALI (Dugi Otok Island). Season Jun.–Sept. *Alga* (I) and annexes, 48 rooms, none with shower. Simple.

ŠIBENIK. Naval base (be careful what you photograph!) and skindiving center. *Ivan* (E), 355 rooms, is best.

Andrija (M), 469 rooms, *Jure* (M), 248 rooms, and *Niko* (M), 223 rooms, are all in the *Solaris* group, about five km. (three miles) out of town, which also provides a therapeutic and recreation center. *Motel Medveščak* (M), on the coastal highway six km. (four miles) north of the town, at River Krka bridge, is a reliable overnight stop. *Jadran* (I), 48 rooms.

STARIGRAD-PAKLENICA. Near Paklenica National Park, on slopes of gaunt Velebit Mountains. *Alan* (M), 217 rooms.

VODICE. *Olympia* (E), 261 rooms. In pine forest on beach, with pool. *Gloriette* (M), 24 family villas. *Punta* (M), 132 rooms. Own beach.

ZADAR. The best choice is found on the Borik peninsula on the far side of the harbor from the old town. *Barbara* (E), 178 rooms. The best. Almost as good are *Adriana* (M), 99 rooms; *New Park* (M), 186 rooms; *Slavija* (M), 127 rooms; and *Zadar* (M), 76 rooms. *Donat* (I), 48 rooms, some with shower.

In town: *Kovolare* (M), 252 rooms, beach; and *Zagreb* (M), 90 rooms, 63 with private bath.

Restaurants. There are a number of pleasant eating houses overlooking the harbor, and also in the old town.

SPLIT AND NEARBY COASTAL REGIONS

BAŠKA VODA. Bathing resort north of Makarska. *Horizont* (E), 200 rooms. *Dubravka* (M), 45 rooms. *Slavija* (M), 52 rooms, some with shower.

BRELA. Seaside village with a long beach backed by woods. *Maestral* (E), 68 rooms, with annexes. The two *Berulia* (M) hotels have 200 rooms; on private beach. *Mirna* and *Marina* both (M), 148 rooms; tennis. *Pelegrin* (M), 23 rooms.

GRADAC. Good beach. *Laguna* (M), 115 rooms in chalets. Own beach. *Pavilions* (M), 170 rooms. Also own beach.

IGRANE. Season Apr.–Oct. *Igrane* (M), 32 rooms. Pleasant.

KARDELJEVO (PLOČE). *Ploča* (I), 46 rooms.

KAStEL ŠTAFILIĆ. On the "Seven Castles" coast near Split; season May–Oct. *Resnik* (M), 229 rooms. Own beach. Near Split Airport.

KASTEL STARI. Another of the "Seven Castles"; season May–Oct. *Palace* (M), 232 rooms. Traditional-style; with pool.

MAKARSKA. *Dalmacija* (M), 200 rooms. Highrise hotel with pool. *Riviera* (M), 265 rooms in small units. *Beograd* (I), 46 rooms. *Motel Kuk* (I), 18 rooms. Just north of town. *Osejava* (I), 44 rooms, some with shower. *Park* (I), 70 rooms.

NEUM. *Neum* (E), 240 rooms. Pool.

OMIŠ. Season May–Oct. *Brzet* (I), 85 rooms. Just south of the town. *Plaža* (I), 35 rooms, none with shower. Adjoins the sandy public beach in the town. At **Ruskamen,** on the coast six km. (four miles) south, *Ruskamen* (M), 171 rooms.

Restaurant. Pleasant excursions from both Omiš and Ruskamen up the Cetina gorge lead to the old mill-restaurant at *Radmanove Mlinice.*

PODGORA. Pleasant old port and modern summer resort; season Apr.–Oct. *Minerva* (E), 169 rooms. Private beach, heated pool. *Aurora* (M), 149 rooms. On a promontory. Again, private beach and heated pool; airconditioning. *Mediteran* (M), 131 rooms. *Podgorka* (M), 142 rooms, with annex *Lovor* (M). *Primordia* (I) and annex, also (I), have a few showers. However, smaller than Podgorka.

SPLIT. *Lav* (E), 469 rooms. With casino, pool, beach. In quiet wooded bay a few kilometers out of the town on the road to Makarska. Highly recommended. *Marjan* (E), 331 rooms. Casino, indoor and outdoor seawater swimming pools on the roof terrace. On the seafront but rather noisy. *Bellevue* (M), 50 rooms. With garden-restaurant. Central. *Park* (M), 60 rooms. Also with garden-restaurant; music in the evenings. Above the Bay of Bačvice. *Central* (I), 40 rooms, some with shower.

Just over 1½ km. (one mile) outside the city, at **Trstenik,** *Split Pavilions* (M), 339 rooms. With private beach and garages. Three km. (two miles) farther south on the sea at **Duilovo** is the *Inex* (M), 237 rooms, 20 chalets.

Restaurants. As usual, all the hotels have restaurants, but we suggest that you explore the following: *Dioklecijan* (on shipboard, alongside main quay); *Marjan,* Marmontova St.; *Sarajevo* (for Bosnian specialties), Domald St.; and *Vidilica,* on Marjan hill north of the town and harbor, with fine views.

Nightlife is catered for at the clubs within the *Lav, Marjan,* and *Park* hotels; also the *Dalmacija* wine cellar; and the *Dioklecijan* restaurant (see above).

TROGIR. Superb little medieval town. 800 meters (half-a-mile) north, on the coastal highway, is *Motel Trogir* (M), 52 rooms, all with bath. 1½ kilometers (one mile) farther on is *Jadran* (M), 152 rooms, all with bath; also *Medena* (M), 663 rooms, pool, and *Medena Apartments* (M), 261 rooms.

TUČEPI. *Alga* (M), 350 rooms. *Jadran* (M), 159 rooms, most with bath. Annexes *Tamaris* (M), 16 rooms, and *Kaštelet* (M), 40 rooms, are modernized older buildings. Located on a fine beach at the foot of beautiful mountains.

Neptun (M) and annex *Maslinik* (M) have 300 rooms between them, all with bath.

ZAOSTROG. *Dalmacija* (M), 56 rooms. Own beach.

ŽIVOGOŠĆE. *Nimfa* (M), 355 rooms. Private beach, heated pool.

THE MAIN ISLANDS
Brač

BOL. Season Apr.– Oct. *Elaphusa* (E), 350 rooms. Pool, pavilion annex. *Bijela Kuća* (M), with dependencies, 200 rooms. All with own beach. *Borak* (M), 148 rooms. *Kastil* (M), 33 rooms.

POSTIRA. *Park* (I), 20 rooms, though old, has modern annexes (M), 40 rooms. *Vrilo* (M), 21 rooms.

POVLJA. Small but picturesque village notable for the skindiving off its coast; season May–Oct. *Galeb* (M), 65 rooms, annex, 130 rooms, half with bath.

SUPETAR. Capital of the island, surrounded by vineyards; season May–Oct. *Kaktus* (E), 118 rooms. Tourist settlements *Palma* (M), 296 rooms; *Tamaris* (M), 27 rooms; and *Vidora Gora* (M), 15 rooms. Also 1,500 private rooms.

Hvar

HVAR. The island's delightful capital. *Adriatic* (E), 63 rooms. Pool. *Amfora* (E), 380 rooms. The outstanding hotel, yet no more pricey than its (E) rivals, even though it can boast an olympic pool and is set on its own beach. *Palace* (E), 75 rooms. Pool. *Bodul* (M), 150 rooms. *Dalmacija* (M), 70 rooms. *Delfin* (M), 55 rooms. *Galeb* (M), 34 rooms. *Pharos* (M), 176 rooms. *Sirena* (M), 150 rooms. Pool.
Restaurants. There are a number of small places specializing in seafood.

JELSA. Charming small port; season Apr.–Oct. *Fontana* (M), 198 rooms. Tourist settlement. *Jadran* (M), 135 rooms, most with shower. *Mina* (M), 208 rooms. Pool. All with own beach.

Korčula

KORČULA. Lovely capital of the island of the same name. *Bon Repos* (M), 329 rooms. On the shore about one km. (half-a-mile) on from Park and Marko Polo hotels (see below). *Korčula* (M), 26 rooms. This renovated hotel is the only one in the old town. Good value. *Marko Polo* (M), 110 rooms. Pool, own bathing area. A short stroll away along the waterfront from Korčula hotel. *Park* (M),

275 rooms. Like Marko Polo, which it is next to, with own bathing area. A new hotel adjacent to Park is scheduled to open in 1984.

Restaurants. All moderately priced are *Adio Mare, Gradski podrum* in the old town, *Mornar* near the waterfront, and just outside the walls, *Planjak.* There is also a disco.

LUMBARDA. Quiet coastal village a few kilometers from Korčula; season Apr.–Oct. *Lumbarda* (M), with nearby annexes *Borik* and *Lovor,* is excellent if you want the quiet life.

VELA LUKA. Charming coastal village in island's north. *Poseidon* (M), 182 rooms. Beach, pool. *Jadran* (M), 61 rooms, with annex *Dalmacija* (M), 27 rooms, *Korkyra* (M), 68 rooms.

Restaurant. *Sunce* can be recommended for its pleasant atmosphere.

Pelješac Peninsula

OREBIČ. Season Apr.–Oct. *Bellevue* (M), 118 rooms. *Orsan* (M), 106 rooms. *Rathaneum* and annex (M), 152 rooms. Private accommodations to rent in nearby Trstenica.

Šolta

MASLINICA. Season May–Oct. *Avlija* (I), 47 rooms. Baroque manor in small fishing village. Full board only.

NEČUJAM. On a lovely bay, renowned for skindiving and fishing; season May–Oct. *Ružmarin* (M), 39 rooms. *Marko Marulić* (I), 21 rooms, none with shower.

STOMORSKA. May–Oct. *Olint* (I), 21 rooms, none with shower.

Trpanj

TRPANJ. On Pelješac's east coast opposite Kardeljevo. *Faraon* (M), 123 rooms.

 HOW TO GET AROUND. To visit the entire coast of Central Dalmatia presents no great problem, thanks to the scenic, if narrow and crowded, Adriatic Coastal Road. However, to visit anything like all the islands by boat would take a long time, but after all most people go to the coast to enjoy themselves on the beach. Perhaps the best solution is to settle in the coastal resort of your choice, and then make a few excursions to one or two of the islands.

Most of the fast coastal vessels, operating from Rijeka, make a call at Split. Some also stop at Korčula and/or Hvar. Regular car-and-passenger ferries operate from Zadar, Split, and several other coastal centers to all the main islands. Pag and Vir are connected to the mainland by bridges. There are also hydrofoil services from Split, and from Split Airport (near Trogir) to a number of the islands during the summer.

Split is a major road and rail center, about halfway between Trieste and Titograd—there are speedy services to Zagreb, Belgrade and other points inland.

The airport at Split handles many international as well as domestic routes, with links to Rome, London, etc., as well as Zagreb, Belgrade, Dubrovnik, and other destinations within Yugoslavia.

 WHAT TO SEE. The Dalmatian coast has not only dozens of first-class seaside resorts, but also many historic towns and buildings. The bustling city of Split sprawls round the walls of the monumental palace built by the Roman Emperor Diocletian. Trogir is a small, unspoiled, medieval city of great beauty and interest. The historic city of Zadar contains Roman and medieval remains, and priceless examples of the art of medieval gold- and silversmiths, while in Šibenik there is of course the splendid cathedral. In addition, there are scores of ancient little towns on the islands where Venice has left her unmistakable artistic and architectural imprint, notably Korčula and Hvar. A special charm is added to the coast and islands everywhere by the peasant costumes, songs and dances you can still see in more remote areas.

Among the beach resorts there are many for those who do not mind crowds. People who like peace and quiet when on holiday should try the islands of Lopud, Brač or Šolta, or the Pelješac peninsula; the coast and islands however are full of unexpected little places that recall the splendid past of this region.

Curiosities of nature are plentiful. For example, the Blue Grotto of Biševo, though smaller, equals (if not actually surpasses) that of Capri in the brilliance of its color.

 SPORTS. Water sports of all kinds are popular along the Dalmatian coast—facilities for water skiing and, increasingly, wind surfing exist in the larger resorts. It would take too much space to list all the beaches of the mainland and islands, but those on Hvar (the Bay of Palmižan) and the island of Brač (Milna and Bol) are justly famous. A number of secluded beaches are reserved for nudist bathing.

In most places the shore is stony or pebbly, but in many resorts cement platforms have been built, which are excellent for both swimming and sunbathing. Quite a few hotels have swimming pools, and these avoid the Adriatic's only real snag—the sea urchins that swarm in still water. In Zadar specifically there is the Olympic pool, while about five km. (three miles) outside the town several good beaches are to be found on the Borik Peninsula. These can be reached speedily by taking a motorboat across the harbor mouth. There are other beaches to the south of Zadar.

Local and international regattas take place during the season at Split, Zadar and numerous other venues of less importance. Sail and auxiliary motorboats can be hired from a number of resorts—enquiries should be made at local tourist offices or travel firms.

Water polo is a traditional sport in Dalmatia.

FISHING. Because of the deeply-indented coastline, and the large number of islands, this part of the Adriatic is particularly interesting to fishermen, and only a meter or two down you can see beautiful shells, giant sponges and strangely shaped coral, where shoals of fish dart to and fro. In the less frequented places fishing becomes quite an adventure.

Some travel firms organize fishing trips, veritable expeditions lasting one or several days. These trips usually take place in the Kornat archipelago, and are for 20–30 persons at the time. Fishingboats, sailboats or motorboats—you can take your pick. All the necessary equipment is provided and an expert goes along to direct the uninitiated. Smaller boats, carrying about 6–14 people, are also available. There is sometimes also a special restaurant boat—if you can tear yourself away from rod and line. All kinds of fish are to be found for underwater sport, whether with snare, net, spear or line.

However, such excursions are for the real enthusiast; most people prefer to settle in the place of their choice, either beach resort or village, and do their fishing from there. In that case you have to go to the local travel firms or tourist office, and obtain a permit for underwater or ordinary fishing. You should also make certain that you know about local restrictions, such as forbidden areas and the like. Local tourist offices can often arrange trips with the fishermen of the area.

Game fish are caught at the mouths of rivers Neretva, Krka and Cetina, also in Lake Vrana.

MUSEUMS. In Zadar. The Art Gallery houses paintings and sculpture, including some good modern work.

The Ethnographic Museum features some lovely examples of the folk art of northern Dalmatia.

The Historical and Archeological Museum on Tito Wharf is the home of regional antiquities: prehistoric, Roman, and "old Croatian" objects. Open 10 to noon and 7 to 9 in the evening.

The Treasure of St. Francis comprises precious musical scores of Gregorian chants.

The Treasure of St. Simon is a unique shrine, with magnificent examples of medieval gold and silver craftsmanship of Zadar.

In Split

The **Archeological Museum** has a fine collection of Roman antiquities that were discovered at Solin. Closed Mon.

The **City Museum** (Papalić Palace) concentrates on statues, coins, and works of art. Closed Mon.

The **Croat Antiquities Museum** displays objects from the Slav pagan period onward.

The **Ethnographic Museum** is for folk art, costumes, embroideries, tools and weapons.

The **Fine Arts Gallery** has plaster casts and sculptures from classical times to the present.

The **Meštrović Gallery** contains more than 200 sculptures by the eponymous artist. In a nearby castle (Kaštelet) is a collection of Meštrović's woodcarvings.

SHOPPING. Visitors to Dalmatia will find plenty of interesting and original things to buy. As it is the most popular area for tourists in Yugoslavia, shops in the larger towns are out to attract customers with handicraft, particularly locally made, and pottery. Lace has been a great specialty of the island of Pag for centuries. However, you will find not only locally made articles, but also many items produced in other regions, such as the coffee grinders and Turkish coffee sets of Bosnia. Leather suitcases, even if somewhat more expensive than a few years ago, remain popular with buyers because of their beautiful finish and still reasonable price. The great Maraska distilleries at Zadar provide a vast and inexpensive choice of liqueurs in decorative bottles, the best probably being the *maraska* (or *maraschino*), which is named after the distillery, the famous plum brandy, *šlivovica,* and the potent local *lozovača.*

USEFUL ADDRESSES. Dalmacijaturist, Titova Obala 5, Split, and other travel firms organize excursions to Trogir, ancient Salona, and to the various islands of Central Dalmatia. They also supply official guides for visits to Diocletian's Palace, etc.

SOUTHERN DALMATIA AND
THE MONTENEGRIN COAST

The World of Dubrovnik

Three features dominate the southernmost stretch of the coast, the ancient but still unspoilt little city of Dubrovnik, the majestic Gulf of Kotor, which carries the sea into the middle of towering mountains, and the final section of coast, part, like Kotor, of the Republic of Montenegro, wild to begin with but subsiding into the longest stretch of sandy shore in all Yugoslavia.

It is hard to decide which among these three areas has the greatest scenic attraction, but if we take architectural criteria into account as well, then Dubrovnik is preeminent—the most striking point of the entire coast, and outstanding not only by Yugoslavian standards but also in comparison with any town and its environs in the whole of Europe.

The city was laid out after a strict geometric plan, but the impression of this classical rigidity is softened by the predominance of Renaissance buildings. The extraordinary harmony of the whole, which unfailingly strikes the visitor, is due partly to the white marble of which the entire town is built, and partly to its homogeneous architecture. The result is that Dubrovnik is still today wholly medieval, and the walls which were unbreached for 1,000 years remain unchanged and intact.

Early in the seventh century, Slav tribesmen sacked the once-Greek, and later Roman town of Epidaurus, which the small town today called Cavtat now occupies. The surviving citizens of Epidaurus fled north to build a new city below the slopes of Mount Srd which dominated a small rocky island. Strong walls were built, and as it grew in importance the town was called successively Lavva, Lausa, Raugium, Ragusium and Ragusa.

On the mainland opposite the island, a Slav settlement called Dubrovnik grew up on the fringe of the oak forests— *dubrava* meaning "oak woods." By the 12th century the narrow creek which separated the two towns was filled up, so that Ragusa and Dubrovnik became one, and in 1205 the united town threw off the overlordship of Byzantium and recognized Venice as the paramount Dalmatian power.

The chief citizen was the Rector, elected each month, who shared the management of the city's business with the Grand Council and the Senate. Most of the military and naval commands were held by members of the nobility (of Roman or Byzantine origin) while the increasingly prosperous middle-class were mostly Slavs. At first Latin was the official language, but the use of Croat soon became general.

The rulers of the Republic were primarily concerned with the promotion of maritime business (the word "argosy," by the way, being a corruption of Ragusa), and the laws governing the citizens were unusually liberal for the period. By the use of farsighted diplomacy Ragusa gradually rose to become one of the greatest maritime and commercial ports of the Mediterranean, with a fleet of as many as 2,000 ships.

After the defeat of Venice in 1358 Dubrovnik decided to place herself under the protection of the Hungarian-Croatian kings, but when the Turks overran Hungary the city sought the protection of the Sultan, paying him a yearly tribute. Later the aid of Spain and the Holy Roman Empire was enlisted for the same purpose, namely to ensure the continued independence of the city.

The conduct of the Republic may strike us as Machiavellian, but it was successful in enabling the city to develop rapidly and to extend its influence to the mouth of the River Neretva in the north and to the Bay of Kotor in the south. Consistent with its policy of deserting its overlords as soon as their power began to decline, Ragusa followed the Turkish defeat in central Europe in 1684 by associating itself with the Habsburgs. So by means of cunning diplomacy and opportunism unceasingly exercised, Dubrovnik remained mistress of her own destiny.

However, toward the end of the 17th century the decline began, and in the same way as her great rival Venice, Dubrovnik was occupied by foreign troops for the first time in her history. In 1808 Napoleon's General Marmont decreed the end of the Republic. When he in turn had surrendered to a couple of Austrian battalions, the Congress of Vienna awarded the city to Austria, and it remained a Habsburg possession until 1918.

Despite the passing of so many centuries, the memory of the greatest days of Ragusa-Dubrovnik is evident in the matchless beauty of its buildings and its liberal institutions, and in the cultural preeminence of its citizens. As early as 1347 Ragusa possessed a Home for the Aged, and the slave traffic was abolished in 1416—more than four centuries before many of the more "advanced" Western nations. Torture was prohibited in the 15th century, and there were a number of endowed schools which offered to all an education far in advance of the general standards of the time.

Peter Bošković made an excellent translation of the works of Molière and Corneille, and while in Paris, was an intimate of the Encyclopedists. His brother Roger became a distinguished astronomer and mathematician, living for many years in London and being elected a member of the Royal Society. Still, even before the time of these distinguished intellectuals, Ragusa had a copious literature of its own, from the 15th century. This was written in Latin to begin with, but soon replaced by "Ragusian Slav"—a language in use until the beginning of the last century, at a time when the Illyrian Movement for the union of the southern Slavs was striving to awake national consciousness of their great historical heritage.

Southward to Dubrovnik

It takes some two hours by boat from Korčula, and rather less than an hour from Trstenik on the Pelješac peninsula to reach the thickly wooded island of Mljet. It is quite different from most of its neighbors, not only because of its rich vegetation, but also due to its freshwater lakes. On a tiny island in Veliko Jezero ("Big Lake"), the hotel Melita, housed in a 12th-century Benedictine monastery, makes an excellent and peaceful base from which to explore. Mljet has one peculiar claim to fame in that it is the only place in Europe where you may find the mongoose roaming about at liberty. One explanation for this is that long ago these little animals were imported from the East to exterminate the snakes with which the island was infested.

The legend is given credence to some extent by the fact that there are still an unusually large number of snakes here—large, that is, by comparison with the numbers on most other Dalmatian islands.

Furthermore, it is claimed that one of the island's snakes bit St. Paul (without doing him any harm) when the apostle was shipwrecked on what was then called Melita while he was on his way to appear before Caesar, and to meet his martyrdom in Rome. Malta, which in those days was also called Melita, disputes this putative honor.

The waters found Mljet are particularly well stocked with fish, and the island is consequently a great favorite with fishermen, though you must bring your own equipment. It's also very popular with discerning foreign yachtsmen. The chief village is Babino Polje, and the old port is called Polače.

The Dubrovnik boat passes between the coast and the three islands of Šipan, Lopud and Koločep. The first is completely covered, almost to the shore, with dense forest, Šipanska Luka being the "capital." There are a number of elegant mansions here, among them the summer homes of rich merchants and sea captains of Dubrovnik. There are also a few little churches, but, most unusually, none of them is of any great architectural distinction. These were built when Dubrovnik was still an independent republic.

Lopud is a bathing resort set among pine woods and olive groves, attractively placed and with several fine, gently sloping beaches. Koločep, less than eight km. (five miles) from Dubrovnik, is small and thickly grown but possesses only one tiny narrow village.

These three small islands are well worth mentioning because of their nearness to Dubrovnik. Most of the large travel firms operate boat excursions to them, and regular steamer services and modern hotels are available if you want an offshore stay.

Along the *Magistrala* southward to Dubrovnik the scenery appears, if anything, even more striking. Following the coast opposite the long peninsula of Pelješac, you will reach the point at which the peninsula juts out from the mainland, and from here there is an attractive detour of some eight km. (five miles) to the strikingly picturesque fortified village of Ston, once the second city of the Republic of Ragusa, whose salt-pans are still being worked. The surrounding countryside is most impressive, and in the village itself are the Gothic Chancellery of the Republic, the Bishop's Palace, the Franciscan Cloister and the tiny 11th-century Church of St. Michael, which is well worth visiting, if only for the beauty of its frieze. The supervening centuries have destroyed part of it, but what remains is ravishing.

Slano lies at the head of a deep inlet, whose waters are serene and sheltered. Here, where a few years ago there was nothing but a tiny decaying village, a fine modern holiday resort has grown up. The only place of real interest between here and Dubrovnik is Trsteno, where there are two enormous plane trees reputed to be 1,000 years old. Trsteno also has a botanical garden, once the grounds of a patrician house where the poet Byron was a guest.

The road continues along the right bank of the Dubrovnik or Ombla river. This appears to be a large inlet of the sea but is, in fact, the River Trebisnjica, which rises far inland, wanders along the *karst* plateau, then suddenly disappears into a swallow-hole, to reemerge at the base of a 400-m. (1,300-ft.) cliff about five km. (three miles) from the sea. The point where it reappears is a magnificent sight, especially in springtime when the cliff is covered with the wild iris *(Iris dalmatica)* which were the ancestors of many of our modern garden-varieties, and with fragrant herbs, like thyme, sage, and lavender. A fine patrician house in the village of Komolac, overlooking the river, is now part of Dubrovnik Marina, a mecca for the boating fraternity with restaurant and other sports facilities. The situation is splendid.

The road continues for a time along the shore of the bay at whose head the Ombla lies. It then enters the industrial harbor area of Gruž, a Dubrovnik suburb and not an especially attractive introduction to one of the world's most beautiful fortified cities. A complex one-way traffic system helps to ease bottlenecks, but motorists will still find themselves in a slow procession at the height of the season.

Exploring Dubrovnik

In 1667 Dubrovnik suffered the worst of several earthquakes throughout its history. The 1979 quake inflicted only minor damage by comparison, but a few of the major buildings in the city are as a result being restored to their pre-1667 condition. However, such natural disasters notwithstanding, Dubrovnik remains an entrancing place, witness to the artistic skills and technical craftsmanship of bygone centuries. Your best plan is to start at the path that makes the entire round of the city's undamaged medieval walls (remembering that they close at 7 P.M.). There's no great distance involved, as the old town was extraordinarily compact. The walls were designed principally by Michelozzi of Florence and George of Dalmatia, and include five great bastions: the Lovrjenac fort and the Minčeta, Bokar, Revelin, and Sveti Ivan towers.

Entrance is restricted to two heavily protected gates by which you may enter, at Ploče on the east and Pile on the west. Incidentally, no private wheeled traffic is permitted within the walls. If you decide to

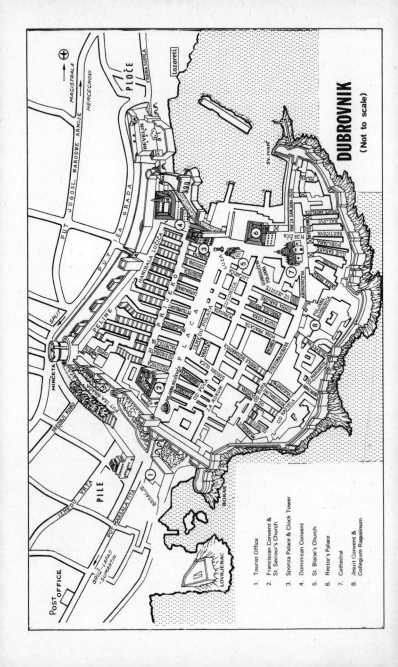

DUBROVNIK
(Not to scale)

1. Tourist Office
2. Franciscan Convent & St. Saviour's Church
3. Sponza Palace & Clock Tower
4. Dominican Convent
5. St. Blaise's Church
6. Rector's Palace
7. Cathedral
8. Jesuit Convent & Collegium Ragusinum

make a round of the walls the main entrance is by the Ploče Gate, close to the Old Port. A small fee is charged.

The old city's main thoroughfare is the Placa—known by the locals as "Stradun"—which crosses it from one side to the other, and runs along what was once the narrow channel separating Ragusa on its island from Slav Dubrovnik on the mainland. It is here that you will find the principal buildings, though there are of course countless narrow medieval streets leading off it which the visitor will find very well worth exploring.

Crossing from west to east, you will soon see the Onofrio Fountain built in the 15th century (at the time of the installation of the city's fresh water supply), which was designed by the Neapolitan Onofrio de la Cava. Behind the fountain is the Convent of the Sisters of Sveta Klara, dating from 1290. Here Europe's first hospice for homeless children was opened in 1432.

Opposite there is the Renaissance-style façade of the Church of Sveti Spas, St. Saviour, designed by the Andrijić brothers after the great earthquake of 1520. Not far away stands an imposing 14th-century Franciscan church, with a remarkable Gothic porch carved by the brothers Petrović in 1498. Inside the Convent itself, there is a small cloister, the work of Miho de Bar. The capital of each one of the cloister columns is ornamented by a different group of grinning or grimacing faces, half nightmare, half humorous, and wholly arresting in their originality.

How incredible the terrifying instruments of medieval medicine seem to us today! The Franciscan pharmacy dates from 1318, and so is one of the earliest in Europe, though one is tempted to wonder how anyone in those days, once ill, was ever cured!

Easier to appreciate is the rich heritage of hand-painted manuscripts, jeweled icons, and remarkable portraits of long-dead Ragusan notables, which is still guarded by the monks. In the convent church there is a 15th-century painting of Sveti Vlaho, Dubrovnik's patron-saint, in which he is shown holding a model of the city. You can see for yourself that the city plan has hardly changed from that of 500 years ago.

The Sponza Palace

Farther along the Placa you will see the 30-m.-high (100 ft.) Clock Tower built in 1445 (recently rebuilt) standing in the center of a small but beautiful square. Nearby is the Sponza Palace, Gothic in style with Renaissance elements. It was built by the architect Miličević in the 16th century.

The main façade is ornamented with an external gallery supported by graceful arches. This particularly attractive and typical building served for many years as Ragusa's Customs House. In the 17th century it was a meeting place for the leaders of all Dubrovnik's greatest educational institutions. Today the ground floor is used for exhibitions and occasional concerts. The upper floors contain the full archives of the old Republic, but a selection of some of the most important documents on display on the ground floor makes fascinating reading. It includes signed statements from almost every head of state, from James I of England to Peter the Great of Russia, confirming or granting privileges to this tiny city-state.

The 18th-century baroque Church of Sveti Vlaho is immediately opposite the Sponza Palace. It replaced the 14th-century church that was destroyed by fire. The only object that escaped the flames was the silver statue of the saint, holding a model of the city, which today stands on the High Altar of the later church.

In the little open square in front of Sveti Vlaho is an attractive fountain, also "Roland's Column," placed there in 1418, from which the Town Crier broadcast decisions of the Senate. The Republic's flag was flown here on public holidays. A local legend, pleasant even if improbable, is that the column and the city's constitution were given to the young Republic by Roland, the famous nephew of the Emperor Charlemagne.

The Rector's Palace

The most remarkable building in Dubrovnik is the Rector's Palace. Built in the 12th century, it was subsequently so severely damaged in several earthquakes that in the 15th century the three architects Onofrio de la Cava, Michelozzi, and George of Dalmatia were charged with the work of designing the present building. It shows a combination of late Gothic and early Renaissance styles. The center of the façade is supported by five massive pillars, each crowned with its capital. In the courtyard there is a bust of a rich 17th-century shipowner, Miho Pracat, who contributed generously to state funds and was the only citizen of his time to be honored with a statue.

On the first floor of the palace are the large rooms where in the days of the Republic the Great Council and the Senate held their meetings, and also the Rector's work-room. One of the Laws of Ragusa was that the Rector might not leave the confines of the palace during his month of office. Deprived of all family and social distractions, it was thought, he would be forced to get on with his job. The Ragusans were obviously fully aware of their own frailties, as the same insistence on hard work is echoed in the inscription over the entrance to the meeting place of the Grand Council, which reads *Obliti privatorum publica curate* or "Forget private affairs, and get on with public matters." The palace holds the city records of over 1,000 years, and houses the Cultural and Historical Museum.

Halfway between the Clock Tower and the Rector's Palace is the Town Hall, containing the municipal theater, which occupies the site of the 14th-century Palace of the Grand Council, destroyed by fire in 1816. The ground floor accommodates a large and popular café. Here the city's war galleys were once stored.

The "Collegium Ragusinum," Dubrovnik's ancient Learned Academy, was convened in a building which may still be seen next to the Jesuit Monastery, at the top of a flight of baroque steps that climb from the statue of the local poet Gundulić.

Also close to the Rector's Palace is Dubrovnik's imposing baroque cathedral. It has church ornaments of immense value and a fine collection of paintings, including one attributed to Titian. If your interests are artistic then be sure to include the 14th-century Dominican Monastery on your list. It is close beside the Ploče Gate.

You may easily overlook the numerous little *lazaretti* just outside the walls near the Ploče Gate where, in the Middle Ages, travelers waited for permission to enter the city, and where if they were merchants they stored their trade-goods. These have now been converted into a complex of shops, tavern, disco, cinema and galleries.

In Puča Street, running parallel to the Placa, there is a tiny Orthodox church containing a collection of icons.

Mercifully Dubrovnik completely escaped physical damage in World War II, though the citizens still recall the day when the Germans, the Italians looking on, drove out 200 members of the city's Jewish colony, not one of whom has ever been seen or heard of again.

Dubrovnik's Summer Festival

Among Dubrovnik's sobriquets is "The Slav Athens," and throughout her long history she has deliberately maintained her cultural traditions. Accordingly, in 1950 she initiated her annual Summer Festival; now every year from 10th July to 25th August an intensive program of concerts, plays, operettas, involving many internationally known guest artists, takes place against the backdrop of some of the city's most beautiful historic buildings. You may be slightly shaken to hear Hamlet, Prince of Denmark, discoursing in Serbo-Croat, but at least the background of the Lovrjenac fortress makes a highly-satisfactory Elsinore.

One word of warning: Dubrovnik's total hotel capacity is considerable, but there is still a summer shortage of top-class accommodations. Note, too, that many of the resort's hotels are on the pleasant Lapad peninsula some distance from the walled town, though linked with it by frequent bus services. If you want to be within strolling distance of the old city, make sure you choose your hotel accordingly.

Farewell to Dubrovnik

Leaving Dubrovnik on the road for Montenegro, we almost encircle her dramatic fortifications, then climb high enough to catch a glimpse of the shrub-covered little island of Lokrum, where Richard the Lionheart was shipwrecked on his way back from the Crusades. It is a National Park, so if you are caught smoking a cigaret (let alone lighting a fire) in the woods you may find yourself in trouble. Otherwise it's popular for peaceful bathing.

The *Magistrala* follows the road built by Napoleon's General Marmont between 1808 and 1813 above the coast for several kilometers until we take a right fork to the village of Srebreno, set in a small bay by an attractive beach. Farther on come the Kupari beach and the village of Mlini, which like Srebreno has good hotels and camping among groves of olive and cypress trees. The village of Plat lies a little beyond Mlini.

The next fork in the road, on the right, leads on to Cavtat, which is one of the most strikingly attractive villages on the Dalmatian coast. It is set among pines in the heart of a bay, and its narrow streets run parallel to each other as they climb steeply from the shore. Each house has its own little garden with orange and lemon trees. One of the best views of Cavtat (the Epidaurus of the ancients, whose surviving inhabitants fled to Dubrovnik in the seventh century following a destructive Avar raid) may be obtained from beside the cypress-guarded tomb of the Račić family, which is on a small promontory within sound of the waves. The mausoleum of this rich family of shipowners (with whom the Duke and Duchess of Windsor used to stay in the 1930s) is the work of Meštrović. A resort-area has developed a little way from Cavtat, in a spot where there is a fine sheltered beach and where the large modern hotels are out of sight of the tiny old town.

The way now lies along the fertile Konavli Valley, where ethnologists claim to be able to detect the classic features of Graeco-Roman Epidaurus in the handsome peasant girls. About ten km. (six miles) from Cavtat (from *civitas*—"township") is the village of Čilipi, which you should visit on a Sunday morning if possible when the people wear their particularly attractive traditional costume. Unfortunately, the men are tending to abandon these reminders of a colorful past. With a busy international airport now dominating their village, this is perhaps understandable.

Next comes Gruda, famous for its wines, and the entrance to the bare Sutorina valley. From here there is a memorable view of the whole of the majestic Gulf of Kotor, the Boka Kotorska.

Practical Information for Dubrovnik and Vicinity

HOW TO GET THERE. By plane. You can reach Dubrovnik from London, Paris, Rome, Vienna and other major European cities by direct flights. In season, there are regular inter-city connections.

By boat. The express boats from Rijeka stop at Dubrovnik, and then continue on to Bar; both Bar and Rijeka are connected by ferry to Bari and Ancona in Italy, and Corfu and Igoumenitsa in Greece.

By bus. Most travel agents operate regular all-in tours between main inland cities and Dubrovnik, lasting two or more days.

WHEN TO GO. The best times to go to Dubrovnik are between the start of April and the end of June, and during September and October. These are the most pleasant periods of the year; generally the weather is ideal and you avoid the July and August crowds. On the other hand, you would miss the Summer Festival, which begins on the 10th July each year, continuing until 25th August.

During the entire six weeks the public can watch one or more performances each day. There is a succession of operas, ballets, plays, concerts, and evenings of folklore music and dances. Yugoslav and foreign artists and ensembles take part. The performances by groups specializing in folk dances and music have a sparkling vitality and fascinating color. Lovely old buildings and other parts of the town serve as backdrop for the festival.

HOTELS AND RESTAURANTS. The city of Dubrovnik contains many excellent hotels, but if you plan on going during the high season—which coincides with the famous festival—it is highly advisable to book well in advance, as the place is packed. Even in the "shoulder" months of May/June and September, hotels are often full. However, an increasing number of them now open year round.

Other accommodations include guest houses and private households—check with the local Tourist Information Center (see Useful Addresses end of this chapter).

The restaurants we have listed below are additional of course to those in the hotels and represent but a selection from the numerous establishments that have sprung up of late. All are moderately priced.

CAVTAT. Old village and summer resort in a beautiful bay, 17 km. (10½ miles) southeast of Dubrovnik, notable for water sports. *Croatia* (L), 480 rooms. Casino, own beaches, pools, tennis, disco, own heliport. *Albatros* (E), 246 rooms. Pool. *Adriatic* (M), 54 rooms. *Cavtat* (M), 109 rooms. *Epidarus* (M), 192 rooms. Older, but well-modernized. *Supetar* (M), 39 rooms. Nearer town than the others in this price range. All these (M) hotels with own beach.

DUBROVNIK. There is actually only one hotel *in* the old town: *Dubravka* (I), 22 rooms, some with bath.

If you want to be within strolling distance of the city, choose somewhere in either the Ploče or Pile district near the walls: *Argentina* (E), 155 rooms; *Excelsior* (E), 211 rooms; and *Villa Dubrovnik* (E), 56 rooms. All three in Ploče district, the first two with swimming pools, and each with own section of artificial beach of rocks and paving stones. On the Pile side of the walls, the grand old *Imperial* (E), 108 rooms, retains an aura of more old-fashioned elegance in the palatial style of 1910, but no beach.

About three km. (two miles) from the city walls and rapidly reached by frequent bus service is the peninsula district of Lapad, dominated by Petka mountain. Here there is a large number of hotels, often with their own lovely gardens, in a marvelously peaceful setting. Fringing a deep bay in the peninsula is a series of accommodations of various categories. On a headland, for example, is *Dubrovnik Palace* (E), 325 rooms, own pool, nudist beach. Nearby is the smaller *Splendid* (M), 61 rooms, set in a small pinewood beside its own artificial beach. A peaceful and pleasant spot.

Several hotels grouped near or above the public beach of Sumratin in this bay are *Kompas* (E), 134 rooms, *Park* (E), 225 rooms, and *Sumratin* (M), 70 rooms. The nearby beach inevitably gets crowded, so if you are in this area check your hotel has its own pool. Otherwise there is bathing off the rocks in various parts of Lapad.

On the farthest part of the peninsula is the Babin Kuk development comprising a number of hotels set by or near a tastefully designed shopping precinct with boutiques, galleries, restaurants and taverns. Among the hotels are *Dubrovnik President* (L), 169 rooms, an impressive structure soaring up from its own bathing area and served by funicular-type lifts. Own pool. *Argosy* (E), 308 rooms, and *Tirena* (E), 208 rooms, are linked by the shopping precinct and both have their own pool.

A delightfully tranquil spot about ten km. (six miles) from town, on the Ombla (Dubrovnik) river at Komolac, is *Dubrovnik Marina* (E), with a few rooms, in a restored patrician house. Restaurants, good sports facilities.

Restaurants and Cafés. *Dubravka,* Brsalje 1. Near Pile Gate, with tables set under shady trees. *Gradska Kavana,* Placa. Popular café rendezvous in the old city from which to watch the world go by; prices somewhat erratic. *Jadran,* P. Miličevića 1. Attractive setting in cloisters of former monastery. *Ohran-Madmaison,* Kolorina 5. French cuisine. *Prijeko,* Prijeko 14. Intimate atmosphere, local and fish specialties. In the old city. *Ragusa II,* Zamanjina 12. Again, local and fish specialties in the old city. *Riblji,* Široka 1. Dalmatian and fish specialties, old city location.

Farther afield but worth the journey are *Konavoski Dvori,* in a renovated windmill at the mouth of the river Ljuta, about 35 km. (20 miles) south of Dubrovnik; and *Soline,* by the sea at Zaton, about 15 km. (nine miles) north. Both serve local specialties.

KOLOČEP. Island near Dubrovnik; season Apr.–Oct. *Koločep* (M), 150 rooms. Villa accommodations.

LOPUD. Island near Dubrovnik; season Apr.–Oct. *Dubrava-Pracat* (M), 94 rooms; *Lafodia* (M), 196 rooms; and *Lopud* (M), 101 rooms. All three with own beach.

MLNI. Pleasant coastal hamlet in fertile area, 12 km. (7½ miles) from Dubrovnik. *Astarea* (E), 221 rooms, annex. *Elapfiti* (M), self-catering villas, pool, overlooking beach. *Mlini* (M), 67 rooms. large garden.

MLJET. Delightful wooded island, part of which is a national park. *Melita* (M), on an islet in a lake of the national park, and housed in a Benedictine monastery founded in the 12th century—an idyllic spot.

In the coastal village of **Pomena,** *Odisej* (M), 160 rooms, overlooks the attractive bay.

PLAT. Hamlet beyond Mlini. *Plat* (M), 648 rooms. Perched on steep hillside above a small beach. A little isolated but near the airport.

Restaurant. By the sea is an excellent small *taverna* with good food at low prices.

ŠIPAN. Island near Dubrovnik; season Apr.–Oct. *Šipan* (M), 72 rooms.

SLANO. A few kilometers north of Dubrovnik; season Apr.–Oct. *Admiral* (M), 225 rooms. Own beach. *Osmine* (M), 152 rooms. Also own beach; facilities for nudists.

SREBRENO. Near Mlini and Dubrovnik; season Apr.–Oct. *Orlando* (M), 275 rooms. (M) and (I) annexes. *Župa* (M), 100 rooms.

STON. Astonishing little walled town at southern end of Pelješac peninsula; season May–Oct. *Adriatic* (I), 27 rooms, some with bath.

Restaurant. Seafood aficionados are recommended to try the attractive *Koruna* eaterie.

HOW TO GET AROUND. By boat. There are regular local services to the islands of Koločep, Lopud, Šipan and Mljet, returning the next day. In summer, a frequent service by motorboat links Dubrovnik with the nature reserve island of Lokrum.

By bus. There are excellent regular buses running up and down the coast and inland to Mostar, Sarajevo, Titograd, Ohrid, Belgrade and beyond. Local buses also link the port of Gruž, Lapad and Dubrovnik with each other.

By cable car. There is a cable car you can take to the top of the Srdj mountain, where the view is guaranteed fabulous.

WHAT TO SEE. First day: Visit the fortifications, the Sponza and Rector's palaces, churches, and the Franciscan and Dominican monasteries, and the Cathedral treasures. A swim at Lapad. Second day: Visit the museum. Excursion by boat to Lokrum. Go for a stroll around the center of town and the outskirts. Third day: A cable-car up to the top of Mt. Srdj, or a coach drive to Žarkovica (wonderful panorama), a swim at Ploče or trip to Trebinje, small Turkish town about 30 km. (20 miles) inland. Stop on the way for a swim at Srebreno or Mlini.

Note: the city walls are closed at 6 or 7 P.M. Allow at least an hour. If you only have time to go halfway round, follow the route on the landward side, it gives by far the best views over Dubrovnik.

SPORTS. The emphasis of course is on the aquatic variety, with a number of hotels having their own beaches. Of several public beaches, the largest is the Sumratin at Lapad, which has a restaurant; elsewhere in Lapad you can bathe off the rocks. The beach of Ploče, near the Excelsior, also has a restaurant. At Pile, at the foot of the Lovrijenac fortress, is a rather narrow creek; if you can find the postern gate behind the Bishop's Palace, you can dive into 6–9 m. (20–30 ft.) of water from the rocks below it. Farther south, at Srebreno, Mlni and Cavtat, the bathing is better and less crowded, and there is good rock bathing on the island (and nature reserve) of Lokrum. (There are also several nudist beaches in the area.)

Water skiing and wind surfing facilities are offered by a number of hotels, notably in Lapad and at Cavtat. For fishing and skin diving, apply to the Tourist Information Center or to the fishing association (Orhan) at Lapad for the latest regulations.

Yachts can be hired, together with crew, from Orsan Yacht Club at Lapad. Yacht services are also available at the Dubrovnik Marina, Komolac, on the Ombla (Dubrovnik) river.

MUSEUMS. In Dubrovnik. The **Cathedral Treasury** contains fine gold and silver reliquaries, including the skull of St. Blaise in the form of a Byzantine crown.

The **Cultural and Historical Museum** is a part of the Rector's Palace, and its exhibits give a picture of life in Dubrovnik from the early days up to the downfall of the Republic, particularly the 18th and 19th centuries. There are vases and procelains, pharmaceutical instruments of the 15th century, and a collection of exotic objects brought home by sailors of the town.

The **Ethnographical Museum, Maritime Museum** and the **Aquarium** are each excellent of their kind.

The **Franciscan and Dominican Libraries** contain ancient manuscripts, early incunabula, books and pictures.

The **Icon Collection** is on Puča St., next to the Serbian Orthodox Church.

The **Rupe Granary** is an historical monument of the 15th-century and features a permanent exhibition of Yugoslav folk art.

The **State Archives,** in the Sponza Palace, house a valuable collection of historical documents from the year 1022 up to the present day. It includes a fascinating permanent display of selected agreements and guarantees signed by most of the heads of state of the great powers over the centuries.

SHOPPING. There are plenty of shops in the Placa in Dubrovnik, and any number of boutiques in the side streets where you will find a wide range of articles, often in very good taste: luggage of pigskin (peccary) and other leathers, trinkets and carved-wood souvenirs, filigree, lace, handwoven textiles and other handicrafts. Prices may be slightly higher than elsewhere but not prohibitive.

USEFUL ADDRESSES. Dubrovnik is the headquarters of Atlas travel agency, at Pile 1, and many of the other major travel firms, such as Centroturist, Dalmacijaturist, Generalturist, Globtour, Kompas, Kvarner Express and Putnik, have branches here and provide full services. The Tourist Information Center is at P. Miličevića 1, at the Pile end of Placa in the old city of Dubrovnik. The head office for the Dubrovnik Summer Festival is od Sigurate 1.

NIGHT LIFE. Most of the principal hotels in Dubrovnik have a nightclub or restaurant with music. Otherwise, a popular spot is the *Labirint* openair bar, surrounded by ramparts, near the Ploče portal. The *Lazaretti,* former city quarantine quarters built in the 17th century just outside the same Ploče portal, have been adapted as a leisure area that includes a disco and tavern. There are casinos at the *Imperial* and *Libertas* hotels.

Frequent and excellent performances of national dances and songs are given by the Lindo folklore ensemble in Fort Revlin.

MONTENEGRO

The Unconquered Land

Anyone who knows Yugoslavia will know too the Yugoslavs' passion for freedom. Nowhere does this passion burn more fiercely and determinedly than in Montenegro. In all the region's history it has never been wholly subjugated—not the inland portions at any rate. And from Roman times these extraordinarily gentle, outstandingly hospitable heroes have been renowned for their valor.

Britain's greatest Liberal statesman William Gladstone, thundering in the House of Commons against the iniquities of Turkish oppression, said of the Montenegrins, "Those are men who, when asked to pay tribute offer stones. These are the men who dress the cowards into women's clothes, and whose wives, when need requires, boldly get hold of the gun."

Their independence lasted for 500 stormy years, and the national spirit of freedom remains unchanged, even though the Turks have gone forever, and even though this tiny mountain land is today no more than the smallest of the six federal republics.

Hemmed in by Bosnia-Herzegovina, the Dalmatian coast of Croatia, Serbia and Albania, Montenegro is the smallest republic not only in area but also in population, with a mere 560,000 inhabitants. The interior is dominated by the rugged Black mountains that led the Venetians to give the whole province the name of Montenegro, which the Yugoslavs have translated literally as Crna Gora. Farther north are the Durmitor, Bjelašica, Komovi and Proketije ranges, each with at least a few green valleys and studded with beautiful lakes.

The especial charm of Montenegro is of something wild, yet warmly human, and there is no lack of surprises. Waterlily-ringed Lake Scutari or Skadar (Skadarsko Jezero), for instance, is not quite what you expect to see among majestically gaunt mountains. Many green Alpine valleys are equally unexpected. And, in further contrast, there is the magical 130-km. (80-mile) stretch of coast, so tragically hit by an earthquake in April 1979. Over 90 lives were lost in this tragedy which did incalculable damage to the region's economic life and cultural treasures. It will take many years to make good all the damage, but already full tourist facilities have been restored in most of the resorts and, stretching from the truly magnificent Gulf of Kotor—among the most remarkable landscapes of Europe—to the Albanian border, the coast has some of Yugoslavia's very finest beaches.

The inhabitants are as remarkable as the country in which they live. Their history is one of unceasing struggle ever since the foundation of the medieval Serb state of which they were originally citizens. While they are peaceful shepherds by choice the Montenegrins in times of war are terrifying fighters—as they showed very clearly in World War II—and have their own strongly individualistic mentality, which defies change. Some of them find it difficult to cope with the complexities of present-day life, and they detest compromise. Fiercely independent, influenced by the harsh conditions of their surroundings, they have something in common with the Highland Scots—mountaineers, and (in their absence only) a favorite subject for wry humor among their neighbors. This strong sense of independence also makes the Montenegrins a little unpredictable, so don't be too surprised if things don't always go according to schedule! But beneath their bluff exteriors, these people are extremely generous and warm-hearted.

The Troubled Past

Montenegro's history is closely linked with that of Serbia, whose first ruling dynasty, the Nemanjas, was originally a noble Montenegrin family. Under the name of Zeta, a semi-independent Montenegro came within the sphere of influence of its northern neighbor, which between 1184 and 1389 was the leading Balkan power. Then, following the Turkish victory at the Battle of Kosovo, the Ottoman domination of southeastern Europe began. Serbia shrank northward and finally disappeared. Though isolated, Montenegro continued to resist, and despite numerous campaigns the Turks never wholly pacified the country.

Late in the 15th century Ivan Crnojević, chief of an important Montenegrin clan, left Žabljak, a fortified islet on Lake Skadar, to move farther away from Turkish pressure, and established himself in Cetinje, making it his capital.

Gradually, Crnojević obtained support from Montenegrin tribes sufficient to form a truly independent principality, which thanks to the heroism of these tough mountain people and the inaccessibility of the whole region, successfully defended itself not only against the Turks, but also against Venice and the Austrian Empire.

From the beginning of the 16th century, the country was governed by Orthodox Bishop-Princes, the family of Petrović-Njegoš particularly distinguishing itself in this office. For a while Montenegro was supported by Russia, but at the close of the Napoleonic Wars Russia opposed the unification of the coast and the Gulf of Kotor with Montenegro, and the tiny country perforce remained isolated.

Petar II, who reigned from 1830 until 1850, was the ablest of all Montenegro's priestly rulers, and introduced a number of reforms into his still very backward country. He used to say of himself, "I am a prince among the barbarians and a barbarian among the princes," which seems to suggest that not only was he an astute leader but he also possessed a sense of humor.

After a successful campaign against the Turks, Montenegro at last won a corridor to the Adriatic in 1878, at Bar and Ulcinj, by driving out the Turkish occupiers. Austria, however, retained the northern coast till the end of World War I. In 1910, Nicolas I declared himself King but, with the creation of united Yugoslavia in 1918, retired to Paris, where he died in 1921.

The Gulf of Kotor

If your approach to Montenegro is from the north by the coastal road from Dubrovnik, you are not likely quickly to forget your first impressions of it. After crossing the "border" at the top of the Naguma-nac Pass, you descend into the bare Sutorina valley and so to one of the most striking and unexpected features of the Yugoslavian coast, the Gulf of Kotor. This extraordinary arm of the sea probing into a seem-ingly impenetrable barrier of mountains consists of two main bays, separated by a strait only 275 m. (300 yards) wide, and subdivided into many smaller bays. The innermost point of this deep, mountain-ringed inlet is some 30 km. (20 miles) from the open sea. The Gulf begins peacefully enough with normal rocky hill-sides sloping down to the sea. But as you progress farther and farther inland along its shores, you find yourself traveling by a curving road suspended a little above sea-level on a steep mountainside that soars away out of sight.

The history of the Gulf of Kotor is closely linked with that of Venice, whose territory it was until Napoleon's abolition of the maritime Republic. The ports of this region sent many great sailors to serve Venice, whose art and architecture are still everywhere apparent.

While the inland parts of Montenegro were never conquered by Turkish invaders, the coast was only partly recovered in 1878, when the Great Powers assigned the northern portion to Austria. In recent years the Republic of Montenegro has made strenuous efforts to devel-op tourism in the region. Some think the efforts made have been too successful in regions such as Budva and the coast immediately to the south. But happily the Gulf of Kotor has acquired nothing to spoil it.

Our first visit is to Igalo, near the Montenegrin "frontier," a spa whose mud is renowned for its curative properties. Nearby is the outer Bay of Topla, where two peninsulas almost close the only outlet to the sea. The small island of Mamula looks like a ship at anchor from here. On our right, is the Oštri Rt—the pointed cape upon the edge of which is perched the village of Prevlaka, with Luštica just beside it. In Topla church there are several ancient and precious icons.

Hercegnovi and Excursions

Hercegnovi, below 150-m.-high (5,000 ft.) Mount Orjen, was found-ed in 1382 by King Tvrtko I of Bosnia with the dual objectives of giving his country an outlet to the sea, and of ensuring a supply of salt. The town was totally destroyed by the Turks at the end of the 16th century, who then rebuilt and fortified it. The Venetians took it two centuries later, and held it until its brief seizure by Napoleon. It was under Austrian rule until 1918.

The main square has a Turkish clocktower and the fountain of Karadža Bey, and the city is crowned by fortifications in three styles—Turkish, Venetian and Austrian. The Orthodox Church, although rela-tively new, is built in the medieval Byzantine style discussed in the chapter on Serbia. The Botanical Gardens are memorable for tropical and subtropical plants. Indeed, Hercegovni is a place of flowers, not least during the Mimosa Festival which lasts several weeks from January to March; the highlight is the special day of the Mimosa Harvest, usually in February, when the blossoms are gathered from tens of thousands of shrubs and there is a procession through the town. Another attractive feature of the resort is the 6½-km. (four-mile) path along the shore to Igalo, with plenty of small restaurants along the way.

From Hercegnovi there is a pleasant full-day excursion from the Španjola Fort to 1,430-m.-high (4,700 ft.) Mount Radostak. From the summit there is a tremendous view across the Bay of Kotor, wild yet beautiful. 16 km. (ten miles) from Hercegnovi, on the slopes of the Subra Mountains, there is excellent skiing to be had as late as the month of May. Après-ski could be to bathe in the warm waters of the Adriatic.

A footpath connects Hercegnovi with the Monastery of Savina, restored in 1839. In the little 11th-century church nearby, there are some remarkable frescos. The monastery is named after the first head of the Serbian-Orthodox Church, St. Sava Nemanja, of the medieval Serbian royal house. The monastery library is of exceptional beauty and value, possessing among many other treasures a collection of manuscripts of church and monastic rules known as the *Savinska Krmčija,* dating from the 13th century and considered unique. The monastery was damaged in the earthquake, but can be visited.

In the days when the sailors of the Bay of Kotor were famous for their long and daring voyages, it was their habit, on their return, to salute the monastery with a salvo of cannon, to which the reply was a peal of the monastery bells.

The coast road now descends to the little Bay of Meljine, and beyond Zelenika we pass the picturesque Kumbor channel. At Baošić, in the Bay of Tivat there is a plaque commemorating the visit of the French novelist Pierre Loti in 1880, when he was a naval officer.

The straits grow steadily narrower, until barely 800 m. (half a mile) separates us from the great out-thrust of the second of the main peninsulas that so forthrightly divide the Gulf into three or four great saltwater bays. In the Middle Ages the men of the Boka used to stretch great chains across the narrowest point in times of war, to prevent enemy ships from penetrating to the inner bays.

This is a fascinating stretch of coast, and you should try to find time to follow the road right round the various creeks. Those who are anxious to reach Kotor and the southernmost coast as soon as possible by car should take the ferry-boat across the narrows from Kamenari to Lepetane, though this will be their loss, in terms of tourist-attraction.

Once past the narrows beyond Kamenari our road turns away sharply westward through Kostanjica to Morinj, with its magnificent view five km. (three miles) across the bay to Risan, passing on the way the waterfall of Sopot, which pours out of a hole in the cliff below the road.

Risan is a pleasant little village, and it is still proudly conscious of its past. In the third century it was already an important Illyrian city. After the Roman conquest, it was here that Teuta, Illyria's last Queen, took refuge. When the remorseless enemy once more caught up with her, she drowned herself in the limpid waters of the bay rather than become their prisoner. The village still possesses some Roman mosaics, of which the most remarkable is that of Hypnos, god of sleep. Much of the town's commercial property once came from the guides it provided to escort caravans into the interior of the country and back.

After Risan, a steep and winding road brings us to Crkvice after a run of 22 km. (14 miles) climbing over a 1,035-m. (3,400-ft.) pass through the Krivošije region dominated by Mount Orjen. From the pass you will see some splendid mountain scenery with glimpses of the blue waters of the bays far below. The inhabitants of the Krivošije are peaceable shepherds who, in time of war, become particularly ferocious soldiers. In the 19th century they refused conscription into the Austrian army. A force of 20,000 trained troops was dispatched by Vienna to break their defiance, and succeeded in surrounding them, but was then forced to retreat in face of intrepid sharpshooters. During World War II the local resistance was probably the most ruthless of any in occupied Yugoslavia.

Back on the *Magistrala,* past the Monastery of Banja, you will see the two small islands of St. George (Sveti Juraj) and Our Lady of Škrpjelo, either of which can be reached by boat in ten minutes. St. George has a sad air, with tall cypress trees marking the sailors' burial ground and the last meager traces of a ruined Benedictine Monastery. The island inspired Böcklin's well-known painting, *The Island of the Dead* (which in its turn was the inspiration for Rachmaninov's hauntingly melancholy music of the same name).

The other island was originally little more than a reef, but the sailors of Boka brought great stones to the place, which they piled upon the rock until they had accumulated enough to provide the foundations for a rather austere looking church, which soon became a popular place of pilgrimage. The interior is a marked contrast however, containing a number of fine 17th-century paintings by the local master Kokolja, and many votive offerings from grateful sailors to their patron saint. There are two popular feasts held here every year, on 22nd July, and 15th August, when in addition to a procession of garlanded fishing boats, there is folk dancing in the local peasant costumes, and various country sports and games are held.

The Boka has always produced the best seafarers of the Adriatic, and the cream of these came from Perast. They founded the earliest maritime fraternity both of that sea and also of the Mediterranean. Their Common Law was already in force by A.D. 809, though this was revised and its statutes codified in 1463. Perast gave Venice some of her greatest admirals and sailors, and on the recommendation of the Venetians, Peter the Great sent 60 young Russian noblemen to the Naval School of Perast founded in 1698. In time, they provided the nucleus for the first Russian fleet in the Baltic which, under the command of Matija Zmajević, three times inflicted defeat upon the Swedes ruling those waters.

However, Perast's past is not solely a tale of naval victories. The Turks launched repeated land campaigns against it, but always in vain, their most crushing defeat being in 1634 when Mehmed Rizvanajić, the Bosnian Moslem convert leader of the Turkish forces, was killed in battle. His prayer carpet may be seen in the Church of St. Nicolas, which also contains some wonderful church robes and ornaments worked by pious country-women, and an exquisite crucifix by Benvenuto Cellini.

Perast today is a museum town and its 17th-century mansions in the Venetian-baroque style are open to visitors. The finest building is the Palača Bujović, once the residence of a Venetian captain, now the town museum. The eclipse of this once-powerful and prosperous city began with the Napoleonic Wars, when embattled British and French squadrons repeatedly disrupted the normal life of the Adriatic with fire and blockade. The coming of steamships sealed the fate of the ancient port, whose past glories can be recalled now only in the Maritime Museum of Kotor.

The farthest of the bays, once barred by a huge chain, is the Bay of Kotor. Continuing east to Orahovac along the shore you should see the fine medieval frescos in its little church before turning south to Dobrota. This is the collective name of a group of villages containing many Venetian-style houses from the period when this section of the Gulf prospered as a merchant shipping center. Several of the churches are worth visiting.

Medieval Kotor

The arrival at Kotor, some 16 km. (ten miles) by road from Perast, is even more exciting if you catch your first glimpse of the extraordinary water-maze from the sea. You will feel that you have come somehow to the World's End when you reach this inmost recess of this inland sea. The town itself, surrounded by formidable medieval ramparts, would be striking anywhere. What makes it seem almost unearthly is its setting at the very end of a long, narrow bay immediately backed by the almost-sheer, pale, 1,770-m.-high (5,800 ft.) wall of Mount Lovčen.

The medieval Serbian Nemanja Kings were quick to realize the immense strategic importance of this almost hidden port, and awarded it a number of special privileges. Later the Venetians did the same, granting the town semi-independence. In 1807 it was occupied by Napoleon's General Gauthier. Encouraged by the English, the Montenegrins and the people of Boka united, rose up against the French and besieged Kotor. Gauthier seized part of the cathedral treasure and minted silver coins with it to buy food for his troops, and some of these numismatic rarities are on view in the Maritime Museum. On one side they bear an N with an Imperial Crown and the motto *Dieu protège la France*—which, by 1813, was very necessary indeed. On the other are the words, *Cattaro en état de siège*—1813. The French surrendered in January 1814, but at the Congress of Vienna the Russians successfully opposed the promised unification of the Gulf region with Montenegro, and the whole coast became Austrian.

Alas, this remarkable little town was among the worst hit by the 1979 earthquake and it will be some years before it is restored to its former glory. Much of the walled town is closed to visitors and the situation concerning its most important monuments is constantly changing so it is wise to consult the Tourist Information office on arrival. One of the first buildings to be restored, however, is the unique Maritime Museum, already mentioned, which should re-open in 1984. It is housed in the Grgurin Palace and gives a very complete idea of the seagoing activities of the Boka region. The Seamen's Guild of Kotor is one of the oldest in Europe, its records going back to A.D. 809. The most interesting building in Kotor is unquestionably its 12th-century Romanesque-style Cathedral of St. Tryphon. This also suffered badly in the earthquake, but is open for a few hours each day (usually mornings). There is a legend that Kotor bought its patron saint with gold. Apparently in A.D. 890 a ship in difficulties sought refuge in the Boka with a cargo of sacred relics for sale in Europe (one of the biggest exports from the Near East at that time), including the head of a Byzantine saint by the name of Tryphon, who had suffered martyrdom by decapitation. The inhabitants of Kotor, who had for some time been feeling the lack of a patron saint of their own, bought the head and other relics of the saint for 300 pieces of gold. The third of February is the anniversary of this strange transaction, and every year it is celebrated with an important fair. The people wear their folk costumes, and there is peasant dancing and other festivities.

The cathedral was built in the 12th century on the foundations of a ninth-century church, and is dominated by its two Renaissance towers, which were added following an earlier earthquake which had almost totally destroyed the town. The ciborium, or baldachin, a kind of sculptured stone canopy over the high altar, is one of a number of such structures in Yugoslavia. The reliefs carved upon it recount the life story of the saint.

In the apse there is another great work of art, a silver panel in bas-relief (1440) by John of Basle, a wandering artist whose condition of chronic bigamy carried him all the way to Kotor by way of escape. There are countless other objects of historic and artistic worth besides the ciborium and John of Basle's bas-reliefs, which can be seen in the cathedral treasury.

Other interesting churches in Kotor were closed after the earthquake, but most will re-open as restoration progresses. They include the small Orthodox basilica of St. Luke, built in the 12th century in Byzantine style, and containing innumerable icons, some of great value; and the more recent St. Mary, built in a style reminiscent of the Serbian monasteries. As far as civil architecture is concerned, there are the patrician homes of the Bysanti, Prima and Drago families. The City Tower was built in 1602 over the ancient "Turris Torturae," or Torture Tower, the clock being added as a peace offering from the French invaders in 1807.

An excursion from Kotor is to the Vrmac Peninsula northwest of the city, perhaps leaving the coast road at Prčanj to climb Mount Vrmac, from which you can see Dobrota across the water. Although only 760-m.-high (2,500 ft.), Mount Vrmac was a landmark familiar to countless great medieval sailors—the welcome sign that yet another dangerous voyage had been safely accomplished. One of the last of these sailors was Ivo Vizin, who sailed away in 1852 in a locally-built ship to make a circumnavigation of the globe. Prčanj reached the peak of its prosperity in the 18th century, and there are a number of fine baroque houses of the period there, also a convent in which the Lord's Prayer is recorded in 166 different languages.

Rounding the northern tip of the peninsula, where the gap separating it from the opposing coastline is so narrow that strong swimmers have swum it despite the current, you come to Lepetane (the name coming from the Italian *le putane* for the ladies of easy virtue who flourished here) set among tall palms and flowering shrubs. In this obviously attractive spot, the Venetian Republic established a sort of glorified brothel to give a welcome to sailors visiting the ports of the Boka.

The circuit of the peninsula from Kotor and back is only some 32 km. (20 miles), and about halfway round, in the southwest, is the industrial town and port of Tivat, once Illyrian Teuta, which has an airport. Its good beaches have also made it a popular tourist center, and there is a big openair summer stage. Just north of Tivat, at Lastva and

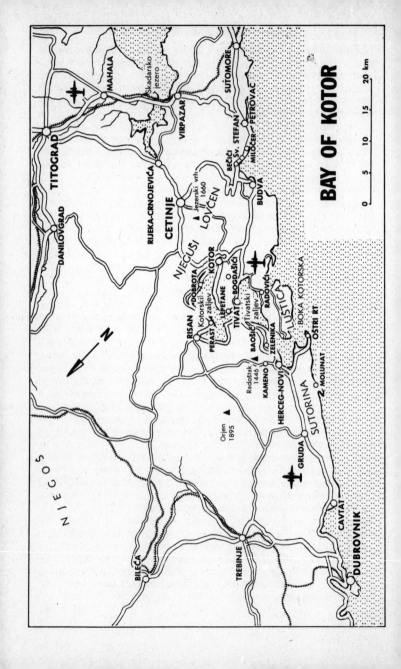

Pržno, are a number of good bathing beaches. Just south of it, near the base of the peninsula, are three small islands, one of which is an important tourist-settlement.

After Kotor the *Magistrala* bypasses both these peninsulas and climbs to Trojica, from which there is a magnificent view of the Budva and Kotor bays. The old fortifications here remind us that this was the frontier between Venice and later Austria, and the tiny independent principality of Montenegro. It was here that Napoleon's General—later Marshal—Marmont had discussions with the Prince Bishop Petar I in 1807, in an unsuccessful effort to bring Montenegro in on the French side.

Trojica, six km. (four miles) south of Kotor, is the meeting place of no less than five roads, and one of them (the renowned Serpentine) takes us on another most attractive excursion from the old city. This is to Lovčen and the 19th-century Montenegrin capital of Cetinje, to be described later.

Budva and Beyond

The *Magistrala* continues from Trojica 20 km. (12 miles) south to Budva, where there are more beaches than can be found on much of the Dalmatian coast to the north. This area was badly hit by two devastating earthquakes in 1979, and most older and many modern buildings were damaged or destroyed. Because of this, the old walled town of Budva is likely to be closed to visitors for some years to come. Nevertheless, the first glimpse of Budva bay is unforgettable: steep, scrub-covered mountains slope down to a beach-fringed shore, and there at the northern end of the bay stands Budva itself.

Once it has been restored, you will find Budva (the "Butua" of the Romans) a charming old town. Built within 15th-century walls on a tongue of land thrust into the southern Adriatic, with a history going back to Phoenician times, it also possesses the remains of an ancient Greek cemetery. When the Roman Empire split in two, Budva was a frontier-town between the halves, ruled respectively from Rome and Constantinople. It was Venetian for four centuries, and it was the architects of the maritime Republic who gave it its present appearance. The so-called "mosaic beach" of nearby Bečiči is acknowledged to be one of the best on the Montenegrin coast, not only because of its perfect setting, but also for the quality and colors of its gravelly sand, so that it ranks among the first half dozen in Yugoslavia. Budva and its surroundings have become one of the biggest tourist-centers of the coast, with a marked degree of sophistication, and most facilities have now been fully restored.

9½ km. (six miles) by road south of Budva (five by sea) is the quite enchanting little village of Sveti Stefan. Originally it was an island, but is now connected to the mainland by an artificial causeway. In 1945 this charming old settlement was virtually deserted. Becoming aware of its potential, the Montenegrins built an original tourist-complex comprising the whole village. Sveti Stefan's bathing beaches are the fringes of the narrow causeway linking the town with the mainland. It once possessed powerful fortifications to withstand Turkish raids from their advanced base at Ulcinj only 65 km. (40 miles) to the south, but war and neglect slowly reduced the little town to a decorative ruin which has been expertly restored, each cottage being beautifully transformed into a self-contained apartment, making this a showpiece of the tourist industry.

On the mainland, north of Sveti Stefan, is Miločer, once the summer palace of the royal family, now a hotel and a particularly peaceful spot. Above Miločer is the tiny Monastery of Praskavica, containing some interesting frescos. A number of large hotels have been built in this once remote and peaceful region.

As you travel farther south, through olive groves and delightful coastal scenery, you are actually on a long and quite narrow bridge of land that separates the sea from the freshwater Lake Scutari. It is only 24 km. (15 miles) as the crow flies from the coast to the lake, but the mountain range of Rumija climbing sharply at your left hand to a height of 1,578 m. (5,177 ft.), keeps the two worlds apart, though linked by an excellent road from Petrovac on the coast to Titograd.

Petrovac is only ten km. (six miles) south of Sveti Stefan but, before we reach it, we skirt the great crag of Skoči Devojka—"maiden's leap"—so called because of the legend that a local beauty, pursued by lustful Turks, leaped from there to her death in the sea far below, rather than suffer a fate that is popularly supposed to be worse than death. Petrovac, surrounded by vineyards and crowned by an old castle, has of late become a very popular holiday resort, now largely restored after the earthquake. Its Roman mosaics prove that it has survived through 20 stormy centuries. Its fine sandy beach is crowded enough during the summer.

18 km. (11 miles) farther on is Sutomore, another modern resort, completely rebuilt since the earthquake; but pause on the way to glance at the Gradište Monastery in which there is a fresco of the "Holy Donkey." No one has the faintest idea what the artist might have had in mind. Two great fortresses, Haj and Nehaj built by the Turks, stand up gauntly against the skyline, just before Sutomore. Some of the inhabitants of the region, known as *Spič,* still wear their attractive peasant costumes.

Beyond Sutomore the *Magistrala* leads to Bar, the terminal point of a spectacular railway linking Belgrade with the extreme southwestern coast of Yugoslavia. This line was completed only a few years ago and is an outstanding feat of engineering, for it penetrates apparently impregnable mountains on its way, in the process passing through over 100 tunnels and across 230 bridges. Apart from being a remarkable achievement, it also provides a scenically unforgettable journey.

Bar is a major and growing port, connected by ferry across the Adriatic with Bari in Italy. Inland from Bar lie the remains of Stari Bar immediately below the highest peak of the Rumija Mountains and the ruins of its Turkish fortress, an area particularly badly hit by the earthquake. The ruins remind us that it was finally seized by the Montenegrins after many fierce skirmishes only as recently as 1878 (seen through the eyes of eternity, that is!). The remains of Stari Bar are quite extensive, with several ruined churches, a medieval palace and aqueduct—all set amidst a tangle of shrubs and wild flowers. Below these remains, the present Stari Bar had a certain picturesque and disheveled charm prior to the earthquake, but will really have no place on tourist itineraries for some time to come.

From Bar the *Magistrala* continues for 30½ km. (19 miles) to its southern terminal at Ulcinj, and into a different world—a world of mosques and minarets and Ottoman corsairs. It was in 1571 that the Sultan Suleiman II based pirates in Ulcinj, with orders to harass Venetian shipping in the Adriatic wherever they might find it. They arrived accompanied by their negro servants, whose descendants are in evidence here, the only colored Yugoslavs in existence. These settler pirates soon began to act entirely on their own account and for their own benefit, without thinking too closely which ships they attacked.

Of its colorful past Ulcinj has little to show except some crumbling fortifications, and a fortress castle, occupied until recently by various Albanian families. They obviously did not feel strongly about the conservation of archeological remains, as they cheerfully employed stones bearing Roman and Greek inscriptions for current domestic needs such as blocking up a drafty window, or as the hearthstone for their cooking. The 1979 earthquake was felt particularly strongly here, too, and the little town was for some time reminiscent of a vast building site. However, most of the restoration work has been completed, and the main tourist area of Velika Plaža ("Long Beach") was very little affected. This lies about four km. (2½ miles) south of the town, with a number of modern hotels set beside a huge beach. The gray silky sands here are radioactive and said to produce remarkable results among those suffering from rheumatic complaints, so it is quite common to see visitors burrowing hollows in the beach in which to lie covered up to their necks in sand.

A few kilometers farther south you come to the River Bojana, the border with Albania. On the island of Ada in the river is a particularly well-equipped nudist center.

Exploring Inland Montenegro

Even in a country as strikingly beautiful as Yugoslavia, inland Montenegro stands out. It is not only the sheer beauty and variety of the scenery and the friendly welcome given by the local people that remain in the mind: there is something, too, in the very atmosphere of this strange, quiet region of remote, towering mountains, lowering gorges, and green valleys, that suggests peace in a land which has rarely known it till recent years.

Cetinje

Our first stop in inland Montenegro is the delightful little former capital, Cetinje, with the embassies and official residences built by the Great Powers little more than a century ago, when Montenegro's independence was formally recognized. There is a good road from Budva, but the route we shall take climbs the mountainside from the former Montenegrin-Austrian frontier-post at Trojica (which we have already called at on our way along the coast), high above Kotor.

This latter road, known as the "Serpentine" because of its innumerable hairpin bends, is one of the most spectacular in Europe, and affords breathtaking views from what feels like the side of a precipice. Not far from the top we come to the fertile fields of Njeguši, birthplace of Montenegro's great poet-ruler, Petar II Petrović-Njegoš: his house is now a museum. From here, it is only a short and comparatively easy run into the old capital of Cetinje, but the journey is a tiring hour or more in a good car, and much longer by bus.

Cetinje lies in a fertile bowl of the bare *karst* limestone mountains, snow-bound for four or five months of the year. Today, it is quite a modern small city, but interesting both for its fine site surrounded by mountains and its historical associations. It was founded in 1485 by Ivan Crnojević as better suited for defense against increasing Turkish pressure. His successor, Juraj, had the country's first printing press brought from Venice in 1494, and it was employed in an Orthodox monastery built by Ivan, in producing religious works of various kinds. The first book printed in a Yugoslav language may be seen here. This monastery was the residence of the Prince-Bishops who ruled the country from the 16th century, though it was repeatedly devastated in Turkish raids on the city. The present building dates from 1785. Close beside the monastery is the sinister round Tablja Tower, where in those fierce days (up to less than a century ago) the Montenegrins used to expose the heads of the Turks they had slain.

Cetinje, too, was badly devastated in the 1979 earthquake, but most of its important historic sights, such as the Biljarda Palace and the former house of King Nicolas described below, will be restored by 1984. The graceful Biljarda Palace adjoins the monastery and was built in the mid-19th century to be a more appropriate residence for Montenegro's rulers; it now contains the Ethnographic Museum, the Njegoš Museum, the Modern Art Gallery, and a giant detailed relief map of Montenegro, illustrating the towering peaks and deep valleys of this fascinating land. The Biljarda (Billiard Table) took its name from the trouble attendant on bringing up from the coast a quarter-size billiard table (still on view) when the palace was built. Close to the Biljarda the former house of King Nicolas, now the State Museum, is preserved almost as it was when occupied by the monarch who reigned for 58 years until his abdication in 1918. Among the exhibits are links with both the American President Roosevelt and the British Royal Family. Also near the Biljarda, the former Parliament now housing the History Museum and Art Gallery, is worth a visit. Scattered through the city are other large houses which served mainly as foreign embassies in the days of Montenegro's independence.

From Cetinje, a modern road leads in about 25 km. (16 miles) almost to the summit of 1,765-m. (5,785 ft.) Mt. Lovćen, now topped by an imposing mausoleum to Montenegro's most famous leader Petar II Petrović-Njegoš. Make sure the monument is open (normally 8 A.M. to 6 P.M.) before you start the beautiful but long, winding drive. When you get there, there is still a stiff uphill walk and about 400 steps to climb to reach the mausoleum itself. It's well worth the effort. Though only 38 when he died in 1850, Njegoš accomplished much for his small country. As Prince-Bishop he persuaded the turbulent tribal chiefs to introduce fair taxation and a codified set of laws based upon common right. As a poet his reputation is worldwide.

There is a story that well illustrates his, and his people's, fierce pride. When he was in Rome he was offered the chains of St. Peter to hold. The monk who was acting as his guide asked him why he did not kiss them in the usual way of a pilgrim and he replied, "No Montenegrin will ever kiss a chain!" His great epic poem, *The Mountain Wreath,* is a hymn to liberty that is still acknowledged as unequaled in the poetry of what is now Yugoslavia.

From the mausoleum there is a stunning view. To the northwest is the intricate outline of the Kotorska Gulf, and northeast the chain of the Durmitor Mountains. Eastward lies the stony wilderness of Montenegro, with Cetinje at its heart, while southeast is the vast, waterlily-ringed Lake of Skadar, with Albania beyond. Southwest you can see the blue of the Adriatic and, on clear days, the faint line of the Italian coast on the horizon—all in one of the most romantic and magnificent views in Europe.

When we have looked round Cetinje, we can continue along the modern road that leads to Titograd, the Republic's more accessible modern capital. This route climbs out of Cetinje's fertile valley over bare mountains, and then drops into a wild valley. The road bypasses the remarkable and remarkably colorful village of Rijeka Crnojevića. It's a sort of tiny rural Venice, with brilliantly painted little boats on the river's backwaters as it flows toward Lake Skadar. The boats really are used for fishing: their colors are traditional. The river is spanned by two stone bridges, mellowed by the years and perfect in proportion.

As you travel this road, you look out across pools and marshes along Lake Skadar's shallow edge, where waterlilies grow in great clusters. In May, when they're in bloom, the colors of the flowers, their dark green leaves, the lake's blue and green water, the stony white mountainsides and a brilliantly clear blue sky make it impossible to pass by without stopping to gaze at the remarkable scene. The marshy banks of the lake are slowly being turned into profitable arable land, a project that will not be completed until the end of the century, but which will provide a rich harvest of grapes, early vegetables, cherries, peaches, figs and melons.

Another modern road links Cetinje to the coast near Budva. This winding route passes through 32 km. (20 miles) of monotonously arid, near-desert mountain stretches alternating with small patches of fertile land. The road eventually zigzags down the side of the mountains facing the sea, to give magnificent views of the coast. If your object is merely to get to the coast—say on a circular tour from Budva or some other coastal resort—this is a useful route. But don't follow it just as a short cut and do yourself the disfavor of leaving the Serpentine out of your itinerary. It's almost worth coming to Yugoslavia just to experience this road and to see the strange sight of large coaches and cars creeping like beetles down a perpendicular mountain wall.

From Petrovac to Titograd

Following this modern road, with the railway never far away, we climb past the northwestern shoulder of the Rumija Mountains, among numerous ruined forts, which bear mute but unmistakable witness to the battles that once swept to and fro across these remote lands. When you reach the top of the Sutorman Pass you should stop to take a last look at the Bay of Bar and the Montenegrin coast before rounding countless hairpin bends to Virpazar. There is a pleasant local-style hotel and restaurant in Virpazar, which also has some attractive old houses, and offers possibilities of boating excursions and fishing on the lake. From here, you cross Lake Skadar on a long causeway and a few kilometers farther on enter Titograd.

Ptolemy mentions a town in this area in the second century by its Roman name of Dioclea. The earliest Slav immigrants settled here and gave the town the name of Podgorica, which it retained until 1944, when it was almost completely destroyed.

Rebuilt and renamed Titograd, it is the capital, cultural, economic and political center of Montenegro: a modern city with some striking architecture. But despite the war damage there is still something of old Podgorica to be seen, notably the castle fortress of the Nemanjić, the medieval kings of Serbia, which stands at the confluence of the rivers Zeta and Morača. Also there are the old Ljubić Mosque, the small tenth-century Church of St. George, the old Clock Tower and various Turkish houses. There are some fragments of Roman water conduits to be seen, and on the banks of the Zeta, the substantial remains of what was once Dioclea—now Duklja—with its forum, baths, temples and early churches.

While rebuilt Titograd, therefore, is not particularly interesting, it is a possible base for excursions into the high mountains of northern Montenegro—the great Durmitor, Bjelašica, Komovi and Prokletije ranges.

Montenegro's Mountain Heart

The Durmitor Mountains afford some of the most magnificent scenery in Yugoslavia, and have been made a National Park. In many ways this region provides a striking contrast with some of the bare mountainsides to be seen not very far away. It is also quite different from the coast. Here you can see vast flowering fields, grazing herds of fat cattle, pine forests, deep canyons, and unexpected mountain lakes.

The road we will follow runs northwest from Titograd, through Danilovgrad. Just short of Bogetići, you will suddenly see among the cliffs the twin monasteries of Ostrog, reached by a branch road to the right, just over 1½ km. (one mile) beyond Bogetići.

This is the eyrie from which toward the end of the 15th century Ivan Crnojević descended into the plain of Cetinje to unite the mountain tribes of Montenegro against the common enemy.

Next comes Nikšić, 56 km. (35 miles) from Titograd, which, although today wholly industrial, is not lacking in interest. It was founded as Anagastum by the Romans, of which traces are still visible together with the ruins of "the Emperor's" bridge. Near the Church of Sveti Petar is another of the strange graveyards of the 16th-century heretic sect of the Bogomils.

Some 70 km. (45 miles) north of Nikšić and west of Žabljak is Plužine in the Piva valley, where there is a newly built mountain settlement. The old town has been submerged under the artificial lake created for the hydroelectric power plant of Mratinje, but the well-preserved 16th-century Piva monastery has been reconstructed elsewhere.

It is only when we are beyond Nikšić that the countryside assumes the wild beauty of the Durmitor Mountains, and we recommend the right-hand road from there to Han Zmajevo, through Gvozd to Šavnik, a run of another spectacular 45 km. (28 miles). The town of Šavnik is divided by the deep gorge of the River Komarnica, from the banks of which there is excellent fishing. From the valley we now climb to the Sinjajevina plateau, 2,180 m. (7,150 ft.) above sea level. Once again the road plunges down over 915 m. (3,000 ft.) before we reach Novakovići, where we take the left fork to Žabljak, itself 1,370 m. (4,500 ft.) high, and a popular base for excursions into the mountains that almost surround the little town.

Here there are several hotels, including the recent Jezera, as well as private accommodations and a good camp site. The setting is idyllic and there are marvelous excursion possibilities, by road, on foot or on horseback. Great mountains and deep canyons are the special features of these landscapes, the canyons including the magnificent Tara tumbling beneath towering rock cliffs reaching up to well over 915 m. Three- or four-day raft trips can be arranged along the Tara (through Montenegroturist); camping along the way with equipment and food provided, it is an unforgettable experience. Winter is also a good time for Žabljak, which now has reasonable skiing facilities.

The famous Black Lake is only three kilometers (two miles) away, hidden in a deep pine forest beneath the mass of Mount Medvjed (Bear Mountain). A path winds its picturesque way through the forest to Lake Zminje and the Durmitor Hotel, from which there is a majestic view of the great peaks of Sljeme, Savin Kuk, Bogaz and, highest of them all, Bobotuv Kuk, 2,500 m. (8,200 ft.) above sea level.

The road from Žabljak to Plevlja, 74 km. (46 miles) away and the northernmost town in Montenegro, crosses the spectacular 163-m.-high (536 ft.) viaduct that spans the River Tara, and then climbs once more through Kosanica to Odžak. Among Plevlja's numerous mosques that of Hussein Bey is outstanding. The Monastery of the Trinity, built at the time of the Nemanjić kings of Serbia is just outside the town.

An attractive alternative road back to Titograd from Žabljak follows part of the magnificent Tara river to Mojkovac and Kolašin—a matter of some 160 km. (100 miles) by road. The gorges are among the most extraordinary sights of their kind in Yugoslavia—and it is a country of many gorges—rising almost sheer to over 915 m. above the river bed.

The road built along the upper course of the canyon follows it across a viaduct carrying the main road from Titograd to Čačak (in Serbia: via Bijelo Polje) near Mojkovac.

Kolašin, just off the main Titograd–Čačak route, is on a ringroad that completely encircles the National Park on the Bjelašica Mountains, where there are a number of delightful lakes—Lake Biograd, 1,190 m. (3,900 ft.) above sea level, being the most attractive of them all. This is the center of the National Park, Biogradska Gora, and there is an inn on the water's edge where you can spend the night.

Kolašin itself is a small town dominated by a Turkish fortress. From Kolašin southward the main highway rises to cross a high ridge, then plunges spectacularly down into the valley of the Morača River. 26 km. (16 miles) from Kolašin you reach the astonishingly well-preserved Morača Monastery, founded in 1252 by Prince Stefan of the Nemanja dynasty. Morača's interior is completely covered with frescos, including remarkably a portrayal of Elijah in the wilderness which dates from 1252. Most of the others date from the 16th and 17th centuries, and are rather traditional in style. South of the monastery begins the 47-m.-long (29 miles) Morača River gorge, reputedly the most picturesque in all Yugoslavia.

Kolašin also serves as the gateway to eastern Montenegro, via the steep mountain road which leads over the 1,585-m. (5,200-ft.) Trešnjevik Pass to the village of Andrijevica, a good center for hunting and fishing trips. To the south stand the Komovi Mountains, rising to over 2,450 m. (8,000 ft.), and forming the frontier between Montenegro and Albania. Most tourists, however, avoid this adventurous route by following the wide, well-surfaced modern road round the Bjelasica Mountains' northern slopes. Another road runs eastward from Ivangrad, Yugoslavia's worst-polluted town north of Andrijevica, through Rožaj to Kosovska Mitrovica, north of Priština in Serbia's Kosovo region. Beyond Kosovska Mitrovica the road joins the main Kraljevo–Priština route that we have already followed along the Ibar Valley.

From Andrijevica we suggest two excursions. The first is north for some 20 km. (12 miles) to the 12th-century Monastery of Djurdjevi Stupovi, close to Ivangrad—not to be confused with the ruined monastery of the same name near Novi Pazar in Serbia. The second is for those who like magnificent scenery and fishing, and takes you south from Andrijevica, through Murino, to Plav, a small mountain resort by a lake in which, believe it or not, the trout often weigh up to ten kilo. (22 lb.).

The last halt before the Albanian frontier is the little oriental town of Gusinje, where in any case the road comes to an end. It is famous for peasant costumes and folk dancing.

It is from Murino that the road leading over the 1,830-m. (6,000-ft.) Čakor pass into Kosovo begins. It was over this terrifying road, covered at the time in deep snow, that the Serbian army—their king at their head—retreated in 1915 from the Austrians all the way into Albania. Scores of men slipped to their deaths from the icy rock-ledges along which they had to struggle—there was no road in 1915—and 1000s more died when they dropped exhausted and tried to sleep in the snow. The Čakor is Yugoslavia's highest pass and the road over it is rugged but scenically magnificent. Its summit marks the boundary between Montenegro and Serbia.

PRACTICAL INFORMATION FOR MONTENEGRO

HOW TO GET THERE. By plane. There is a daily air service each way between Belgrade–Titograd and Belgrade–Tivat. During the summer season there are flights from Belgrade to Ivangrad and to Žabljak.

By train. There is a rail link with the port of Bar and Belgrade (and, thus, the rest of the Yugoslav railroad system). See Facts At Your Fingertips at the start of the book for more information.

WHEN TO GO. Like the adjoining coast of southern Dalmatia, Montenegro's has a long season, and it is best if possible to avoid the hottest, most crowded months of July and August. Winter can be pleasant unless your visit coincides with a spell of *bura,* the cold north wind (though this usually clears the skies and heralds a dry spell) or with the *jugo,* a warmer but wet south wind. Prices in winter are very reasonable. Inland Montenegro is a place in which to visit the mountains, and to enjoy a remarkable but little known range of monuments and museums. In the bare mountain areas of the interior mid-summer may be too torrid for a holiday. However, you only pass through these arid zones briefly on your way to the alpine climate of the Durmitor Mountains, where hot days are followed by delightfully cool and refreshing nights, one of the region's greatest attractions. There is also a developing winter sports season, the main center being Žabljak.

HOTELS AND RESTAURANTS. There has been a rash of hotel development along the coast, not all of it beautiful, but providing good amenities against a usually fabulous backdrop of profuse vegetation and soaring peaks. Following the 1979 earthquake, the establishments listed below are those that escaped damage or have been restored at the time of going to press, or which are expected to have been reconstructed by 1984. Greater attention is now being given to self-catering facilities, while accommodations in private houses are also available in a number of resorts (enquire through Montenegroturist).

Except at a few centers, hotel accommodations in inland Montenegro are still relatively scarce, and often simple. However, establishments in categories (E) (M) will have all or many rooms with bath or shower, and provided you are prepared to manage without a few luxuries for a night or two, you will find the others quite adequate for a short-term stay.

Apart from those within the main hotels, the choice of restaurants is fairly limited. One regional specialty you might like to try, if you can get it, is a whole sheep cooked in a vast cauldron filled with milk. It's an excellent gala dish, particularly if cooked over charcoal in the open air.

ANDRIJEVICA. On the road to Kosovo. *Komovi* (I), 26 rooms.

BIJELO POLJE. *Sandžak* (M), 82 rooms.

BIOGRADSKO JEZERO (Lake Biograd). *Biogradsko Jezero* (I), 15 rooms.

BUDVA. Popular resort with several beaches of coarse sand or stones. However, access to the old walled town is temporarily prohibited as the town was particularly badly hit in the 1979 earthquake. *Avala* (E), just outside the walls, has been rebuilt and is ultramodern, with all facilities, also some villas. *Mogren* (M), next door to Avala, although affected by the earthquake, has now been reconstructed.

Hotels by the more extensive beach of **Slovenska Plaža,** a few minutes' walk away, were destroyed and for the moment there is only a campsite there. A little farther on, by the large beach of **Bečići** (a few kilometers south of the old town) is a complex of hotels set in pleasant gardens: *International,* with own pool; *Mediteran,* 220 rooms; *Merkur,* 260 rooms; *Montenegro,* 280 rooms; and *Splendid,* 190 rooms. All upper (M).

Restaurants. The *Vidikovac* on the main road offers a marvelous view overlooking the old town. Otherwise, *Sunce* in town near the harbor, and *Obala* on the outskirts.

CETINJE. The intriguing former capital of Montenegro. *Park* (E), with pool, in the Castle Park. Reconstructed since earthquake.

Restaurant. *Gradska Kafana,* fairly basic but with terrace and dancing. Well-placed for visiting the monuments.

DANILOVGRAD. *Zeta* (M), 70 rooms.

HERCEG-NOVI. Attractive resort with splendid gardens set steeply on slopes by Bay of Kotor. *Plaža* (E), 320 rooms. Rebuilt hotel with pool, mini-golf, shops; rises like a massive glasshouse from the shore (stony and paved bathing beach). *Topla* (M), pavilion-type villas on terraces by the sea. *Rent-a-Ville* near the town center is a modern complex of self-catering accommodations. Private rooms also available in town.

At **Njivice,** reached by motorboat across the bay in about seven minutes: *Riviera* (M), over 200 rooms. Guests may share the facilities of other hotels in the town. Njivice lies a little beyond neighboring *Igalo,* and *Tamaris* are both large (M)s, with pools and all facilities. (The Institute of Physiotherapy and Rehabilitation at Igalo offers cures through radioactive water and mud, but the resort lacks the charm of Herceg-Novi.)

Restaurants. The following are all recommended: *Glicinia,* with terrace; *Gradski Restoran,* with shady terrace; and *Škver,* for fish specialties.

KOLAŠIN. *Bjelašica* (E), 200 rooms. Reconstructed.

MANASTIR MORACA. *Morača* (I), 20 rooms. Adjoins the monastery. Simple.

MILOČER. Peaceful small resort linked with Sveti Stefan. *Miločer* (E), housed in the former summer residence of the Yugoslav royal family. Small, gracious, very quiet in extensive grounds which also contain the *Novi Miločer* (E). *Maestral* (E), 160 rooms. Near the first two hotels; own pool, casino.

MOJKOVAC. Useful and attractive transit point near the Tara River in the heart of the interior. *Mojkovac* (M), 70 rooms. Modern.

NIKŠIČ. A handy stop-off point en route to the Durmitor Mountains. *Onogošt* (M), 60 rooms, all with bath. Comfortable.

PETROVAC. Pleasant resort just off the main road with good facilities. *Castellastva* (M), 175 rooms. Friendly atmosphere, near the sea. *Pallas* (M), 180 rooms. Newly rebuilt; even closer to the sea. *Rivijera* (M), 80 rooms. *Vile Oliva* (M), 110 rooms.

About five km. (three miles) to the north: *As* (L), 210 rooms. In splendid isolation beside the shore. Pool.

ROŽAJE. An embryo winter sports center in the mountains near the South Serbia border. *Motel Turjak* (M), 13 rooms. *Rozaje* (M), 38 rooms.

SUTOMORE. Attractive small coastal village, almost entirely rebuilt, with beach of coarse sand and stones (also waterfront). *Nikšić* (M) and *Sozina* (M), the former new, are both near the waterfront.

Just south of the village, by the larger beach, is the *Zlatna Obala* (M), a complex of hotels including *Juzno More* and *Korali,* 870 rooms. Direct access to the main road which passes above the resort.

SVETI STEFAN. A former fishing village within medieval fortifications on a tiny island linked to the coast and Miločer by a modern causeway; now converted into 110 apartments of a luxury holiday village. With casino, sports center, openair theater; utterly charming.

TITOGRAD. The entirely rebuilt capital of Montenegro. *Crna Gora* (M), 130 rooms. Modernized. *Podgorica* (M), 60 rooms. Situated on the bank of the River Morača, with its restaurant terrace overlooking the Nemanja fortress. Attractive stone building. *Zlatica* (M), 64 rooms.

Restaurant. *Mareza,* 9½ km. (six miles) from the town on the Cetinje road, specializes in fish and has its own fish tanks to prove it.

TIVAT. Resort and small port on the Bay of Kotor, now also the site of an international airport. Indifferent beach. *Mimoza* (M), 69 rooms. In the town overlooking palm-fringed waterfront. *Palma* (M), 21 rooms.

Toward neighboring **Lastva** is *Tivat* (M), 26 rooms. 1½ km. (one mile) farther on, at Lastva, are *Kamelija* (M), 95 rooms, and *Park* (M), 66 rooms. On the island of **Sveti Marko** is a *Club Méditerranée.*

ULCINJ. The southernmost seaside resort in Yugoslavia, close to the Albanian border. Much post-earthquake restoration has taken place in this appealing town stacked around a bay and sandy beach. There is a distinct oriental atmosphere to the place. *Galeb* (M), now reconstructed, and *Mediteran* (M), 244 rooms, are both in the town. About 1½ km. (one mile) out is *Albatros* (M), 75 rooms. Three private beaches, one reserved for nudists.

Around four km. (2½ miles) south of town is the 11-km.-long (seven miles) Velika Plaža ("Long Beach") of very fine, gently shelving sands, Yugoslavia's most extensive. Here there is the *Olympic* (E), 130 rooms. Own pool. *Bellevue* (M), 370 rooms. Beach-side restaurant. *Grand-Hotel Lido* (M), 52 rooms and many bungalows. Best-placed of the three, on edge of the sands. A big new luxury complex, *Otrant,* is under construction by the beach, with casino, sports center and marina all planned.

16 km. (ten miles) to the south is the large and splendid *Ada Naturist Complex* (E) and (M), set on an island in the River Bojana forming the border with Albania. Offers a wide range of water sports and riding facilities.

Restaurants. There are several small pleasant private restaurants, among them *Stijena,* set in the rocks overlooking the Bay of Ulcinj from the south.

ŽABLJAK. Mountain resort at around 1,370 m. (4,500 ft.) in spectacular setting among the highest peaks of the Durmitor range. *Planinka* (E), 105 rooms. New. *Jezero* (M), 103 rooms. Recent. *Žabljak* (M), 31 rooms. *Durmitor* (I), 20 rooms plus bungalows.

HOW TO GET AROUND. By coach. There is a far-flung network of coach services operating from Titograd's bus station. You can reach any sizeable town in Yugoslavia within 24 hours of leaving the Montenegrin capital.

Montenegroturist and the other main travel firms run a full range of excursions, and will make all your bookings and reservations.

By car. All major roads are surfaced, but narrow, and because of Montenegro's mountainous nature they are very winding. The main axes lead northward from Petrovac on the coast road across the northern edge of Lake Skadar, via Titograd and Bijelo Polje to Titovo Užice; with a lateral connection from south of Bijelo Polje to Kosovo. A rugged branch southward from this route climbs the spectacular Čakor pass and descends to Peč.

WHAT TO SEE. Great chains of mountains scored by torrential rivers that plunge into deep canyons and gorges, clear mountain lakes, sunny, sandy beaches and ancient towns revealing the story of the centuries—the choice is infinite, despite the fact that Montenegro is the smallest of Yugoslavia's six federal republics. The best known area, inevitably, is along the coast with its string of beach-side resorts and many hotels, some of them adjoining charming little old towns with ancient traditions, such as Kotor and Budva, and Ulcinj with its oriental ambience. The luxury tourist-center of Sveti Stefan, converted from an old fishing village on a promontory, is a showpiece. Note that Montenegro has many of Yugoslavia's best beaches.

The touristic mountain zone lies in the north and northwest of the country. Žabljak is the obvious center for excursions into the Durmitor range. The 88-km.-long (55 miles) Tara canyon is one of the most remarkable in the world, and although much shorter, that of Morača is equally beautiful, and has been made readily accessible by the opening of the Titograd–Bioče–Kolašin road. The Prokletije Mountains, which guard the frontier with Albania, are also very beautiful.

The south of Montenegro is centered on the north of mighty Lake Skadar, while its heart is in its interesting former capital of Cetinje. Westward, Mount Lovčen gives a tremendous view across the intricate network of deep bays known as the Gulf of Kotor, with Lake Skadar also just visible to the south.

SPORTS. Hunting and fishing are at their best in northern Montenegro. There are a number of state-run hunting preserves—for permission apply to the Secretariat for Agriculture in Titograd. The best fishing is in the rivers Lim and Tara, and their tributaries the Morača and Piva; also in the upper reaches of the Zeta near Nikšić. Biograd Lake near Kolašin, Black Lake near Žabljak, and the other neighboring glacial lakes are excellent for trout. Permits for fishing are granted at the Town Hall of the nearest town or village.

Spectacular rafting trips (usually three to four days, with camping equipment) through the Tara river gorges are arranged by Montenegroturist. Also, water skiing and wind surfing, notably in Budva (Bečići), Sveti Stefan and Ada (near Ulcinj).

 USEFUL ADDRESSES. Montenegroturist are to be found in the majority of resorts. Their principal office is in the town of Budva. Most resorts have a local Tourist Information office, though the actual information dispensed is rather limited.

BOSNIA-HERZEGOVINA

Approaching the Orient

The domes and slender minarets scattered across the landscapes of Bosnia and Herzegovina lend them an oriental air, hardly to be wondered at when you recall that they formed part of the Ottoman Empire for no less than four centuries.

The Turkish heritage is evident not only in the architecture. A good many of the present-day inhabitants have also kept the faith of their former masters, although there are, and always were, numerous Christian districts and enclaves. The Moslems built their houses in the Turkish style, with balconies and interior gardens or patios. Their townships are crowded closely round the mosque and public fountain, with narrow, winding, haphazard alleys typical of all old oriental towns. The Christian villages, on the other hand, have wider streets. Their houses are far more spaced out. There are also a large number of modern towns that have been built since World War II, to replace others destroyed during the fighting.

Despite the harsh and rocky aspect of its treeless hilltops, the province of Herzegovina, in the south nearest the coast, is not inhospitable, for there are green mountain hollows *(polje),* and its rainfall and high sunshine record allow it to produce three crops of tobacco in a single year. In addition there are everywhere disciplined ranks of olive groves and sturdy fig trees to testify to the fertility of this rough-looking soil.

There is no lack of distraction if you decide to spend a few days in this part of the country, among some of the most striking scenery in all Yugoslavia—but it is not a place in which to try to force the pace. Although the main routes are good, you will find secondary roads vary from adequate to poor.

Herzegovina affords magnificent scenery and fascinating towns. It also provides good rock climbing and mountaineering, and no shortage of well-equipped refuges and chalets to serve as bases for such activities. The forests which cover the lower slopes are rich in game such as chamois, deer, bear and wild boar, not to mention a great variety of partridge, pheasant and other game birds. Packs of wolves add an element of danger. The rivers are teeming with trout, and trips can be made by raft or kayak down the moderately easy but exciting rapids of the Drina Gorge, and other reaches of the mountain rivers.

In certain of the more isolated and lonely parts of Herzegovina, you will come across large and curiously carved tombs, placed there in the Middle Ages by the religious sect of the Bogomils who inhabited these remote places during periods of persecution.

The capital of the combined provinces of Bosnia-Herzegovina is the picturesquely situated city of Sarajevo, architecturally a blend of East and West, though Herzegovina's principal town is Mostar, farther south. Mostar is largely Turkish in appearance, its houses and mosques clustering upstream from its famous Turkish bridge.

Away to the northeast is Travnik, the home of the Turkish Vizirs or Governors of Bosnia for 150 years. Other interesting towns include Jajce at the junction of the rivers Vrbas and Pliva. The rivers meet at a dramatic waterfall below the ruined castle captured by the Turks after many attempts in 1528. Banja Luka is one of the few other large towns, and is largely Western-looking, despite its many minarets. Everywhere in this little-known corner of Yugoslavia you will be captivated by reminders of its Roman, Islamic and Christian past.

A Brief Historic Background

During the sixth century there was a massive influx of Slav tribes from the northeast into what is today Yugoslavia. They were early converted to Christianity, and sovereignty over them was a matter of long-drawn-out dispute between Rome and Byzantium. After a time the western area, made up of Slovenia and Croatia, became Catholic (though employing the Slav Liturgy), while Serbia and Macedonia in the east favored the Orthodox religion. The dividing line of this marked difference in religious development therefore ran directly through Bosnia.

The Slav tribes were ruled by patriarchal chieftains *(pleme)*. Bosnia, at least during the tenth and 11th centuries, fell within the Serbian sphere of influence. Later it was one of the founder members of the little semi-independent state of Duklja, which was to become Montenegro. By the 12th century, Bosnia had allied itself with the Hungarian-Croat monarchy, which upon becoming wholly Hungarian, extended its frontiers into the mountainous south. The province was given the status of a duchy—Herzegovina deriving from the Hungarian word *herceg,* meaning "duke."

In 1463, the Turks under Sultan Mohammed II occupied the country and converted many to Islam—there are still, today, well over a million Moslems in the province—especially members of the schismatic Bogomil sect. The Bogomils followed the ascetic beliefs and dualism of the Manichees, a fourth-century Christian heresy prevalent in this region during the late Roman Empire, colored by the desire for a national church. They maintained connections with the forerunners of the Reformation in Western Europe—the Albigensians or Cathars (the Pure Ones) of northern Italy and southern France. But that is about all we know for certain, except that their western cousins lived very simple lives that demanded much more self-sacrifice than the official religions.

The Bosnian chieftains adopted the Moslem faith and continued to wield wide administrative powers. Their example was slowly followed by many of the common folk.

The Turks had come to stay for over four centuries, and it was not until 1875 that Bosnia raised the standard of revolt, abetted by Serbia and Montenegro. The Great Powers were engaged in the struggle to gain influence in the Balkan Peninsula, and Bosnia's fight for independence was discussed by Bismarck and Disraeli during the Congress of Berlin in 1878. Britain, France, Russia, Prussia and Italy, however, destroyed the hopes of the Bosnian patriots by doing no more than changing their masters from Constantinople to Vienna. Bosnia fought on for three months to prevent the completion of Austro-Hungarian occupation, but matters became still worse when the Emperor Franz Josef annexed both Bosnia and Herzegovina to make them part of the Habsburg Empire in 1908.

This produced increased tension between the Entente Cordiale and members of the Triple Alliance.

In Bosnia, university students formed themselves into a secret society called *Mlada Bosna* (Young Bosnia). One of its members was Gavrilo Princip, who in 1914 assassinated Archduke Franz Ferdinand, heir to the throne of Austria-Hungary, during his state visit to Sarajevo —launching a series of events which led to World War I.

Austria accused Serbia of complicity in the assassination, and the four years of death and destruction that was World War I followed. With the demise of the Austro-Hungarian Empire, Bosnia and Herzegovina became a province of the new Kingdom of Yugoslavia. During World War II it was one of Tito's principal partisan strongholds.

Yugoslavia's stormy past does much to explain the varieties of religions to be found within its frontiers. There is a misleading habit of classifying Moslems as "Turks." Actually, the Turkish population voluntarily returned to Turkey as the power of the Ottoman Empire declined. The present inhabitants of Bosnia and Herzegovina, Christian and Moslem, are Slavs.

Exploring Bosnia-Herzegovina

If you have chosen Sarajevo as your destination in this region, leave the *autoput* near Okučani to cross the River Sava which marks the boundary between Bosnia and Croatia. After a run of some 60 km. (38 miles) you will reach Bosnia's second town of Banja Luka, rebuilt after a severe earthquake in 1969. There is an Old Town and a New Town divided by the river, but the latter has not much to show the casual visitor. The town's most remarkable building is the 16th-century mosque of Ferhad Pasha Sokolović, erected with the 30,000 ducats which the Turks received from the Austrian General Auersperg by way of ransom for his son. The Sahat-Kula (Clock Tower) is also of interest. 35 km. (22 miles) southeast along the Vrbanja River, Kotor Varoš lies below an impressive castle that long withstood the Turks. The main road to Jajce closely follows the Vrbas River south through increasingly striking scenery, winding round the edge of precipices and diving through tunnels as it passes rocky peaks, crowned by ruined medieval strongholds. The first town after Banja Luka is Jajce, where early in the 15th century Hrvoje Vukčić Hrvatinić, Duke of Split and Governor of Bosnia, built a great fortress on the site of a still earlier building. Excavations in the town and its surroundings have uncovered traces of numerous Roman villas, and a magnificent bas-relief of the god Mithras from a temple that must once have stood there. Nearby the River Pliva flows over a great fall into the Vrbas.

As you pass through Jajce you may be interested to glance at the crypt—locally called a catacomb—cut into the rock below the fortress, which contains several unusual bas-reliefs. Other local curiosities are the old wooden Turkish watermills near the waterfall, which provide a typical Bosnian touch to the scene.

Jajce, with its mosques, medieval fortifications and typically oriental houses and streets, has great charm, and you cannot fail to notice the 30-m.-tall (100 ft.) belfry of St. Luke, which was built early in the 15th century in an amalgam of the Gothic and Romanesque styles. When the church was converted into a mosque the bell-tower served as a minaret.

Since early in the 15th century Jajce has played an important rôle in the country's history. It was here that the Turks executed Bosnia's last king, Stjepan Tomašević, in 1461. His remains are buried in the small Franciscan Church. It was in Jajce, in 1943, that the Partisans met under the very noses of the Germans and worked out the constitution of the new Yugoslavia when—not if—the war was won.

There are several attractive excursions to be made from Jajce, notably to Jezero, only 9½ km. (six miles) away along the banks of the River Pliva. The town is set amid beautiful scenery beside a lake, in which the fishing is excellent. Be sure to try the delicious cray fish.

Šipovo, farther upstream, preserves several bas-reliefs from its Roman past. Travnik, at the foot of Mount Vlašić, is where the Turkish Vizirs, or Governors, of Bosnia ruled from 1700 until 1852. Once a busy seat of government, immortalized in Ivo Andrić's novel *The Time of the Consuls,* it is today little but a sleepy, predominantly Moslem village, of which the old quarter is wholly Turkish in appearance. A new quarter was created at the beginning of the present century following a serious fire. Some of the fortifications built by the Bosnian King Tvrtko II may still be recognized, and the tombs of the Consuls of Travnik, the Colored Mosque and the still older Mosque of Hadji Ali Beg (with Bosnia's only sundial) and the Turkish cemetery are all of great interest. Today Mount Vlašić is a well-equipped winter sports center.

During ancient times there was a caravan route linking Sarajevo with Central Europe along the Bosna Valley. The present railroad follows this old track to the terminus at Vrpolje, the entire 240 km. (150 miles) having been laid immediately after the war by volunteer bands of Yugoslav youth, helped by student delegations from 42 different nations.

Incidentally, the novel method by which this stretch of track was so quickly constructed was also employed in building the *autoput* that joins Zagreb with Belgrade. In those days almost all roadbuilding had to be done by hand, and this highway represented a very considerable achievement. Over recent years it has been widened and improved.

Of the two minor roads branching south off the Zagreb–Belgrade *autoput,* farther east, the one starting at Slavonski Brod and connected to Bosanski Brod by a bridge is preferable. Both roads leave the plain of the Sava to converge on the Bosna Valley, which leads into the heart of the country, which is itself dotted with attractive little towns, guarded by the crumbling walls of medieval fortresses. The roads meet shortly before Doboj, where there are the remains of a large Roman camp.

Continuing south, Maglaj is perched on the side of a cliff, its ancient houses huddled round the Kuršumli Džamija (Mosque). Farther up the valley is the medieval royal village of Vranduk, with its magnificent castle.

Approaching Sarajevo, you reach Visoko, Roman Bistua Nova, which has Yugoslavia's biggest iron and steel complex and is thus badly polluted, but nearby are the remains of the Bosnian kings' medieval capital, Kraljeva Sutjeska, with ruins of a castle and of the palace, as well as the Franciscan monastery dating from 1340, which contains priceless manuscripts. Visoko is a center of the leather industry, but in the 15th century it was the residence of the Bosnian kings.

Sarajevo, Heart of Bosnia

Sarajevo, a city of nearly 500,000 people, is known to everyone as the setting for the events that led to World War I. Today it is a city of many differing aspects. In the center you feel that you are in the middle of the Orient. The mosques, the craftmen's little shops, the narrow streets and cobbled lanes suggest an Eastern country. A few of the buildings left over from Habsburg rule, however, indicate curious attempts to mingle East and West. Then, when you travel out to Sarajevo's suburbs, you find yourself among the squared-off modern apartments and public buildings that might be found almost anywhere. More recently the city has expanded enormously with districts of highrise and other modern architecture and, of course, has now achieved new international renown as the venue of the 1984 Winter Olympics. These have meant the construction of a number of fine installations, such as the great stadiums of Skenderlija and Zetra, and the Olympic Village.

The name "Sarajevo" is of Turkish origin, deriving from *Saraj Ovasi,* or "Field round the Governor's Palace," though it has been an inhabited site from time immemorial, as is proved by the Neolithic remains and the ruins of Roman baths. After the diminution of the power of Byzantium, Slav tribes established themselves here, but it was under the Turks in the 15th century that the town first became important. Despite present developments and large-scale Austro-Hungarian building during the last century, the older part of Sarajevo retains its secretive and oriental character. Under the Sultans it became one of the most active military and administrative centers in the Ottoman Empire, and the 16th century, coinciding with further Turkish expansion, was the city's Golden Age. The great builder of Sarajevo was Gazi Husref Bey, who was its governor from 1521 until 1541, and he brought fine taste as well as great energy to his task, so that by the 17th century the city possessed a number of palaces and public baths, and 73 mosques.

This period of expansion and prosperity was followed by one of disaster. Sarajevo was captured in 1697 by Prince Eugene of Savoy, fighting in the service of Austria. His troops did great damage, and deported or conscripted many of the inhabitants, so that it was not for a long time that the city regained anything of its former animation and beauty. Under pressure from the Western Powers, the Turks introduced a number of reforms in 1850, which encouraged the city's recovery, and the Austrians, when they took control of Bosnia in 1878, carried out extensive plans for its modernization. Today, its many historical buildings are lovingly preserved.

Exploring Sarajevo

The old town, with its narrow streets bordered by oriental-style houses, is perched on the steep slopes of the Miljacka Valley, and the new quarter has spread across the plateau of Sarajevsko Polje, situated at the mouth of a fortified gorge at a height of over 490 km. (1,600 ft.). The whole is encircled by mountains gradually dropping down into small hills, upon which are laid out the many delightful Turkish-style gardens for which the city is famous.

Undoubtedly one of the most interesting quarters of Sarajevo is that of the *souks,* or oriental market, which begins at Baščaršija (Market Square) and is approached from there down a maze of narrow alleys seething with a colorful motley crowd, a spectacle that seems to belong wholly to North Africa or the Near East. Just behind the *souks* is the Baščaršija Mosque, whose dominating aspect makes it even harder to realize that you are still in Europe.

Farther on you will come to the Brusa Bezistan, built in 1551, where the carpets, silks and brocades were stored to await the departure of the next caravan for the north, and now housing displays of Bosnian folk costumes and crafts. These caravans always stopped at Morića Han, which was one of the oldest caravanserais in the Balkans, and which has been restored after a recent fire. *Hans,* though now often ruined, may still be seen throughout Anatolia, Syria, Iraq and Persia.

Some were often little more than sheltered stopping-places for man and beast, set about a day's march of 30–40 km. (20–25 miles) apart for 100s, sometimes 1000s, of kilometers along main caravan trade routes. Some, however, are quite elaborate.

It was the energetic Gazi Husref Bey who built among other things the magnificent Begova Džamija (Mosque of the Bey) in 1530, which you will see from Sarači (Saddlers') Street. It has exquisite Persian carpets and prayer rugs, as well as one of the earliest-known copies of the Koran. After his death a tomb was erected for Gazi Husref by the mosque, where he is buried beside his greatest friend, Murat Bey Tardić, a Christian converted to Islam, and subsequently Governor of the province.

Close beside the mosque is the Clock Tower, or Sahat-Kula, upon the face of which the hours of prayer are marked in Arabic numerals. Inside the gates is the fountain whose waters are used for the ritual ablutions demanded by Islamic law as a preliminary to prayer.

If you turn west from this courtyard into Mudželiti Street, you will come to the *Imaret,* built at the same period to provide food for poor students. Here, too, is Musafirhana, a hostel maintained as a religious duty by the richer citizens, in which any poor traveler had the right to claim free bed and board for three days. The great bakery of the Imaret of Sarajevo is still intact.

Another reminder of the golden days of Turkish rule is the Kuršumli Medresa, a theological High School facing the mosque. Unfortunately it was restored in 1910 in such a way as to disguise the beauty of the finely worked doors and windows. Inside, the building is divided into 12 separate classrooms. Its tall chimneys are designed to resemble minarets.

There are so many remarkable mosques to be seen in Sarajevo that a full list would make lengthy reading, but two more at least must be mentioned. The first is the Mosque of Ali Pasha, and the second the Mosque of the Emperor (Careva Džamija), which are close to each other and near the center of the city.

The Ali Pasha Mosque, built in 1560 after the death of the general, is small but beautifully proportioned—an outstanding example of 16th-century Turkish architecture. In the mosque garden are the tombs of two Moslem patriots, Sumbul and Mutelević, executed by the Austrians.

The Emperor's Mosque, on the left bank of the River Miljacka, was built by the Sultan Suleiman in 1566 on the site of an earlier mosque destroyed in 1480 by Bosnian Christians. Next door is Husref Bey's Library. Founded in 1537, it contains a magnificent collection of illuminated manuscripts almost unique in the perfection of their lettering and binding.

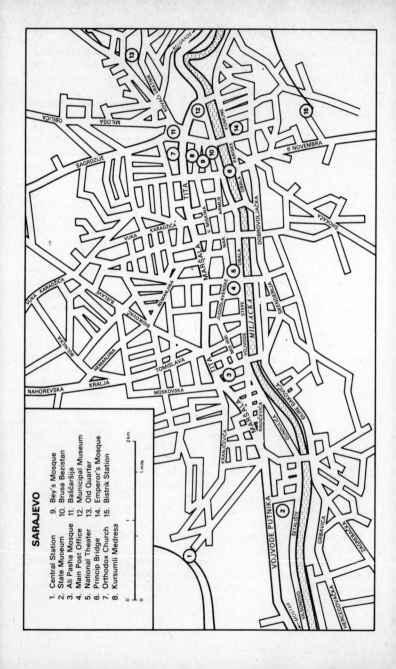

SARAJEVO

1. Central Station
2. State Museum
3. Ali Pasha Mosque
4. Main Post Office
5. National Theater
6. Princip Bridge
7. Orthodox Church
8. Kursumli Medresa
9. Bey's Mosque
10. Brusa Bezistan
11. Baščaršija
12. Municipal Museum
13. Old Quarter
14. Emperor's Mosque
15. Bistrik Station

0   1 mile

0   1   2 km

The call to prayer goes out now on tape recordings (except from Gazi Husref Bey Mosque) and sightseers often outnumber the faithful in the mosques. Nevertheless, although the Moslem religion has in large part succumbed to Communism, it still has some influence in this area.

Other points of interest include the pseudo-oriental building intended by the Austrians to serve as the Town Hall, and the strange little Orthodox Church reconstructed when the Turks were in occupation, with a wall that hid those who visited it from view. It has no campanile in order not to break the Turkish law that no Christian church might be built higher than the mosques of the faithful, but its little treasury contains 14th-century manuscripts, various valuable reliquaries and some beautiful icons. It also has a magnificent iconostasis.

Opposite Princip Bridge, on the wall of the Young Bosnia Museum, is a commemorative plaque marking the spot from which the young Gavrilo Princip fired those fateful shots at the Austrian Archduke, that sparked off World War I.

Do not fail to take a stroll through the picturesque residential quarters of Benbaša and Dariva, which climb the steep slopes of a hill. From the walls of the ancient fortress that crowns Benbaša you will see what were the homes of the Turkish aristocracy of four centuries ago. Even better, admire the view across the city while drinking a very thick, very black, very strong Turkish coffee on the terrace of a *kafana.* On the hill facing you are the white stones of the Turkish cemetery of Alifakovac. The more important graves, those of civic dignitaries and highly-placed families, are roofed with stone canopies to distinguish them from the simple graves of their subjects.

Sitting there as it grows dark, with the swifts screaming overhead as they seek out a late supper, you may well feel that you are a very long way indeed from Times Square or Piccadilly Circus.

Allow some time, too, to explore the surrounding mountains: Trebević, Jahorina, Igman, Bjelašnica, scene of many of the 1984 Winter Olympics events, and Treskavica a little farther afield. The fine modern park-like War Memorial on Vrace on the way to Trebević is well worth a halt.

The Road to Mostar

Both the railway and the road from Sarajevo to Kardeljevo run through the thermal spa of Ilidža. It's a popular excursion point, linked by a regular tram service with Sarajevo. From there, three km. (two miles) along a sideroad, are Vrelo Bosna and the source of the River Bosna, with horse-drawn carriages available to cover the distance. Both are extraordinarily pleasant and green. At Vrelo Bosne, woods and water combine to make the place seem cool, even in summer. The train next turns south to climb Mount Ivan, and you then come into the beautiful sheltered valley of the Neretva, with superb views, passing through many small tunnels and crossing great viaducts.

In this short distance the whole character of the country has changed dramatically, and the climate from temperate to almost subtropical. Here you are in a land of cotton plantations set among fig, almond and olive trees, that also produces the famous yellow Herzegovina tobacco.

Konjic is a charming little town set under the shadow of the great mountains, and despite damage during World War II it still retains something of its former wholly-oriental character. The old bridge close to the fort dates from the 13th century. Some 21 km. (13 miles) from Konjič, near Borci, the lake Boračko Jezero lends green charm to otherwise rather arid scenery.

We now enter the district of Jablanica (also the name of the lake that we have been following for over 30 km./20 miles) which is a center for hunting trips in the Prenj Mountains and the surrounding forests. The great hydroelectric dam retains the waters of three rivers, along whose banks vast Bogomil cemeteries are scattered.

Beyond the town of Jablanica, over whose bridge Tito led 4,000 wounded partisans to safety (there is a museum to the battle near the bridge), the scenery becomes austere but impressive, until once over the pass, the valley again widens to bring us at last to Mostar. On the way you pass more recently built dams and their attendant lakes whose waters are also being exploited for recreational purposes.

Mostar's Mosques and Minarets

Mostar *(most:* bridge, and *stari:* old) is the provincial capital of Herzegovina. Despite high-rise blocks on the outskirts, the view of the town is still dramatic. The countless thin pencils of its minarets, backed by wild and rocky mountains, lend the old town an enchanted air.

The single-span, hump-backed bridge over the Neretva was built by the Turks in 1556, and is one of the most famous and delightful civic works in the whole of Yugoslavia. Local youths prove their manhood by diving or jumping from the highest point into the swift green waters below, and every 4th July there is a competition dedicated to this feat.

Probably Mostar's most attractive mosque is Karadjoz Beg's from the 16th century, which is graceful architecturally and has a richly decorated interior, with carpets presented by many Moslem heads of state. Also worth seeing is the History and Ethnographic Museum near the old bridge. It contains an attractive model of the old town and is housed in Inad Mosque.

There is a very ancient and unusual Orthodox Church in Mostar where you can see the special grille behind which women were screened from the sight of the male worshippers in the same way as they are in a mosque—a Byzantine custom adopted by the Turks. Also well worth visiting is the dwelling of Bišćevića Ćošak, a masterpiece of Turkish-local architecture.

In the middle of so much that is old, it is sobering to note that Mostar's memorial to the dead of World War II must be one of the most striking and moving constructions in the whole of Europe. It is not something you stand and look at, for to see it you have to walk through its stone-flanked lanes and symbolic little artificial gorges. The memorial makes one apprehend especially clearly the sacrifices of the men and women it commemorates.

There are a number of attractive excursions from Mostar. One is to the nearby village of Blagaj, where the River Buna emerges suddenly from the base of majestic cliffs after running underground for nearly 20 km. (12½ miles). On the slopes still stand the ruins of the great fortress of Stjepangrad, built by Herceg (Duke) Stjepan Kosača on the site of the impregnable Roman city of Bone. Blagaj is the original home of the Žilavka grape, and produces the best heavy white Žilavka wine and Blatina red wine. Both were supplied to the Habsburg court. Another is to the rocky plain of Mostarsko Blato—a haunt of every kind of water fowl, since it forms a shallow depression which is flooded each year, attracting great quantities of wildfowl at the nesting season.

From Mostar along the valley of the Neretva, both road and railway are flanked by cliffs rising to well over 915 m. (3,000 ft.). The 16th-century Žitomislić monastery near here has some precious icons. About 30 km. (20 miles) south of Mostar you will see the fortified village of Počitelj. It is set on the banks of the river and was for many centuries a Turkish frontier post. This picturesque spot, abounding in delightful cherry trees, has been painstakingly restored stone-by-stone. It has become an active artists' colony of international standing, with a charming restaurant and accommodations in the village houses.

Traveling through the picturesque Neretva Valley, where once there were many busy water mills, we soon reach Gabela. Not far away is the Hutovo Blato marsh, where again you may find first-rate fishing and wildfowling. No less than 223 species of waterfowl are shot here. The main road and rail continue to follow the river. At Metković, a road branches off to climb the hills and to give the traveler from the north his first unforgettable view of the Dalmatian coast, the Adriatic, and its chain of islands. The road descends before joining the Magistrala.

An alternative route from Mostar to the coast is the newly built road from Buna via Stolac, Ljubinje and Trebinje. At Stolac there is a remarkable Bogomil cemetery with its typical, strangely-carved tombs. A larger necropolis is to be seen at Boljuni. Altogether there are over

2,300 tombs in this area. Popovo Polje, the region some 32 km. (20 miles) beyond Stolac, is an interesting spot. In winter, this plain used to become a shallow lake fed by subterranean streams which forced their way to the surface through a number of craters. Hydroelectric projects along the Trebišnjica river have changed this, though irrigation is planned to keep the plain the green, fertile place it had always been as a result of regular flooding. The road continues to Trebinje, a small town famous for its tobacco, called *trebinjac,* and also a popular excursion center. Market days on Saturdays are fun to watch.

If Turkish architecture interests you, you should certainly make it a point to see Begova Kuća (the Bey's house) and the Mosque of Osman Pasha at Trebinje. The fine, seven-arched, 76-m.-long (250 ft.) Turkish bridge, Arslanagića Most, has been reconstructed about 800 m. (half a mile) from its original site before the damming of the Trebišnjica river. Fishermen should note that California trout are plentiful in the upper Trebišnjica during the months of July and August. It is an odd river, as it disappears underground in the Popovo Polje to reemerge close to Dubrovnik, as the Ombla, described in our chapter on Southern Dalmatia.

Wild Grandeur

Trebinje is only 32 km. (20 miles) northeast of Dubrovnik, on the scenically lovely road inland, roughly along first the border of Herzegovina with Montenegro, then of Bosnia with Serbia. The 17th-century frescos of the monasteries of Dobrićevo and Zavala have been preserved, even though the former had to be moved and painstakingly reerected when the Bilećko Lake was created. Round Bileća, where the Turkish invaders suffered in 1388 their first defeat, are 1000s of Bogomil tombs.

After some kilometers through forbidding Karst, there is a dramatic change to luxuriant vegetation at Gacko, due to the presence of innumerable little streams. Tjentište on the River Sutjeska lies in a National Park framed by Bosnia's highest mountains. Beside excursions to Europe's only virgin forest, at Perućica, the 72-m. (240-ft.) Skakavac Waterfall and the seven glacier lakes of the Zelengora Mountains, Tjentište offers unusually extensive athletics facilities and an artificial lake for watersports.

Foča, at the confluence of the Cehotina and Drina rivers, was the seat of the Turkish Sandžak Begs of Herzegovina, and is thus endowed with fine buildings, outstanding among them the remarkable Aladža (Colored) Mosque. From June through August Foča is the center of rafting on the Tara and Drina. Newly-felled tree trunks from the endless forests are lashed together for a thrilling journey over the rapids of the fast-flowing currents in an evocation of past times. More modern, but no less exciting, are the kayak regattas.

The road crosses and recrosses the Drina on its way northeast between Bosnia and Serbia, through the apple and plum orchards of the Goražde district. Here is one of the most ancient of all the Orthodox churches of Bosnia-Herzegovina, that of St. Juragi. It was built in 1446, when the region was still part of Serbia, by Herceg Stjepan Kosača. It was later to house Serbia's first printing press which, between 1529 and 1531 and under the direction of St. Juragi, produced missals and prayerbooks in the Cyrillic script. The road east to Sarajevo is rough, as indeed are all those colored green on the map.

The Goražde Valley is effectively sheltered from rough winds. All the slopes leading down to the river are thickly wooded, so that the houses are almost hidden by the trees, and the apples and nuts grown in this happy part of the land are in demand even beyond the frontiers of Yugoslavia.

Both Foča and Goražde provide superb fishing—no less than 18 different species being found in the Drina. The locally caught trout and salmon have an exquisite flavor; their average weight runs to around three kilo. (six to seven lb.), though salmon weighing as much as ten kilo. (22 lb.) have been caught.

However you reach Višegrad you will pass through the most beautiful mountain scenery in central Bosnia, and the town itself is no anticlimax. It was once a great Turkish stronghold, and in the 16th century, Mehmed Pasha Sokolović, Vizir of Bosnia, commissioned (in 1571) Turkey's greatest architect, Sinan, to span the Drina. The monumental 11-arched bridge, 165 m. (180 yards) long, inspired Ivo Andrić's Nobel Prize-winning novel *Bridge over the Drina.*

The road from Sarajevo via Kladanj to Zvornik is for those in search of the high mountain passes that lead to the forest regions of Romanija and Jahorina—the partisan stronghold during the German-Italian occupation of 1940 to 1945.

Zvornik is Moslem in appearance, and is linked with Serbia by a bridge over the Drina. The Friday markets are colorful not least because of the variety of local peasant costumes.

Practical Information for Bosnia-Herzegovina

HOW TO GET THERE. By plane. There is a service linking Sarajevo with Belgrade all year, and with Zagreb, Dubrovnik and Split during the summer; also a Mostar–Belgrade schedule all year.

By train. Trains link Kardeljevo on the coast via Mostar and Sarajevo with Zagreb and Belgrade.

WHEN TO GO. The mountains of Bosnia attract many winter visitors, as the area for snow sports is extensive and the terrain relatively easy. As a result, Jahorina in the center of the province, just south of Sarajevo, is becoming increasingly important. Owing to the mountainous and thickly wooded nature of the province, summer is moderate in Bosnia. On the other hand, in Herzegovina it can be unpleasantly hot. The best time for Bosnia-Herzegovina as a whole is late April and May through June, and Sept. to early Oct.

If you are staying on the Dalmatian coast do not fail to set aside two or three days to see something of the exotic hinterland—it is well worth exploring at any time of the year.

HOTELS AND RESTAURANTS. There are very few (E) hotels in Bosnia-Herzegovina, but those in the (M) price range are generally reliable. We would suggest, however, that you try to avoid accommodations in the lowest category. Every hotel listed here has all or at least some rooms with bath or shower, unless otherwise stated. Most are open year-round.

There are in addition mountain refuges and alpine inns in the Bosnian mountains, notably at Bjelašnica, Prenj, Romanija, Trebević, Treskavica, Vlašić and Zelengora. Numerous camping sites are also to be found in the area.

Food and Drink. Most Bosnian food specialties are of partly Turkish origin, and thus exclude pork. *Musaka* is fresh meat minced and roasted in an oven with egg-plant and covered, before cooking, with Béchamel sauce; *kapama* consists of mutton cooked together with spinach and green onions and served with a yogurt sauce; and *kalija* is a mixture of finely chopped cabbage and mutton prepared after the manner of pot-au-feu. Bosnian *lonac* is a ragout of the vegetables currently in season, while *sarma* is minced beef rolled in a leaf of cabbage or vine.

For those who like their dessert to be sweet, the Turkish specialties of Bosnia will be most appreciated. *Baklava* is a wafered pastry containing nuts and covered with syrup. *Kadaif* is a pastry cut into thin strips and, as always, covered with syrup. *Lokum* is our childhood friend, Turkish Delight, *alva* is better known to us as halva or hulva. Stewed fruits are called *rošaf* or *zerde*.

Yugoslavia's best white wine comes from Mostar, and is called *Žilavka.*
Blatina is a pleasant red Bordeaux type. *Žilavka*, like Traminer, Riesling, Sylvaner and other well-known wines, is actually the name of the grape, so wine made anywhere from *Žilavka* grapes can use the name. Much is of extremely poor quality, but the original is superb; it comes from the village of Blagaj and is labeled accordingly.

BANJA LUKA. *Bosna* (E), 208 rooms. Central. *Motel International* (M), 68 rooms. About five km. (three miles) on main road to north. *Palace* (M), 75 rooms. *Slavija* (M), 44 rooms.

BIHAC. 35 km. (22 miles) from the Plitvice Lakes. Popular fishing center. *Ada-Garni* (M), 86 rooms. *Park* (M), 110 rooms.
Restaurant. The *Pavillon* café-restaurant is on the banks of the River Una.

DOBUJ. *Bosna* (M), 87 rooms. *Motel Tourist* (I), 7 rooms. At the confluence of the Usora and Bosna.

FOČA. *Zelengora* (M), 87 rooms. On the banks of the River Čehotina, with a natural bathing beach, terrace and garden.

GORAŽDE. *Gradina* (M), 68 rooms. *Drina* (I), 34 rooms.

ILIDZA. Spa a few kilometers out of Sarajevo. In a lovely park are four tastefully reconstructed hotels in the (E) or (M) category: *Bosna, Hercegovina, Jadran,* and *Srbija.* These make excellent alternatives to those actually in Sarajevo, particularly if you have your own transport, though there are frequent and inexpensive connections with the city by tram. Other accommodations in Ilidza include an autocamp, complete with bungalows.

JABLANICA. *Jablanica* (M), 33 rooms.
Restaurant. If traveling between Sarajevo and Mostar, stop for lunch or a snack at **Aleksin Han,** at the popular little *Bife Vrelo,* 9½ km. (six miles) south of Jablanica. Here your lamb roasts on a spit powered by a stream which plunges down toward the Neretva River.

JAHORINA Part of the splendid 1984 Winter Olympics venue near Sarajevo. *Jahorina* (M), 130 rooms. Young travelers will find inexpensive accommodations at the three youth hotels.

JAJCE. *Jajce* (E), 85 rooms. Indoor pool. *Hotel Turist* (M), 52 rooms. *Plivska Jezera* (I), 32 rooms, 18 chalets. Out of town, on the lakeside.

KISELJAK. Spa near Sarajevo. *Dalmacija* (M), 113 rooms.

KLADANJ. Spa on the road between Sarajevo and Belgrade, whose waters are said to restore virility. *Bosna* (I), 55 rooms.

KONJIC. Starting point for climbing 2,048-m. (6,718-ft.) Mount Bjelasnica and 4,705-m. (7,004-ft.) Mount Prenj. *Motel Konjic* (I), 32 rooms.

KOŠEVO. At the northern entrance to Sarajevo. Autocamp accommodations.

MOSTAR. *Ruža* (E), 75 rooms. Fine new hotel a short stroll from the famous bridge and the old part of town. *Bristol* (M), 56 rooms, and *Neretva* (M), 40 rooms, Moorish-style, face each other across the Neretva river, but some rooms are noisy. *Hercegovina* (I), 20 rooms.

Restaurants. *Aščinica* is a small private restaurant offering national dishes in the town center. The popular *Labrint* has a terrace overlooking the river, and is to be linked with the *Pečina* ("Cave"), a tavern actually located in a natural cave. *Stari Most* is by the old bridge.

MOSTAR-BUNA. *Buna* (I), 42 rooms. On the River Buna, 9½ km. (six miles) from Mostar. Also campsite and chalets.

MRKONJIČ-GRAD. *Krajina* (M), 39 rooms. *Motel Balkan* (I), 24 rooms.

PALE. 16 km. (ten miles) from Sarajevo. Starting point for excursions to Jahorina and Romanija mountains. *Koran* (E), 42 rooms. Pool. *Panorama* (M), 59 rooms.

POČITELJ. Well-known artists' colony. Accommodations available in various houses in the village.

Restaurant. Charming old *Han* (inn) has been restored as an attractive restaurant.

TJENTIŠTE. In a wild and beautiful national park. *Mladost* (M), 41 rooms. *Sutjeska* (I), 31 rooms, a few with bath. Large youth center.

TREBINJE. 26 km. (16 miles) from Dubrovnik. *Leotar* (M), 110 rooms.

TUZLA. *Bristol* (I), 84 rooms, some with bath.

VIŠEGRAD. *Bikavac* (M), 44 rooms. *Vilina Vlas* (M), 68 rooms. Pool.

ZENICA. *International* (M), 62 rooms. *Metalurg* (M), 73 rooms.

ZVORNIK. *Drina* (M), 72 rooms.

HOW TO GET AROUND. By car. Roads are adequate, except for the atrocious last stretch from Sarajevo to Višegrad, and the scenery is mostly superb. The main highway ascends along the Neretva north from the coast at Metković through Mostar to Jablanica, then strikes east to Sarajevo, from which there are three connections with the Zagreb–Belgrade *autoput*. The shortest is due north to Županja; the second, branching east at Kladanj, leads straight to Belgrade; and the third, running through Jajce, joins the *autoput* much nearer Zagreb. The branch from Jajce to Bihać and on to Karlovac in Croatia is the quickest route to Zagreb, which can also be reached via Banja Luka. The Dubrovnik–Belgrade road via Trebinje, Foča, along the Drina to Višegrad, where it turns east to Titova Užice in Serbia, is scenically the loveliest. Filling stations are adequate.

By bus. An excellent network of bus services radiates from the modern bus station at Sarajevo.

WHAT TO SEE. The oriental influence is paramount, with nearly every town and village revealing the effects of 400 years of Turkish rule. The older core of Sarajevo, the capital, built along the narrow valley of the River Miljacka, is both picturesque and fascinating. Mostar, the capital of Herzegovina, with its stone-built houses, is even more so. And the former provincial capitals of the Turkish Vizirs, Jajce, Banja Luka and Travnik, have all retained their historic atmosphere.

Počitelj, a charming restored Moslem village, is now an artists' colony. The mountainous countryside of the region, scored by dramatic river gorges, is often magnificent and is peppered with historic remains—notably the cemeteries of the distinctive Bogomil sect.

Regional Costumes. These are often worn on market days which, in Bihać, Bosanski Šamac and Visoko, are on Mondays; in Modriča on Tuesdays; in Foča, Višegrad, Jajce and Sarajevo on Wednesdays; Travnik on Thursdays; Tuzla, Zvornik and Žepče on Fridays, and Trebinje on Saturdays.

SPORTS. The winter variety inevitably predominates, with the choice of Sarajevo as the venue for the 1984 Winter Olympics. This has given a tremendous boost to facilities available in the nearby mountains, making it one of the top areas outside traditional Alpine skiing haunts. The resorts of Jahorina and Bjelašnica are particularly well-developed for downhill skiing, with several ski-lifts, and Igman for cross-country skiing. Buses provide regular links between the city and the skiing grounds for those who prefer to stay in the town.

The huge areas of forest in Bosnia-Herzegovina make it one of Europe's most varied natural preserves for hunting. Here hunters frequently come across brown bear grown to the size of small grizzly, not to mention wolves. Wild boar, bear, red deer, fox, and wild cat are all plentiful, and in the Maglić, Zelengora and Prenj mountains there are herds of chamois. You will find developed sites in all hunting zones, and most provide accommodations, with electricity, running water, and bathroom facilities. Mountain refuges, though simpler, are also well-equipped. Guidebeaters with dogs, saddle horses and row-boats are available. Arrangements for hunting can be made through the local travel agency, Unis Turist.

There are few more exciting or romantic experiences that to make the descent by kayak from Šćepan Polje on the Tara, via Foča and Višegrad on the Drina—a distance of about 95 km. (60 miles). You can also do it by raft. Other suitable rivers for this form of sport are the Neretva, Una and Vrbas. The tourist offices in Foča and Višegrad sell tickets for one-day excursions by raft between the two centers every Saturday in July and August. There is also a four-day trip which takes place twice a month; this can be booked through Unis Turist.

 FISHING. The numerous fast-flowing mountain rivers of Bosnia-Herzegovina provide excellent fishing, with no less than 18 different varieties of fish being caught in the Drina alone, and everywhere there is an abundance of trout, salmon, and grayling.

Rivers Una, Vrbas, Neretva, Drina and their tributaries offer splendid possibilities, as do the glacial lakes in the Treskavica and Zelengora area. Bihać, Martin Brod, Ključ, Jajce, Mostar, Buna, Foča, Zvornik and Tjentište are among the important centers. Permits are obtainable from tourist offices and some hotels, but you must bring your own equipment.

 SHOPPING. You will find a variety of interesting and original things to buy as souvenirs in Bosnia. The oriental handicraftsmen in the souks of Sarajevo produce attractive metalwork, and everyday household utensils in beautifully carved wood make an appealing and useful gift. If you are interested in hand-loomed carpets, embodying traditional peasant designs, then you can examine them without obligation to buy at one of the numerous shops specializing in rugs and carpets. Colorful Turkish slippers with knitted stocking tops are another specialty of the area.

 USEFUL ADDRESSES. Every town possesses a Tourist Information office and at least one travel agency. The main agency in Bosnia is Unis Turist, whose head office is at Morića han, Sarač 77, Sarajevo.

The motoring organization is Auto Moto Savez Bosne i Hercegovine, Boriše Kovačevića 18, Sarajevo.

PRACTICAL INFORMATION FOR SARAJEVO

 HOTELS. Preparations for the 1984 Winter Olympics have included a sharp boost in hotel accommodations. Generally speaking, most visitors in the past have been transient, a situation which the tourist organizations are anxious to change—and certainly, longer stays are justified in this fascinating and beautiful region. In addition to those listed below, a score of privately run hotels is being built (bookings through local travel agencies), and there are plenty of private accommodations (handled by Unis Turist).

Expensive

Bristol, Josipa Sigmunda 10. 250 rooms. Near the Sarajevo.

Sarajevo, close to the rail station. The latest, complete with ultramodern facilities.

Moderate

Evropa, 225 rooms. Upper end of the price range. Service is a bit erratic but they've been accommodating travelers for about 100 years now. Just round the corner from the lively Baščaršija (bazaar) area; has a pleasant garden restaurant.

National, Obala Pariške komune 5. 73 rooms. Across the river from the center.

Inexpensive

Beograd, Slobodana Principa 9. 45 rooms. Fairly central boarding house.

Central, Zrinjskog 8. Adequate and inexpensive. Near the Evropa.

Stari Grad, Maršala Tita 126. Again, adequate for the price. In the old town.

 RESTAURANTS. Two restaurants with lots of atmosphere are *Daira,* Halači 5, in a charmingly converted complex of 17th-century Turkish storehouses; and *Morića Han,* Sarači bb, formerly an old inn. Both serve national dishes, are moderate, and have openair sections. The *Dalmacija,* Maršala Tita 45, near the old town, specializes in fish; pleasant garden. *Kula,* at Butmir out near the airport, has a beautiful situation, good food, and very reasonable prices. *Lovački Rog,* Nicole Tesle 24, is another moderate place. Two self-service restaurants for the budget-minded, both central, are *Bosna* and *Marin Dvor* (latter also has waiter-service section), at respectively Maršala Tita 36 and 1. The *Peking,* Obala V. Stepe 21, is of course Chinese, and fairly expensive with it.

Otherwise, there are numerous small private eateries and food bars where you can get national or local specialties, *čevapčiči, burek,* etc., as quick and inexpensive meals.

There is dancing in the *Plavi Podrum* restaurant in the Evropa hotel (see above) and nightlife in general at the *Carmen* nightclub in the Bristol hotel (above again). There are innumerable discos packed with the young, many small coffee bars, and the more sophisticated *Hamam-bar,* the latter attractively adapted from a 16th-century Turkish bath at Maršala Tita 55.

 WHAT TO SEE. A tour of Sarajevo's monuments and museums will occupy a day or two, especially if you add in a cable-car trip to the top of 1,500-m. (5,000-ft.) Mount Trebević, which dominates the city. You will find a number of inns and cafés at the summit to sustain you on the descent. Other attractions without the city include the thermal spa of Illidža, a mere 20 minutes away. Known since Roman times, the exquisite mosaics discovered there have been removed to the State Museum of Sarajevo, but the site is still worth a visit. The source of the River Bosna, at Vrelo Bosna, some 14½ km. (nine miles) from Sarajevo, is located in a lovely park. You can reach it by horse-and-carriage ride from the popular spa of Ilidža, itself some 9½ km. (six miles) southwest of the city. Other small resorts in the area are Pale, and the spa of Kiseljak.

Buses for the ski grounds and mountain resorts of Jahorina start from the central bus station. The artificial lake Jablanica, about 80 km. (50 miles) to the southwest, begins at Konjic and stretches for around 20 km. (12 miles). Climbers leave from here to scale Mount Prenj. Farther afield, there are fascinating excursions to Mostar, Višegrad, and the Tjentište National Park.

 MUSEUMS. The Jewish Museum, Maršala Tita. Housed in an old synagogue and excellent of its kind.

The Municipal Museum, Remzije Omanovića 51. Contains objects dating back to the Iron Age, utensils employed in Turkish medicine, a reproduction of a Turkish barber shop—also vestments, tools and harness dating from Turkish times, icons and frescos.

The Museum of National Revolution, Vojvode Punika 9.

The Museum of Young Bosnia, Vojvode Stepe Obala 36. The theme is the revolutionary student group whose activities sparked off World War I. On the pavement outside are the footprints marking the spot from which the fatal shots were fired that killed Archduke Franz Ferdinand.

Orthodox Church, Maršala Tita 83. Houses a rich collection of Orthodox artefacts.

The State Museum, 7 Vojvode Putnika St. (not far from rail station). One wing contains prehistoric, Greek, Roman and medieval objects; another a truly remarkable ethnographic collection, including reproductions of Bosnian peasant houses and feudal Turkish dwellings. In the gardens of the museum are a number of the unique burial steles of the Bogomils.

Svrzo's House, Jovana Kršića 6. A typical Turkish feudal house; three rooms are fully furnished with 17th-century articles.

ENTERTAINMENT. The National Theater on Vojvode Stepe Obala, also features opera and ballet. Performances at the several other theaters in Sarajevo are in Serbo-Croat of course, but the Puppet Theater might be of more general interest. In summer, folkloric evenings of good standard are common—details from the Tourist Information Center. There are also a number of concert halls.

USEFUL ADDRESSES. The Tourist Information Center is at Jugoslovenske Armije 50. All the larger Yugoslav travel agents have offices in Sarajevo; the principal Bosnian one is Unis Turist, Morića han, Sarači 77.

The main post office is at Obala V. Stepe 8. The First Aid Center (Hitna Pomoć) is at ugao Ž. Jošila i Darovalaca krvi.

INLAND SLOVENIA

An Alpine Land

This region is much like Alpine Austria, though only half its size. Set between Austria and Italy, it is the obvious entry to Yugoslavia for any visitor coming from the north or west by road or rail. It is a land of excellent hill-walking and good climbing. Its mountain roads are of good quality.

Slovenia's northern borders are the abrupt peaks of the Karavanke Mountains. The Julian Alps lie in the northwest, and to the east the mountains gradually descend to the great Hungarian plain. In the southwest lies the Adriatic, and the southern limits are marked by the Croatian hills. The white limestone mountains of Slovenia are dominated by majestic Mount Triglav (Three Heads) which rises to a height of over 2,835 m. (9,300 ft.). There are several fairly easy climbing routes to the peak. Old Three Heads watches over the province—one looking to the past, one to the present and the third to the future, or so say the peasants of Slovenia.

There are many charming lakes both in the mountains and amid the thickly wooded valleys, most famous of them all being Lake Bled, with its castle and the high mountain valley of the Seven Lakes of Triglav nearby. Waterfalls and twisting little trout streams break up the landscape, and here it is easy to realize how Slovenia alone in bygone years furnished enough hydroelectric power for the needs of the greater part of the country.

The mountains in the east and south of the province did not provide such a good defensive barrier as those in the west and north, but at the time of the Turkish invasions they formed the boundaries of the Christian world, as you will realize from the profusion of castles and fortified churches.

The level uplands are characterized by a number of shallow basins in which soil has collected, where the peasants cultivate their smallholdings. The region has other, rather special characteristics, chief among them the famous Postojna Caves, which experts consider one of the most extraordinary underground curiosities in Europe—a series of halls pillared with stalactites and stalagmites, that continue for over 19 km. (12 miles).

Until recently, Slovenia was more advanced than any of Yugoslavia's other five Republics, because of its long contact with the West in those centuries when Turkey ruled most of the rest of Yugoslavia. Its capital, Ljubljana, differs little in architecture from such capitals as Vienna or Budapest. The countryside resembles neighboring Austria. The snowy peaks, the wooden-tiled chalets clinging to the mountainsides, the long sloping green fields, the gardens bright with roses, geraniums, carnations and dahlias, unmistakably recall the Austrian Alps.

However, the illusion, strong though it is, soon vanishes when you meet the inhabitants, whose way of life is Alpine, but whose main language is Slav. Older folk speak German, particularly in Lower Styria; many speak Italian, especially in the area near Trieste; French is generally understood by the intellectuals; and most young people learn English at school.

Slovenia's History

Someone who knew his subject once remarked: "Geography is the key to history." Lying along the easiest route to and from the Adriatic, Slovenia witnessed the Romans marching north (and had Roman legions quartered on it in the second century), and later the Germans and Huns pushing south toward the Mediterranean. Local tribes put up a long and fierce resistance to the Romans, but once the Pax Romana was established the country became one of the richest colonies of the Empire. However, as the power of Rome waned in the fourth century the Germanic hordes swept into the Balkans and were followed by the Slovenes who took possession of the mountainous east, replacing the Celto-Romans whom they found there.

After a period of political uncertainty, Slovenia became a frontier province of Charlemagne's great empire, later to pass for over 1,000 years under Austrian rule, fighting for the Habsburgs against the Turks. While the other southern Slavs were overrun by Turkey, Slovenia remained an Austrian province. Neglected by absentee landlords, the Slovenes' sense of national identity developed very slowly.

The first Slovene books of Primož Trubar were published in 1551, but it was not until the introduction of reforms by Joseph II at the end of the 18th century, and the Napoleonic occupation of 1809–13, that the Slovene literary Renaissance developed.

Napoleon recreated the Roman province of Illyria, and the Slovene language was revived, but once the French interlude ended Austrian hegemony was reestablished. However, the Illyrian Movement had by now drawn up a truly nationalistic program that inspired both Slovene and Croat literature to their full flowering, defying the Habsburg determination to Germanize the country.

Slovenia was annexed by Hitler and Mussolini in World War II. Many of her young men fought in the anti-Axis guerrilla units.

Exploring Slovenia

Visitors coming to Slovenia from Austria mostly cross by the nearly 1,070-m.-high (3,500 ft.) Koren (Wurzen) Pass—the easiest of the few passes through the Karavanke barrier. After the frontier the road begins to descend to the little mountain town of Podkoren. Farther east, the Ljubelj tunnel on the Klagenfurt–Ljubljana road saves traffic some mountain-climbing.

If Slovenia is entered from Italy by way of the town of Tarvisio, the first Yugoslav village will be Rateče, which is almost at the exact point where the frontiers of Yugoslavia, Italy and Austria meet. Only a little farther on is Planica, with one of the best ski-jumps to be found anywhere in Europe.

Returning to our road along the upper reaches of the River Sava, we wind along a narrow, mountain-bordered valley, through scenery wholly typical of the Karavanke and Julian Alps, until we come to the village of Podkoren and, next, Kranjska Gora, an extremely popular winter sports resort, which itself standing at a height of some 800 m. (2,630 ft.), is close to some of the highest peaks. Not far from there is Gozd Martuljek, from whence you can look across the great mountain mass of Martuljek. The Martuljek Waterfall at the foot of 2,475-m. (8,125-ft.) Mount Spik is another local attraction.

If you are tempted to take a closer look at Mount Triglav after reaching Mojstrana, there is a narrow road that turns off to the right for a distance of some 13 km. (eight miles). Within five km. (three miles) of leaving Mojstrana, you will see the impressive 50-m. (160-ft.) Peričnik Waterfall. Near the end of the valley, under the northern flanks of Triglav, is the small mountain hut of Aljažev Dom, set at a height of 1,005 m. (3,300 ft.) above sea-level, an acknowledged head-quarters for both Yugoslav and foreign mountain climbers. From there two tracks set out for the 2,835-m. (9,300-ft.) summit. On the way you can rest, or stop the night, at another refuge (open only in summer) at a height of 2,380 m. (7,800 ft.). For less experienced mountaineers, the Škrlatica ascent from Aljažev Dom is relatively straightforward.

Returning again to the Sava, the road takes us past the great metal-working town of Jesenice. From there we follow the railway that leads to the romantic and world-renowned Lake of Bled.

From Austria to the Istrian Peninsula

Having entered by the Koren Pass and reached the village of Kranj-ska Gora, we find a secondary road over the Vršič Pass, linking up with the Tarvisio road, and then skirting the River Soča, formerly known by the Italian name of Isonzo.

You will pass the site of important World War I battles, along a green mountain valley of great beauty, where there are various Alpine refuges, until you reach the 1,600-m. (5,252-ft.) Vršič Pass. Winding wildly through the foothills to the west of Mount Triglav, and occa-sionally plunging into tunnels, the road now enters the famous Trenta Valley. Close to this there is a narrow but passable track that leads you in a few moments to the impressive site of the quick-flowing River Soča's source.

Following the course of the river, which bursts through a fault in the rock, you will see a sign drawing your attention to the Botanical Gardens of the Julian Alps, founded in 1927 by Albert Boise de Chesne. Here you will find every variety of flower that grows naturally in these mountains and a simple church containing some remarkable mural paintings.

Mountain Resorts

The little village of Na Logu through which we now pass is set in a vast circle of mountains close beneath Mount Triglav, and with every kilometer the scenery becomes more majestic. The Soča is here divided into various separate falls before the currents rejoin to flow together through the valley and run swiftly to the summer mountain resort of Bovec. From there a road branches off to the Adriatic.

Motorists who wish to see something of the high mountains guarding the Italian frontier should take a right turn just before reaching Bovec, which leads to the Koritnica Valley and the village with the delightfully rustic name of Log. From there the road climbs rapidly to the frontier at the Predel Pass.

The Predel Pass, originally a Roman military road to the north, was also the route taken by the Lombards when they in their turn invaded the fertile plains of northern Italy. It then became the "Amber Caravan Route" of the Middle Ages which later served to link Trieste with the great cities of central Europe. Naturally enough the road is lined with old fortifications that last served Austria in delaying the Napoleonic advance toward Vienna.

Beyond Bovec the main road continues to follow the River Soča, giving us a delightful glimpse of the 60-m. (195-ft.) Boka Waterfall before descending into the quite distinct atmosphere and quite different towns of the coast.

At Kobarid the road from the Udine-Robič Pass comes in from the west, and we pass the 2,275-m. (7,465-ft.) mass of Mount Krn on our left. On reaching a fork in the road, our way is to the left, crossing the River Soča, to Tolmin. This is another small summer resort, and only four km. (2½ miles) farther to the south the rivers Soča and Idrija meet. Here a dam has been built to create a charming little lake, in which bathing is permitted. Needless to say, the whole area is famous for the excellence of its fishing and, more humble but still not to be despised, the most delicious sheep's milk cheeses.

A few kilometers south of Tolmin is the village of Most na Soči, from which we have the choice of three roads; the first following the river south to the frontier town of Nova Gorica in the vicinity of which very good white wine is produced; the second running southeast through Čepovan and Vipava to the famous Teran vineyards and Postojna; the third branching off from the road leading to Čepovan, a few kilometers from Most na Soči, and running east along the beautiful Bača valley toward the Slovene capital of Ljubljana.

Between Grahovo and Podbrdo you will have plenty of opportunities to admire the peaks of Črna Prst and Porezen, both of which, incidentally, can be reached by easy paths. This remote region was one of the principal hideouts of the Slovene underground during World War II. After climbing a pass our route descends to Železniki, formerly famous for its excellent ironwork. The road forks here, the left-hand leading to Bohinjska Bistrica and Bled, and the right to Češnjice and Škofja Loka.

Škofja Loka is a charming little medieval town, with a baroque castle which is now the regional museum. From here it is only another 20 km. (13 miles) to Ljubljana.

At Most na Soči we are already in the *karst* area—a rugged, rough, broken kind of limestone—and the river is flanked by plateaux over 915 m. (3,000 ft.) above sea-level. From here we now take the main alternative route already mentioned, through Kanal to Nova Gorica, a summer resort with a full-size swimming pool and a number of good camping sites.

If you spend a little time there you may visit the Franciscan Monastery perched on a neighboring hill and pay your respects to the memory of the last of the Bourbon kings of France who, after fleeing from the Revolution of 1830, spent his declining years in England where he surprised his hosts by his passion for shooting sparrows. In due course, this became the last resting place of King Charles X, brother-in-law of France's ill-fated Marie Antoinette.

Of Wine and Lippizaners

On the 915-m.-high (3,000 ft.) plateau of Trnovo, not far from Nova Gorica, is the little winter-sports resort of Lokve, and neighboring Vipava and Podnanos are both picturesque. The limestone soil supports vines of excellent quality, and all the way to the Italian frontier you will be passing through little villages whose livelihood depends on the vines of Teran.

One such place is Štanjel, built of the local stone and perched, for defense, on top of a hill. Another is Sežana, popular with visitors because of its huge park containing exotically scented plants, and a third, Lipica. It was in Lipica that the Lippizaner breed of white horses originated, and where they first received their training. The establishment was founded by the Habsburgs in the Middle Ages, and from 1580 it was from here that all the horses came that took part in the intricate, ballet-like maneuvers of the Spanish School of Riding in Vienna. The stud farm had difficulty in starting again after the last war, but there are now over 200 excellent horses in the stud book. A visit is well worthwhile, especially in the morning, when the horses are being trained. Some of these superb steeds are available for hire and seven-day riding courses are arranged. In summer there are twice daily performances by the Spanish Riding School. There are, of course, stud farms in Austria and Hungary.

The next town is Divača and, if you are a caving enthusiast, you should take the opportunity to visit the Caves of Skocjan near the village of Motovun, though if your enthusiasm for underground marvels is limited, then save your energy for Postojna later. From here we return to the main road at Kozina, and soon are rewarded by our first view of the Gulf of Trieste.

Bled and Its Castle

To miss Bled would be a pity. It has become one of Yugoslavia's best-known tourist attractions—and rightly so. The golf course (18 holes) is magnificently situated above the River Sava gorge: guest players are welcome, and indeed golfing holidays here are becoming popular.

When you reach the lake itself, 460 m. (1,500 ft.) above sea-level, you have only to lift your head to get an impressive view of the whole mass of the Julian Alps, backed by Triglav. In the foreground, set in the wooded hills, the still waters of the lake reflect a stately castle at the summit of a steep cliff. In the middle of the lake there is a romantic little island, with an ancient church close to the shore, which can be visited by gondola-like boats.

Legend has it that Živa, the Slav goddess of love and life, made this island her home. In Christian times it became a place of pilgrimage, as it still is today, seven centuries later. Unfortunately, the church has been deconsecrated. The local people will assure you that any wish expressed while the bells are ringing will be granted, and visitors are allowed to ring the bell while making their wishes.

The island itself has only the church and a café, but along the shores of the 1½-km.-long (one mile) lake there are numerous first-rate hotels, in one of which there are a large number of trout from the lake swimming about in an aquarium, happily unconscious that they are on the menu.

Bled was founded at the time of Charlemagne, but remained nothing more than a feudal stronghold for nearly 1,000 years, and it was only with the advent of modern transport facilities that it suddenly became an internationally famous tourist resort. It was the favorite home of the Regent Prince Paul of Yugoslavia during the years before World War II, and the late Marshal Tito observed the precedent by spending several weeks each summer in his villa there. Probably because of deep hot thermal springs the temperature of the lake in summer is around 68°F. despite the Alpine streams feeding it.

The fortified castle which dominates the lake may be reached in half an hour, and from it you will have a dramatic view across the lake and mountains. It is an extraordinary example of 11th-century architecture, set on the top of a bluff that rises vertically from the edge of the water. Today part is a museum containing some indifferent paintings and a most terrifyingly malevolent carved wooden devil. In another part you will find the restaurant, famous for its smoked ham.

The Country Round Bled

There is an exciting half-day excursion to the Vintgar gorges and waterfalls, and to the winter sports resort of Pokljuka, returning via the Savica Falls, Bohinj Lake and its nearby summer resort of Bohinjska Bistrica.

Gradually, as we continue toward Bled the surroundings become more and more attractive. The road enters the narrow valley of the Sava Bohinjska and passes through the hamlet of Sv. Janež, in whose 14th-century Gothic church there are some very interesting frescos. Lake Bohinj lies silent beneath the peaks of the Julian Alps, but there are a few pleasant hotels not far from its shores—it is an ideal place for anyone really wishing for peace, rest and quiet "far from the madding crowd," but with fresh-water swimming, boating, pleasant walks or climbing excursions into the mountains available. Bled is the starting point for mountain trips in the Triglav reservation.

At the far end of the lake and the valley the waters of the Savica make a tremendous leap over a 60-m. (195-ft.) fall. This is the source of the River Sava, which grows into an important tributary of the Danube.

Anyone coming from Bled who wishes to climb Mount Triglav could reach it up the Valley of the Seven Lakes and the Komna plateau—but don't forget that the excursion takes a full 12 hours.

The Roads to Ljubljana

Ljubljana, the center and capital of Slovenia, is a university town of some 330,000 inhabitants. It is also an important center for coach and rail communications, and its airport receives visitors from many countries.

Coming from Klagenfurt by car you may enter by the 1,356-m. (4,453-ft.) Karavanke Mountains. A tunnel has been dug beneath the top of the pass, thus making all-the-year-round traffic possible. The very good road descends in a series of loops and turns to the old city of Tržič. Beyond that we join the main Ljubljana highway.

There is another more direct and interesting route which begins some 13 km. (eight miles) east of Klagenfurt. At the main crossroad you turn right, continue immediately beneath the shadow of the Austrian Karavanke range, pass through Eisenkappel, and then climb the 1,690-m.-high (5,560 ft.) Seebergsattell to enter Yugoslavia.

This leads you through the attractive little winter-sports resort of Jezersko. Only five km. (three miles) farther on is Zgornja Kokra, which is the point of departure for those wishing to climb 2,484-m. (8,147-ft.) Mount Grintavec. With a good guide the ascent takes six hours, and if you are lucky you may see herds of chamois somewhere near the summit. Ibex are there, but rarely seen.

The descent, always steep, leads through a narrow valley, and after passing Kranj, rejoins the main Ljubljana highway.

If you approach Ljubljana from Bled, the road runs southeast through the 17th-century city of Radovljica, which lies on a terrace at the meeting place of the rivers Sava Bohinjka and Sava Dolinka. From here you will have a tremendous view of the Karavanke and Julian Alps. If you continue by the main road you will be in Ljubljana, some 40 km. (25 miles) away, in no time but, if you like to make an occasional picturesque detour, then you may enjoy the secondary road along the right bank of the River Sava.

Alternatively, you can stop and explore the old center of Kranj. Basically it is, or rather was, a little Alpine town. But it has grown now into an industrial center where important experiments in town planning were carried through.

Ljubljana, Slovenia's Capital

Ljubljana was founded by the Romans with the name of Aemona, though the only trace of their presence is a wall and complex of foundations, including mosaics and central-heating system, in the Mirje district of the city. The original town was destroyed by the barbarian hordes that swept out of Asia in the fifth century, and reconstructed by the Slavs with the name of Luvigana. Later it became the capital of the Duchy of Carniola and is known in German as Laibach.

Nearly 2,000 years old, Ljubljana is one of the most ancient cities in Yugoslavia, but in appearance it is wholly central European and not Balkan. The city lies on both sides of the River Ljubljanica and is in a position of unusual strategic importance, since it commands the "Ljubljana Gap" through the mountains.

Exploring Ljubljana

The city has been subject to many earthquakes, the last serious one in 1895, and has few old buildings of interest for the present-day visitor to see, apart from the citadel.

The modern quarter is dominated by the 13-story Nebotičnik building, built 1930–33, which the townspeople like you to call the skyscraper. The two top floors accommodate a café-restaurant, from which you can obtain a pleasant view over the city and surrounding country—and there is dancing at night. The old quarter, mostly built in Austrian baroque style, lies between the hill upon which the castle stands and the Ljubljanica River. Although, as mentioned above, it is not a particularly beautiful city, it does possess a pleasant busy charm, which becomes gradually apparent. And, indeed, it contains much attractive detail, such as the Robba marble fountain opposite the Town Hall, and—dominating the city—the intact medieval citadel, in appearnace reminiscent of Salzburg. From the top of the old ramparts, where incidentally there is a good restaurant, you get a marvelous view of not only the city and its many bridges, but also the tremendous backdrop of the Julian Alps.

If you are a determined sightseer then you will find the baroque cathedral, the church of the Franciscans and the rococo church of the Ursulines with a fine painted ceiling by Quaglio, the Bishops' Palace and the Seminary, well worth a visit, as are the National Art Gallery and the Modern Art Gallery. One of Ljubljana's great attractions is undoubtedly its opera; another is its International Summer Festival which extends from late June through August. Main venue for this is the interesting complex of Križanke, adapted in the 1930s by the architect Jože Plečnik from an old monastery.

To the Kamnik Alps

There is a delightful excursion by car north from Ljubljana which will show you the best of the Kamnik Alps in one day. After crossing the Sava River, drive about 23 km. (14 miles) to the town of Kamnik, set amid rich and smiling uplands. It is a quaint little place beneath the ruins of the old castle of Stari Grad and the romantic-looking little fortress of Mali Grad, with its curious three-story chapel. The large number of other old castles in the neighborhood clearly shows the great military importance attached to this road in medieval times.

Continuing north, we keep company with the little River Kamniška Bistrica for the five km. (three miles) to Stahovica, and there turn left. We climb from the narrow valley, parallel with the series of rapids and falls that carry the river from the heights, until we come to the mountain refuge of Dom pri Kamniški Bistrici, which is named after the small river that rises nearby. From the little inn there is a majestic view of the Kamnik Alps, dominated by 2,484-m. (8,147-ft.) Mount Grintovec and Mount Ojstrica (2,329 m./7,638 ft.).

From here we return to the fork in the road and turn east, over the 8,930-m.-high (2,931 ft.) Crnilec Pass and down to Gornji Grad, a popular mountain resort surrounded by deep forests facing the highest ridge of the Kamnik Alps. 6½ km. (four miles) brings you to Radmirje, where you turn left to Ljubno and Luče, a matter of another 12 km. (7½ miles). Both nestle beneath the mountains in the valley of Savinja. The road follows the winding channel of the river through the Robanov Kot valley, of glacial origin, cut into the base of Mount Ojstrica.

Following the Logarska Dolina (valley), the road struggles on through scenery of ever-increasing grandeur, reminiscent of the famous *Cirque de Gavarnie* near Pau in the central Pyrenees. Here, beside the source of the River Savinja, are various hotels and inns, and in the surrounding mountains climbers' refuges and shelters, for it is a popular center for all kinds of excursions by foot.

In the Path of the Roman Legions

Celje lies almost due east and 76 km. (47 miles) from Ljubljana. The road between the two towns was taken by the Roman legionaries as they thrust toward the plains of what is now Hungary and the banks of the mighty Danube. It is a smiling, undulating countryside through Trojane and Vransko to Šempeter, only a few kilometers from Celje, and it is there that important archeological discoveries have been made in the ruins of what was once the thriving second-century Roman city of Claudia Celeia.

Celje itself was seriously damaged during World War II, but still retains something of the medieval charm it had when the Counts of Celje made it the capital of their domain. Opposite the Town Hall is the Romanesque Church of St. Mary, and the museum has a Lapidarium containing Roman stone carvings of considerable interest, its most attractive exhibit being an exquisite statue of a warrior. The Count's Palace, or *grafija,* is a fine late Renaissance-style building, its courtyard bordered by a double-tiered arcade.

Other interesting sights of Celje include the museum housed in the former town castle of the Counts of Celje, and there is a delightful half-hour walk to the ruins of the ancient castle that dominates the whole town.

Celje on E93, halfway between Ljubljana and Maribor, with the spa Dobrna to the north, is the starting point for roads leading either south to the valley of the Savinja or to the east. The former leads to Laško, where a castle perched on the conical hill of Hom has a fairy-tale air, and thence to the popular spa of Rimske Toplice. Almost next door is Zidani Most, where the Savinja joins the River Sava, and if we follow the river southeast, we shall be on the road to Zagreb, a total run of 106 km. (66 miles).

Some 26 km. (16 miles) before Zagreb, soon after passing Brežice, is Čateške Toplice, another spa with radioactive water at a constant temperature of 131°F. Almost the last glimpse of Slovenia before crossing into Croatia is of the Castle of Mokrice on our right.

Maribor and the Pohorje Mountains

There are two other main roads from Austria which will bring you to Maribor, second only to Ljubljana among the cities of Slovenia.

The first is east from Klagenfurt, through Völkermarkt to the frontier beyond Lavamünd, after which the first Yugoslav village is Dravograd in the valley of the River Drava. Following the winding course of the river on its way to join the Danube, we pass through pleasant rustic scenery where the centuries seem to have wrought few changes even though, paradoxically, rapid industrialization is taking place. On our right the Pohorje Hills can be seen, the last gentle foothills of the Alps, sweeping down between partially wooded slopes.

It is some 14½ km. (nine miles) from Dravograd to Muta, with its tiny medieval church, and another four km. (2½ miles) to Radlje ob Dravi. Here steep, forest-clad cliffs close in above the valley, but fall away before we come to Fala, one of the main centers for trips into the Pohorje. Near Selnica is the hydroelectric dam that supplies Maribor with all its electricity.

The second route from Austria cover the 71 km. (44 miles) on E93 from Graz to Maribor, passing Leibnitz and the Yugoslav frontier village of Šentilj. From there it is less than 16 km. (ten miles) through Slovenske Gorice to Maribor, a city of 130,000 inhabitants. Maribor is the economic and cultural center of the northeast of Slovenia (Lower Styria), though its fame outside Yugoslavia is chiefly for its splendid apples. The district is virtually one vast apple orchard—and a sight beyond description when all the trees are in blossom.

Maribor was founded in the 11th century, though there is evidence of prehistoric settlements in the neighborhood. It was a Christian outpost and bastion, built to stem the repeated tides of Turkish conquest that swept into central Europe and which twice threatened the walls of Vienna itself.

There is a monumental pillar which commemorates the Great Plague of 1643, which followed the ravages of the Thirty Years War. The 16th-century Town Hall is unusual because of its Renaissance balcony, and the Audience Chamber has interesting baroque ornamentation. If you want a pleasant impression of the town as a whole you should cross the old bridge over the Drava, from which you can easily pick out the 15th-century Municipal Law Courts and various other fine old buildings.

The 12th-century Romanesque cathedral has suffered from Gothic and baroque additions, but is still worth a visit. The impressive Maribor Castle was built in the 15th century but it too has been deprived of some

of its original character by the grafting on to it of a 16th-century
Renaissance loggia and 18th-century baroque enlargements.

Some of the halls of Maribor Castle are now used as the regional
museum, and that reserved for archeological exhibits contains a good
collection of Celtic and Roman antiquities, while elsewhere there are
some beautiful wood carvings and a magnificent display of medieval
arms and armor.

Excursions from Maribor

Maribor is an excellent center for all manner of excursions. One of
the most popular begins some 6½ km. (four miles) south from Hoče,
from where a twisting mountain road climbs to a holiday region at a
height of over 1,200 m. (4,000 ft.) above sea-level, whence (while sampling the superb smoked mountain ham) you can look across the valley
of the Drava and the vineyards of Slovenske Gorice to Croatia and
Austria.

You will almost certainly make the 24-km. (15-mile) trip to the little
medieval town of Ptuj, if only to sample some of the best wine found
anywhere in Yugoslavia, and to admire the giant cask to be seen there,
which is said to hold over 30,000 liters (7,000 gallons).

Ancient Ptuj, dating from Roman times, is a compact little town, so
you will not find it tiring to take in the sights while enjoying an
unguided half-hour stroll. There is the Orpheus Pillar, which was the
pillory in the Middle Ages, the 13th-century Dominican monastery,
now an archeological museum, and the Municipal Museum in the great
castle that dominates the town.

Of a different era, but none the less remarkable, are the ruins of the
Temple of Mithras, the Persian sun-god, built in Roman times, when
the town was called Paetovium.

Dating from over 1,000 years later, there is the 15th-century priory,
and close beside it, the city tower in the old defensive walls. There is
also the Wine Museum in one of the medieval towers on the banks of
the Drava.

You can combine sightseeing and accommodations if you stay in the
Castle of Štatenberg, today the Grad Štatenberg Hotel, as all the original installations have been kept intact, though of course modern ad-
juncts have been added for the comfort of the 20th-century visitor. The
frescos in the Hall of the Equerries are extremely fine.

It is only 37 km. (23 miles) southwest from Ptuj to Yugoslavia's
best-known spa, Rogaška Slatina. The climate and scenery are particularly agreeable, and the mineral water is not only good for you, but also
pleasant-tasting.

The great Kazan Gorges, not far from the Iron Gates on the Danube River

The Slovenian mountains high above Kranjska Gora

The Sveti Petar Church near Novi Pazar in the Raska Valley, built in the 10th century; and below, Golubac Castle ruins on the Danube east of Belgrade

A picturesque bridge in the Slovenian capital, Ljubliana

Another 15th-century castle that has been turned into an attractive hotel is that of Borl, east of Ptuj on the road to Varaždin. The terrace of its restaurant affords a peaceful view across the valley of the Drava to green pastures and rich vineyards.

This northeastern part of Slovenia (Lower Styria) close to the Austrian and Hungarian frontiers, is famous for its wine, and in addition to Ptuj, other great vineyard-centers of the Slovenske Gorice are Ljutomer, Jeruzalem, Ormož and Radgona. These wines are without doubt among the best in Yugoslavia.

Farther north, at Murska Sobota, the character of the country changes. With the long balanced wooden arms standing high above the wells, and the gipsy orchestras that play on every important occasion (including funerals), the atmosphere becomes very much like that of the villages of the Hungarian *puszta* or Great Plain.

Toward the Sunny Adriatic

A favorite itinerary for visitors to Ljubljana is southwestward to the shores of the Adriatic. E93 widens and becomes a toll-highway for about half the distance, and it is just off this road that you find Postojna and its famous caves in the heart of a fascinating *karst* area characterized by extraordinary underground formations and disappearing rivers. There are good accommodations right by the most famous caves of Postojna if you want to explore the region at greater leisure.

The Postojna Caves are the second largest and in some respects the most extraordinary in the world, being no less than 19 km. (12 miles) long, of which the first seven km. (4½ miles) are easily accessible and illuminated by electric light. As the distances are so great there is a miniature railway that carries you through a representative three km. (two miles) with the minimum effort, and from its "terminus" you will be led by a guide on a figure-of-eight circuit after which you emerge once more into the light of day. But do not lose the guide, or you may disappear forever into this fantastic world of stalactites and stalagmites that have been growing for a million years in a darkness that has only quite recently been disturbed by man.

It is a predilection of all guides to underground grottos to find resemblances between the formations of blind nature and something within human experience. If you cannot accept them for what they are, tremendously strange and impressive forms, then there are the "Cathedral," "the Concert Hall, " "Paradise Grotto," "the Great Ball Room" (with rock clusters than might be giant chandeliers), all strangely-colored, glittering and slightly warped, as though seen in some waking dream. There is the stalagmite like a monkey or a cockerel, or the leaning tower of Pisa, and no doubt if your imagination is vivid enough, like the Brooklyn Bridge or Winston Churchill! Fantasy aside, however, probably the most impressive hall is the first to be visited, called the "Grotto of Mount Calvary."

Entirely in keeping with the strangeness of this underground world are the snake-like creatures, the size of a pencil, called Proteus Anguineus, which may be examined—we will not say admired—in a floodlit aquarium in the "Great Hall," next door to a small picture-postcard shop and post office. Eyeless and colorless because of countless centuries of life in total darkness, the proteus is both fish and mammal. It is a biological conundrum, and can live for up to 60 years.

Parts of the Postojna Caves are blackened and scorched by fire. During the Axis occupation of World War II, the German High Command decided to use this perfect bomb-proof shelter for the storage of a great part of their reserves of gasoline and oil. Slovenian guerrillas discovered this, and making use of an unmapped entrance unknown to the enemy, a small band of them entered secretly to rig up a time-bomb, with the result that 10,000 tons of strategically vital fuel went up in smoke.

The River Pivka and the Postojna Caves end abruptly, to reappear some kilometers farther north as the Unec River and the Planinska Jama Caves.

Around 24 km. (15 miles) north and then east of Postojna, near the village of Cerknica, is another curiosity of nature, the disappearing Cerkniško Jezero. In winter it is some 26 km. (16 miles) long by 1½ km. (a mile) wide, but in summer it drains away through fissures in the limestone bed of the lake, and the peasants harvest the thick grass that grows there.

Not far from Cerknica is the national park of the Rakova Dolina valley, in beautiful scenery. Close by the Križna Jama Caves, near to Stari Trg, can only be reached by boat, and with the assistance of a guide. This grotto is several kilometers long and contains no less than 22 small lakes.

The entire area is riddled with caves and grottos, some of them barely explored, so that any visitor will find even a short excursion an adventure. We have already mentioned the Škocjan Caves close to Divača, which although smaller than those of Postojna, are of an even wilder beauty, and echo ceaselessly to the sound of two great waterfalls. The caves in the region of Kras provide valuable material to expeditions by teams of professional speleologists.

From Ljubljana to Zagreb

The main link between Slovenia and Croatia and Serbia is the 160 km. (100 miles) or so of road between Ljubljana and Zagreb, which is designated an *autoput* or express highway. This cuts across fertile, agreeable country, with small churches and chapels perched on the top of its low hills. The road runs southeast through marshes that mark the extent of what, long ago, was a great lake.

If you are more interested in seeing something of the district through which you are traveling rather than in reaching your destination by the shortest possible route, then we would advise you to turn right and follow the valley of the Krka. The river bursts from the mouth of a cave, then flows below numerous impressive medieval castles. Leave the river, and a turning to the left will bring you to the well-equipped spa of Dolenjske Toplice.

15 km. (nine miles) northeast is Novo Mesto, capital of Lower Carniola, and built on a steep promontory worn from the rock by the action of the river. The Church of the Chapter-House contains a *St. Nicholas* by Tintoretto. The 15th-century Franciscan Abbey and Municipal Tribunal are interesting. To the north is yet another spa, Šmarješke Toplice.

As we continue east, the powerful walls of the Castle of Otočec, rising from the shores of a small island in the River Krka, come as an agreeable surprise even in this land of ancient fortresses. It has been restored and adapted as a well-equipped hotel. 24 km. (15 miles) farther along the main road from Novo Mesto to Zagreb is the typical Lower Carniolian town of Kostanjevica, built upon another island in the Krka. Nearby is a powerful castle within whose unbreached walls there is a series of deep galleries and arches of unusual design.

21 km. (13 miles) east from Kostanjevica we reach the borders of Slovenia and the highway to Zagreb.

PRACTICAL INFORMATION FOR SLOVENIA

HOW TO GET THERE. By plane. Ljubljana is linked by air with the major cities of Yugoslavia and with many cities in Europe, including London.

By train. The Slovenian capital lies on the route of main expresses running between various countries. The through rail route links Ljubljana also to Zagreb, Belgrade, Niš and Skopje.

By bus. Buses from Ljubljana go to major towns throughout Slovenia.

WHEN TO GO. There are two separate tourist seasons in Slovenia, the winter for skiing, etc., and the summer, to be spent either by the sea or in the mountains. Winter sports begin at Christmas and continue until mid-April, and the summer holiday season is from early June until the end of September or mid-October. Here is a list of annual events which may help you to make your choice.

March (second half). International Skiing Competitions (slalom and giant slalom), Vitranc Cup at Kransjka Gora.

March (end). Ljubljana International Fair Alp-Adria.

May–September. Bled. Artistic, folk and sports events.

June–Aug. Ljubljana Festival, with openair performances of opera, ballet, and symphony concerts.

August (early). Folk Festival at Bohinj (Ohcet—peasant wedding).

September (beginning). Ljubljana: International Wine Fair. *(Middle)* Maribor: Merry Autumn (market, folklore and exhibitions).

HOTELS AND RESTAURANTS. Most Slovenia hotels listed here are open year-round; unless otherwise stated, all have rooms with bath or shower—except in the lower (I) establishments. Note that Slovenia is also well-provided with privately run guest houses (look for the sign *gostilna).* In addition, farmhouse accommodations are now widely available and a special booklet from Kompas travel agency (see Useful Addresses) gives full details.

Food and Drink. In Slovenia you meet Balkan cuisine, immediately noticeable from the number of dishes served, and the ubiquitous Turkish coffee. Slovene cooking reveals the influence of Austria, and this is particularly evident in the delicious pastries and cakes. You can also get a *Wiener schnitzel* or *escalope Viennoise* (Dunaiski Zrezek) the equal of any to be had in an Austrian restaurant. Similarly, the famous sausages of Kranjska are unmistakably Germanic, and are called *kranjske klobase.* In northern Slovenia, the influence is more Hungarian, as is clear from such dishes as chicken fried in breadcrumbs *(pohovano pile)* and the "gipsy roast" called *cigansko pečenje,* flavored with garlic.

Slovenia is fortunate with her wines, which are among the best in the country. The red *Teran,* grown not far from Trieste, was appreciated by the Romans nearly 2,000 years ago. Those who prefer white wines should try Slovenia's *Ljutomer* or *Jeruzalem. Radgona* is excellent, whether still or sparkling. "Vin ordinaire" in Slovenia is never bottled; it is a powerful rosé known as *cviček.* It is very cheap, and is served in every little roadside inn or tavern, drawn straight from the cask.

BLED. A delightful lakeside resort in the Julian Alps. *Golf* (E), 150 rooms. Open and covered pools, tennis, golf. *Park* (E), 186 rooms. The newest in Bled, with indoor pool. *Toplice* (E), 121 rooms. Private beach, covered pool. A long tradition. Annex *TRST,* 48 rooms. *Jelovica* (M), 146 rooms. Annexes of varying prices. *Kompas* (M), 97 rooms. *Krim* (M), 100 rooms. *Lovec* (M), 72 rooms.

BOHINJ. A pleasant resort in the Julian Alps. *Bellevue* (lower M), with annexes, 120 rooms. *Pod Voglom* (lower M), with modern annex. *Zlatorog* (lower M), with annex, 74 rooms. *Ski Hotel* (I), on Vogel Plateau, 1,000 m. (3,280 ft.) above the village. 60 rooms, 14 with bath.

BOVEC. A mountain resort in the Julian Alps and Trenta Valley. *Alp Hotel* (M), 65 rooms. *Kanin* (M), 130 rooms. Sauna, indoor and outside pools.

CELJE. Great archeological center roughly equidistant from Maribor, Ljubljana and Zagreb. *Evropa* (M), 110 rooms. *Merx* (M), 26 rooms. *Celeia* (I), 86 rooms, some with bath.

DOBRNA. *Dobrna* (M), 172 rooms. Pool. *Zdravilíski Dom* (I), 82 rooms, a few with bath.

DOLENJSKE TOPLICE. *Kopaliski Dom* (M), 90 rooms. *Zdravilíski Dom* (M), 54 rooms. Both with pool.

GOZD MARTULJEK. *Pension Spik* (I). *Spik* (I), 93 rooms. Neither has private baths.

JEZERSKO. On the Austrian border; a good center for excursions into the Kamnik Alps. *Garni Planinka* (M), 31 rooms. *Kazina* (I), 27 rooms, some with shower.

KAMNIK. Good mountain center. *Malograjski Dvor* (M), 26 rooms. *Planinka* (I), 15 rooms, a few with bath.

KRANJ. *Creina* (M), 94 rooms. Pool. *Jelen* (I), 48 rooms.

KRANJSKA GORA. Summer mountain resort and winter sports center. *Kompas* (E), 155 rooms. Indoor pool; convenient for 18-hole golf course. *Alpina* (M), 101 rooms. *Larix* (M), 130 rooms. Indoor pool. *Lek* (M), 75 rooms. Pool. *Slavec* (M), 48 rooms. *Prisank* (I), 65 rooms. *Prisank-Garni* (I), 50 rooms.

LIPICA PRI SEŽANI. Original home of the famous Lippizaner horses. *Lipica* (M), 102 rooms. *Maestoso* (M), 84 rooms.

LJUBELJ. Near Yugoslav entrance to Alpine road tunnel. Two-stage chair lift; fine skiing and walking. *Kompas* (M), 36 rooms.

LJUBINJE. *Ljubinje* (M), 25 rooms.

LJUTOMER. *Jeruzalem* (M), 43 rooms.

MARIBOR. An excellent center for excursions to the Pohorje mountain region nearby. No truly first-class accommodations. *Habakuk* (M), 40 rooms. *Motel Jezero* (M), 15 rooms. 6½ km. (four miles) out on the Dravograd road. Bungalows. *Orel* (M), 150 rooms. *Turist* (M), 133 rooms. *Zamorec* (I), 36 rooms, none with bath.

MARIBORSKO POHORJE. Winter sports center near Maribor. *Areh-Sport Hotel* (M), 25 rooms. *Bellevue* (I), 51 rooms, some with bath.

MOST NA SOČI. In the Julian Alps. *Soča* (I), 10 rooms.

MURSKA SOBOTA. Near the Hungarian border. *Diana* (M), 103 rooms. *Zvezda* (I), 34 rooms.

NOVA GORICA. Near the Italian frontier. *Park* (M), 80 rooms. *Argonavti* (I), 80 rooms. *Sabotin* (I), 60 rooms, 35 with shower.

NOVO MESTO. *Metropol* (M), 78 rooms. *Kandija* (I), 28 rooms, a few with shower. *Pri Vodnjaku* (I), 13 rooms.

OTOČEC. *Grad Otočec* (M), 21 rooms, 10 with bath. Annex with 90 rooms. A charming castle on an island in the Krka River, now converted into hotel accommodations. Pool. Situated 400 m. (¼ mile) off the *autoput* between Ljubljana and Zagreb. *Motel Otočec* (I), 40 rooms, 24 bungalows. Actually on the *autoput*.

PODVIN PRI BLEDU. Stopover near Bled. *Grad Podvin* (E), 33 rooms. Pool.

POKLJUKA. Mountain resort near Bled. *Šport* (M), 39 rooms.

POSTOJNA. Europe's largest caves, with fantastic stalactites and stalagmites, and an internal railroad. *Jama* (M), 128 rooms. *Kras* (M), 54 rooms. *Motel Erazem* (I), 12 rooms. *Motel Proteus* (I), 233 rooms. On Ljubljana–Trieste highway. *Šport* (I), 56 rooms.

PREDDVOR PRI KRANJU. Near Kranj. *Bor-Grad Hrib* (M), 54 rooms. A former castle.

PTUJ. Archeological and wine-growing center. *Poetovic* (I), and annex, 43 rooms, some with bath.

RADENCI. Spa. *Radin* (E), 137 rooms; *annex* (M), 169 rooms. Both with pools.

RADOVLJICA. Southeast of Bled, starting point for canoeists on the River Sava. *Grajski Dvor* (M), 76 rooms. Pool. On the road to Ljubljana.

ROGASKA SLATINA. One of Yugoslavia's best-known thermal spas. *Donat* (L), 152 rooms. Pool. *Sava* (E), 260 rooms. *Boč* (M), 40 rooms. *Ljubljanski Dom* (M), 45 rooms. *Park* (M), 35 rooms. *Slovenski Dom* (M), 90 rooms. *Soča* (M), 49 rooms. *Styria* (M), 64 rooms. *Zagrebski Dom* (M), 62 rooms.

SLOVENJ GRADEC. Mountain resort. *Korotan* (I), 28 rooms, 5 with bath. *Pohorje* (I), 42 rooms, 15 with bath. There are two refuges on Planinski Dom, one at 1,370 m. (4,495 ft.) with 21 rooms, the other at 1,450 m. (4,757 ft.) with 36 rooms.

ŠMARJEŠKE TOPLICE. Thermal spa in Eastern Slovenia. *Smarješke Toplice* (M), 51 rooms. Pool. *New Hotel* (I), 70 rooms. Pool.

ŠTATENBERG. *Grad Štatenberg* (I), 30 rooms, a few with bath. In a former castle.

TOLMIN. *Krn* (M), 54 rooms.

VRŠIČ PASS. Leading from Kranjska Gora to Trenta Valley. *Erjavčeva Koča* (M), 45 beds. *Tičarjev Dom* (M), 70 beds. Modern, situated at top of the pass. These are but two of the four mountain inns located here, each set among fine scenery.

 WHAT TO SEE. The mountains, with their beautiful lakes, are Slovenia's greatest tourist attraction. There is a large number of thermal spas, of which the only one known outside Yugoslavia is Rogaška Slatina. However, you may prefer Dobrna, Radenska Slatina, Čateške, Dolenjske, or Šmarješke Toplice. Ljubljana, capital of Slovenia, contains some of the finest museums in the country, and many delightful baroque buildings.

Celje and Ptuj are important regional centers, where remarkable discoveries of Roman art treasures have also been made. If you prefer a quieter holiday then you will find what you want, plus superb scenery, in the Kamnik Alps and Pohorje Mountains.

The caves of Postojna and Škocjan reveal a fantastic subterranean world to visitors—and they are only two of the best known of the dozens that have been formed in Slovenia's limestone soil. The Slovene coast has the fishing port-resorts of Koper and Piran, and the smart international resort of Portorož.

 SPORTS. Slovenia is Yugoslavia's best winter sports area, largely because the various resorts are relatively accessible, well-organized, well-served with hotels— *and* charges are reasonable. The Olympic ski-jump is at Rateče Planica. There are chiar and ski lifts at Kranjska Gora to the choicest slopes of Vitranc Mountain, also a great number of inns and mountain cabins where everyone is very helpful. The Pokljuka Plateau, 1,200–1,585 m. (3,900–5,200 ft.) above sea-level, affords perfect conditions for beginners. In Bohinj there are ski lifts to extensive *pistes* on Vogel and Komna plateaux (1,370–1,645 m./4,500–5,400 ft.). Others from Kamniška Bistrica to Velika Planina. In the Pohorje Mountains, near Maribor, the terrain is even easier—and the prices lower.

In summer months climbing and mountaineering attract many visitors, the principal centers being Kranjska Gora, the valley of the Trenta, Bohinj, Bled, Kamnik, Jezersko and Solčava. The last stages of the European Footpath, E6, from the Baltic to the Adriatic passes through Slovenia, crossing the Pohorje Mountains, then continuing east of Ljubljana and over Snežnik Mountain to reach the coast west of Rijeka.

There is a fine golf course (18 holes) about 1½ km. (a mile) from Bled, situated above the River Sava gorge, with splendid views of the mountains. Season is from mid-April to mid-October, and equipment may be hired—green and caddies' fees are reasonable.

Swimming and boating are popular on the lakes, particularly rowing on Lake Bled. For kayak enthusiasts Slovenia offers marvelous opportunities: from Žužemberk, on the River Krka, through a countryside dotted with ancient castles, or from the junction of the two rivers Sava to the frontiers of Croatia; either is outstanding.

PRACTICAL INFORMATION FOR LJUBLJANA

 HOTELS. Apart from the hotels listed below, Ljubljana has a good selection of inns and guest houses, as well as five student hostels—details from the Tourist Information Center. Camp sites are: Autocamp Ježica, Titova 260, and Camp Dragočajna, Zbiljsko jezero, on the lake shore, a short drive north of the town.

Deluxe

Holiday Inn, Miklošičeva 3. 132 airconditioned rooms. Pool.

Expensive

Lev, Vošnjakova 1. 209 airconditioned rooms.

Moderate

Ilirija, Trg prekomorskih brigad 4. 136 rooms.
Motel Medno, on the Kranj road, 9½ km. (six miles) north. 42 rooms.
Slon, Titova 10. 185 rooms. Those looking out on to the main street are not recommended for light sleepers.
Turist, Dalmatinova 13. 192 rooms.
Union, Miklošičeva 1. 270 rooms.

Inexpensive

Gostilna Pri Mraku, Rimska 4. 27 rooms. Inn.
Motel Tikveš, Draga. 14 rooms, some with shower.

 RESTAURANTS. Food is excellent in the listed hotels. Ljubljana has in addition numerous restaurants, many of which are extremely attractive and with good service. *Maček,* Cankarjevo, Nabrežje 15, is outstanding. It overlooks the river that flows through the heart of the town, as does *Pri Vitezu,* at Breg 18–20. The first specializes in fish, the second in game. *Majolka,* Vodnikova 35, has reliable Slovenian cuisine. *Šestica,* Titova 16, has been a flourishing inn for almost 200 years, while *Zlatorog,* Zupančičeva 9, concentrates on game, and indeed can be found in the same building as houses the Hunting Association of Slovenia.

The Ilirija, Lev, Slon and Turist hotels all have nightclubs with floorshows and dancing; so too has the Nebotičnik, which is on the top floor of the first tall building to be built in Ljubljana.

The town has a good selection of cafés where you can drink coffee and eat huge cream cakes in the best central European manner. Two are in the Lev and Slon hotels. Self-service restaurants include *Emona* and *Triglav,* which are conveniently close to the Slon and Union hotels respectively.

 HOW TO GET AROUND. Kompas and other Ljubljana travel agents organize circular tours that visit the Julian Alps, the Kamnik Alps, the Logar Valley (Logarska Dolina), and the caves and grotto country around Postojna.

WHAT TO SEE. International country-style weddings have become an event here in the latter part of May, with parades and colorful costumes. From June to August there is the annual Summer Festival, which includes openair performances of opera, ballet and orchestral music at Križanke, a former monastery of the Crusader knights. The Wine Fair in September is very popular, with plenty of tastings and free samples.

MUSEUMS. The National Gallery, Cankarjeva 20, contains the best works of the particularly prolific baroque school of Slovene artists.

    The National Museum, Trg Herojev 1, has one ethnographic and one archeological section. Its greatest treasure is almost certainly the Vače Situle, a bronze urn discovered in Vače in Slovenia. Dating from the fifth century B.C., it is a wonderful example of Ilyrian workmanship of the best period, and illustrates the high degree of civilization attained by the original inhabitants before Roman, or even Greek, influences had made themselves felt.

    The National and University Library, Turjaška 1, includes first editions of all books printed in Slovene, also a number of interesting incunabula.

THEATERS. Most of the summer is taken up by the Ljubljana Summer Festival, with performances at Križanke, Trg francoske revolucije 2, and other historic settings. The main concert hall is the Slovenian Philharmonic Hall, Trg Osvobodite 9, while the Opera House is in Župančičeva and is well worth visiting for performances of a high quality.

USEFUL ADDRESSES. The Tourist Information Center is at Titova 11. The main Slovene travel agency, Kompas, has its headquarters at Pražakova 4. All the other main Yugoslav travel firms have offices in the center of town. Ljubljana Airport is at Brnik near Kranj, 40 minutes from the town. Auto-Moto Zveza Slovenije is the principal motoring organization, and is at Titova 138. The main post office is at Cigaletova 15. First Aid Service, Bohorićeva; 24-hour pharmacy, Prešernov trg 5.

INLAND CROATIA

Prosperity, Hills and Plains

Inland Croatia is very different from its great length of coast—except in prosperity, which both parts of the region share. While the coast is stony and fierce and elemental, tree-clad in Istria but bare and glaring over the rest of its length, Croatia inland is a region of rolling hills, fertile rivers and rich plains. We can distinguish four main sub-areas: the Zagorje hill area; the Gorski Kotar; the hills and valleys stretching south from Zagreb to Karlovac, the Plitvice Lakes and the Lika Valley; and the flat plain of Slavonia.

Varaždin, to the north, is the heart of Zagorje. Between the rivers Drava and Sava, east from the latter, lie the fertile plains of Slavonia that spread away unbroken to the banks of the Danube. Zagorje and Slavonia together make up northern Croatia. Between them and the long limestone ridge of the Velebit, which lies between inland Croatia and the Adriatic, the Gorski Kotar is east and northeast of Rijeka, north of the road to Karlovac. The Plitvice Lakes and the Lika, as it is usually called, occupy the south, having a common border with the Republic of Bosnia-Herzegovina.

The Historical Background

What is the modern province of Croatia was colonized by the Romans and formed part of the Pannonian province of the Empire, a vast territory stretching to the present Hungarian border. The arrival of the Croats, members of the great family of Slavic peoples, occurred over the sixth and seventh centuries. Established between the rivers Sava and Drava, the Croats were still subject to the Avars (who had conquered them before their arrival in their new home), and remained so until they liberated themselves in the middle of the eighth century.

The following years saw the gradual fusion and unification of the various Croat tribes, until in the year 924 they created their own kingdom. Though Catholics, the Croats adopted the Slav liturgy fought for by Bishop Gregory of Nin. Their greatest kings were Tomislav, Petar, Krešimir and Zvonimir. Later, the Croat nation associated itself with the Magyar Kingdom, recognizing the royal house of Hungary as their overlord.

In 1527 the Turks occupied Hungary, and the Croats therefore transferred their allegiance to Austria. Throughout this alliance with—and subservience to—Vienna, the nobility were all-powerful, and there were repeated unsuccessful peasant revolts against their dominance, that of Matija Gubec in 1573 being suppressed with particular ferocity. Others that followed met the same fate, nor did the revival of the Croat-Magyar union in 1779 remove feudal injustice.

The Prussian defeat of Austria in the war of 1866 brought about great changes, among them the creation of the dual monarchy of Austria-Hungary. Austria took the overlordship of Slovenia and Dalmatia, while Hungary obtained control of Croatia, to which she granted autonomy in 1868. Under this arrangement, Croatia directed her own internal political affairs, including education. She was also allotted a certain number of seats in the Budapest Parliament. These concessions increased the determination of Croatia to achieve full independence, and her aims found expression in the Illyrian Movement, whose objective was that of the union of all southern Slav peoples. However, various pan-Slav attempts to realize this end failed to produce positive results, the long-awaited opportunity presenting itself only with the collapse of the Austro-Hungarian monarchy in 1918. The map of the Balkan peninsula was redrawn at the conclusion of World War I, and

Croatia became an integral part of the new Kingdom of the Serbs, Croats and Slovenes.

Between the two world wars, certain Croat pretensions brought about the formation of an extreme nationalist political party under Ante Pavelić, which degenerated into the Fascist movement known as the *ustaše,* more concerned with killing Serbs and Jews—if necessary with the aid of Axis troops—than with the struggle for independence.

The assassination of King Alexander and the French Foreign Minister Louis Barthou during the former's official visit to Marseilles was the work of the *ustaše,* which seized power after the occupation of the country by German and Italian troops in 1941. The reality of an "independent" Croatia rapidly vanished, however. It became a mere puppet state.

After 1944 Croatia took its rightful place in the federation of Yugoslav Republics and struggled, like all the country's other regions, toward a viable economic existence. Partly through large tourist revenue from its coast, the Republic soon began to outstrip the rest of the country in prosperity—and new trouble began. Many Croats objected to being compelled to contribute funds for the economic development of non-Croatian backward areas (which was an essential provision of the new, increasingly decentralized Constitution adopted in the early 1970s) and voices were raised in favor of secession from the Federation, specifically permitted by the new Constitution. It required the personal intervention of President Tito, himself a Croat, to stop nationalist separatism.

Zagreb, Capital of Croatia

Zagreb's 850,000 inhabitants live on the fringe of a rich and fertile plain where maize, tobacco and wheat are cultivated under the lee of the wooded heights of Zagrebačka Gora.

The second city of Yugoslavia, Zagreb is in effect a second capital of the country. It has an intense cultural life of its own, and vies with Belgrade in the profusion of its concerts, theatrical performances of all kinds and literary and artistic exhibitions, including folklore festivals.

Exploring Zagreb

The city's attractive center is surrounded by a rapidly growing belt of undistinguished and indistinguishable suburbs. This results in a striking contrast between the lower town, with the spacious avenues and flower-filled gardens which divide up the new residential districts, and the two ancient quarters of the upper town, Kaptol and Grič. Here you will find the palaces of the former nobility, and such churches as have survived the city's two major earthquakes and one disastrous fire.

Zagreb is a main road, rail and air junction, and is unmistakably busy and prosperous, with its two famous International Trade Fairs (Spring and Autumn), by far the most important in the entire country, as the events of the year. If you are in search of the past, then remember that within a quarter of an hour's journey from all the bustle of Zagreb main station, you can still find ancient villages which the passage of the centuries has left largely untouched.

Zagreb—meaning "behind the hill"—claims to be the cultural capital of Yugoslavia. Its theaters, Opera House and various orchestras are justly famous. Here, too, is the headquarters of the Yugoslav Academy of Arts and Sciences, and the university attracts the most talented among the youth of the nation. Zagreb's art galleries are particularly rich in examples of the French Impressionists, notably Degas and Renoir.

Centuries ago Zagreb comprised two neighboring but separate towns, one secular and the other religious. Perched on the summit of a hill, the former dominated the latter as it did the whole valley. In the 13th century it was named Gradec, meaning "fortress," and was walled to protect the citizens against the Tartars. The other town, named Kaptol or Chapter House, was also fortified in the 16th century, at the time of the great Turkish drive to the Danubian plain, though as it happened the enemy never came within 65 km. (40 miles) of the town. The separation of the two towns continued until the time of the Napoleonic Wars, and it was only in the 19th century that new building at last united them into the single city of Zagreb.

The lower town is centered around Ilica, the main street that crosses it for a distance of some 4 km. (2½ miles). It is full of shops and cafés, and leads you to the center Trg Republike—Republic Square. From there you should climb Radićeva Street and Štrosmajer Promenade to the quarter of the upper town known as Gornji Grad. This route affords fine views.

Alternative ways up are by Radićeva Street and the Kamenita Vrata, the ancient Stone Gate (where, legend has it, a devastating fire was miraculously halted), or by the funicular that leaves from Ilica Street.

If you choose the funicular, you will be put down opposite the Dverce Tower, or Little Gate, which is the entrance to the fortress of Gradec. In memory of the days when all the gates of the fortress were closed against the perils of the coming night, a bell is still rung every evening at the hour of sunset.

Beyond the Dverce Tower you will see two churches. The first was built in the 17th century as a monastery dedicated to St. Catherine, the second, built in the center of Radićev Trg (Radić Square) is the Church of St. Mark the Evangelist, its roof brilliant with red, white and blue tiles depicting the emblems of Croatia (on the left) and Zagreb. It was

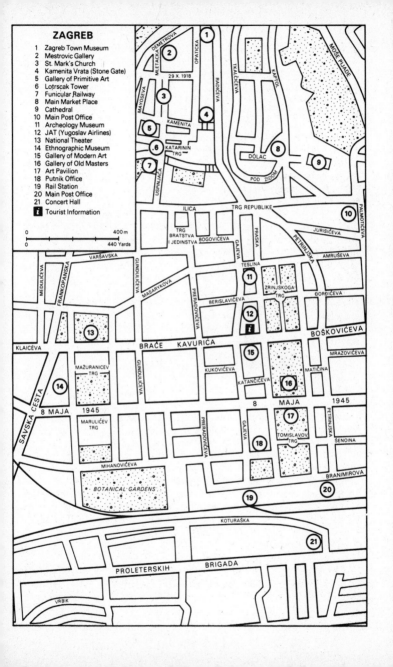

in front of St. Mark's that Matija Gubec was executed after the defeat of his peasant revolt in 1573.

The interior of St. Mark has been decorated by the best modern Yugoslav artists, including the sculptor, the late Ivan Meštrović, who lived in the United States. The modern frescos and various other works of art blend quite harmoniously with the 14th-century Gothic sanctuary. Do not miss the tenth-century painting in the unfinished chapel, of King Tomislav holding his first Council of State.

The slightly out-of-date elegance of Gornji Grad has a certain charm, but Kaptol as a whole is disappointing. The Catholic Cathedral of St. Stephen is imposing, but has little of interest to offer except, perhaps, the inscription of the Ten Commandments on the north wall, written in 12th-century Glagolitic characters.

A pleasant local custom is for the townspeople to take a morning walk, more often than not a few turns of the cathedral building. Among the chattering throng you will recognize the peasants who have come in from the neighboring villages, the women sometimes dressed in their traditional costumes. Very near the cathedral, too, is the bustling and colorful openair market of Dolac, doing business seven days a week.

Zagreb has comfortable hotels, restaurants and cafés to suit most tastes and pockets. In addition, because of the long period of war and isolation, the town has not grown in such a way as to demand the sacrifice of its many parks and gardens, which are beautifully kept. It is a further attraction that most of these small parks are in or near the center of the city, notably those of Maksimir, Zrinjevac, and Tuškanac —this last providing splendid open spaces where children seem always to be noisily at play.

This is not only a city worth a visit on its own account, it is also a first-rate center for excursions, particularly to the hills of Zagrebačka Gora. Many visitors like to climb Mount Sljeme (also accessible by cable car), from the slopes of which there are unforgettable views across the city of Zagreb, as well as the scenic River Sava valley.

The only worthwhile detour on the short Croatian section of the *autoput* is to Samobor, a pleasant little town much visited on weekends from nearby Zagreb and reached by narrow-gauge railway. It is popular in summer for the attractive scenery, in winter for the skiing—and all year round for the excellent local wine.

Zagorje

A most picturesque district lies north of the Zagrebačka Gora hills and is known as Zagorje which, roughly translated, means "the land beyond the mountains."

Zagorje is full of wooded heights with vineyards among them. Between are park lands through which wind fast-running trout streams. At intervals there are villages, still somewhat remote from the world of today, where ancient ways and customs thrive in the place of their birth, presided over by the crumbling walls of an ancient castle.

There are many of these crowning the heights of the Ivančica range, which rises to over 990 km. (3,250 ft.), and you will certainly notice the castles of Oštre, Labor, Milengrad and Bistra, and numerous others. Since it is impossible to list them here, we shall just mention a few of the most interesting, chief among them being Trakošćan in the northwest of Zagorje. It crowns the summit of a wooded height and is reflected in the still waters of a lake. Trakošćan Castle houses a magnificent collection of medieval arms—and also a most welcome restaurant.

Januševac Castle not far from the town of Marof is now little more than a ruin. Built in the 14th century, it successfully survived the passage of time only to be partially destroyed during the last war. On the other hand, 13th-century Varaždin Castle, which witnessed important events in the country's history, has been more fortunate and now serves as one of the most remarkable historical museums in Croatia. It stands within the old walled town of Varaždin, some 75 km. (47 miles) north and east of Zagreb, which has many charming little baroque palaces. Nearby is the romantic old castle of Maruševac, with its slender towers rising high against the sky. Another charming Zagorje castle is Veliki Tabor, built in the 15th century, but still fairly intact.

While you are in this part of the country you may care to visit the little town of Krapina where the remains of Paleolithic man now on exhibition in Zagreb were discovered in a nearby grotto. Krapina was the birthplace of Ljudevit Gaj, famous at the beginning of the last century as the founder of the Illyrian Movement. Lepoglava, just northeast of Krapina, was the site of Croatia's first university, founded in the 17th century.

The Sutla Valley which stretches from a few kilometers west of Zagreb and runs north, reaches its greatest magnificence as it approaches Klanjec, and the Zelenjak Gorge, where the river has worn a narrow way through the solid rock, is quite startlingly beautiful. Beside it is a small monument dedicated to Antun Mihanović who was inspired here to write the poem *Our Lovely Land* which became the Croat national anthem.

Marshal Tito was born in a little village called Kumrovec, about eight km. (five miles) northwest of Klanjec. The house where he was born has been converted into a museum. In the courtyard there is a statue of him by Augustinčić, a disciple of Meštrović, and the rooms contain mementos of the great leader's early days.

Zagorje's thermal spas, famous since Roman times (their *Aquae Vivae* being the Krapinske Toplice of today), include the sulphurous waters of Varaždinske Toplice (136°) which, judging by the numerous Roman remains found in the district, enjoyed a great reputation as *Aquae Jasae.*

Gorski Kotar

Leading southwest from Zagreb to the sea is the E96, a toll motorway for its first 43 km. (27 miles). This takes it as far as Karlovac, a flourishing town at the confluence of the Koranc and Kupa rivers. Karlovac was once one of the Christian world's bastions against the Turks and today its 16th-century fortress is still impressive.

The town is an important crossroads. To the northeast, back along the road to Zagreb, is Jastrebarsko, still dominated by its 15th-century castle. To the south is Slunj Castle, where Napoleon billeted his troops and, beyond Slunj, are the Plitvice Lakes. To the west of Karlovac is Dubovac, another stronghold and reminder of the region's bloody past.

West from Dubovac and only a few kilometers inland from Rijeka is the wildly picturesque district of Gorski Kotar. Separated from the Adriatic coast by the hills inland from Rijeka, the heights of Gorski Kotar are everywhere thickly covered with silent forests of pine, though there are frequent grassy clearings. Lower down, the land is gashed by countless ravines, with fast-running streams.

Some of the peaks in this area, such as Risnjak and Sniješnik (or Snežnik), reach a height of nearly 1,525 m. (5,000 ft.). They are popular with ski enthusiasts, who can indulge in their favorite pastime well into the month of May, when bathing in the neighboring Adriatic is already possible.

One of the most attractive places in Gorski Kotar is the waterfall of Zeleni Vir, near to the town of Skrad, which hurls itself, with the noise of thunder, from a height of almost 90 m. (300 ft.). There is an unusually interesting grotto on the fringe of a neighboring lake.

We have mentioned only in passing that winter sports facilities are available in the heights of the Gorski Kotar. One of the most popular centers for skiing is the little town of Delnice, set between mountains and forests, and at Platak regular ski-competitions are held every season. Incidentally, if winter sports are not in your line, it may be worth remembering that the River Kupa, a tributary of the Sava, is not far away, and is a favorite with fishermen.

Delnice is conveniently central, and from it you can easily reach the various other sporting centers and beauty spots of the Gorski Kotar. An area of rocky hillsides, deep gorges and forest of giant pines is to be found near Lokve, and is strikingly beautiful in its wild grandeur.

You should try to visit the 1,370-m. (4,500-ft.) Mount Bitoroj if you can. Its ascent is definitely worthwhile.

From Delnice, the shortest run to the shores of the Adriatic is via Fuzine, a village attractively positioned beside a pine-fringed lake. However, the road is still only partly paved and you would do better to take the E96 which leads all the way to Rijeka, Yugoslavia's principal port, and widens into a motorway as it nears the coast.

The Plitvice Lakes and Lika Valley

These 16 lakes are among the greatest tourist attractions in Yugoslavia. Each is on a different level, and the water cascades from one to the other in a series of extraordinarily beautiful falls, gleaming and making rainbows of spray in the sunshine. Scenically speaking, the serene and romantic countryside round the lakes is, though relatively little known, one of the most beautiful districts in Europe. Today it has been declared a National Park to preserve it from ugly buildings or thoughtless commercial exploitation.

In this remote place, each season of the year has its special enchantment. In the spring, the melting of the heavy snows of a Balkan winter fill to the brim the higher lakes, creating a tremendous flow to the lower ones. In the summer, this thunderous series of waterfalls gradually quietens, and the special charm of autumn is that the utterly still surface of each lake perfectly mirrors every shade and leaf of the shores. Even the harshness of winter seems softened when the immaculate white of the snow is reflected in those quiet waters, and summer and winter alike there is the music of the falls between lake and lake. Their beauty aside, the Plitvice Lakes abound in fish and that gourmet's delight, freshwater crayfish.

You will probably notice the gigantic waterweeds and vegetation of all kinds that grow around the innumerable falls with such exuberance. Some of the trees in the surrounding forests are more than 490 m. (160 ft.) tall.

Near the village of Ljeskovac, two little streams unite to form the River Matica, which less than 1½ km. (a mile) farther on flows into the highest of the Plitvice Lakes, Prošće. This vast expanse of water is at a height of well over 610 m. (2,000 ft.) above sea-level, and flows into a far smaller lake which in turn supplies a third no less than 13 m. (42 ft.) below it. Next comes a group of four, connected by a whole series of magnificent cascades, and so, step by step, the chain descends to the third largest, and quite the bluest of the 16, Lake Galovac, which is at a height of 580 m. (1,900 ft.).

Past the last houses of Velika Poljana, Lake Kozjak narrows toward a mountainous canyon. From far off you can hear the roar of the great waterfall by which the upper lakes thunder down into Lake Kaludero-vac, 530 m. (1,650 ft.) above sea-level. At the heart of the current the water is still the deepest blue in color, though the edges of the stream are dark gray.

There are a number of caves, one of which may be reached by a series of rough steps cut in rock for the purpose. From the head of these falls there is a magnificent view across the lower lakes.

The water from the last lake of all flows into a remarkable natural dam at the foot of the magnificent fall known as "watersmeet." From there it forms the little River Plitvice which gathers momentum for another series of cascades which together fall nearly another 70 m. (230 ft.). Various terraces provided for the visitor make it possible to appreciate the extraordinary sight of the sun shining with every color of the spectrum through the curtain of falling water which is to form the River Korana.

If you take the westward-leading coast-bound road from Plitvice Lakes and turn south at the junction near Prezor, instead of toward the coast, you come into a region called the Lika. Most of it lies in fact in the valley of the River Lika. Tiny Gospić is the area's main town. Till recently few visitors came to Gospić and the Lika because the roads were so bad. Though fertile, it is not a part of Yugoslavia that offers very special attractions, apart from the views from roads leading in and out of the area.

At its northern end you approach or leave either from Plitvice or by one of the two roads leading from the sea at Senj and Karlobag over the mighty, 80-km.-long (50 miles) Velebit ridge. The Velebit encloses the Lika on its seaward side, and the huge 1,525-m.-high (5,000 ft.) mountain gives the valley a very different climate from that of the coast. In October it is possible for the Lika to lie under ten cm. (four in.) of snow while people are still bathing and complaining of the heat a bare 30 or 40 km. (20–25 miles) away. The Velebit also provides superb views of the Kvarner Gulf and all its islands—once you have crossed one of the passes at the top of its ridge. Rab, the nearest of the islands, seems to be within a stone's throw, though it is in fact some 25 km. (15 miles) distant.

The road at the Lika's southern exit takes you over the magnificent Alan (or Halan) Pass, with the town of Obrovac at its southern approach. The Alan affords stupendous views from whichever side you approach. If you come from Obrovac toward the Lika you have the experience of crossing suddenly from a bare landscape to one filled with forests. If you travel southward you climb up out of the thick trees and suddenly see, spreading for kilometer after kilometer below you, the enormous and unforested sweep of the Velebit's southern end continuing all the way down to Obrovac.

It is also worth noting that a different southward-leading side road from Plitvice takes you quickly into a mountain area previously accessible only to the tough and determined, but now popular with both mountaineers and Yugoslav summer tourists. Its focal point is the little town of Udbina, where you can find modest lodgings. It lies east of the Lika Valley.

Slavonia

The final part of inland Croatia that we must consider is the region called Slavonia. Unlike the rest, it is flat—or very nearly so.

The province is really of greater economic interest than it is in terms of tourist attraction. It stretches from Zagreb to Belgrade, and is watered by both the rivers Drava and Sava, and crossed by the *autoput* linking the two capital cities. The land here is extremely fertile, with rich grasslands, vines and oak forests. Despite its industrialization, Slavonia is not without its attractions, notably at Daruvar, the *Aquae Balissae* of the Romans, and at Lipik, set in the romantically beautiful Pakra Valley. The two towns are only 26 km. (16 miles) apart on the road that runs from the *autoput* at Kučani.

Daruvar and Lipik are thermal spas, their waters leaving the spring at a temperature of 142°F, and containing a high concentration of iodine. Fortunately, or unfortunately, according to your point of view, oil has been found locally, and the exploitation of the wells during the next few years seems certain. Of the many fortifications built along the River Drava during the Middle Ages, few have survived. Among those that have is the fortress at Djurdjevac.

Another 160 km. (100 miles) east is the industrial city of Osijek, Slavonia's greatest manufacturing center, with a population of 100,000. It is situated on the banks of the Drava, and its history goes back to Roman times. South of Osijek and only 21 km. (13 miles) north of the Zagreb–Belgrade highway is the town of Dakovo, which grew round an elegant 18th-century castle, and was once the home of the priest Štrosmajer, one of the champions of Yugoslavia's 19th-century renaissance, and founder of the Academy of Arts and Sciences in the Croat capital. Today Dakovo is the seat of a bishopric. There is also a Lippizaner Stud Farm. An International Riding Tournament is held here in July.

Despite its present peaceful air, Slavonia was the scene of many great battles in the past. Conquered by the Turks early in the 16th-century, the region remained under Ottoman domination for a century and a half. The Habsburgs subsequently fortified the whole of the province against the threat of further Turkish invasion. To achieve Croat cooperation, they were granted various special privileges, among them the right of soldiers to possess their own land, and exemption from all feudal taxes. Like the men of the Swiss Confederation, these peasant soldiers organized themselves so that they could muster many thousands of men at a few hours' notice, and their bravery and efficiency soon became famous throughout Europe. This military régime was maintained until toward the end of the last century. It is an amusing historical digression to recall that the members of a cavalry regiment of these soldiers in the service of Louis XIV of France were the inventors of the necktie. They wore a kind of white handkerchief round their necks, a fashion which was copied by the courtiers of Versailles—the French word *cravate* being a corruption of *croate (hrvat* in Serbo-Croat).

PRACTICAL INFORMATION FOR INLAND
CROATIA

 WHEN TO GO. Yugoslavia's two most important international fairs take place in Zagreb. The first, in April, concentrates on consumer goods; the second, in September, focuses on science and technology. On the cultural front, the Zagreb Evenings, from July to mid-September, attract a large audience for a varied program of entertainments mounted in openair theaters. At the end of July is the International Review of Original Folklore.

 HOTELS AND RESTAURANTS. In the selection of accommodations below, where no dates are indicated it means the establishment is open the year round. All hotels have bath or shower facilities unless otherwise stated—but not necessarily will *all* rooms. Croatia is also well provided with privately run guest houses or pensions (look for the sign *gostionica).*

Food and Drink. Croatian cooking is simple, tasty, and slightly sharp. It is not especially original, resembling central European cuisine in general. You can order just about anywhere such Balkan specialties as breaded chicken *(pohovano pile)* and gipsy roast *(cigansko pečenje),* both particularly good. The latter dish has a little garlic in it. As for pastries, Croatia is justly proud of its *štrudla,* a flaky crust with cherries *(sa trešnjama)* or apples *(sa jabukama),* which is delicious if eaten when still warm—but watch out for your digestion. Noodles *(rezanci)* are eaten as dessert with chopped walnuts or poppy-seed, or with white pot-cheese and sugar. Cakes are typically central European—excellent. Whipped cream is used freely.

Light Croatian wines include *Žumberak* and *Moslavina.*

ČAKOVEC. A good hunting area near the Hungarian border. *Park* (M), 120 rooms.

ČATEŽ OB SAVI. *Terme* (E), 150 rooms. *Bungalows* (M), 60 rooms. *Zdraviliški Dom* (M), 60 rooms.

DELNICE. Mountain resort. *Delnice* (M), 43 rooms. *Risjnak* (M), 21 rooms. At **Petehovac**, some 1,025 m. (3,360 ft.) up, is *Pension Petehovac* (I), 18 rooms, none with shower.

KARLOVAC. *Korana* (M), 192 rooms. Terrace on the bank of the Korana River. *Central*, *Mrežnica* and *Park* are all (I), but with no baths. At **Dubovac** is a *castle-hotel* with 11 rooms, 2 with bath. At **Duga Resa**, 6½ km. (four miles) west of Karlovac, on the road toward Rijeka, is *Motel Roganac* (I), 11 rooms.

KRAPINSKE TOPLICE. Spa. *Toplice* (M), 164 rooms. Spa.

LIČKO LEŠĆE. *Gacka* (M), 60 rooms.

NOVA GRADIŠKA. *Slaven* (M), 34 rooms. On the *autoput, Motel Turist* (I), 16 rooms.

OBROVAC. *Kanjon Zrmanje* (M), 24 rooms.

OSIJEK. Good stopover in the northeastern section. *Osijek* (M), 182 rooms. *Central* (I), 36 rooms, a few with bath. *Royal* (I), also 36 rooms.

OTOČAC. *Park* (I), 44 rooms.

PLITVICE LAKES (Plitvička Jezera). *Jezero* (E), 250 rooms. Sauna, indoor pool. *Plitvice* (E), 70 rooms. *Bellevue* (M), 90 rooms.

SAMOBOR. *Šmidhen* (M), 50 rooms. Pool.

SLAVONSKI BROD. Conveniently located halfway along the *autoput* between Zagreb and Belgrade. *Motel Marsonia* (M), 63 rooms, half with bath. On the *autoput. Park* (M), 49 rooms, most with bath. In the town. *Motel Vinogorje* (I), 39 rooms, a few with bath. Also on the *autoput.*

SLUNJ. In the narrow valley of the Korana River. *Park* (I), 14 rooms. *Slunjčica* (I), 34 rooms, none with shower.

STUBIČKE TOPLICE. Spa. *Matija Gubec* (M), 96 rooms. Pool.

TRAKOŠĆAN. Lovely *castle* (M), in the Zagorje. 50 rooms.

TUHELJSKE TOPLICE. *Mihanović* (M), 178 rooms. In new recreation and sports center.

VARAŽDIN. *Turist* (M), 207 rooms, most with bath.

ŽUPANJA. On the *autoput* between Zagreb and Belgrade. *Motel Rastovica* (I), 50 rooms, most with bath.

WHAT TO SEE. During the summer, the most popular inland resort in Croatia is unquestionably Plitvice, with its 16 lakes lying like terraces one above the other linked by waterfalls, in the midst of a National Park. It is one of nature's rare wonders. In the northeastern section of the country are most of the watering places, the best-known being: Varaždinske Toplice *(Aquae Jasae* of the Romans), Sisak, Daruvar *(Aquae Balissae)*, Krapinske Toplice and Stubičke Toplice, which is quite near Zagreb, at the foot of the Sljeme.

Admirers of arms and armor will find some beautiful collections of the medieval period in the castles of Trakošćan and Ozalj.

SPORTS. If you are interested in kayaking, spend some time on the Kupa, Korana and Mrežnica rivers, set in wonderful woodland scenery. The Croat Krka can be reached from Knin, where you can also start the descent of the Cetina, as far as Šibenik. These rivers additionally provide excellent fishing.

Inland Croatia has tremendous hunting reserves, especially in Slavonia. The main quarry are deer and wild boar. Game birds also abound. Hunting in Croatia, one of the best grounds in Europe, is very well organized and offers all facilities to the amateur.

PRACTICAL INFORMATION FOR ZAGREB

HOW TO GET THERE. By plane. Zagreb is covered by the international air routes and can be reached direct from London, Paris, Amsterdam, Zürich and other cities. In summer, the city has air connections with all Yugoslav tourist centers that have airports.

By train. Of the numerous through trains stopping at Zagreb, many continue on to Belgrade, Niš and Skopje, or to towns on the coast such as Zadar, Šibenik and Split.

By car. The *autoput* connecting Ljubljana via Zagreb with Belgrade goes through the Slavonia region for a stretch of nearly 300 km. (190 miles), before entering Serbia. Zagreb can be bypassed on a motorway. There is a turnpike from Zagreb to Karlovac, where E96 continues to Rijeka. And there is a branch southeast from Rakovica, just before Plitvice to Jajce in Bosnia-Herzegovina. The usual access from Croatia to Bosnia-Herzegovina is from various branches off the *autoput* farther east. North of Zagreb, E96 leads to Varaždin and Budapest.

By bus. Regular bus services connect Zagreb with all main centers.

WHEN TO GO. April or September is the time to choose if you are interested in major international trade fairs; and either month is also a good time for the surrounding countryside. Cultural events are year-round, with the emphasis on openair and street entertainments in the summer months. Otherwise, like all big cities, Zagreb has plenty to offer at any time. But do remember that on the edge of the central European plains, it can be very hot in summer—and cold in winter.

HOTELS. The hotels listed below have all or most rooms with bath or shower unless otherwise stated. Private accommodations can be booked through the travel agencies Croatiaturist, Generalturist, and TD Novi Zagreb (see Useful Addresses end of chapter). Youth accommodations are provided through Omladinski turistički centar, 73 Petrinjska Str., near the main rail station in Zagreb. Camp sites: Mladost, Horvćanski zavoj, on the north bank of the River Sava; and Zagreb, Partizanskih pilota, next to the motel of the same name, near the fairground south of the Sava.

Deluxe

Inter-Continental Zagreb, 1 Krsnjavoga Str. 457 rooms. Restaurants include one in national style; also casino, nightclub, pool.

Expensive

Esplanade, 1 Mihanovićeva Str., opposite main rail station. 197 rooms. An imposing turn-of-the-century building, modernized; nightclub, and dancing on the terrace in summer—which can make some rooms noisy. One of the restaurants is in regional style.

Palace, 10 Strossmayerov Sq., near main rail station. 91 rooms.

Moderate

Beograd, 71 Petrinjska Str. Large and central.

Dubrovnik, 1 Gajeva Str. 279 rooms. Beer tavern but no restaurant. Recently renovated; very central, overlooking Republic Sq.

International, 24 Miramarska Str. 420 rooms. Away from the center in less attractive newer district. Nightclub.

Laguna, 29 Kranjčevićeva Str. 180 rooms. Out of the center.

Inexpensive

Bristol, 12 Gajeva Str. 30 rooms, only a few with bath. No restaurant, but very central.

Central, 3 Branimirova Str., opposite main rail station. 103 rooms, some with bath.

Jadran, 50 Vlaška Str. 32 rooms, half with shower. Near the cathedral.

Turopolje, Velika Gorica, Trg slobode 38, four km. (2½ miles) from Zagreb Airport. 40 rooms, none with bath. Modest but good value for transit stop.

Motels and Pensions

Dvorac Brezovica, 28 rooms, all with bath or shower. First-class pension in old "castle" (bungalows) out of the town. Very inexpensive.

Šumski dvor (M), Prekrizje. 9 rooms, none with bath or shower. A pension in a quiet and particularly attractive district on the outskirts of Zagreb.

Zagreb Motel, Dubrovačka aleja. 51 rooms. South of the River Sava, near the fairground.

 RESTAURANTS. There is a wide choice of places to eat in Zagreb, covering the whole price spectrum; those below are but a small selection. Additionally, there are any number of self-service restaurants, milk bars and snack bars. Three good ones among the latter are *Corso,* 2 Gundulićeva Str.; *Medulić,* 2 Medulićeva Str.; and *Splendid,* 15 Zrinjevac Sq. All three are central. For quick and cheap snacks, look for *čevapi u somunu* (selling *čevapčići* with bread) or *buregdžinica* (for tasty Bosnian pastries known as *burek*).

Otherwise, inexpensive food can be obtained at the beer halls, that in the Dubrovnik hotel, for example (address, see above); also, at *Stari fijaker,* Mesnička Str.

Dubravkin put, on the road of the same name. A lovely situation among woods near the city.

Kaptolska klet, 5 Kaptol. Central and good.

Korčula, 17 N. Tesle Str. Specializes in fish and Dalmatian dishes. Central.

Okrugljak, 28 Mlinovi. A little out of the center of Zagreb, but in a pleasant setting. There is an openair section in the garden.

Pod mirnim krovovima, 7 Fijanova Str. Lamb-on-the-spit here is particularly good; also freshwater fish.

Split, 19 Ilica. Fish and Dalmatian specialties. Very central.

 HOW TO GET AROUND. By bus/tram. There is a good network of trams serving the center, and there are buses out to the suburbs. The price is the same regardless of distance, and you can change as often as you like while traveling in the same direction, including from tram to bus, within a time limit of 1½ hours. Tickets are best bought on board the vehicle (second or third car).

By train. A narrow-gauge local train, beloved of the Zagreb townspeople, links the city with Samobor.

By coach. Generalturist and other travel firms in Zagreb run comfortable coach excursions to such tourist areas as the Plitvice Lakes and Dubrovnik.

By cable car. There is a cable car from the Gračani district to the top of Medvednica Mountain. The lower and upper levels of Zagreb are connected by a venerable funicular in less than a minute, saving you a short but steep haul.

Note. Car parking in the center of Zagreb is a big problem and best avoided if possible.

WHAT TO SEE. Only a short distance from the center of Zagreb are the 120 sq. km. (75 sq. miles) of Maksimir Park, once a wild forest and now a pleasant oasis for relaxation which also contains a zoo. The village of Samobor to the west of Zagreb is a favorite excursion spot. Also easily reached is the splendid mountain district of Medvednica (highest peak Sljeme, at 945 m./3,105 ft.), reached in 25 minutes by cable car from Gračani (trams 14 and 21 from the city center), by car or on foot. Beyond the mountains lie the wooded hills and vineyards of the Zagorje region, dotted with old castles, churches, and a number of excellent spas such as Stubičke Toplice, Krapinske Toplice, and Tuheljske Toplice (with large new sports and recreational center). Not far from the latter is the village of Kumrovec, where the simple home in which the late President Tito was born is now a museum.

SPORTS. There are facilities for swimming, sailing, and wind surfing at Jarun Recreation Center by an artificial lake in the suburbs, and water skiing at Čiče lake near the airport. In Zagreb itself, you can swim in the pool at Mladost, by the River Sava.

Of non-aquatic sports, tennis is popular. And from a spectator point-of-view, football is the favorite, as elsewhere in Yugoslavia. The first clubs in Zagreb were organized in 1903, and the Dinamo stadium, where big international matches are played, seats 60,000 persons.

Winter sports are practised on beautiful Mount Sljeme, Zagreb's natural playground rising to the north of the city. It is reached by cable car to Medvednica from the Gračani district in about 25 minutes.

The area also offers excellent hiking.

MUSEUMS AND ART GALLERIES. These are usually open six days a week, with Monday the common day of closure; Sunday is mostly mornings only.

Archeological Museum, 19 Zrinjski Sq. From prehistory to the 19th century. Fine coin collection.

Arts and Crafts Museum, 10 Marshal Tito Sq. Furniture, musical instruments, textiles, clothing, and handicrafts—all from the 15th century to modern times.

Ethnographic Museum, 14 Mažuranić Sq. Admirable collection of folk costumes, crafts, instruments and other artefacts; also interiors of peasant homes.

Gallery of Primitive Art, 3 Cirilometodska. Memorable display of foreign and especially Yugoslav naive painters, many of international repute.

Meštrović Gallery, 8 Mletačka Str. Sculptures and drawings by Ivan Meštrović most famed of Yugoslav sculptors.

Mimara Gallery, housed in a former Jesuit monastery in the Upper Town. Notable private art collection of Ante Topić Mimara.

Modern Gallery, 1 Braće Kavurića Str. Croatian art over the past 150 years.

Strossmayer Gallery of Old Masters, 11 Zrinski Sq. Yugoslavia's largest gallery of Old Masters, including Italian, Flemish, Spanish and Dutch schools from the 14th to 19th centuries.

Zagreb Town Museum, 20 Opatička Str. Excellent displays showing the development of the city through the ages.

ENTERTAINMENT. Your best bet is to get the latest calendar of events from the Tourist Information Center. There is a lively program of summer happenings throughout the city, but especially in the attractive settings of the old Upper Town, with music, drama and folklore performances taking place in courtyards and old buildings, or often in the open air. In July, an International Folklore Festival unfolds in the streets and squares of the city.

Zagreb has a number of theaters (and 40 theater groups), though these do present most visitors with a language problem. Music, however, has no barriers. There is opera and ballet at the excellent National Croat Theater, and at the Conservatory of Music you can hear the Croat Symphony Orchestra or the Zagreb Soloists, an internationally known chamber music ensemble. There are also top-class performances in the modern Concert Palace (Vatroslav Lisinski). Musicals, rock operas, etc., are the specialties of the Komedija at 9 Kaptol. There is music every afternoon in Zrinjevac, and organ recitals are given in the church on Palmotićeva Str.

MARKETS. Zagreb has 15 openair market places where fresh food, household goods, textiles and souvenirs can be bought seven days a week—and where prices for handicrafts are likely to be substantially lower that in the popular coastal resorts. The biggest and most colorful market is at Dolac, which is very central and near the cathedral.

TRADE FAIRS. Zagreb, as has already been mentioned, is the setting for one of the world's oldest trade fairs, which takes place in the well-laid-out fairgrounds just to the south of the River Sava. The two principal events are the Spring Fair in April and the Autumn Fair in September, but minor or specialized shows continue almost throughout the year. The emphasis is on modern products, such as computers and highly sophisticated office equipment.

 USEFUL ADDRESSES. Consulates: U.S., Braće Kavurića 2; British, Ilica 12. Tourist Information Center, 14 Zrinjevac. Travel agencies: Astratours, J. Gajeva Str.; Atlas, 17 Zrinjevac; Croatiaturist, 17 Tomislav Sq. and at bus terminal, Držićeva Str.; Dalmacijaturist, 16 Zrinjevac; Emona Globtour, 40 Gajeva Str.; Generalturist, 18 Zrinjevac, also several other branches; Kompas, 6 Gajeva Str.; Putnik, 6 Preobraženska Str. Motoring: Auto-moto savez Hrvatske touring service, 25 Draškovićeva Str. Main post offices: 13 Jurišićeva Str., Zagreb 1; and 4 Branimirova Str., Zagreb 11. Central pharmacy: 3 Trg Republike.

 NIGHT LIFE. The *Inter-Continental* hotel has a casino and dancing in its top-floor Opera restaurant. There is also dancing at the Ruma restaurant in the *International* hotel, on the openair terrace of the *Esplanade* hotel in summer, and at the *Ritz Cabaret* nightclub, 4 Petrinjska Str. (See Hotels section for other addresses.) The Esplanade also has a disco—the *Zlatni Lavovi*—in the basement. Several clubs provide disco music and a convivial atmosphere till midnight or later; the Tourist Information Center or your hotel porter can give you the latest position. Two openair clubs in summer are *Studenski Centar* and *Scena,* both popular meeting places for the young. Other include *Kalušić, Lapidarij, Number One* and *Saloon*—the first one with many visiting bands and a theater stage.

SERBIA

Hub of the Modern State

Despite considerable tourist attractions, the Socialist Republic of Serbia is still given relatively little attention by travelers. Nevertheless, Serbia has both attractive scenery and historic towns and buildings, dating from medieval times, the period of Turkish occupation and the independent state.

Anyone who has ever seen the towering Iron Gates of the River Danube will know why they have been called the greatest natural wonder of the Balkan peninsula, if not of all Europe. Elsewhere, too, rivers through the ages have worn deep gorges through living rock. You cannot fail to be impressed by the Gornjak Gorges in the east, by the Rugovo Gorge in the west or those of the Ibar in the center. In addition, there are a number of excellent thermal spas.

In the remotest fastnesses you will come unexpectedly upon beautiful medieval Serbian churches and monasteries, many with polychrome brick and stone exteriors, and often containing exquisite frescos that reveal the influences of the Renaissance at work here long before the movement reached its first flowering in Italy. Neglected in the first years of the Communist régime, but now undergoing much-needed restoration, the priceless artistic treasures that these churches have guarded for so many centuries are now becoming better-known to the outside world.

History

Archaeological excavations are uncovering some remarkable prehistoric sites that show a very advanced level of culture in the Danube basin between 2500 and 3000 B.C. Several of these are near Belgrade. In Roman times, Serbia formed part of the provinces of Lower Pannonia and Moesia, and comprised the basins of the rivers Morava, Ibar and Upper Vardar. When the Empire was divided it came under the rule of Byzantium. But by the seventh century the Slavs had penetrated this far and established their own rule.

The new state almost replaced Byzantium as the dominant power in the Balkans when Serbian Tsar Dušan, in 1349, promulgated his famous Code of Common Law—the most important document of the medieval Slav state. But at his death there was a serious deterioration in the situation, and the Golden Age ended at the great Battle of Kosovo in 1389, when a much larger Turkish force was victorious. During the next two centuries unceasing warfare drastically reduced the population, and the gradually weakening military power of the Ottoman Empire only served to make things worse, with the provincial governments of the Pashas becoming increasingly arbitrary and oppressive in their efforts to maintain control. There was a series of popular uprisings during the 17th century against the provincial government of the Turks, which had in the supervening years become more and more tyrannical. They were crushed with ferocious violence, leading to the two Serb migrations across the Danube and the Sava in 1690 and 1739.

At the order of the Pasha Pasvan Oglu, a cruel massacre of the leading Serbs was carried out in 1804. A national revolt of protest led to the capture of Belgrade by Karageorge, the ancestor of the Karageorgević dynasty. Karageorge was elected the national leader, but unfortunately rivalries between the leaders of the revolt made it possible for the Turks to reoccupy Belgrade. In 1815, Miloš Obrenović led a second insurrection, and then, before the Turks had time to mass sufficient forces against him, imposed on them an agreement under the terms of which Serbia received autonomy.

In 1867, bowing to international pressure, the Turkish garrisons gradually withdrew from the few fortified towns still in their possession, and ten years later Serbia achieved full independence, again adding to her territory at the expense of Turkey. In 1882 Serbia elected an Obrenović king. When his descendant was assassinated in 1903, the Karageorgević house was restored, ruling until 1941.

In 1912 Serbia, Montenegro, Greece and Bulgaria formed an alliance to expel the last remaining Turks from the Balkan peninsula. This led to the two Balkan Wars that troubled the years just prior to the outbreak of World War I, when notable Serbian successes made a strong impression upon those future Yugoslavs still under foreign rule. The growing power of Serbia was a hindrance to Habsburg plans for further expansion, and when Gavrilo Princip assassinated the heir to the 84-year-old Emperor Franz Joseph of Austro-Hungary at Sarajevo in June 1914, Vienna was not slow to send an ultimatum. What the Emperor meant to be a "preventive war" against Serbia rapidly expanded into a world war, that was to destroy the Habsburg Empire itself, together with so much else.

Serbia was already exhausted by her rôle in the Balkan Wars, but before she was crushed by her still mighty enemy, she earned the admiration of the world for the fierce courage with which her soldiers fought on the long and bitter retreat across the mountains of Albania to Corfu, where, thanks to her allies, they could safely reequip.

The Treaty of Versailles recognized the new Kingdom of the Serbs, Croats and Slovenes, but the Kingdom was weakened by internal dissension and outside pressure. Her people's decision in 1941 to remain loyal to the Allies cost her nearly a million dead before she finally regained her independence.

Today, Serbia has lost the position of political preeminence she held between the wars, when the overwhelming majority of important appointments in every branch of public life went almost automatically to Serbs. But this is not so much a loss for Serbia as a gain for the whole country: all the Republics now stand on an equal footing, and all bid to gain from Yugoslavia's prosperity and stability. Belgrade, in particular, now has the advantage of being not only the capital of Serbia, but also a truly federal center for the whole of Yugoslavia.

Belgrade, the Capital

Today Serbia has within its boundaries two autonomous zones with large national minorities. In the north, the Vojvodina, Yugoslavia's granary, has an important Hungarian element. In the southwest, the area formerly called Kosmet and now Kosovo (*Kosovo i Metohija* is the full title) is inhabited largely by Albanians.

Under the present régime of six federated Republics, Serbia has very largely lost the leadership that was hers in the years between the two world wars, but which had been the cause of much friction (for example, of the country's 169 generals in 1939, all but three were Serbs). However, she remains the heart of the country, and the capital city of Belgrade (Beograd) is here, which phoenix-like has risen from its ashes to become one of Europe's modern capitals.

Since Herodotus first mentioned it 25 centuries ago the city has been repeatedly destroyed—the price it has had to pay for its strategic position, spread out as it is on hills commanding at the junction of the rivers Sava and Danube, a crossroads between the West and the Orient, and the gateway to central Europe. However, Belgrade today has relatively little to show of her stormy past, almost the only ancient building still in existence being parts of the great Turkish fortress Kalemegdan, which dominates the Vojvodina Plain.

The Celts founded the first settlement here, which had become a fortified town by the fourth century B.C. The Romans occupied it some 300 years later and named it Singidunum, but the Huns razed it in the fifth century, and it was abandoned for over 100 years, when the Emperor Justinian ordered it to be rebuilt. A period of prosperity followed, until the Slavs overran the city in the seventh century and gave it its present name.

The city is briefly mentioned in connection with the Crusades of the 11th century, and it then appears as the capital of the first Serbia under King Dragutin. 300 years later, in 1521, it was captured by the Turks. However, being right in the path of the perpetual ebb and flow of the Christian crusade against the penetration of Islam into Europe, Belgrade was repeatedly burned, sacked and almost destroyed, and suffered again heavily in the reprisals for the Serb uprisings against the Turks at the beginning of the 19th century. When in 1867 the last Turkish Governor handed over the keys of the city to Prince Michael of Serbia, it was at last free to develop into the political, economic and cultural capital of the new Serbia.

Since that Palm Sunday in 1941, when 300 Nazi bombers killed 25,000 people in one morning, Belgrade has grown again to a city of 1,500,000 people, with broad avenues, modern, airy houses and vast blocks of apartments that crowd upon the occasional pre-war survivor, and the carefully tended parks, so that it once more justifies its name made up from *belo* (white) and *grad* (town). There is acceptable and even occasionally interesting architecture of the 1970s among the abortive high-rise experiments of the 1950s. But the city is still suffering acutely from growing pains, as the building program cannot keep pace with the demands of the expanding population.

Exploring Belgrade

The great fortress of Kalemegdan is Belgrade's most notable ancient building. Its superimposed Celtic, Roman, Serbian and Turkish stones make of it a mute history of the city's life for some 2,000 years. There is a museum in the citadel, which houses relics from each of the many previous cities. If you follow the street named Usun Mirkova you will reach the hilltop crowned by the fortifications of Gornji Grad. Crenellated walls and creeper-covered turrets give the old citadel a romantic air, and from its terraces you can look out across Zemun toward Hungary to the north, or east to the Romanian frontier, less than 80 km. (50 miles) away. On one of these terraces is one of Meštrović's best-known works, *The Messenger of Victory,* which was placed there soon after the end of World War I.

A pleasant path leads to the baroque gate of Prince Eugene of Savoy, who temporarily liberated the city from the Turks in 1717. Close beside it are the remains of a Roman bath destroyed in the 1941 air raid, and also an octagonal tower known as *Nebojša*—meaning "fear nothing." From there, cross the drawbridge, and climb to the lofty Kalemegdan restaurant, from which you can comfortably enjoy both the attractive view and the thick, strong, sweet Turkish coffee. According to the archeologists, the present upper fortifications are built partly on the site of a Roman *castrum* dating from the times of the Flavian Emperors. The Austrians built a barracks on the same site, but this was later demolished.

Inside the boundaries of the surrounding park there is an openair exhibition illustrating the Yugoslav resistance movement of the last war, with a replica of the cabin in the mountains of Bosnia which served as Tito's headquarters. In another corner of the park is the Artist's Pavilion, where contemporary Yugoslav painters and sculptors hold exhibitions of their works.

From Kalemegdan a short stroll will bring you to the Serbian Orthodox Cathedral of Belgrade, dedicated to the Archangel Michael, built between 1836 and 1845. The cathedral's architecture is neoclassical with a baroque tower. The church contains the tombs of several Serbian princes; just outside its main entrance are the graves of the two great Serbian educators, Vuk Karadžić and Dositej Obradović. Across the street from the cathedral is the Patriarchate of the Serbian Orthodox Church.

The interesting frescos that are to be seen in the widely scattered monasteries of Serbia are usually only to be found in somewhat remote

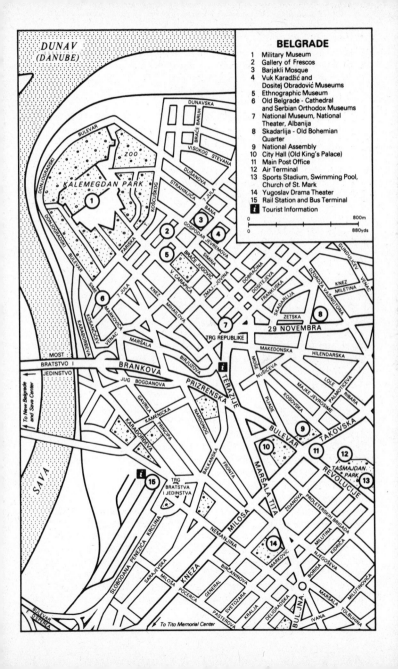

BELGRADE

1 Military Museum
2 Gallery of Frescos
3 Barjakli Mosque
4 Vuk Karadžić and
   Dositej Obradović Museums
5 Ethnographic Museum
6 Old Belgrade - Cathedral
   and Serbian Orthodox Museums
7 National Museum, National
   Theater, Albanija
8 Skadarlija - Old Bohemian
   Quarter
9 National Assembly
10 City Hall (Old King's Palace)
11 Main Post Office
12 Air Terminal
13 Sports Stadium, Swimming Pool,
   Church of St. Mark
14 Yugoslav Drama Theater
15 Rail Station and Bus Terminal
i Tourist Information

| 0 | | 800m |
| 0 | | 880yds |

places, and may be under restoration. While the original is, of course, always better than the copy, it is an advantage to find good reproductions of some of the best of these monastery frescos in the special Fresco Art Gallery of Belgrade. The originals date from the 11th up to the 15th century. Many have been exhibited in the West.

There were 20 mosques in Belgrade in the 18th century, of which only one has survived until today. This is the Bajrakli Džamija, the Mosque of the Flag, so called because, in Turkish times, it used to fly a signal flag to show the moment when the *imams* of the other mosques should make their five daily calls to prayer to the faithful.

This mosque and the Kalemegdan fortress are the only relics of Turkish occupation though, perhaps not surprisingly in view of its comparatively younger age, much of the 19th-century capital has survived.

A general impression of the center of the city can be gained by the following itinerary. Start in Trg Republike, or Republic Square, where you will find the National Museum. Opposite is the National Theater, where there is an opera season each year. Not far from here is the narrow cobbled street called Skadarlija, a favorite haunt of the Bohemian set in the 19th century. It has now been restored to provide a very popular dining-out area, as well as being animated by various forms of street entertainment during the summer months. There are several crowded, lively restaurants with good folk music. Pass by the building called Albanija, and you will come to the nerve center of the capital, the street called Terazije. Here two main streets meet, and we follow the Bulevar Revolucije which is 6½ km. (four miles) long. It brings us soon to the impressive Parliament House, or, more properly now, the Federal Assembly Building. Then we come to the Tašmajdan Park, and glimpse the Church of Sveti Marko (St. Mark): it is a copy of the church at Gračanica. Here lie the bodies of King Alexander and Queen Draga, brutally murdered by the followers of the Karageorge faction in 1903, when the Obrenović line was exterminated. The former Royal Palace, incidentally, is not far from here; it stands in the former royal gardens, facing Parliament House.

In a quiet suburb to the south of the center is a museum complex of significance to all those interested in Yugoslavia's modern history. This is the Josip Broz Tito Memorial Center. Here is the house where the late President Tito lived and is now buried, and close to it the Museums of 25th May and 4th July, so closely connected with his life.

Across the Sava River from the main part of Belgrade, on land which before World War II was swampy and desolate, a vast expanse of modern buildings, collectively known as Novi Beograd ("New Belgrade") has been built. According to the plans which have been drawn, Novi Beograd will grow to accommodate a population of a quarter-million. Aside from its modern residential areas, Novi Beograd is also the site of a number of government and cultural institutions. One of its most imposing structures is the 24-story headquarters of the Central Committee of the Federal Executive Council. The Modern Art Museum, on the bank of the Sava River, adds a contemporary esthetic touch to Novi Beograd's neat appearance. So does the brand spanking new and most impressive Sava Center, a huge congress and concert hall complex with the Belgrade-Intercontinental Hotel adjoining it. It has already provided the venue for many major international gatherings.

The most popular local excursion is to 520-m.-high (1,700 ft.) Mount Avala, 20 km. (12 miles) south of the city, in the hilly, forested region called the Šumadija. On the summit of Avala the Monument to an Unknown Soldier was built in 1938. The memorial is of dark polished granite and is especially notable for its sculptured figures of eight women symbolizing the eight nationalities of Yugoslavia. It is the work of Yugoslavia's famous sculptor, Ivan Meštrović.

Not far from the monument stands a 200-m.-high (660 ft.) tower, topped by the principal radio and television antennae for the Belgrade area. Resting on a tripod base, the tower has, halfway up, a restaurant and observation platform, which offers visitors a magnificent view of the surrounding region.

East from Belgrade

After the Danube has been augmented by the Sava at Belgrade it becomes Europe's greatest river. It then flows for some 105 km. (65 miles) through the fertile Serbian plain, marking for the next 210 km. (130 miles) or so the Yugoslav-Romanian frontier. During the last stage of this part of its course it runs through the tremendous gorge that it has worn through the living rock, known as the Iron Gates, one of the most famous stretches of river in the world. The roads to the Iron Gates are not all in very good condition, and in any case they don't follow the river completely through the most interesting parts of the gorge. Therefore, by far the best way to see the Iron Gates is from the river itself. You can make a one-day excursion from Belgrade as far as Kladovo by hydrofoil. There is a road bridge across the dam which considerably shortens the journey to most parts of Romania.

Exploring the Danube Valley below Belgrade

From Belgrade to Smederevo, the Danube flows lazily past numerous low-lying islands, and along the banks the vines still grow that give us the *smederevka* wine, which has been produced for the past 2,000 years. The immense fortress of Smederevo is one of the most imposing military constructions of the Middle Ages. It was built by Prince Djuradj Branković in about 1420, and was destined to change hands many times in the succeeding centuries. Its original form was triangular, and even today its five-m.-thick (17 ft.) walls and fortified towers convey a tremendous sense of ancient power and durability—despite massive damage caused in 1941 when explosives stored there by the Germans inexplicably blew up.

Soon the River Morava flows into the mighty Danube, which wends its way through a countryside where roads are still very poor. River traffic pauses at Kostolac, a small town today but an important base for the Danubian fleet in Roman times, when it was called Viminatium.

Shortly before reaching the Romanian frontier on the left bank, we pass the 15th-century Turkish fortress of Ram.

The entrance into the gorge was defended in the old days by the fortress of Golubac, which now stands deserted but still impressive, its ancient turrets crowning the crest of a hill against the skyline. Golubac was built upon the site of the Roman Castrum Calumbarum, and retained its strategic importance for nearly 2,000 years.

From here a road follows the Danube, which has been of imposing width, but at this point a spur of the Carpathian Mountains reaches out and forces it into a channel between rocky cliffs, some bare and some forest-covered, rarely more than 400 m. (¼ mile) apart for the entire 40 km. (25 miles) of the "Little" Djerdap, part of the 130-km.-long (80 miles) artificial lake which has resulted from the building of the Djerdap (Iron Gates) Dam.

Soon we pass the site of one of the most important archeological finds of recent years, known as Lepenski Vir. Here, on the former banks of the river, the remains of one of the oldest and most complete neolithic settlements in the world were found in 1965. To preserve it from the waters of the lake, it has been transferred to the site of the Roman camp of Thallus which is on higher ground. The substantial remains have been roofed over and there is an excellent museum. Particularly interesting are the strange human faces, carved with primitive stone tools by the community of Danube fishermen who lived here 8,000 years ago.

As we continue downstream, following the brief break in the rocky walls at Donji Milanovac, we enter the Kazan—the Cauldron—the "Great" Djerdap. Imprisoned by sheer rock, the Danube is compressed at times into a width of barely 150 m. (500 ft.), between cliffs rising to over 610 m. (2,000 ft.). Innumerable lives were lost over the centuries in these once-turbulent waters that are now deep and mostly calm as they approach the massive Iron Gates dam.

On the right, or Yugoslav, bank was the Roman road that once linked Golubac with Orsova, and which has now disappeared under water. Work was begun on it during the reign of Tiberius. The living rock had to be cut away to a depth of two m. (6½ ft.).

Precisely at the river's narrowest point, graven upon a sheer wall of rock, is the *Tabula Traiana,* or Trajan's Tablet, which commemorates both this extraordinary engineering achievement and the victorious campaign against the Dacians made possible by it. This too has been moved above the risen waters of the Danube and may only be seen by river travelers. Not far beyond the tablet the narrows come to an end and the Danube widens, separating the opposing Romanian and Serbian towns of Orsova and Tekija.

The river then narrows once again for the approach to the Djerdap Hydroelectric Dam, a joint Yugoslav-Romanian project and the largest scheme of its type in Europe. Regular guided tours of the Dam installations are arranged. Soon after comes Kladovo, the end of our hydrofoil-excursion from Belgrade, where the well-preserved fortress of Fetislam dates from the 16th century. A little beyond Kladovo, facing the old Romanian city of Turnu Severin across the river, you can see part of the massive pillars of Emperor Trajan's bridge over which he led his legions to the conquest of Dacia, as Romania was then called. By the bridge, excavations are currently revealing the presence of a substantial Roman settlement.

If you have done the trip by car, you can continue beside the Danube through the rich Wallachian plain. The local inhabitants, the Vlachs, called *Kučovlasi* in Serbo-Croat, who gave their name to the Romanian principality of Wallachia, speak a dialect even closer to the Latin of their ancestors than the Romanian language. Their costumes, songs and dances further accentuate their difference from the Serbs.

This whole area is relatively seldom seen by visitors. From Prahovo, the farthest point on the Yugoslav Danube, you could return by road through the vineyards of Negotin near the border with Bulgaria, which produce a full-bodied wine like a young Burgundy. Besides the usual museum, an old church, the Bukovo monastery and a Hajduk tomb, Negotin has a Stevan Mokranjac museum, commemorating the locally-born composer. Just southwest of it, at Bor, are the largest copper mines in Europe, of great importance in these days of "strategic metals." Nearby is the pleasant little thermal spa of Brestovačka Banja.

The way back to Belgrade leads along the valley of the River Mlava to one of the most extraordinary locations in Serbia, the Gornjak Gorge. In deep forests nearby there is a monastery, on the left bank of the river, which dates from the 14th century. The route continues through the town of Petrovac, which lies in the center of a region of rich orchards. We continue on to Požarevac, briefly Prince Miloš' capital, the agricultural center of eastern Serbia, famous for its early fall horse-riding competitions. From here it is an easy 80-km. (50-mile) run back to Belgrade, and our circuit of this region of Serbia is complete.

South of Belgrade

The tourist wishing to explore Serbia can distinguish four regions on his southward routes from Belgrade. Directly south of the capital is a charming area of wooded hills and rolling farmland known as the Šumadija (*Šuma* in Serbian means "forest"). It is a fertile area, much fought over in the past but now notable mainly for its farming and as an excursion region for the people of Belgrade.

The *Ibar Magistrala* leads south past Avala through the Šumadija, to Kraljevo. Beginning from the city of Kraljevo (which means "Kings' Town"), a valley formed by the Ibar River extends due south. It was this "Valley of the Kings" which constituted the heart of the original independent Kingdom of Serbia (then known as Ras) at the end of the 12th century. And in this valley the earliest Serbian kings built the monasteries which were to give spiritual cohesion to their young nation. This oldest group of Serbian monasteries, identified as the School of Ras, holds place of honor among all the cultural and spiritual achievements of the Serbian people. The Ibar Valley forms our second region.

Our third is made up of what is called the Morava Valley, though the name is a little confusing. At Kraljevo the north-flowing Ibar joins the Western Morava which here flows east. After some 110 km. (70 miles) the Morava joins the Southern Morava (Južna Morava), northbound on a course roughly parallel to the Ibar's, to form the Great Morava (Velika Morava). We treat all three Morava valleys as forming one region, which extends as far south as Niš and the Macedonian frontier. But when art historians talk of the Morava Valley, they are referring only to the Western and Great Morava's regions. Here you can find other examples of early Serbian monasteries and Serb-Byzantine art.

Western travelers of the 19th century, when the Turkish Iron Curtain was being slowly lifted from the Balkans, have stories to tell of their visits to a chain of monasteries and churches hidden away in almost inaccessible mountain country. These extraordinary places, remote and mysterious, are built in a Byzantine style that tends to mix Western influences with those from the East.

Inside them is a great wealth of unique frescos in which the artists broke away from the rigidity of formal Byzantine mosaics, and employed firm yet sweeping lines to portray more ample movement and nobler figures than seen in frescos of this period elsewhere. The final and most highly developed stage of Serbian-Byzantine architecture is to be found in the valley of the Morava River, and is known as the Morava School.

There remains one more important region of Serbia proper. It extends from the Sava River in the north down to the border with Montenegro in the south, and on its western side adjoins Bosnia-Herzegovina; it runs from rich farmlands across deep valleys to dry and sparsely populated hills. We will consider this diversified region as "Western Serbia."

Exploring Šumadija

The *Ibar Magistrala* is the westernmost and scenically most attractive of the three roads leading south from Belgrade. Bypassing Lazarevac, 55 km. (34 miles) south, is an important crossroads, the western (right) branch following the railroad up the Kolubara Valley to Valjevo amidst densely forested mountains, and Divčibare, a resort 997 m. (3,270 ft.) up in the Maljen Mountains, where in late May the White Narcissus Festival is held; the eastern branch leads via the spa of Bukovička Banja—which produces the Knjaz Miloš mineral water and holds the Marble and Harmony Festival July to September in conjunction with an International Sculpture Symposium—to Topola; the *Ibar Magistrala* climbs south over the Rudnik Mountains and through the plum orchards of Gornji Milanovac to Kraljevo, where it is joined by the middle road from Belgrade.

Topola was the home of the leader of the First Serbian Insurrection against the Turks (in 1804), whom the Turks named Karageorge ("Black George"). Karageorge's family home, as well as the village church and school, have been restored.

This First Serbian Insurrection ultimately failed. In spite of this, the Karageorge family reclaimed the leadership of Serbia in 1903 in the course of another political upheaval. From that year onward, a Karageorge was to sit on the throne of Serbia, and ultimately all Yugoslavia, as king.

As the Karageorge family mausoleum, a remarkable church of Venčac marble with a graceful gilt dome was built on the Oplenac hill overlooking Topola. The interior of the church, as well as of the crypt below, is completely covered with stunning mosaics, almost unique in quantity and workmanship. Each is a faithful reproduction of one of the masterpieces of Serbian medieval frescos. Thus a visit to Oplenac is like a summary of a tour to all the greatest of the Serbian monasteries, as here you see faithful copies of the same pictures which were painted centuries ago on the walls of remote monasteries.

From Topola it is a further 42 km. (26 miles) to Kragujevac. The town was the family home of Miloš Obrenović, leader of the Second

Insurrection. Following his success against the Turks he made Kragujevac his capital from 1818 to 1842. Interesting as an example of Serbian architecture of the 19th century is the house known as "Amidžin Konak," once belonging to a member of Prince Miloš' train, and now part of the Kragujevac city museum. This is not merely a city of 19th-century history. It occupies a uniquely tragic place in the Serbians' memory of World War II, for it was here that on 21st October 1941, a Nazi punitive expedition shot 7,000 citizens, including 300 secondary school pupils who were taken directly from their classes to the place of execution in the fields of Šumarice. The site has been made into a memorial park. Today, Kragujevac is a thriving industrial center; its most important factory is the Crvena Zastava enterprise, Yugoslavia's main manufacturer of automobiles.

From Kragujevac, a drive of 58 km. (36 miles) will take you to Kalenić monastery, the least accessible of the major monasteries of the Morava School. Kalenić was founded in about 1413 by the nobleman Bogdan, a cupbearer at the court of Prince Stefan Lazarević. Inside the church are some fine frescos depicting apocryphal scenes from the life of the Virgin Mary and the principal incidents in the life of Christ. These were only rediscovered in 1877 after the removal of the coating of whitewash with which the Turks nearly always treated Christian works of art. They are in an excellent state of preservation. The warlike saints at the lower end of the choir and the particularly moving image of Christ on the left of the altar are among the best of Yugoslavia's many beautiful medieval mural paintings.

Exploring the Ibar Valley and the Sandžak

At the confluence of the Ibar and the Western Morava rivers, surrounded by the Stolovi and Goć mountain ranges, stands the busy city of Kraljevo. Among its historical monuments, the 19th-century Gospodar Vasin Konak now houses a museum, which includes a fresco gallery that gives the visitor in Kraljevo an opportunity to become acquainted with the art of the Raška School monasteries before he sets out to visit the monasteries themselves.

The first turn-off from the road following the Western Morava eastward takes us up the right bank of the Ibar River to the Monastery of Žiča, characterized by its red walls. The best of the frescos here is the *Last Supper*, though that of the founder, the crowned figure of Stefan Nemanja Prvovenčani, is extremely fine. The remainder are of a later period, and depict 40 martyrs being tortured by the Turks.

The background of Žiča is more interesting than the building itself. Soon after the coronation of Stefan by the Pope, a certain dualism between state and church developed in Ras, core of the new Serb empire. The king's brother, Sava, was a monk and writer, and also emissary to the Greek Patriarch of Nicea. He advised the Patriarch to authorize the establishment of an autonomous Serb Orthodox Church, which would be able to counteract the Latin influence of Rome. Sava himself became the first archbishop of the new church, which established its seat in 1219 in Žiča, where seven medieval Serbian kings were crowned.

The two brothers cooperated successfully in their government of both the spiritual and secular administration of the country, and it was principally the work of these two remarkable men that laid the foundations for the great days of Serbian rule. Žiča became the cradle of the Serbian Orthodox Church. Sava died in 1233, shortly after returning from a pilgrimage to the Holy Land. His hold upon Serb religious sentiment was so strong that even 300 years later the Turks thought it necessary to remove his bones from the Monastery of Mileševa and have them publicly burned in Belgrade. Close beside Žiča is the little Church of St. Peter and St. Paul, with yet more beautiful frescos. A little farther along the Ibar is the spa Mataruška Banja, near the Ljubostina Monastery.

The main road from Kraljevo to the south runs along the left bank of the Ibar River and this is the route we must follow to explore the monasteries of this region. Where the valley narrows to form a dramatic gorge, 29 km. (18 miles) from Kraljevo, stand the eight towers of the Maglič fortress perched like an eagle's nest upon a separate spur of the mountains. Although the fortress dates from the 15th century, it is still in a pretty good state of repair.

Another 21 km. (13 miles) from Kraljevo brings us to the village of Ušće, from which we turn off to make the 11-km. (seven-mile) drive to visit the village and monastery of Studenica, along a winding road beside the brook of the same name. The monastery, gray-white marble and completely surrounded by walls, is richly ornamented with sculptures.

It was established in about 1190 by the first king of Serbia, Stefan Nemanja, whose remains, as well as those of his son, King Stefan the First Crowned, are still venerated in the largest of its three churches, the one dedicated to the Virgin Mary. This contains a number of beautiful frescos, the best of which date from the 13th century. The procession of the church-fathers, behind the altar, is remarkably well preserved, but the greatest of the frescos is the incomparably moving Crucifixion. This church also displays various interesting treasures, such as gold and silver liturgical vessels, richly illuminated Gospels and copies of a number of Turkish decrees.

The smallest of the three churches is dedicated to St. Nicholas, and likewise dates from about 1190. The third church was built by King Milutin in 1315, and is known as the King's Church.

14½ km. (nine miles) south of Ušće, a road branches off southeast (left) to the spa of Jošanička Banja, and into the Kopaonik Mountains, where Suvo Rudište is being developed into an important skiing resort. Back on the *Magistrala* the ruins of the Turkish fortress of Brvenik come into view. Here, a side road leads 11 km. (seven miles) west to the Monastery of Gradac, founded by Helen of Anjou, wife of King Uroš. The Gothic pillars and open flying buttresses were probably designed by architects from Helen's homeland. Built in the 13th century, Gradac was abandoned 400 years later at the time of the Turkish invasions. Since the end of World War II, work has been done on an enormous scale to restore the building and the frescos.

After visiting Gradac, we push on farther south through the village of Raška, in whose vicinity are the ruins of the Stara and Nova Pavlica churches. The next side road southwest leads to Novi Pazar, in the area called the Sandžak. This is a Turkish word signifying that it is under the jurisdiction of a Bey acting on behalf of the Pasha—in this case the Pasha of Belgrade. Novi Pazar was built by the Turks in 1460 and was devastated by a fire started by the Serbian insurrectionists in 1809. The Altum-Alem mosque is a fine example of Moslem architecture, and the *mihrab* niche is beautifully worked. A large caravanserai in the main square is well worth visiting.

There are many sights in the neighborhood of Novi Pazar, outstanding among them the oldest religious building in Yugoslavia, the seventh-century Petrova Crkva (Church of St. Peter). It is designed in the form of a Greek cross set amid circular walls and is a perfect example of pre-medieval Slav architecture, but is unfortunately the only one still standing. There are, however, a few ruined remains from the same period on the Dalmatian coast. As long ago as the tenth century, the Byzantine Emperor Constantine Porphyrogenitus mentioned in the account of his travels "the curious little churches lost in the forgotten places of my vast empire." If they struck the Emperor as "curious" nearly 1,000 years ago, then this surviving example here in Novi Pazar today is truly extraordinary.

Five km. (three miles) north of the town there are the ruins of another foundation of Stefan Nemanja, the Djurdjevi Stubovi Monastery, which was in good repair until damaged in 1912 during the first Balkan War. The two world wars virtually completed its destruction, and it has only been possible to save fragments of its frescos which are to be found below the walls. On the east wall there is a warlike St. George seated on a noble white horse, and in the little chapel you will find effigies of kings Dragutin and Milutin with their families.

16 km. (ten miles) away to the southwest is the Monastery of Sopoćani, which has been more fortunate. Its undamaged 13th-century frescos
are among the finest in the country. Situated amid impressive scenery,
the monastery is quite shut away from the world. The immense building houses vast mural paintings, and each person portrayed seems to
radiate some inner power. The subjects are from the Gospels—the most
strikingly beautiful of them all undoubtedly being the *Ascension* and the
Death of the Virgin on the west wall of the church. On the north wall
there is a painting of the dramatic death scene of Anne Dandolo, the
Venetian mother of the founder of the monastery, King Uroš I. The
mural paintings of Sopoćani are the work of a master hand.

The Morava Valley

For today's traveler, the Morava Valley is one of the most readily
accessible areas of Yugoslavia. The *autoput* which leads from Belgrade
in the direction of Niš and Skopje closely parallels the Morava River
and its tributaries for some 370 km. (230 miles). The main railroad to
Greece and Istanbul also runs along this valley.

After leaving Belgrade, the road passes a number of colorful villages
and crosses fertile agricultural country. We suggest that you leave the
autoput at the Požarevac junction for a side-trip of 13 km. (eight miles)
over a rather bumpy road to Lozovik, where there is an interesting
wooden church built between 1804 and 1831. It is especially distinguished because of the carvings on its portal and ceiling. A little farther
on, close to Velika Plana, is the Monastery of Koporin, built in the 15th
century, where the building itself is of far less interest than the frescos
it contains. Three km. (two miles) west of Velika Plana is the interesting Pokajnica ("Repentance") Monastery. It was built in 1818 by
Vujica Vuličević, who took part in the assassination of Karageorge,
leader of the First Serbian Insurrection against the Turks.

Returning to the *autoput* and continuing south, you soon reach the
Markovac junction, some 103 km. (64 miles) from Belgrade, where you
turn off for the Monastery of Manasija, 35 km. (22 miles) off the
highway on a side road (through Despotovac), and one of the greatest
achievements of the Morava School.

It was founded by Prince Stefan Lazarević and built as a fortress in
the 15th century; its massive walls rise sheer above the rapid waters of
the River Resava. The mountains that dominate the walls of the defile
make a perfect setting for our brief return to the stormy days of the
Dark Ages.

The frescos in the Manasija church contain an unusual wealth of
detail. They represent the Holy Trinity, and also Prince Stefan, holding
a model of the monastery in his hands. Warlike saints in sumptuous

vestments brandish their swords, handsome and nobly at ease in their finery.

24 km. (15 miles) south is the little town of Ćuprija, which is the starting point for the excursion to the Monastery of Ravanica, set in a secretive narrow valley some 9½ km. (six miles) to the northeast. It was founded by Prince Lazar toward the end of the 14th century, but was abandoned by its monks at the time of the Serb migration into the Vojvodina in 1690. On their return 27 years later, after the Turkish defeat by Prince Eugene of Savoy, they restored the original building.

The façade is covered with rich bas-relief ornamentation in stone, and flowing small columns surrounding the polygonal extremities that typify the work of this school. The frescos have been gravely damaged: those on the west wall representing the family of the founder are the best preserved. Of the old fortified walls practically nothing now remains. As a complete contrast, a few kilometers west of Ćuprija, beyond the Morava River and the *autoput,* an unusual art gallery in the town of Svetozarevo offers an excellent opportunity to study the works of Yugoslavia's naive painters, many of them of international repute.

At the Pojate junction, 160 km. (99 miles) from Belgrade, you may wish to leave the *autoput* for another side trip, which will bring you to two more of the greatest treasures of the Morava School. The first is in Kruševac, 24 km. (15 miles) southwest (right). During the reign of Prince Lazar, the Serbian leader who lost the decisive battle to the Turks at Kosovo Polje in 1389, Kruševac was the capital of Serbia. Some of the ruins of the fortifications which once guarded the hill from which Prince Lazar exercised his rule can still be seen; but, most important, you will see Prince Lazar's small church, known as Lazarica, now fully-restored. Built about 1375, this church exemplifies the original pattern of Morava School construction, after which the various Morava School monasteries were designed in the next several generations.

Carry on from Kruševac, now going up the valley of the Western Morava River, to the village of Trstenik, from whence it is five km. (three miles) north to Ljubostinja Convent. Incidentally, the word *manastir* is used in the Serbo-Croat language to mean either a monastery or a convent; so don't be surprised when you are looking for a *manastir* (monastery) to discover that it houses nuns instead of monks. Ljubostinja was endowed by Princess Milica, the wife of Prince Lazar. Following Prince Lazar's death at the Battle of Kosovo Polje, Milica decided to become a nun and chose this place to build the new convent where she would spend the rest of her life. The convent was finished in 1402, and in spite of the historical changes which the passage of centuries have brought about, the visitor can still well appreciate the reasons that influenced Milica's choice of this location. There is something almost mysteriously peaceful about the quiet, thickly wooded vale, set beside its small brook. The interior of the church is less interesting than it might be, because most of its frescos have been damaged or destroyed in the course of the various waves of destruction which have passed this way. There is one curiosity, however, in that the name of the architect, which in Orthodox monastery construction is usually enveloped in anonymity, is here clearly inscribed on the church threshold for all to see.

The Sisters sell their superb carpets, which are hand-made, from the spinning of the yarn from the sheep's wool to the final stitch of decoration, and intricate basketwork, painstakingly woven from reeds gathered nearby. In these Orthodox convents and monasteries matins and vespers are sung in the church every day, and if your schedule coincides, you can find in the chanting of the nuns or monks an extraordinary sense of peace and inspiration.

After completing your visit to Ljubostinja, you will have to return over the same road to the *autoput,* in order to resume your way in the direction of Niš. The branch-road follows the Western Morava to Kraljevo, while the motorway ascends the Southern Morava of Niš, among the sloping hillsides garlanded with vineyards and flowering pastures.

Niš

Set on the banks of the River Nišava, the city of Niš has always been an important center of communication between east and west. As a Roman city it was known as Naïssus, and it was here that the Emperor Constantine was born. During the barbarian migrations it was destroyed, to be rebuilt by the Emperor Justinian. It was included in the Serbian state ruled by the Nemanja dynasty toward the end of the 12th century.

The importance of the town declined under the Turks, and prosperity returned to it only when they left in 1877. It was repeatedly bombed during World War II, since which time it has been rebuilt as a flourishing city of 160,000 inhabitants, making it the second largest city in Serbia proper. Its rôle as a transportation center is still as significant as ever, for it is in Niš that both the main road and rail lines from Western Europe divide into two branches, the one to Thessaloniki and Athens and the other to Sofia and Istanbul.

The great fortress to the north was built by the rulers of the Byzantine Empire, and its massive walls and two great gates, ornamented with Arabic characters, are in an excellent state of preservation.

In the Jagodina quarter, close to the bridge, a fifth-century Byzantine crypt was discovered not long ago—the means by which the date could be accurately fixed being in the many contemporary coins found around the site. Another interesting local discovery came to light four km. (2½ miles) outside Niš near the little thermal spa of Niška Banja, where at a hamlet called Brzi Brod the remains were found of a luxurious Roman villa with beautiful mosaic floors, gardens with fountains—in fact, every indication of the grace and luxury that had been achieved in this town of Mediana in the fourth century B.C. The villa might indeed have been Constantine's summer residence.

There are still two more unusual sights to be seen before leaving Niš. The first, on the site of the original town, is the Monastery of St. Panteleimon, largely rebuilt after the departure of the Turks. The second is the macabre Tower of Skulls (Čele Kula), raised after the Serb revolt of 1809 on the spot where Stefan Sindjelić, realizing that he and his forces could hold out no longer, set fire to the powder magazine and died together with his men and such Turks as had already forced their way into the stronghold. As a warning, so that the Serbs would never again attempt to throw off Turkish dominion, the Pasha of Niš built a tower in which he set the skulls of 952 of the insurgents, that all might see and understand the lesson. The result achieved was the reverse of what the Pasha had intended it to be.

Beside the Nišava River

The radioactive waters of Niška Banja, just outside Niš, have resulted in the establishment of a small spa and the consequent modernization of the little town, which possesses several good hotels. Excavations in the neighborhood revealed that the Romans also took the waters here.

The road turns into E5N east along the Nišava to Bela Palanka and farther on to Pirot, which crouches beneath 1,783-m.-high (5,850 ft.) Mount Trem. This is a sleepy little town of handicraft workers, despite the fact that it is on the main road linking Western Europe to Istanbul and the East. Between it and the Bulgarian frontier, peaks over 2,135-m. (7,000-ft.) high pile up against the sky.

The pressure of huge flocks of sheep has led to the local production of most attractive rugs. These are made by hand on special looms by the womenfolk, and their designs show kinship with their Greek neighbors and their former Turkish rulers.

Near Dimitrovgrad (formerly Caribrod), almost on the Bulgarian frontier, is the 15th-century Monastery of Poganovo, where the frescos in the chantry are particularly beautiful.

This is the end of the road, if you are not driving the 58 km. (36 miles) on to Sofia, and we return to Niš.

From Niš toward Macedonia

E5 follows the Southern Morava to Leskovac, 45 km. (28 miles) from Niš, with many factories, but also possessing both ethnographic and archeological museums. There are several dwellings typical of the region which it is possible to visit and where the old way of life is still a living reality. A notable place of interest is the town's repertory theater, where it's always "standing room only." Seats are free: local firms pay the running costs.

A detour of some 29 km. (18 miles) southwest from Niš will take you to the villages of Prekopčelica and Štulac immediately below the Veliki Jastrebac Mountains. Close by is the Byzantine fortress of Caričingrad (the Empress' fort) where excavations have brought to light much valuable information about the Emperor Justinian's city that surrounded it.

In 1949, the remains of a basilica 30½ m. long by 20 m. wide (100 × 65 ft.) were discovered, with fragments of the original columns and capitals, upon one of which are engraved the titles of the Emperor Justinian I. The ruins of the rooms and living quarters, and the complex water conduits contained in the walls, make Caričingrad of exceptional interest.

On the main road south from Leskovac, the character of the country changes abruptly as we approach the Grdelica Gorge. After 44 km. (27 miles) comes the rather oriental little town of Vladičin Han. Before Vranje, 26 km. (16 miles) farther on, is a side road to the left leading to the large thermal spa of Vranjska Banja, hidden away in a gorge at the foot of steep wooded hills.

Vranje has a fine Turkish bridge, Turkish baths, the harem and palace of Rajif Bey dating from the 17th century, but in a sufficiently good state of preservation to give us a graphic picture of the life of a Turkish Bey 300 years ago.

Northwest of Vranje you may see the ruins of the fortress of Markovo Kale. Marko Kraljevic, who ruled in the 14th century, is a great figure in Serbian song and legend because of his private war against the Turks long after his people's great defeat at the Battle of Kosovo. Riding a black stallion which drank nothing but wine, he and his small band of followers harassed and raided the Turks, yet somehow always escaped back to their stronghold—or so the legend claims. 9½ km. (six miles) south is the branch road heading east to the 11th-century Prohor Pčinjski Monastery, with its fine 14th- and 15th-century frescos.

Western Serbia

We enter this region from the city of Čačak, northwest of Kraljevo, proceeding up the Western Morava River through the dramatic Ovčar-Kablar gorge, and past various new hydroelectric dams. It is a pleasant countryside, and there are in the immediate vicinity no less than eight well-known monasteries, most of them dating from the period of Turkish domination. They are all rather inaccessible, but stand out vividly white among the thick surrounding woods. At Požega we turn south along the Moravica Valley to Arilje, with its Raška-School church and remarkable frescos. Among these last the Procession of the Archbishops and the Council of King Stefan Nemanja are not only great masterpieces but also extremely valuable historical records.

Though it is off our present route, it is worth mentioning here that Karan, some 9½ km. (six miles) north of Titovo Užice, can be reached by a short stretch of country road beginning right in Užice. Its small church is one of the most perfect examples of medieval Serbian architecture. Because of the inclusion of certain historic personages portrayed in its frescos, it has been deduced that the church was built in the first years of the 14th century.

Užice (as it was called before it honored President Tito by prefixing the "Titovo") was the political and military center of the resistance movement founded to combat the German-Italian occupation of the country in 1941, and it has a small patriotic museum of souvenirs of those days. The surrounding country is particularly pleasing, and on a height above the River Djetinja you will see the remains of an ancient fortress abandoned by the Turks as late as 1867.

Bajina Bašta on the Drina, 37 km. (23 miles) northwest of Titovo Užice, is the starting point of an exciting excursion across the 1,524-m.-high (5,000 ft.) Tara plateau, which can easily be reached by a road that passes close to the Monastery of Rača. In these high places there are many unusual kinds of flowers and plants, for instance the extremely rare Red Fir trees, a species which was officially classified only in 1875. In winter the slopes of this great plateau provide perfect conditions for skiing, but have not yet been equipped for winter sports enthusiasts.

Going south from Titovo Užice we cross the deep vales of the Zlatibor plateau through the villages of Partizanske Vode and Nova Varoš to Bistrica, from where we circle back north to Priboj. However just before reaching the Monastery of Banja there is the little thermal spa of Pribojska Banja, which dates from the time of St. Sava. There are some fine frescos here.

On the way to the marvelous Monastery of Mileševa, joining E27 at Ribarevina, you will pass the massive Tower of Jeriningrad, all that remains of the fortress which used to command the mouth of the narrow valley worn by the River Lim. Close to Prijepolje we find the monastery standing majestically beside the River Mileševka.

Mileševa Monastery enjoyed all the special privileges reserved for a royal foundation, and ranks second in the land only to that of Studenica. It was repeatedly profaned and pillaged by the Turks, and its present outward appearance dates but from the last century, when large-scale restoration was made. Internally, however, the frescos are the original works of Dimitrije and other great artists of the time of the foundation of the building in 1235. The special technique of the fresco is brilliantly achieved, the colors warm yet clear, the subjects portrayed with immense vitality. The lines are bold. The angel at the Tomb of Christ, and the Descent from the Cross, are outstanding and among the supreme achievements of medieval Serbian art. Of special interest, too, is the portrait of the founder, King Vladislav, holding in his hand a model of Mileševa Church. The mural paintings in the open galleries are also extremely fine, though of much later date, the work of 16th-century artists.

With the visit to Mileševa Monastery, we conclude our explorations of Serbia proper. From Prjepolje the road we were following continues on up the valley of the Lim River into Montenegro, joining E27 at Ribarevina.

It remains to describe two further regions very different both from each other and from the Serbia we already know. Like the Vojvodina, Kosovo is an autonomous, self-administering region, distinct both politically and culturally from the main part of Serbia.

Exploring the Autonomous Region of Kosovo

Because Kosovo is an area which has repeatedly changed hands in the course of history, it is, like the Vojvodina region, ethnographically very mixed. The main racial group is the Albanian which forms 73 percent of the population. After 1945, large numbers of Montenegrin partisans were also given holdings in the area. Albanian and Turkish are official languages in addition to Serbo-Croat, and broadcasting and education are carried on in all three languages. The Albanians or Sjiptars are temperamentally quite different from their Slav compatriots, and among some of them blood ties with their relatives in austere little neighboring Albania run deep, a factor encouraged by the literature in their own language which comes from across the border. A desire for greater independence on the part of an active minority led in the early 1980s to considerable unrest and even violence, and order was only restored by a hasty dispatch of the army.

When you are in Priština or Peć it is easy to know if it is a market day by the Sjiptars' custom of wearing skullcaps or large white turbans, and dressing in black-braided white cloth suits. The women are often very handsome when young, and are treated with great respect in their homes, but have virtually no contact whatever with the outside world. This race of former shepherds and farmers has its own extraordinarily animated dances in which only the men take part.

Priština, the capital of Kosovo, was under Turkish rule until 1912, and you can still see some of the Turkish mosques and old houses lying off the main road. The Tzar (Emperor) Mosque was built by Sultan Mehmet II in 1461, in the form of a square surmounted by one large and three small cupolas. The interior is richly decorated. Almost next door is the old *hammam* (Turkish Baths) with its installations completely modernized. Sultan Bajezit constructed the second mosque immediately after the Battle of Kosovo. The Emindžika is a rare example of Turkish 19th-century architecture.

There is plenty to see of historical interest around Priština. The Kosovo Polje (Field of Kosovo) lies a few kilometers outside the town. On this vast area of open rolling plain the biggest battle—in terms of the numbers engaged—in all medieval Europe was fought between Serbs and Turks. A simple Turkish mausoleum marks the tomb of Sultan Murad I, who was killed in the moment of victory. Not far off stands another memorial, the Monument to the Heroes of Kosovo, honoring the Serbs who died here in defense of their nation in 1389. Tales of this battle, glorifying Prince Lazar and his outnumbered troops, are still recounted in the chants of the few remaining wandering minstrels.

Not far from the village of Laplije Stavo recent excavations have brought to light remains of an important Roman town. Nearby, standing quite by itself in open country, is a small church with alternating red and white stones used in the construction of its walls.

A more distant excursion to the north of Priština takes us through the industrial town of Kosovska Mitrovica to the Monastery of Banjska, built of delightfully blended white, red and blue marble, at the orders of King Milutin in the opening years of the 14th century. Inside it houses fabulously rich frescos decorated with gold, which were unfortunately allowed to deteriorate during the Turkish occupation. As with so many other similar foundations, it was transformed into a mosque, with the usual thick whitewash covering the Christian frescos. This has now been removed and the frescos restored.

9½ km. (six miles) southeast of Priština is one of the most striking of all Serb medieval buildings, the Monastery of Gračanica. Its church is in the compact form of a Greek cross with powerful, polychrome walls. It is a typical "five-cupola" building, in which four small domes surround the large central dome, but one of particularly complex yet harmonious design. The narthex at the entry into the basilica contains the portraits of King Milutin of the Nemanja dynasty, though the subjects of the other frescos are drawn from apocryphal religious literature and poetry. One can only describe them as epic paintings.

The little town of Lipljan, 18 km. (11 miles) south of Priština, was once the Roman Ulpiana. Later it was the frontier post between medieval Serbia and the Byzantine Empire, and under the Turks an important halt on the caravan-route linking Niš and Skadar (Scutari, on the Albanian side of the frontier with Montenegro). The battered, humble little church was built on Roman foundations in the 17th century.

13 km. (eight miles) beyond Lipljan, at Štimlje, we take the right fork of the road through Sava Reka southwestward of Prizren, one of the most fascinating cities in Yugoslavia, only some 18 km. (11 miles) from the Albanian frontier.

Prizren was already a prosperous town in Byzantine times, and the coin of the medieval Serb state was minted here. The Turks captured it in 1454, the year after the fall of Byzantium, and left it only in 1912. Prizren is still an important market town, and retains much of its oriental appearance. The fortress of Kaljaja dominates its mountain setting. Make a point of seeing the splendid view from its walls.

The River Bistrica flows into Prizren from the south, and leaves it by way of a dramatic gorge, and to follow its course is a favorite Sunday walk with the citizens. Because of the river, Prizren is a city of fountains, and these lend a special charm to its ancient squares and strangely attractive streets. The hub of the place is the Mosque of Sinan Pasha, built in 1615 of masonry from the Monastery of the Holy Archangel. The Church of Our Lady of Ljeviška, built at the order of King Milutin in 1307, was converted into a mosque, and it was not until 1950 that the covering plaster was removed from nearly 460 sq. m. (500 sq. yards) of magnificent medieval frescos. They are particularly notable for their free composition, their clever handling of detail and the charm of the portraits included in them.

Fine gold and silver filigree work has always been, and still is today, a specialist art of Prizren, and it is probable that many similar articles that you see offered for sale in Belgrade or Opatija were made here. Every Wednesday, which is market day, the play of color from the beautiful metalwork exposed for sale in the streets is a delight to the eye. South of the town one of the loftiest mountain ranges in the country piles up magnificently to mark the border with Macedonia. These are the Šar-Planina Mountains, the highest point, some 32 km. (20 miles) away, being "Titov Vrh" (Mount Tito), nearly 2,750 m. (9,000 ft.) above sea-level.

Church Land

We now turn away to the northwest of the Kosovo region; this is called the *Metohija,* a word meaning "church land"; in the Middle Ages, the land here was the sole property of the Serbian Orthodox Church. We pass through another Moslem town famous for its filigree work, Djakovica, which is only 39 km. (24 miles) from Prizren, and keep on for a further 21 km. (13 miles) to Dečani. Here we take a mountain road to the left, along savage gorges and through magnificent mountain and forest scenery, to arrive at the Monastery of Visoki Dečani set beside the River Dečanska Bistrica.

In 1335 a Franciscan friar named Vid of Kotor was ordered by King Stefan Uroš III (nicknamed *Dečanski* because of the monastery's construction) to build this Orthodox church. The style that he chose incorporates certain Western elements into its fundamentally Byzantine structure. Its lively polychrome exterior, high soaring lines and magnificent interior frescos make it one of the most impressive of all Serbia's striking monastery churches. Once inside, among ascending pillars, you will be struck by the fact that it is a much larger building than it appears from a distance. The frescos were executed by artists from the shores of the Adriatic, one of them, called Srdja, having signed his work.

The themes illustrated in the Visoki Dečani Monastery are not solely religious. They also portray the way of life, the costumes, customs, morals and manners of the people of Serbia in the 14th century. There is also a veritable portrait gallery of all the Serbian kings. The scale of these wall paintings is such that there are no less than a thousand figures included in the Last Judgment alone. However, the Church Calendar or Almanac, with every day of the year separately shown, takes up more wall space than anything else. The halos of the saints were not painted, but made from gold dust set in the surface of the wall.

Despite the various wars and pillaging raids that the monastery has suffered through the centuries, the church treasure is still remarkably rich. Outstanding are the ancient parchments and holy books, a series of priceless icons and a great, engraved wooden 14th-century cross.

The Brothers of Visoki Dečani do not possess a guest house, only a rather uncomfortable dormitory. But there is now a quite charming but fairly modest motel a few 100 meters uphill from the monastery. The surrounding pinewoods are cool even in the hottest months of the year. A campsite is attached to the motel. Returning to the main road at Dečani we have a run of only 16 km. (ten miles) to the sizeable town of Peć.

Patriarchal Peć

This town, the capital of the *Metohija,* takes its name from the caves (*pećine*) in the surrounding rocks. The narrow and twisting streets of the Okolj quarter are lined with cavern-like little shops and stalls which never seem to shut, and you will find them surprisingly like the *souks* of North Africa, a likeness heightened by glimpses of numerous mosques and minarets, the open gutters of running water that line each street and by important Turkish potentates' dwellings, with their interior gardens. This is the "Orient" as television would have us know it, even though we are in Europe, and it is in marked contrast with the modern installations of the newer part of town.

The town became important in the 14th century when the Patriarch of the Serbian Church made it his permanent residence. Before that time the Patriarch had lived in the Monastery of Žiča, but this had become too close to the Hungarian war zone. Following their normal practice, the Turks allowed the conquered people to retain their old religion. Their Grand Vizir, Pasha Mehmed Sokolović, nominated his cousin, an Orthodox monk, for the position of Patriarch in 1545.

The Serbs, however, were in no way placated by this move. Successive Patriarchs of Peć became the focal points of all the plots and intrigues that led to the revolts which periodically convulsed the country. On one occasion emissaries were sent to Russia to beg for help against the Turks. Two great uprisings promoted by the Patriarchs failed, and in order to avoid the mass extermination of the population, they led a migration to the Austrian side of the Danube in 1690, and in 1737 settled in the Vojvodina, where the Patriarchate continued more or less in exile. The abbeys and churches they built are in the Fruška Gora region.

The ancient monastery and residence of the Patriarchs is less than 1½ km. (a mile) from the town, not far from the main road leading west to Montenegro. It is a curious building of which the main church, that of the Holy Apostles, dates from the 13th century. No less than four other churches or chapels were built on to the original church at various dates. Most still possess their original frescos, which are especially fine. The outlines of the Patriarchate's original fortified quadrangle can still be made out, as can the foundations of smaller, older chapels. An 18th-century residential block continues to be used by priests and monks. The whole unit, with the churches' fantastic tiled cupolas and the high wooded mountains that look down into the little fortress, enjoys an extraordinarily picturesque setting. Immediately to the west there is the mouth of the gaunt Rugovo Gorge.

The family tree of the Nemanja kings preserved here is a fascinating study in medieval genealogy. In the Treasury the Patriarchate keeps a great number of precious objects, illuminated manuscripts and icons.

The Vojvodina

From Serbia's southern borders with Albania and Montenegro we return once more to the Republic's northern extremities. The plain of Vojvodina, immediately north of Belgrade, is Yugoslavia's granary. Only the hilly vineyards of the Fruška Gora, between Ruma and Novi Sad, interrupt the green or golden sea of grain that during spring and early summer spreads away endlessly toward the Hungarian and Romanian frontiers.

This remarkably fertile area has in the past been the lure for countless conquerors, and has also known pacific invasion. Various German colonies were brought from Swabia by the kings of Hungary to settle there toward the end of the Middle Ages, and today 50,000 of their descendants are still there. There would be more if, in 1944, many of them had not chosen to retreat with the German Army while others were expelled after the war.

Last century roughly 100,000 Slovaks (racial cousins of the Yugoslavs) were transported from northern Hungary to the Vojvodina, and along the frontier there is a considerable Romanian minority. However, by far the most important ethnic minority in the district is Hungarian. Some are descendants of Magyars who arrived in the ninth century, others were settled there in the days of the Austro-Hungarian Empire. Some Serbs also migrated to the Vojvodina region between the 16th and 18th centuries, seeking so to escape from Turkish repression in Serbia proper.

Some years ago, the Yugoslav Government granted the Vojvodina region internal autonomy, so that all ethnic minorities have their own schools, newspapers, theaters and cultural associations. As a result this part of the country is a fascinating pattern of different customs, costumes and music.

Exploring the Vojvodina

The Autonomous Region of Vojvodina includes three quite distinct parts: roughly speaking, the area north of the Danube and east of the Tisa River is referred to as the *Banat* (the name, used also in Romanian, means an area ruled by a military governor); the area north of the Danube and west of the Tisa is the *Bačka;* and the segment of the Vojvodina which lies south of the Danube is known as Srem. This multinational melting-pot reflects the long history of social upheavals and population migrations which have crisscrossed the Balkans over the past 2,500 years.

Srem

The visitor from Belgrade generally arrives first in the neighborhood of Srem. This territory has a long history. The Roman settlement of Sirmium, whose remains dating from the early centuries A.D. are now being excavated at the modern city of Sremska Mitrovica, was a fine provincial town with luxurious buildings.

Between the Sava River Valley, where Sremska Mitrovica is sited, and the Danube River, there rises a range of mountains running the full length of Srem, called the Fruška Gora. The highest point of this range is 533-m. (1,750-ft.) Mount Crveni Čot. In the pleasantly wooded hills of the Fruška Gora there are numerous historic buildings, such as the 14th-century Tower of Vrdnik and 16 monasteries dating from the great Serb migration of 1690, when it became a place of refuge for Orthodox priests and monks. The most remarkable of these monasteries are Krušedol, Hopovo, Jazak and Beočin, where there are many precious manuscripts and icons. They are well worth making a special visit to see.

On the Danube side of the Fruška Gora is a string of agricultural villages, including some famous for their vineyards. Some are of major historical importance for the several national groups which have made their home there. Stara Pazova, on the main highway between Belgrade and Novi Sad, for example, is a leading center of Slovakian culture. Its women and girls wear colorful full skirts and aprons, hand-embroidered and puffed out by a half-dozen starched petticoats.

On the same highway, farther along toward Novi Sad, is the historic town of Sremski Karlovci, where in 1699 the treaty was signed by Turkey abandoning a great part of her European conquests. Soon thereafter, Sremski Karlovci came to be the center of the cultural and political life of the dispossessed Serbian people, since Serbia proper continued under Turkish control. Thus, Sremski Karlovci was the seat of the Patriarchate of the Serbian Orthodox Church, and hence the seat of most Serbian church assemblies of this period; it was the place where Serbian newspapers and books were published; and it was the site (in 1791) of the first Serbian secondary school. The best of the architectural reminders of this period are in baroque style, and include the former Town Hall, cathedral, and Patriarchal Palace. This, considered by some the most imposing 19th-century building in the Vojvodina, houses the charming Patriarchal Chapel.

Novi Sad, the Bačka, and the Banat

Eight km. (five miles) farther on from Sremski Karlovci brings you to Petrovaradin, set in a sudden turn in the course of the Danube and dominated by a great fortress captured by Prince Eugene of Savoy from the Turks in 1716. Later it was to serve as a link in Austria's so-called "military frontier." From the Petrovaradin Fortress there is a memorable view of the capital of the Vojvodina, Novi Sad, a city of over 200,000 inhabitants. It was a great intellectual center during the decisive years of the struggle against the Turks early last century, and the Literary Association called Matica Srpska, formed in 1828, still exists.

The Town Hall is in the main square, facing the Orthodox Church and Bishop's Palace. The Orthodox churches in Novi Sad contain particularly valuable iconostases. Because of the mixed population of the Vojvodina, Novi Sad serves uniquely among the cities of Yugoslavia as a meeting-place of various groups and cultures.

A major center of Slovakian culture in the Bačka is the village of Bačka Petrovac, 34 km. (21 miles) west of Novi Sad. Especially on Sundays during the month of August, you will find yourself caught up in a whirl of bright colors, and strange, half-wild music and dancing.

Srbobran is on the main highway leading into Hungary; from it, it is 67½ km. (42 miles) to Subotica, the last major city before the frontier. This drive will take you across flat country indistinguishable from the *puszta* landscape so typical of Hungary. Subotica's population of 150,000 is predominantly of Hungarian origins. Eight km. (five miles) from the city is Lake Palić, in a vast area of park-like country. Here you will find a hunting museum, showing all the species of animals and birds once shot here, when it was the preserve of a Hungarian noble family, and also a small zoo.

The Banat is less frequented by visitors than the other parts of the Vojvodina. Nevertheless, some of its villages—notably Kovačica and Uzdin—have produced a number of remarkable native artists whose work has become known far beyond Yugoslavia's borders. In Kovačica an art gallery displays a selection of these vivid paintings and it is possible, by arrangement, to visit some of the artists' homes. Part of eastern Vojvodina consists of uninviting sand flats. The major city of the Banat is Zrenjanin, but most of the Romanian minority live at Vršac, less than 14½ km. (nine miles) from the Romanian frontier. Vršac has a Bishop's Palace and many of its churches have interesting iconostases. Just over 35 km. (22 miles) to the south is another frontier town called Bela Crkva, justly renowned for its Romanian carnival costumes on high days and holidays.

PRACTICAL INFORMATION FOR SERBIA

WHEN TO GO. Serbia is extremely hot in summer and many parts of it can be very cold indeed in winter. Nevertheless, it is mainly the summer season which attracts visitors. However, the best time to go to Serbia is in spring or autumn.

FOOD AND DRINK. Serbia offers a wide variety of exciting dishes—that is, if you can persuade the chef to concentrate on the local recipes. Information on the regional specialties is given in the *Food and Drink* chapter. Many dishes use red peppers and have the highly spiced quality of Oriental cooking. But Serbia is also fish country, and you will find the product of the local rivers cooked in many delightful ways. Soups may be presented either in the accepted Western manner, or as a *čorba*, common throughout the Balkans—a fish *čorba* can be a real experience. Chicken (*pile*) is served with bread noodles swimming in the sauce. *Sarma, musaka, čevapčići* and *ražnjiči*, all of them inspired by the Turkish occupation, are also delicious, and the Serbs will be delighted if you try them.

There are a number of local wines, but the beer is very weak. Some of the best wines come from Smederevo, and are drunk cold for preference. *Prokupac* and *Negotinsko* resemble light Burgundies.

The atmosphere in Serbian restaurants is usually very cheerful.

HOW TO GET AROUND. By car. Roads between all major Serbian towns are adequate, if often narrow. However, avoid all those marked green on tourist maps, unless you are prepared for some rough rides. An *autoput* from Zagreb to Belgrade widens into a motorway 16 km. (ten miles) west of the capital; this road now connects to the toll motorway which forms part of the route to Niš and which is being extended. A scenically rewarding and uncrowded route from Belgrade to Skopje is the *Ibar Magistrala* farther west. You will find gasoline stations satisfactory, and there are plenty of motels etc. close to the main roads.

By coach. Comfortable long-distance coaches operate to most destinations. If you decide to take one of the exciting "Monastery Tours" you will find the deluxe vehicles used by the big Yugoslav travel firms give you a very relaxing ride.

WHAT TO SEE. Its scenery varies from the almost flat Danubian plain in the north to impressive mountains and mountain gorges in the south, with large stretches of fertile rolling hills in between. The Iron Gates, where the might Danube plunges into a narrow gorge, with Yugoslavia on one side and Romania on the other, is one of the most magnificent spectacles in all Europe.

Lovers of medieval art will be delighted with the Serbian painting and architecture of the Middle Ages. The most beautiful churches, often surrounded by mountains which greatly enhance their appearance, are found in the region of the Morava and the Ibar. When the Turks pushed on toward the north, the monks who took refuge in the Pannonian Plain established, between the 16th and 18th centuries, several monasteries set on the highest points of the Fruška Gora, which are easily reached from Belgrade. You will find an abundance of folklore throughout Serbia. The Turkish heritage remains strong in cites like Novi Pazar, Prizren and Peć. Poverty is still apparent in some of them, though standards of living are rising fast, and changes are apparent after the lapse of only a few months. Much of the region is, of course, thoroughly Western, and there are large areas which are extremely fertile and beautiful.

SPORTS. In general, the thick forests of Serbia abound in game. Hunting is especially good in the Obed swamps, which are a favorite stopping place for migratory birds, while bear hunting is popular on the slopes of the Šar Planina hills and on the Tara plateau. Fishing is possible in a large variety of rivers.

For those who like swimming, there are numerous lovely beaches along the Danube. And the Ibar lends itself admirably to a descent by kayak. You can even go skiing in Serbia, though facilities only exist at relatively minor resorts.

PRACTICAL INFORMATION FOR BELGRADE

HOW TO GET THERE. By train. All the chief European express trains leaving Paris, Ostend, Basel and Vienna, en route to Athens or Istanbul, go through Belgrade. As behoves the capital, Belgrade is also the hub of Yugoslavia's internal railroad system. The main trans-European line runs from Zagreb to Belgrade, then turns south to Niš, where it divides—one branch going on to Sofia and through Bulgaria, the other continuing south to Skopje, and on through Greece. A more westerly line likewise links Belgrade with Skopje, but in this case via Kraljevo and Pristina. From northeastern Europe, there is another international line to Belgrade which goes by way of Subotica and Novi Sad. There is also a connection between Belgrade and Bar, on the Montenegrin coast. This runs through some splendid scenery and being new is also comfortable. Trains between Bosnia-Herzegovina and Belgrade are very slow and should be avoided if possible.

By plane. Belgrade has air connections with all Western European capitals and also New York. In addition, there are regular flights between every Yugoslav provincial capital and main tourist center and Belgrade, by the national airline, JAT.

By boat. An original way to get to Belgrade is by taking a cruise ship from Passau or Vienna, and going down the Danube via Hungary.

 HOTELS. Economic and political center, seat of all the national government agencies, Belgrade has many visitors but not enough hotels. Therefore it is wise to reserve rooms in advance. Hotel prices are very different from those in the rest of the country, being in general higher in all categories than the average rates given in the *Facts at Your Fingertips* section at the start of the book. Hotels here need to be chosen according to location as well as by price and comfort, however—that is, if there are enough beds available to give you a choice. If you have any difficulty, the Tourist Information Office in the Pedestrian Underground Passage at the Albanija Skyscraper, Terazije (tel. 635–343), or at the railroad station, will help you find an available room. But note that in low season these two offices close fairly early.

There are camp sites at Košutnjak and near the National hotel (see below). For youth accommodations, enquire in advance from Mladost-Turist, Kosovska 49. Private accommodations can be booked through Turist Biro Lasta, Trg bratstva i Jedinstva 1a, and Putnik, Požeška 45.

Deluxe

Beograd-Intercontinental, 420 rooms. Across the River Sava in Novi (New) Belgrade, adjoining the glossy new Sava Center. Modern accommodations, and very elegant if you don't mind being away from the city center. Pool.

Jugoslavija, Bulevar Edvarda Kardelja 3. 577 rooms. Again, across the Sava, but in a rather dull area of apartment blocks on the banks of the Danube. Pool, garage.

Expensive

Excelsior, Kneza Miloša 5. 81 rooms.

Metropol, Bulevar Revolucije 69. 206 rooms. Smartest hotel in the town center, sumptuous in a slightly old-fashioned way. One of the few with a garage.

Moskva, Balkanska 1. 140 rooms. On a busy corner in the city center. More expensive than 1974 modernization merits.

Palace, Topličin Venac 23. 78 rooms. Garage.

Moderate

Balkan, Prizrenska 2. 95 rooms, 76 with bath. Central, but older.

Central, 31 rooms. In the charming old "suburb" of Zemun by the Danube.

Kasina, Terazije 25. 96 rooms. Central but somewhat noisy

Lipovačka Šuma, 20 rooms. Motel on the road to Kraljevo.

National, Bežanijska kosa bb. 70 rooms. Across the Sava, on the motorway from Zagreb.

Park, Njegoševa 2. 131 rooms. Garage. Central, but noisy.

Prag, Narodnog fronta 27. 131 rooms. Central, noisy.

Putnik, across the River Sava, near the Jugoslavija (see above).

Romeo i Julija, 14 rooms. Motel on the road to Kraljevo.

Slavija, Svetog save 1. 332 rooms. Comfortable modern hotel a little outside the town center, near the Belgrade motorway.

Splendid, Dragoslava Jovanovića 5. 50 rooms. Central, but can be noisy; no restaurant.

Srbija, Ustanička 127. 337 rooms. Without the town center, by the Belgrade motorway. Comfortable and modern.

Šumadija, 106 rooms. Near the fairground on the way to Avala.

Toplice, 7. jula 56. 90 rooms. Central, but inclined to be noisy.

Turist, Sarajevska 37. 93 rooms. Near the main railroad station. Again, central though can be noisy.

Union, Kosovska 11. 74 rooms, 59 with bath. Central.

Inexpensive

Astorija, Milovana Milovanovića 1. 77 rooms, 36 with bath. Older but central.

Grand, 21 rooms, 14 with bath. In Zemun, by the Danube.

At Avala

Avala pension.
Beograd pension.
1000 Ruža, 52 rooms.

 RESTAURANTS. In Belgrade, virtually all the hotels have restaurants. The cuisine in the large hotels is very international (though the restaurant attached to the Metropol hotel—*Arhiv,* on Karnedžijeva—is one that can be recommended). In general, it is much more fun to go to other restaurants, especially in the evening when musicians and singers create the atmosphere which is peculiar to the city. At many restaurants, the grilled meats, such as the *ražnjići, ćulbaštija,* and *pljeskavica,* are prepared in front of the guests. We will not repeat the long list of Serbian specialties, but just remind you that in Belgrade you may have your only chance to taste excellent sturgeon (and caviar) fresh from the Danube. Sturgeon is a gastronomic delicacy and is prepared in different ways. Menus are often printed in French; if not, you can ask for *jesetra.* To go with this dish or the sturgeon, we recommend *Smederevka,* a greenish wine from the vineyards of the Danube, or *Žilavka:* the genuine Žilavka comes from Blagaj, and should be so labeled.

Belgrade's restaurants, outside of the hotels, are as varied as you would expect in a capital city. The most popular ones at the moment are the Bohemian spots in the city's old Bohemian quarter centered on the street called Skadarlija.

Ima Dana heads the list, with *Dva Jelena* (one of the latest to open), *Tri Šešira* and *Skadarlija* close behind. The first and last provide openair dining, and all four have entertainments in addition to music.

Other central restaurants include *Beogradjanka,* Masarikova 5, for fish specialties; *Dušanov Grad,* Terazije 4, pleasant if not very exciting; *Dva Ribara,* Narodnog fronta 21, again, pleasant; *Madera,* Bulevar Revolucije 43, with lovely garden; and *Romani Tar,* Terazije 27, which is an outstanding gipsy restaurant, but more expensive.

Some way out of the center are *Dunavski cvet,* T. Koščuškog 63, with fish specialties; *Grafičar,* Vase Pelagića 31 (five km./three miles out of center), charcoal grills and lamb-on-the-spit; *Kumbara,* Beli Potok (9½ km./six miles out), spicy grill specialties; *Milošev Konak,* Topčider (6½ km./four miles out); *Trojka,* Triše Kaclerovića 24, Russian food; and *Vinogradi,* at Grocka (26 km./16 miles out), on hill overlooking the Danube, for roast-on-the-spit specialties.

Three useful self-service restaurants, all in the center, are *Atina,* Terazije 28; *Kasina,* Terazije 25; and *Zagreg,* Obilićev unac 29. There are cafés everywhere —and very crowded they become on sunny days. A historic one is the *Café of the Question Mark,* 7. jula 6, opposite the Orthodox cathedral, and typical of Serbian homes of two centuries ago.

 HOW TO GET AROUND. To travel about the city of Belgrade, if you do not have your own car, the best bet is to take a trolleybus, streetcar or bus. It is a little cheaper to buy your ticket in advance from a tobacconist near the bus or tram stop; the ticket must then be punched in the correct machine when you have boarded the vehicle (watch how others do it). To get a taxi, call 765–666 (Belgrade City Transport) or 443–443 (private operators).

 WHAT TO SEE. The Vuk and Dositej Museum, at Gospodar Jevremova 21, is housed in what was the first Serb high school at the beginning of the 19th century. The building probably dates back to the 17th century. Home of a wealthy Turkish family, it is a typical Moslem house, characteristically divided into two parts: the first where the family lives (*harem*), and the second where male visitors are received (*selamluk*).

Bajrakli Džamija, at Gospoda Jevremova 11, was built in the 17th century and is the only mosque left in Belgrade. During last century it was converted into a church. The Mound of Sheik Mustapha, at the corner of Jugovićeva and Višnjićeva streets, is the mausoleum of the head dervish of the order of Sadi, who was born in Baghdad and died in Belgrade during the 18th century. Engraved on a slab over the entrance is an epitaph in Turkish, indicating the name of the founder. The Palace of Princess Ljubica is at Kneza Sime Markovića Street 8, and was built by Prince Miloš for his family around 1830. In typical Serbian style; on the roof is a turret which used to serve as an observation post.

SPORTS. The following sports centers have swimming pools and, in some cases, tennis and other recreational facilities: Ada Ciganlija, on an island in the River Sava but accessible by road; Banjica, Crnotravska 4; Hala sportova Pionir, Čarli Čaplina 39; Košutnjak, Kneza Višeslava 72; and 25 maj, Tadeuša Košćuškog 63. There is rowing at the Crvena Zvezda Club or the Belgrade Nautical Club (Veslački Club). Horse racing takes place at the Hippodrome, Pastrovićeva Street. And devotees of football (soccer) will doubtless know of Belgrade's famous clubs, Red Star and Partizan.

MUSEUMS. The Ethnographic Museum, Studentski Trg 13, contains national costumes, rugs, and articles in everyday use throughout Yugoslavia. Also models and typical interiors of peasant houses, ancient Slav pottery etc. Closed Mondays.

The Fresco Gallery, 20 Cara Uroša St., has copies of the finest frescos of the medieval Serbian and Macedonian monasteries.

The Historical Museum of Serbia, Prince Miloš Palace, at Topčider.

The Jewish Historical Museum, 2nd Floor, Sedmog Jula 71.

The Josip Broz Tito Memorial Center. This comprises the house where the late President Tito lived and is now buried; the nearby *Museum of 4th July,* Bulevar Oktobarske Revolucije 10a, which is concerned with the early days of the Yugoslav Communist Party and the national uprising; and the *25th of May Museum,* Botićeva 8, which has a collection of birthday gifts presented to President Tito, including many beautiful handicraft items from both Yugoslav and foreign sources.

The Modern Art Museum, on the River Sava in Novi Beograd, has a good display of 20th-century painting and sculpture, with the emphasis on the work of Serbian artists. In addition, it frequently holds special exhibitions of particular interest.

The Museum of Applied Arts, Vuka Karadžića 18.

The Museum of the City of Belgrade, Zmaj Jovina 1, depicts the history of the city.

The Museum of the Serbian Orthodox Church, in the Patriarchate, Sedmog Jula 5, displays some of the best examples of icons, vestments and other art work from Serbian churches.

The Museum of the Underground Press, Banjički Venac St. 12.

The National Museum, Trg Republike, was founded by Prince Miloš Obrenović. It houses archeological, historical and numismatic collections, as well as a picture gallery. Among the pre-classical material are many vases, statuettes, gold jewelry, and the famous Duplja cart. The antique art section contains Greek and Roman items found on Yugoslav territory. There are gold objects from Trebeniište, a late copy of the Athena Parthenos by Phidias, two dancing satyrs from Stobi (all from Macedenia), gold Roman jewelry from Kostolac in Serbia, etc. In the section representing the Middle Ages, besides fragments of frescos from Serbian monasteries, there are superb icons from

Ohrid and elsewhere. The Gospel of Miroslav written in 1190 and a 14th-century copy of the Code of Emperor Dušan are the most valuable documents in this collection.

The numismatic section contains unique gold Roman coins, silver pieces of the Byzantine Emperor Nicephorus, etc. Paintings include some fine canvases by Renoir and Degas. The two great Yugoslav sculptors, Meštrović and Rosandić, are also well represented. Closed Mondays.

 OTHER ENTERTAINMENT. Belgrade has seven theaters: the leading one is the National Theater, Trg Republike. In addition to its dramatic repertory, this theater possesses a very good opera and ballet company. Otherwise, there are a number of Yugoslav folkdance and folksong groups; one based in Belgrade is known as the Kolo Company, and if an opportunity presents itself for you to see their program be sure to take it. The FEST International Film Festival is in February, and in September there is the BITEF, the Belgrade Theater Festival.

Summer months see openair concerts in the parks, at Kalemegdan and in the Fresco Gallery. There are also classical concerts in the Zuzorić Art Pavilion, Kalemegdan, and in winter at the Kolorac Hall, Studentski Trg. Many movie houses show French, English or American films, and in summer there are a few outdoor cinemas. The Children's Theater at Trg Republike is justly famous.

 SHOPPING. A handy booklet about shopping in Belgrade is available from the Tourist Information Center (see Useful Addresses). Of the major department stores, you can't miss the high-rise block of the Beograd Palace on Maršala Tita, which houses the largest of them all, Beogradjanka. Another big one, Beograd, is at Trg Terazije 15–23, with its drugstore (look for the phonetic spelling *Dragstor*) in the Underground Pedestrian Passage in Nušićeva, open round the clock. A chain of handicraft shops known as Narodna Radinost is worth seeking out: at Knez Mihailova 2 and 4, Knez Mihailova 19, and Terazije 45. The Galerija Primenjenih Umetnosti, at Uzun Mirkova 12, has a permanent display of the work of the Association of Applied Artists of Serbia. Leather goods are other recommended good buys, and there are specialist shops for these in Knez Mihailova and Terazije.

The main bookshop in Belgrade is Jugoslovenska Knjiga, at Knez Mihailova 2. Museums can be a valuable source of unusual souvenirs. Try the National Museum, the Fresco Gallery, the Ethnographic Museum, the Museum of Applied Arts, and the Museum of Contemporary Art.

There is a number of very lively openair markets that sell handicrafts from many parts of the country, as well as fresh produce, household goods, clothes—in fact, pretty well everything you can think of. Such markets open daily from 5 A.M., including on Sundays. The principal one is at Zelenci Venac.

NEWSPAPERS. Depending on the current state of the economy, foreign newspapers and magazines, including most English-language publications common in Western Europe, are sold in the large hotels in Belgrade, also at the Central Railroad Station, and at some kiosks in the center of the city. One such kiosk is in the pedestrian subway near the Beograd cinema, another in Knez Mihailova in front of the American Reading Room.

USEFUL ADDRESSES. The Tourist Information Center can be found at the Central Station, also in the subway passage at the end of Terazije below the building called Albanija, and in season on main roads into the city. Of the numerous travel agencies in Belgrade, Putnik (the main Serbian travel firm) has its headquarters at Dragoslava Jovanviča 1; Inex is at Trg Republike 5; Kompas, Brankova 9; Centroturist, Bulevar Revolucije 70; Dalmacijaturist, Makedonska 35; and Kvarner Express at Balkanska 8. Naromtravel, specializing in youth travel, is at Moše Pijade 12.

Embassies: U.S., Kneza Miloša 50; Canada, Proleterskih Brigada 69; British, Generala Ždanova 46. Motoring organizations: Auto-moto savez Jugoslavije, Ruzeltova 18; and Auto-moto savez Srbije, Ivana Milutinovića 58. Pharmacies open round the clock: Prvi Maj, Maršala Tita 9; Savski Venac, Nemanjina 2; and Zemun, Maršala Tita 74.

NIGHT LIFE. Yugoslavs in general and Belgrade people in particular like to dance. Almost all the good hotels have a bar with dancing, while the former Bohemian quarter of Skadarlija is an especially lively area on summer evenings. Nightclubs that can be particularly recommended include that at the *Metropol* hotel, which also has a casino; the *Lotus,* at Zmaj jovina 4; and *Topčiderska noć,* Bulevar Vojvode Mišića bb. Discos and jazz clubs worth a visit are *Disko-Videoteka,* at Bezistan, and *Dom omladine* (Youth Center), at Makedonska 18.

PRACTICAL INFORMATION FOR SERBIA

OUTSIDE BELGRADE

HOTELS FOR SERBIA EAST OF BELGRADE

DONJI MILANOVAC. By an artificial lake in the Danube defile, well-placed for visiting Lepenski Vir, the Kazan Gorge, and the Iron Gates. *Lepenski Vir* (E), 262 rooms. On a hill overlooking town; modern.

GOLUBAC. Overlooking the Danube defile. *Golubački Grad* (I).

KLADOVO. Terminus of the hydrofoil excursion through the Iron Gates. *Djerdap* (M), 100 rooms. Modern.

SMEDEREVO. Medieval fortress on the Danube. *Smederevo* and annex *Palma* (M), 165 rooms.

ZAJEČAR. In the Timok Valley. *Srbija* (E).

HOTELS FOR SERBIA SOUTH OF BELGRADE

ALEKSINAC. *Motel Morava* (M), 104 rooms. On the *autoput.*

DIMITROVGRAD. On the Bulgarian frontier. *Motel Dimitrovgrad* (M), 38 rooms.

GORNJI MILANOVAC. *Šumadija* (M), 116 rooms.

KRAGUJEVAC. Principal city of Šumadija. *Kragujevac* (M), 109 rooms. *Šumarice* (M), 103 rooms. *Zelengora* (M), 25 rooms. *Dubrovnik* (I), 33 rooms, 3 with bath.

KRALJEVO. Near Ziča Monastery. *Turist-Pariz* (M), 75 rooms. In the city center.

KRUŠEVAC. *Rubin* (E), 110 rooms. *Evropa* (I), 36 rooms, a few with bath.

LESKOVAC. Near the ancient city of Caričingrad. *Motel Atina* (M), 40 rooms. Pool. *Beograd* (I), 107 rooms, 34 with bath. In the town.

NIŠ. *Ambassador* (M), 162 rooms. In the town center. *Niš* (M), 87 rooms. *Park* (I), 87 rooms, 6 with bath. A block away from the Niš, beside the large city park.
Outside the town, *Motel-Camp Mediana* (I), 52 rooms.

NOVI PAZAR. *Vrbak* (M), 65 rooms.

PARTIZANSKE VODE. *Lovac* (M), 60 rooms, 43 with bath. *Palas* (M), 40 rooms. *Palisad* (M), 412 rooms. A complex of hotel units and individual cottages, on a ridge of the Zlatibor plateau at an altitude of 960 m. (3,150 ft.). Pool; excellent restaurant, music in the evenings.

PROKULPJE. *Hammeum* (I), 35 rooms.

RASKA. *Motel Putnik* (I), 60 rooms, half with bath.

SOPOČANI. *Sopoćani* (M), beside the monastery.

STUDENICA. *Studenica* (M), 24 rooms. In idyllic mountain valley.

SVETOZAREVO. Near Manasija and Ravanica monasteries. *Jagodina* (M), 152 rooms. Pool.

TITOVO UŽICE. *Zlatibor* (E), 150 rooms. *Motel Zlatiborska Noć* (M), 40 rooms. *Turist* (I), 38 rooms.

TOPOLA. *Oplenac* (M), 53 rooms. Situated near the Karadjordje mausoleum church in the Optenac park on a hill overlooking Topola.

TOPOLA JARMENOVCI. *Karadjordje* (M), 32 rooms.

VALJEVO. *Beli Narcis* (M), 75 rooms.

VELIKA PLANA. *Pokajnica* (M), 108 rooms. Pool. *Velika Plana* (I), 36 rooms. Motel on the *autoput.*

VLASINSKO JEZERO. *Vlasina* (M), 49 rooms, 10 with bath.

VRANJSKA BANJA. Serbia's premier spa. *Fontana* (M), 228 rooms. Indoor pool. *Zvezda* (M), 122 rooms. Pool.

VRANJE. 11 km. (seven miles) from the thermal spa of Vranjska Banja. *Vranje Motel* (M), 64 rooms. One of the best between Niš and Skopje; on the *autoput.*

HOTELS FOR KOSOVO

DEČANI. *Visoki Dečani* (M), 39 rooms. In a pine forest just above the monastery, three km. (two miles) west of the village of Dečani. Excellent for fresh trout.

PEČ. Principal city of Metohija. *Metohija* (E), 85 rooms. An attractive stone-and-wood design characteristic of the area, on the bank of the Bistrica River. *Korzo* (M), 40 rooms. *Motel Dardania* (I), 16 rooms.

PRIŠTINA. The main city of Kosovo, and capital of the Autonomous Region. *Grand Hotel Priština* (E), 370 rooms. *Kosovski Božur* (M), 120 rooms. In the center. *Union* (I), 20 rooms, none with shower.

PRIZREN. Photogenic oriental city. *Vlazrimi* (M), 29 rooms. Motel. There is a good restaurant, *Maraš,* overlooking the river.

UROŠEVAC. *Ljuboten* (M), 30 rooms.

HOTELS FOR THE VOJVODINA

BAČKA PALANKA. Fishing center on the Danube. *Motel Poloj* (I), 10 rooms. *Turist* (I), 32 rooms, some with bath.

KIKINDA. *Narvik* (E), 100 rooms. Pool.

NOVI SAD. Capital city of the Vojvodina. *Park* (E), 120 rooms. *Trdjava* (E), 52 rooms. Across the Danube in the renovated Petrovaradin Fortress, on a bluff overlooking the river and Novi Sad. Scenic. *Novi Sad* (M), 124 rooms. *Putnik* (M), 86 rooms. Convenient for the city center. *Vojvodina* (M), 66 rooms. *Auto Camp Ribarsko Ostrovo* (I), 30 rooms, none with shower. Restaurants include the *Mala Gostiona* inn and *Velika Terasa.*

SREMSKA MITROVICA. *Sirmium* (I), 54 rooms.

SUBOTICA. *Patria* (M), 200 rooms, nearly half with bath. Comfortable. At Palić, *Park* (M), 30 rooms, and *Sport* (M), 27 rooms. Both pensions.

VRBAS. A short distance off the Novi Sad–Subotica highway. *Backa* (M), 85 rooms.

ZRENJANIN. *Vojvodina* (M), 109 rooms.

WHAT TO SEE. An excursion through the famed Iron Gates is the number one attraction here. The hydrofoils which make the Danube River excursions between Belgrade and Kladovo are operated by the Yugoslav River Shipping enterprise (Jugoslovensko Rečno Brodarstvo). Tickets and reservations for the trip should be secured a few days in advance at any Belgrade travel agency, or through your hotel.

Normally, there are departures from Belgrade every day at 6 A.M., with return the same evening. This schedule includes a two-hour stopover in Kladovo for lunch. However, you should be warned that if there is a delay for any reason the Kladovo stop is canceled, since there is no navigation on the river at night and the "boats" must return to Belgrade by sundown. Thus, if you plan to make the roundtrip in one day, it is advisable to fortify yourself with a few snacks and to be prepared for any contingency. Another, and perhaps more relaxing, alternative is to stay overnight at the riverside Hotel Djerdap in Kladovo, returning to Belgrade by hydrofoil the next day.

MACEDONIA

Cradle of Slavdom

It is strange how the name of Macedonia has survived. 23 centuries ago it became the most powerful nation in the world of ancient Greece under Philip and his son, Alexander the Great, and somehow it has conserved its name through 2,000 years of Roman, Byzantine and Turkish occupation.

Today, as one of the six federal republics of Yugoslavia, the portion of Macedonia lying inside Yugoslavia has recovered something of its independence. It had been a Turkish province until just before World War I, and was unknown to the outside world until the 1920s. It is still to a large extent off the main communication lines, so that modern development has started only recently. Progress, however, has been striking, and today you will find excellent modern hotels in a number of towns and resorts, as well as the other organized amenities (excursions, sports facilities, etc.) that go with expanding tourism. Hunting, fishing, spas and winter sports especially are being developed, together with "village" tourism aimed at bringing the visitor into closer contact with the Macedonian way of life. Youth, too, is being given a fair share of consideration, with the construction of more hostels and camp sites.

So, though it is still quite an expedition to reach Macedonia across the full length of Yugoslavia, any visitor who makes the effort will reap a rich and stimulating reward. He will find here one of the few remaining corners of Europe where the old way of life still survives, a silent land of fertile valleys given over to the cultivation of tobacco, cotton and rice. The roads connecting these valleys one with another penetrate a countryside of abrupt mountain peaks of startling beauty, and in the far south there are three exquisite lakes: Ohrid, Prespa and Dojran, brilliant beneath a southern sun.

The Islamic culture and religion imported by the Turks are still quite widespread amid a setting of mosques, minarets and Moslem cemeteries. After the Ottoman invasion, the Orthodox priests and monks withdrew to the remotest mountains and there, in their monastic strongholds, kept the flame of Christianity alight. As in Serbia, a large proportion of these remote monasteries have magnificent Renaissance-style frescos, as well as precious icons and rich wood carvings.

Many were the civilizations that lingered in Macedonia until their fortunes declined, so that the country has much of historical interest to show, principally along the riverbanks of the Vardar and near Lake Ohrid. There are Macedonian-Greek towns such as Heraclea Lyncestis (near Bitola) and Lychnis (Ohrid), and Roman Stobi. Excavations at Scupi and Stobi have revealed two cities of the Roman province of Macedonia Salutaris. Once the barbarian invasions came to an end and the Slavs settled here great changes took place, the people of these new tribes adapting Byzantine culture to meet their own needs and tastes.

Macedonian folklore, folk arts and crafts are relatively pure and untouched by outside influences, so that the songs, dances, embroidery, carpet-weaving and wood-carving are unequaled in their abundance. The popular dances are a delight to the eye, the most striking being those from the mountainous west of the province.

Here you will enjoy all the pleasures and interests of a voyage outside Europe, though without much sacrifice in personal comfort. There are good hotels in all the larger towns and summer resorts, and the roads, though still sometimes bumpy, are relatively free of wheeled traffic.

Something of its History

The rise of the great Macedonian kingdom began in the fourth century B.C., when both Athens and Sparta had passed their zenith and had exhausted themselves with 30 years of fighting against each other. The Greeks regarded the Macedonians as "barbarians," i.e. people who could not speak proper Greek, and looked down on them accordingly. Nevertheless, by using a mixture of brilliant diplomacy and armed force, Philip II and his son, Alexander the Great, brought the whole of Greece under the control of Macedon.

One secret of their success was the adoption by Philip of the "phalanx," a squad of heavily-armed soldiers carrying strong pikes of different lengths and constituting, in effect, a sort of human tank. At the same time, the Macedonians perfected the employment of lightly-armed troops and cavalry, who could easily outmaneuver military formations of the time. Once all Greece had been brought under Macedonian control, Alexander, universally considered one of the greatest military geniuses of all time, then set out upon his extraordinary conquest of the known world. First he took Asia Minor, then the mighty Persian Empire of Darius. Pressing ever eastward, he next subdued Babylon and continued to the Punjab in India before his homesick troops finally compelled him, much against his will, to turn back. He himself died at the age of 33 without ever seeing his native country again. The generals whom he had left in charge of various provinces seized control for themselves and began to quarrel with each other. After 175 unsettled years, in 146 B.C. Macedonia became a Roman province.

Centuries later, Byzantium tried to check the Slavs' infiltration from the north, but was unable to prevent their settling there, and in the tenth century the newcomers formed themselves into an independent state under Tsar Samuel. After several victories over the Byzantines, he added other Slav provinces to his kingdom, whose central portion was what is now Bulgaria. But Byzantium, once fully mobilized, was too powerful for him.

In a terrible battle in 1014, the Byzantine Emperor, Basil II, took 14,000 prisoners, blinded them and sent them back to Samuel. Stunned by the horror of this monstrous act, Samuel died soon after, and for a time Byzantine power was assured.

With the expansion of the Serb state under the brilliant Nemanja dynasty, King Dušan occupied Macedonia in the 14th century, but this unification of the two Slav countries was not fully achieved before the Turks made themselves masters of both, staying there for 500 years.

Following the growth of nationalistic sentiment in Serbia early in the 19th century, Macedonia began to hope that her long subjection was nearly ended, but her case aroused little support abroad. Her attempts at a national uprising, such as that of Kruševo organized by the Macedonian revolutionary movement known as "VMRO," were mercilessly suppressed. In 1909 there was a state of open warfare for three months, but the insurgents, poorly armed and led, were beaten.

The first Balkan War (1912) liberated Macedonia from the Turks, but the Greeks, Bulgarians and Serbs immediately embarked upon the second Balkan War of 1913. In World War I this unhappy backward province was a theater of operations. The Treaty of Neuilly in 1919 again divided it, the new Yugoslavia being awarded the lion's share, Greece keeping Thessaloniki and its environs, and Bulgaria a small strip in the northeast. In 1941 the Germans presented the whole of Macedonia to Bulgaria, but the 1919 frontiers were restored in 1945. While the province was probably better-off in the period between the two world wars than she had been under the Turks, the kingdom of Yugoslavia was particularly active in its efforts to bring the region up to date and repair the damage of its long neglect.

However, after World War II, schools were opened for the first time. In them instruction is given in the Macedonian language, which is in many ways different from Serbo-Croat. Macedonia is still in some respects more backward than the northern region of Yugoslavia, but industrialization is going ahead fast, agriculture has been drastically reorganized, and excellent new roads have been built. There remains much to do, but it is significant now that the people are at last free of foreign rule, and painters, musicians and writers are very actively asserting the country's highly individual artistic outlook.

Exploring Macedonia

There are two principal routes to the Macedonian capital of Skopje from Belgrade, one via Niš, and the other via Kraljevo and Priština. The first is the faster route, the second more interesting, passing close to several outstanding medieval monasteries referred to in the chapter on Serbia.

By the Niš route you cross the Kumanovo plain just inside Macedonia, where the Serbs in 1912 revenged themselves on the Turks for their enslavement after the defeat of Kosovo over 500 years before, finally destroying the Turkish Balkan Empire. From the town of Kumanovo we recommend a detour 9½ km. (six miles) to the east, to Staro Nagoričano to visit the church of St. George (Sveti Djordje) built in 1318 by the Serbian King Milutin, one of the loveliest small churches in Yugoslavia. The magnificent frescos were damaged up to the height of a man by Bulgarian soldiers during the Balkan wars. The finest illustrate the "Legends of St. George," and scenes of "The Passion," the best of which is "The Flagellation."

If you are interested in Serbian art, you will be prepared to go farther afield into the mountains of Kumanovo to Matejic Monastery. It is not easy to find, but is an example of the "five-cupola" style. It was built early in the 16th century.

If you come by the road from Priština through Stimlje, you will without noticing it cross the watershed of the rivers of southern Yugoslavia: everything south of the line flows into the Aegean. Just before entering Macedonia is the oriental-looking little town of Kačanik, and the road then immediately enters the long gorge formed by the Lepenac River, which divides the Šar-Planina Mountains from the Skopska Crna Gora that climb to 2,440-m. (8,000-ft.) Mount Ljuboten on your left.

If you have time to take a closer look at the Šar-Planina, take the road leading off from the village of Cučer to the tiny Church of Sveti Nikita, which despite its uninspiring outward appearance, contains some of the most delightfully spontaneous and realistic medieval mural paintings in the country. A similar detour into the Black Mountains on the other side of the river will give you a glimpse of colorful peasant costumes, still in regular use in this unsophisticated region.

Skopje City

Capital of Macedonia and thriving city of some 500,000 inhabitants, Skopje suffered severely in the earthquake of July 1963. However, it was mainly the city center that was affected, and in the suburbs you can still see the innumerable streets of tiny houses, seemingly no stronger than packs of cards, which survived with fairly little, if any, damage.

The first tremor took place at 5.17 A.M. It was followed swiftly by another, and between them they did the damage, though 82 more tremors were recorded that day. In all, 85 percent of the total number of houses were affected to a greater or lesser degree.

Within hours help was pouring in from all over the world, and the city had been transformed into an international salvage camp. Women and children were evacuated; only those who could work remained. By the autumn of 1963, 150,000 people were living in Skopje again, many in tents, before they could gradually be rehoused in the prefabricated lodgings which were arriving from various countries. Since then, rebuilding has continued apace, producing some very fine architecture and practical facilities for the inhabitants, such as the huge modern covered shopping precinct in the center of town and many cultural, educational, commercial and sports buildings; in fact, all the amenities that go to make a thriving modern city.

There is a tremendous first impact if you arrive by rail in Skopje. The ruined station has been left as it was, the hands of the clock still pointing to 5.17 A.M.

A new city plan for the whole of the center of Skopje has been completed and extensive seismographic tests have been carried out to ensure its future solidity. A permanent Club of Solidarity, for all those concerned with the reconstruction, has been created in the center of Skopje.

Although so much was destroyed, there are still several historical and religious monuments to see. These are situated on the left bank of the River Vardar, crossed by a narrow stone bridge believed to have been originally built in 1368. This leads you into the Caršija or bazaar, a maze of cobbled streets and alleys.

Places of interest include the old Orthodox Church of Sveti Spas (St. Saviour) with its glorious bas-relief iconostatis; the Mustapha Pasha Mosque, dating from 1492; and Daut Pasha's bath, now an art gallery. The huge Kuršumli Han, an enormous caravanserai built in the 16th century, which housed the archeological museum, was badly damaged, but has now been completely restored. The Skopje Fortress was built in Turkish times, though its history goes back to the sixth century B.C. Its ruined mass still dominates the town from its hill. Near the openair market, a fine modern building houses the cultural center for the Albanian and Turkish national minorities.

Excursions around Skopje

There are three interesting excursions from Skopje, all of them of only a few kilometers. The first is to the hill-top Church of Nerezi, dedicated to St. Panteleimon, which was built in the 12th century. It contains some of the most beautiful and best-known Byzantine frescos to be found in Yugoslavia. The most famous of these is the *Bathing of the Infant Christ*, which forms part of a *Nativity*. Some of the painters responsible for these works may have come from Constantinople itself. They were court painters, who did not adhere to the conventions of their monastic colleagues.

The Sv. Marko Monastery is today silent and apparently deserted, standing dramatically on a sudden hill, but despite its lonely air you will find yourself at the center of a warm welcome from the caretakers, anxious to show you round their exquisite little church, with its wonderful frescos (but enquire at Skopje tourist office about opening times, etc., before making the journey).

The third excursion takes you west into the beautiful gorge of the Treska River. You set out on the road to Tetovo, then, 9½ km. (six miles) from Skopje, follow the paved road which forks off to the left along the Treska. Five km. (three miles) from this junction is Matka Monastery, with its tiny Byzantine church dedicated to the Virgin Mary, dating probably from the 14th century.

From Matka continue on along the river for 1½ km. (one mile) farther to the Treska River Dam, at the narrowest part of the gorge, which is also the end of the road. A five-minute walk past the dam brings you to the Church of St. Andrew (again no longer used), formerly a monastery, built in 1389. St. Andrew's was once inaccessibly high on the mountain slopes, but with the building of the dam it now finds itself picturesquely situated at the level of the lake behind the dam. The extraordinary frescos in this church are the work of the 14th-century Metropolitan Jovan and Deacon Grigorije; their painting here displays much greater humanism than the strictly formalized productions of the monastic Byzantine style. Historians are now beginning to realize that the Renaissance began in Constantinople in about A.D. 1100, not in Italy. Much of the evidence of this comes from Yugoslavia.

The Mountain Road to Ohrid

Of the two routes between Skopje and Ohrid, the northern road is both the more strenuous and the more interesting, as it traverses territory still dominated by Turkish traditions. It first runs westward to Tetovo, in its early stages crossing not particularly interesting cotton-and-tobacco plantations, but soon the Šar-Planina Mountains, rising to well over 2,440 m. (8,000 ft.), break the skyline ahead. Tetovo itself is a markedly picturesque little town of almost 40,000 people set beside the River Pena. It is animated and colorful enough in the morning, but if you see it for the first time during a summer afternoon, you will find that all the 40,000 inhabitants are invisible, enjoying a siesta.

The Sarena Mosque has a particularly graceful minaret. It is unique in Yugoslavia because of its colored exterior decoration and also because of the delicate beauty of the arabesques to be seen inside it. A further peculiarity is that unlike all others that we have so far seen it possesses no cupola. Tetovo's Turkish Baths have been completely modernized, as the people have not changed their personal customs with the departure of their former rulers. Do not fail to visit the Konak, the once luxurious oriental residence of Pasha Haki, and also the Regional Museum installed in what used to be the Moslem convent of Arabati Baba Teke. The atmosphere of the town is vividly Eastern, and this is emphasized by the long chaplets of tobacco leaves hanging up to dry from the gables of many of the houses. In winter Tetovo is the base for visits to various neighboring winter sports resorts, of which Popova Šapka, nearly 1,830 m. (6,000 ft.) above sea-level, is the most popular.

Our road runs 26 km. (16 miles) south from Tetovo to Gostivar, with an occasional glimpse of snow-capped 2,635-m. (8,650-ft.) Mount Borislajec away to our right. Gostivar is inhabited principally by Albanians, but is gradually losing its oriental appearance though it still has an elegant mosque. From there the road climbs steeply to cross a ridge, then descends to the lake of Mavrovo, which is formed by a hydroelectric dam. At the dam itself, a side road to the left leads to the village of Mavrovo across the lake and beyond it. At evening, when the sun is setting over the lake, the view from the restaurant terrace is one of the most charming in Macedonia. Mavrovo is on the way to becoming a popular winter sports center.

After the Mavrovo dam, the highway descends into a wild gorge, between the cliffs of the Bistra Planina and the 2,745-m.-high (9,000 ft.) chain of the Korab Mountains, where the rushing waters of the River Radika come hurtling down from the black crags of Albania. 32 km. (20 miles) from Mavrovi Hanovi, a small sign directs you to a side road on the left, which climbs the steep slope to the extraordinary Monastery of Sv. Jovan Bigorski—St. John on the Rocks. The term "bigor" refers to the steep crags upon which the church is built. Once inside your attention will immediately be caught and held by the exquisite iconostasis of carved wood worked by the Filipovski brothers, among the greatest masters of woodcarving of this country. This iconostasis is divided into six horizontal bands, each one portraying a different subject, and all revealing an extraordinary originality and brilliance.

The refectory is built to seat 200 persons, though today there are few monks left to tend this 11th-century foundation. There is something enchanting about every detail of this ancient building: its setting high on its tall rock, the entrance gates, the carved wooden galleries hanging in a dark confusion one above the other, and the closed-in, secretive little inner courts all combine to leave a deep impression. After your visit, continue a little farther along the road and then look back at the ancient, mysterious building sitting on the rock: it will be an impression that will stay with you for a long time.

Eight km. (five miles) after Sv. Jovan Bigorski you will see set into the mountainside on the left side of the valley the oriental-looking village of Janče. From here a path climbs up the mountain to Galičnik, one of the many picturesque villages to be found off the beaten track in Macedonia.

The architecture of the houses you will come across in the villages and also in the suburbs of larger towns, such as Titov Veles, is common to the whole of Macedonia. That is to say it is the same as the style found in Bulgarian and Greek Macedonia. The houses are built into the hillside and climb the slopes in clusters.

On the main road we soon reach the frontier town of Debar, which also suffered severe destruction in the earthquake of November 1967. As in the case of Skopje, relief assistance from all parts of the world helped to rebuild and rehabilitate this area. From Debar we proceed along the Crni Drim River, running parallel to the frontier with Albania, through a countryside with stark cliffs eroded by the subtropical rainstorms, and bright with the many different-colored stata laid bare to the sun. Lazy water-buffaloes heighten the sensation that this is no longer Europe, but some forgotten part of Asia.

44 km. (27 miles) south of Debar is the typically Albanian village of Velišta, with its baked-clay houses, brightened on Sundays by the brilliant peasant costumes of the inhabitants. Another 9½ km. (six miles) brings us to the simple little lakeside town of Struga at the head of giant Lake Ohrid. On a Saturday, Struga's market day, you will see women from the surrounding countryside in their attractive local garb.

The Shores of Lake Ohrid

At Struga we have arrived at the northern end of magnificent Lake Ohrid, which like Lake Scutari (or Skadar), Prespa and Dojran, is only partly Yugoslav. In this case, two-thirds of Ohrid belong to Macedonia and the rest to Albania. It sweeps away for nearly 30½ km. (19 miles) of still water, so clear that the bed of the lake for as much as 20 m. (65 ft.) down is usually visible. In certain places the depth is greater than in almost any other lake in the world, soundings at 293 m. (962 ft.) having been recorded, and the geologists assure us that it is one of the world's oldest lakes, having been formed in the tertiary age. Although you are now in the deep south, the surrounding mountains and the altitude tend to keep the temperature within bounds.

The underground springs help to keep the water permanently at a temperature of between 56° and 75°F, so that bathing is agreeable all the year round, but it is to its very good fishing that most visitors are attracted. And there are various species in the lake unknown elsewhere. It is fascinating to watch the professional fishermen in their ancient boats, each day following the ritual observed by their ancestors for generations. The environs of this strangely timeless lake harbor rare species of birds. Just so that no picturesque note, natural or human, shall be missing, there is a chain of romantic little Byzantine churches set among tall and ancient cypress trees, or groves of figs, idyllic and seeming hardly to belong to this latter day and age.

Nowadays, Ohrid is a popular resort, with a number of modern hotels both in and around it, but it probably pre-dates the coming of the Romans, who built the Via Egnatia through it, the great highway linking the Dalmatian coast with the Aegean. From the second century it was the See of a Bishop—one of the earliest—and it was from Ohrid that locally-born St. Clement and St. Naum, pupils of St. Cyril and St. Methodius, undertook their great missionary work to Christianize the early Slav settlers. (St. Cyril and St. Methodius had invented a new alphabet in order to be able to transcribe the Scriptures into a script capable of reproducing the sounds of the Slav tongue.) Here pilgrims came from all over the Christian world to study some of the earliest known examples of the new calligraphy and the art of mural painting.

The huge frescos painted in the churches of the towns and the surrounding district were famous as far afield as Russia, and in the time of the feudal Bulgarian ruler, Tsar Samuel, Ohrid became the fortified capital. Later it was under Byzantine, Bulgarian or Serbian rule, until the Turkish invasion of the 14th century. After this date a few of the frescos were damaged and most were covered in whitewash. Only relatively recently were many of these extraordinary masterpieces uncovered. Most, since then, have been painstakingly and excellently restored. In the case of the specially important Church of Sveti Kliment (St. Clement) the frescos had to be first laboriously copied and recorded, and then physically removed from the crumbled walls, and the walls themselves had to be rebuilt before the frescos could be replaced and restored. This complex operation was undertaken in the early 1950s, when a great number of Yugoslavs were still workless, homeless and hungry as a result of the war.

Modern Ohrid has numerous old houses of typically Turkish appearance, a colorful market, several mosques, impressive remains of the old fortifications, a large and fascinating number of small monastery churches and a smart new resort area. Many who know it consider it one of the most beautiful in Europe.

Exploring Southern Macedonia

A road has been built from Peštani over the Galičica Mountains to Otevo near the northwest corner of Lake Prespa. It continues on the main Ohrid–Bitola road at Resen.

Lake Prespa is at an even greater height than Lake Ohrid, being some 840 m. (2,760 ft.) above sea-level. Until the mid-1960s it was completely unknown and neglected by holiday makers. Now, however—since it is, if possible, still more strikingly beautiful than Ohrid—this long-forgotten spot is losing its former solitude and mystery. Like Ohrid, the lake is famous for its fish. It is also well known to ornithologists, for its rich variety of avian species includes the pelican which breeds here.

The deserted island of Golem Grad has remains of a small Byzantine town. The eastern shores are equally empty of human life. There are a few ancient and ruined monasteries scattered among the steep hills.

A good road links Lake Prespa with Bitola, second city of Macedonia, set in a plain dominated by 2,575-m. (8,450-ft.) Mount Pelister, now part of a National Park. The city of Heraclea Lyncestis, capital of Pelagonia, flourished on a nearby site long before the birth of Christ. The modern town of Bitola lies about 2½ km. (1½ miles) from ancient Heraclea.

The still visible Monastery of Obitelj in Bitola played an important rôle in the country's history until the city was captured by the Turks in 1382 and renamed Monastir.

Only about a dozen of the 60 mosques built by the Turks during their 530-year occupation of the city remain, of which undoubtedly the finest is that built with the last of the fortune of a rich merchant by the name of Isaac and still called Isaac's Mosque. Do not fail to see the wonderful wood carvings in the Church of St. Dimitri, and Bezistan covered market. During the few days up to 2nd August, Bitola celebrates the Ilinden Day Festival, during which groups of dancers from all parts of Macedonia converge to commemorate the short, fierce uprising against the Turks in 1903.

Archeologists continue to make valuable discoveries of Greek and Roman remains among the ruins of the neighboring city of Heraclea, which are well worth seeing, though some of the best have been removed to the museums of Belgrade, Skopje and Bitola. 16 km. (ten miles) farther on, on the road to Prilep, there is the great circular burial-shaft of Vissovi, similar to the one at Mycenae in Greece and, like Mycenae, dating from about 1500 B.C.

Prilep is some 44 km. (27 miles) north of Bitola and is today a thoroughly modern-looking town, though some old corners and several mosques still stand. The entire population makes its living from tobacco, and it is the Macedonians' ambition to transform Prilep into one of the world's great tobacco-marketing centers.

However, the surroundings are more attractive than the town itself. Just to the northeast are the ruins of the fortress of the redoubtable 14th-century Prince Marko, set on a volcanic rock shaped by nature in the form of an elephant's head. The impressive Monastery of the Archangel nearby is still intact. The lower buttress of the rock, today called Stara Varoš, encloses the two little churches of St. Dimitri and St. Nicolas. Many of the stones in their walls were dressed by the masons of Rome and Byzantium, and were collected centuries later for fresh use by stonecutters of the Middle Ages.

If you enjoy a couple of hours' walk through mountain scenery then you should make the excursion to the Convent of Treskavac, situated among the ravines of Mount Zlatovrh.

Some 30 km. (20 miles) west of Prilep is the mountain resort of Kruševo. Imagine a series of vivid colors splashed over the flanks of a southern valley beneath a radiant sky, and you will have some idea of Kruševo's first impact upon the senses. Oddly enough for this part of the country there is not a single mosque to be seen, due probably to the fact that the only Ottoman presence here consisted of a small resident garrison. Perhaps for this reason it was possible for the inhabitants of this eagle's nest to organize the 1903 rising against the overlords. The Kruševo Republic lasted for exactly 12 days before it was smashed in the stark tragedy of mass slaughter, when the expelled Turks returned in overwhelming force to avenge themselves.

From Prilep we continue northeast for 55 km. (34 miles) to the site of the Graeco-Roman city of Stobi, near which we meet the main road between Skopje and Gevgelija

Stobi and Demir Kapija—A Breath of Ancient Greece

The main road from Skopje to Titov Veles, which we have now joined, follows the River Vardar southeast for 53 km. (33 miles). Titov Veles on the river's right bank is not without interest, particularly those quarters spread out upon the two slopes of the valley, which contain a large number of characteristically Macedonian houses as well as a good deal of building of the Turkish period. Here, as in Prilep, tobacco is the main crop. Apart from the typical old houses, the main buildings of interest are the Orthodox churches of St. Dimitri and St. Panteleimon.

26 km. (16 miles) farther down the Vardar valley, though now with the river on our left instead of our right, brings us to Gradsko. Where the rivers Vardar and Crna Reka meet lies ancient, ruined, yet still impressive, Stobi.

Alexander the Great's father, Philip II of Macedon, made Stobi the capital of Peonia in 358 B.C. after his conquest of northern Macedon. Two centuries later, when the country became the Roman province of Macedonia Salutaris, Stobi continued to be its capital. It was sacked by the Goths in the fifth century, and in 518 a particularly violent earthquake brought about its final and complete ruin. It is last mentioned in history, briefly, in connection with the Slav-Byzantine wars.

The present excavations of the ancient city have brought to light only the Forum and its immediate environs, but already results far exceed all anticipations. Today you may see the West Gate, five churches and the remains of several palaces. The amphitheater, built entirely of marble, is still only partly uncovered, but is known to be one of the largest yet discovered, the stage alone measuring over 53 m. (175 ft.) in length. This was a Greek theater in the second century B.C., and was transformed by the Romans to mount gladiatorial and wild-animal combats. An interesting detail is that certain of the seats have names carved upon them—a regular practice in Roman times.

If you are interested in exploring Macedonia beyond the limits of the ordinary foreign visitor then we advise a detour of 16 km. (ten miles)

or so from Gradsko to the ancient little town of Negotino. Then turn off right for another 11 km. (seven miles) to Kavadarci, marvelously picturesque among its abundant vines. Only 16 km. more from Negotino on the main road is the Demir Kapija Gorge (the name means "Iron Gates" in Turkish) which is remarkable both naturally and archeologically. The River Vardar, forcing its way between the rocks here, narrows to a mere 50 m. (165 ft.) of swift-flowing water, almost as spectacular as the striking gorge farther north.

Demir Kapija was a natural fortress, surrounded on all sides by high hills particularly difficult to scale, and has been used to control the passage of the river and keep watch over the surrounding plains since remotest times, every summit being crowned with some kind of fortification. From any of these you will see all the way from the distant hills in the west to the confluence of the rivers Bašava and Vardar. When the railroad and, later, the road were being constructed, traces of ancient buildings and tombs were uncovered, some of them containing magnificently-wrought votive vases. As a result systematic excavations were carried out during 1951–2, which brought to light a number of Greek, Roman and Slav tombs.

The road to the Greek frontier, 48 km. (30 miles) to the south of Gevgelija, is without touristic interest, but if you are in the mood for one more adventure before you leave Yugoslavia, you can make an interesting side-excursion by turning left at the village at Udovo. After a run of about 32 km. (20 miles), you will find yourself on the shores of Lake Dojran, where fishing with cormorants is still practiced in a manner that cannot be seen anywhere else outside China or Japan.

PRACTICAL INFORMATION FOR MACEDONIA

HOW TO GET THERE. By plane. There are frequent air services from Belgrade, Zagreb, and other major Yugoslav cities to Skopje; there is now also an airport at Ohrid, with air connections to Dubrovnik, Skopje etc.

By train. You can reach Skopje from Belgrade by boarding one of the international express trains that travel the length of Yugoslavia on their way to Greece, though you are likely to find accommodations more crowded and less comfortable than on the average luxury long-distance coach. Certain trains from Belgrade do, however, operate direct to Bitola, and there are other towns and villages which can be reached more easily from Belgrade by stopping trains (though these are slow) than by coach.

WHEN TO GO. Inland Macedonia has a Continental climate, with cold winters and very hot summers. The southeast, however, toward Gevgelija, enjoys an equable Mediterranean climate. In winter its mountains offer sports conditions which, even if they cannot equal those found in the Slovenian Alps, are still good enough to attract many Yugoslav skiers. In summer the shores of Lake Ohrid are relatively cool, because they are well over 610 m. (2,000 ft.) above sea-level and surrounded by mountains. For these reasons the best seasons for visiting Macedonia are spring and autumn.

 HOTELS AND RESTAURANTS. Hotels have been vastly improved in recent years, and there is a far greater realization of visitors' requirements—though standards of service do not always match modernity of style and amenities in the newer establishments. However, the local people's innate hospitality will overcome some of the defects you are likely to encounter. The moral of this is simply—don't expect too much. Advance bookings are advisable. All hotels in the (E) and (M) categories have all or many rooms with bath. Accommodations in private homes are available through some local travel bureaux, notably in Ohrid and Struga. Not the least of the pleasures awaiting you in Macedonia, incidentally, are the performances of folk music and dancing put on by many hotels in the evenings.

The best restaurants are attached to the hotels. However, in addition, we recommend that in Ohrid you visit the *Orijent* restaurant, in the old Moslem quarter. And at Sveti Naum, the restaurant on the island in the Beli Drin River is excellent for Ohrid trout. At Skopska Crna Gora, 13 km. (eight miles) north of Skopje in lovely rural surroundings, is the *Čardak* restaurant in old rustic style, with music. There is also a good national-style restaurant in the St. Panteleimon Monastery at Nerezi, with splendid views over the city.

In the pastry-cooks' shop you will find a number of Turkish specialties, all very sweet, and the non-alcoholic drink called *boza,* sharp, but extremely refreshing, and made from maize flour. Regional dishes we can recommend include *bamnja* (lamb stew with peas), *sarma od vinivog lišća* (vine leaves stuffed with minced meat and rice) and *sarma u jagnjećoj maramici* (eggs and minced lambs' liver).

The *čevap* and other grilled meats are generally excellent in Macedonia, as in Serbia. The trout of Ohrid (*belvica*) is a variety of salmon-trout found nowhere else in Europe. *Alva,* made with crushed nuts and honey, makes a wonderful dessert. *Kačkavalj* is a hard cheese, common throughout the Balkans.

Macedonia produces a number of very palatable wines, mostly red. *Mastika* is an agreeable aperitif. There is also good beer.

BITOLA. Second largest city in Macedonia. *Epinal* (M), 155 rooms.

GEVGELIJA. Principal frontier town between Yugoslavia and Greece. *Inex Motel Vardar* (M), 48 rooms. A good stopover.

GRADSKO. Near the Stobi excavations. *Motel Stobi* (I), 20 rooms. On the Titov Veles–Gevgelija road.

KIČEVO. *Union* (M), 52 rooms.

KRUŠEVO. *Montana* (E), 94 rooms. Pool. *Ilinden* (I), 54 rooms, a few with bath.

MAVROVI HANOVI. *Mavrovo* (I), 28 rooms, a few with bath. Attractive lakeside location.

MAVROVO. *Bistra* (M), 44 rooms.

NEGOTINO. *Park* (M), 60 rooms. *Auto Camp Antigona* (M), 80 rooms, none with shower.

OHRID. *Grand Hotel Palace* (E), 137 rooms. Does not justify its prices. *Metropol* (E), 125 rooms. Pool but no beach; on the lake a few kilometers outside the town. The best. *Palace Annex* (M), 88 rooms, 56 with bath. On the lakeside, but still in the town. *Slavija* (M), 61 rooms.

At **Gorica,** three km. (two miles) south of Ohrid, are *Gorica* (E), 60 rooms, pool; and *Park* (M), 37 rooms. Both are under the management of the Inex enterprise, and set on a wooded peninsula, one of the best locations on the lake, with bathing beaches. Also 20 chalets (M), with pool.

OTEŠEVO. Summer resort on the shores of Lake Prespa. *Oteševo* (M), 250 rooms. Complex of hotels and bungalows. Beach.

PEŠTANI. On Lake Ohrid, 13 km. (eight miles) south of Ohrid on the east shore. *Desaret* (M), 136 rooms. Beach.

POPOVA ŠAPKA. Winter sports center 22½ km. (14 miles) from Tetovo. Two ski lifts; mountain cableway from Tetovo to Popova Šapka. *Popova Sapka* (M), 60 rooms. *Skopje* (I), 25 rooms.

SKOPJE. *Continental* (E), 200 rooms. *Grand Hotel Skopje* (E), 180 rooms. Beside the Vardar River. *Olympic* (E) tourist village, 260 rooms in hotel and chalets. *Bellevue* (M), 65 rooms, 15 chalets. *Jadran* (M), 23 rooms. In a quiet location; built in Turkish style. *Panorama* (M), 96 rooms. *Turist* (M), 82 rooms. On the main business street.

Out of the town are *Saraj* (I), 18 rooms, eight km. (five miles) west on the road to Tetovo; and *Vodno* (I), 26 rooms, in the hills above Skopje to the south. 11 km. (seven miles) to the south, is *Motel Katlanovo* (I), 18 rooms and a campsite.

STARI DORJAN. Summer resort on the shores of the lake of the same name. Perhaps the best fishing in Yugoslavia. *Stari Dorjan* (I), 26 rooms. Beach.

STRUGA. Small town on the northern shore of Lake Ohrid. *Biser* (E), 51 rooms. In attractive local style on lake shore near the Albanian border. *Inex Hotel Drim* (M), 180 rooms. Pool, beach.

TETOVO. Starting point for mountaineering and skiing in the Šar-Planina. *Makedonija* (I).

TITOV VELES. *Internacional* (E–I), 88 rooms. *Motel Mladost* (I), 8 rooms. On the Skopje road.

 HOW TO GET AROUND. By car. The main road to Greece (Skopje–Gevgelija) is excellent, part of it being a motorway. The route from Skopje to Ohrid through Tetovo, Gostivar and Debar is metaled. The alternative route, through Titov Veles, then southward along the main road to Greece as far as the ruins of Stobi (where you can turn off for Prilep and Bitola) is fully surfaced the whole way, and is extremely picturesque. A good road continues to Oteševo on Lake Prespa—a beautiful stretch of water shared by Yugoslavia, Greece and Albania—as well as to Ohrid. Almost all of Macedonia's main routes of necessity pass through deep gorges, so that building any road—let alone a fast motorway—is a major feat of engineering. Minor roads, climbing up the steep mountainsides, are usually rough, but an excellent stretch of metaled road now ascends the steep hillside immediately south of Skopje to the Motel Vodno and the St. Panteleimon Monastery at Nerezi.

Filling stations are frequent on the main through road to Greece, and can also be found in each of the main towns through which you are likely to pass—nevertheless, don't miss a chance to fill up your tank, and a spare can of gasoline is a good idea.

By coach. For comfort at a relatively economical price, the extensive luxury coach network is your best bet. On all long-distance journeys you can, and indeed should, reserve your seat well in advance. Shorter journeys may mean sharing the coach with a multitude of people and, sometimes, animals. It can be fun if you don't mind crowds; the worst factor is usually the heat.

 WHAT TO SEE. Macedonia's loveliest town is the gem-like Ohrid. In medieval times it was a major center of the Orthodox religion, and still possesses many ancient churches, with a number of frescos and some beautiful icons. This popular lake resort now has good hotels and other holiday facilities. Skopje, beautifully-situated capital city, has survived the terrible 1963 earthquake: though some fine ancient buildings were lost, the majority are now almost completely restored. Numerous other towns, such as Titov Veles and Bitola, are well worth visiting.

The remains of a considerable number of Greek and Roman towns have been discovered. Many have been partially excavated, and work is in progress on important discoveries on the site of Heraclea Lyncestis, just south of Bitola. Here you can see the previously shattered design of third-century Roman mosaics reassembled by Yugoslav scholars.

South of Skopje is the enchanting little Monastery of St. Panteleimon, at Nerezi, which has stupendous views over the capital in the fertile hollow 305 m. (1,000 ft.) below. There are other ancient Orthodox monasteries and churches nearby.

Macedonia's natural beauties include the three great lakes of Ohrid, Prespa and Dojran, and the Treska, Radika and Demir Kapija gorges. From the summit of Mt. Pelister you can gaze across all of ancient Pelagonia, while from that of Mt. Solunska Glava (Head of Thessaloniki) you can see the whole of southern Macedonia to the Aegean.

Around mid-July is the famous Galičnik Wedding, an outstanding folkloric event featuring old wedding customs. But Macedonia's most important artistic event is the Summer Festival, held each year at Ohrid from mid-July to mid-August, including in July the Balkan Festival of Original Folk Dances and Songs performed on the openair stage of the fortress. Toward the end of August is Ohrid's Festival of Old Town Songs and the Evenings of Poetry at Struga, an international event.

Major plans are in progress to develop the Republic's particular attractions: notably its splendid medieval art treasures, its hunting and fishing potential, its health spas, and its folk traditions.

 SPORTS. Swimming is possible on beaches fringing Lake Ohrid and Prespa, though lake water tends to be rather cold outside high summer and early fall. Both lakes offer good fishing. A special fish-breeding station has been established at Struga, on Lake Ohrid. Boats for lake fishing can be hired by private arrangement from on-the-spot professionals, and information about permits, etc., can be obtained from the local Tourist Offices.

There is an increasingly popular little winter sports resort in Macedonia, Popova Šapka, at 1,783 m. (5,580 ft.), near Tetovo, where, every March, a ski contest known as the Sarplaninski Smuk is held. At Tetovo you board the new cablecar which lifts you in a few minutes to Popova Šapka. There is a halfway station near the village of Lisac from where it's a 90-minute walk. There are many excellent slopes available also on the flanks of 2,575-m.-high (8,450 ft.) Mount Pelister. Mavrovo is another developing winter sports center. The 2,530-m. (8,300-ft.) Solunska Glava, south of Skopje, is ideal for mountain climbing.

Macedonia has two native sports of its own which you should try to see. One is *pelivani,* a kind of Graeco-Roman wrestling, and the other *biška,* which is played on grass and resembles hockey.

SHOPPING. There is a great variety of attractive souvenirs on sale in Macedonia. Embroidery is the richest in Yugoslavia, the ornamental designs employed being of Slav, Byzantine and Turkish origins. Pottery and ceramics generally can be bought more cheaply direct by the tourist in the small towns or villages where they are made, such as Titov Veles and Resen. The Macedonians are past masters in the art of woodcarving, and you will find delightful examples in the shops and markets. In Kruševo, near Prilep, you can buy beautiful hand-made woolen carpets.

 USEFUL ADDRESSES. (All in Skopje.) Tourist Information and Reception Center, Kej Dimitar Vlahov 1. Auto Motor Association, Ivo Ribar Lola 55. Centroturist, Generalturist, Kompas and Putnik all have office in Skopje, as well as in other towns and resorts in Macedonia.

TOURIST VOCABULARY

THE ALPHABETS. Here are the Cyrillic and Latin alphabets, to help you pronounce the place names in Yugoslavia.

А а	A (a)	as in f*a*ther		Н н	(N) (n)	as in *n*o
Б б	B (b)	„ „ *b*rother		Њ њ	Nj (ny)	„ „ *n*ews
В в	V (v)	„ „ *v*odka		О о	O (o)	„ „ *o*rb
Г г	G (g)	„ „ *g*o		П п	P (p)	„ „ *p*op
Д д	D (d)	„ „ *d*o		Р р	R (r)	„ „ *r*od
Ђ ђ	Đ (dj)	„ „ *j*ump		С с	S (s)	„ „ *s*od
Е е	E (e)	„ „ *l*et		Т т	T (t)	„ „ *t*oo
Ж ж	Ž (zh)	„ „ plea*s*ure		Ћ ћ	Ć (tch)	„ „ *t*ube
З з	Z (z)	„ „ *z*ero		У у	U (u)	„ „ r*oo*m
И и	I (i)	„ „ *i*f		Ф ф	F (f)	„ „ *f*a!
Ј ј	J (y)	„ „ *y*ear		Х х	H (gh)	„ „ a*ch*
К к	K (k)	„ „ *k*eg		Ц ц	C (ts)	„ „ lo*ts*
Л л	L (l)	„ „ *l*ad		Ч ч	Č (tch)	„ „ *ch*urch
Љ љ	Lj (ly)	„ „ mi*lli*on		Џ џ	Dž (j)	„ „ *J*ohn
М м	M (m)	„ „ *m*ap		Ш ш	Š (sh)	„ „ *sh*oe

PRONUNCIATION. The vowel sounds in the Serbo-Croat languages (the chief languages of Yugoslavia: Serbian is written in the Cyrillic alphabet and Croat in the Latin) are uniform and do not vary from word to word as is the case in English. They are pronounced as follows:

a - as in f*a*ther
e - as in l*e*t
i - as in *i*f
o - as in *o*rb
u - as in r*oo*m

GENERALITIES

Is there anyone who speaks English . . . French . . . German?

Ima li neko koji govori engleski? . . . francuski? . . . nemački?

Yes — no

Da (or) jest — ne

Impossible

Nemoguće

Good day — Good morning

Dobar dan — dobro jutro

Good evening	Dobro veče
Good night	Laku noć
Goodbye — *Au revoir*	Do vidjenja
Mister — Madam — Miss	Gospodin — gospodja — gospodjica
Please — Don't mention it	Molim vas — molim
Excuse me	Izvinite
How are you?	Kako ste?
How do you do (Pleased to meet you)	Milo mi je
I don't understand	Ne razumem
Thank you	Hvala

TRAVELING

I am traveling by car . . . train . . . plane . . . boat	Putujem automobilom . . . vozom . . . avionom . . . parobrodom
Taxi, to the station . . . pier . . . airport	Taksi, na stanicu . . . na pristanište . . . na aerodrom
Porter, take the baggage/luggage	Nosač, iznesite stvari
Where is the filling-station? (gas) (petrol)	Gde je železnička stanica? Gde je benzinska stanica?
When does the train leave for . . . ?	Kada polazi voz za . . . ?
Which is the train for . . . ?	Koji je voz za . . . ?
Which is the road to . . . ?	Koji je put za . . . ?
Where is the ticket-window?	Gde je blagajna?
A first-class ticket, please	Molim vas jednu kartu, prve klase
No smoking (compartment)	Zabranjeno pušiti
Ladies — Men	Zene — Muškarci
Where? — When?	Gde? — kada?
Sleeping-car — Dining-car	Kola za spavanje — restoran
Compartment	Kupe
Entrance — Exit	Ulaz — izlaz
Nothing to declare	Nemam ništa za carinjenje
I am coming for my holidays	Dolazim na godišnji odmor
Nothing	Ništa
Personal use	Za ličnu upotrebu
Must I pay duty?	Treba li da platim carinu?
How much?	Koliko?

ON THE ROAD

Straight ahead	Pravo
To the right — to the left	Desno — levo
Show me the way to . . . please	Molim vas pokažite mi put za
Where is . . . ?	Gde se nalazi?
Stop!	Stoj!

One-way (no entrance)	Ulaz zabranjen
Crossroad	Raskrnica
Danger	Opasnost
Drive slowly!	Vozi lagano!
Look out for the train (railroad crossing)	Pazi na voz

IN TOWN

Will you lead me? take me?	Hoćete li me pratiti?
Street — Square — Place	Ulica — Trg
Where is the bank?	Gde je banka?
Far	Deleko
Quickly	Brzo
Police station	Stanica milicije
Consulate (American, British . . .)	Konzulat (Americki, Britanski ، . .)
Theater	Pozorište
At what times does the film start?	Kada počinje bioskop?
Will you dance with me?	Hoćete li da igrate?
Where is the travel office?	Molim vas gde je turistički biro?
Where is the tourist information office?	Gde je turistički informativni biro?

SHOPPING

I would like to buy	Želeo bih da kupim
Show me, please	Molim vas možete li mi pokazati
How much is it?	Šta staje ovo?
It is too expensive	To je skupo
Have you any sandals?	Imate li sandale?
Have you foreign newspapers?	Imate li stranu štampu?
Show me that blouse, please	Pokažite mi onu bluzu
Show me that bag	Pokažite mi onu torbu
Envelopes — writing paper	Koverte — papir za pisanje
Roll of film	Film
Map of the city	Plan grada
Something hand-made	Ručne izrade
Wrap it up, please	Molim vas upakujte mi
Cigarets, please	Molim vas, cigarete
Matches, please	Dajte mi šibice
Ham	Šunka
Sausage — salami	Kobasica — salama
Sugar	Šećer
Grapes	Grožđe
Apple	Jabuka

Pear	Kruška
Orange	Pomorandža
Bread — Butter	Hleb — puter
Peach	Breskva

AT THE HOTEL

A good hotel	Jedan dobar hotel
Have you a room available?	Imate li slobodnu sobu?
A room with one bed, with two beds	Soba sa jednim krevetom, sa dve kreveta
With bathroom	Sa kupatilom
How much is it per day?	Šta staje dnevno?
A room overlooking the sea	Soba prema moru
For one day, for two days	Za jedan dan, za dva dana
For a week	Za nedelju dana
My name is	Ja se zovem
Here are our papers	Evo vam naših isprava
What is the number of my room?	Koji je broj moje sobe?
The key, please	Molim vas ključ
Where is the chambermaid?	Gde je sobarica?
Breakfast, lunch, supper	Doručak, ručak, večera
The bill, please	Molim vas račun
I am leaving tomorrow	Ja putujem sutra

AT THE RESTAURANT

Waiter	Kelner
Where is the restaurant?	Gde je restoran?
I would like to have lunch, dinner	Hoću da ručam, večeram
The menu, please	Molim vas jelovnik
Fixed-price menu	Molim vas meni
Soup	Supa, juha
Bread	Hleb
Hors d'oeuvre	Mešano predjelo
Smoked ham	Dalmatinski pršut
Ham omelet	Omlet sa šukom
Roast chicken — roast duck	Pečeno pile — pečeno patka
Roast pork	Svinjsko pečenje
Veal cutlet	Teleča šnicla
Potatoes	Krompir
Tomato salad	Paradajz salata
Vegetables	Povrće
Cakes	Kolači, testa
Fruit Cheese	Voče Sir
Fish Eggs	Ribe Jaja

Serve me on the terrace	Servirajte mi na terasi
Where can I wash my hands?	Gde mogu da operem ruke?
Red wine, white wine	Crno vino, belo vino
Rosé wine	Ružica
Beer — bottled water	Pivo — Mineralna voda
Turkish coffee	Turska kava
Fruit juice	Vocni sok

AT THE BANK — AT THE POST OFFICE

Where is the bank? . . . post office?	Gde je banka? . . . pošta?
I would like to cash a check	Ja želim da promenim ček
I would like to change some money	Ja želim da zamenim novac
Stamps	Poštanske marke
I want to send it by airmail	Hoću da pošaljem avionom
I would like to telephone	Hoću da telefoniram
Postcard — letter	Dopisnica — pismo
Letterbox	Poštansko sanduk
I would like to send a telegram	Hoću da pošaljem telegram

AT THE SERVICE STATION

Service station—Gasoline	Garaža — benzin
Filling station	Benzinska stanica
Oil, please	Molim vas ulje
Change the oil	Promeniti ulje
Look at the tires — a tire	Pregledati gume — guma
Wash the car	Oprati kola
Grease the car	Podmažite kola
The car broke down — I have a flat tire	Imam automobilski defekt — guma mi je pukla
Can you tow it?	Možete-li nas vući?
Spark(ing) plug	Svečica
The brakes	Kočnice *or* bremse
The gear box	Menjać brzine
Carburetor	Karburator
A headlight (headlamp)	Farovi
Starter	pokretać
Axle	osovina
Spring	pero

VOCABULARY

NUMBERS

1	jedan	8	osam	60	sezdeset
2	dva	9	devet	70	sedamdeset
3	tri	10	deset	100	sto
4	četri	20	dvadeset	200	dve stotine
5	pet	30	trideset	300	tri stotine, etc.
6	šest	40	četrdeset	1000	hiljada
7	sedam	50	pedeset	2000	dve hiljade

INDEX

GENERAL INFORMATION
See also Geographical listings for additional details.

GEOGRAPHICAL
**The letter H indicates hotels and other accommodations.
The letter R indicates restaurants & other eating facilities.**

**(The Geographical Index also provides practical information
for each chapter and major cities.)**

YUGOSLAVIA ①

② AUSTRIA
③ HUNGARY
⑥
⑦ RUMANIA
Slovenia
Ljubljana
Zagreb
Trieste
Istria
Rijeka
Croatia
Vojvodina
BELGRADE
⑤
Zadar
④
Bosnia-Hertzegovina
Dalmatia
Sarajevo
Serbia
Split
⑧
Ancona
ADRIATIC
Mostar
Monte-negro
Niš
Ancona
Dubrovnik
Peć
Kosovo
Pescara
Titograd
Bar
ALBANIA
Skopje
ITALY
SEA
N
Macedonia
Bari

CONTENTS

Maps

KEY

〰〰 Motorways
━━ Main roads
⌇ Other roads
┼┼┼┼ Railways
- - - Car ferries
● Cities
• Large towns
· Other towns
✳ Airports
▒ Land over 1,200 feet
   (Map 1 above only)